AF361249

WEAVING WORDS AND BINDING BODIES

The Poetics of Human Experience in Old English Literature

Weaving Words and Binding Bodies

The Poetics of Human Experience in Old English Literature

MEGAN CAVELL

UNIVERSITY OF TORONTO PRESS
Toronto Buffalo London

ISBN 978-1-4426-3722-1

Library and Archives Canada Cataloguing in Publication

Cavell, Megan, 1985–, author
Weaving words and binding bodies : the poetics of human experience
in Old English literature / Megan Cavell.

(Toronto Anglo-Saxon series)
Includes bibliographical references and index.
ISBN 978-1-4426-3722-1 (bound)

1. English literature – Old English, ca. 450–1100 – History and criticism.
2. Figures of speech in literature.   I. Title.   II. Series: Toronto Anglo-Saxon series

PR179.F53C39 2016   829'.09357   C2015-908264-1

This book has been published with the help of a grant from the Federation for the Humanities and Social Sciences, through the Awards to Scholarly Publications Program, using funds provided by the Social Sciences and Humanities Research Council of Canada.

University of Toronto Press acknowledges the financial assistance to its publishing program of the Canada Council for the Arts and the Ontario Arts Council, an agency of the Government of Ontario.

Funded by the   Financé par le
Government   gouvernement
of Canada   du Canada

Canada

Contents

Acknowledgments

I would like to sincerely thank everyone who has supported and advised me throughout the research, writing, and revision of this monograph. In particular, I am grateful to those who have taken the time to read this work more times than they perhaps would have liked: Richard Dance, Hugh Magennis, Rosalind Love, William Robins and my anonymous reviewers. My thanks go to Suzanne Rancourt and the editorial team at the University of Toronto Press, as well as to readers and mentors in the wider medievalist community: Matthias Ammon, Helen Foxhall Forbes, Alaric Hall, Antonette diPaolo Healey, Fabienne Michelet, Britt Mize, Andy Orchard, Simon Patterson, Russell Poole, M.J. Toswell, and Judy Quinn.

I also owe a great debt of gratitude to the Social Sciences and Humanities Research Council of Canada, whose funding of my postgraduate degrees and postdoctoral fellowship allowed me to pursue my passion for Old English literature and eventually wrestle this study into its current form. The final stages of this publication took place during my time as a Cofund Junior Research Fellow at Durham University, and I am likewise grateful to the fellowship programme and my colleagues for their support and collegiality.

Finally, to all my friends and family – you know who you are – thank you so very much!

Abbreviations

ASE	*Anglo-Saxon England*
ASPR	Anglo-Saxon Poetic Records
BAR	British Archaeological Reports
CCSL	Corpus Christianorum Series Latina
CSASE	Cambridge Studies in Anglo-Saxon England
CSEL	Corpus Scriptorum Ecclesiasticorum Latinorum
DOE	*Dictionary of Old English* (eds. Antonette diPaolo Healey et al.)
DOE Corpus	*Dictionary of Old English Web Corpus* (eds. Antonette diPaolo Healey et al.)
EETS	Early English Text Society
ELH	*English Literary History*
ELN	*English Language Notes*
ES	*English Studies*
JAF	*Journal of American Folklore*
JEGP	*Journal of English and Germanic Philology*
Klaeber Four	The fourth edition of *Klaeber's Beowulf* (eds. R.D. Fulk et al.)
MÆ	*Medium Ævum*
MLN	*Modern Language Notes*
MLR	*Modern Language Review*
NM	*Neuphilologische Mitteilungen*
OED	*Oxford English Dictionary Online*
OEN	*Old English Newsletter*
PMLA	*Publications of the Modern Language Association*
PQ	*Philological Quarterly*
RES	*Review of English Studies*

Editions

Unless otherwise stated, all Old English poetic quotations refer to the ASPR editions. (Their numbering is also used for the *Exeter Book* riddles.) However, quotations from *Beowulf*, *Judith*, *The Metres of Boethius*, and *Solomon and Saturn I* and *II* are from Klaeber Four, Griffith's, Godden and Irvine's, and Anlezark's editions, respectively. All references to the *Vulgate* are from the *Biblia Sacra* (eds. Fischer et al.), and those to *The Hêliand* are from Behaghel's edition, while the various Latin enigmata are quoted from Glorie's CCSL edition. Unless otherwise stated, all Old English and Latin translations – which I have tried to keep as literal as possible – are my own.

WEAVING WORDS AND BINDING BODIES

Construction and Constriction: Introducing Human Experience in Old English Poetry

The aim of this study is to provide a comprehensive survey of material and metaphorical weaving and binding in Old English poetry. There are several hundred instances of such imagery invoked in relation to objects, humans, elemental forces and complex abstract concepts in the poetic corpus. Despite its frequency of appearance and despite its use in a wide range of overlapping and contradictory (nevertheless intriguing) metaphors and thematic clusters, such connective language has received a great deal of passing or partial comment, but no thorough and exhaustive critical treatment. It is perhaps because of the scholarly reduction of the metaphorical use of binding terminology in Old English poetry to mere "cliché"[1] that the significance of the imagery has been overlooked. Given the sheer scale of this formulaic diction and imagery, however, the lack of a comprehensive analysis prevents scholars from engaging in nuanced discussion of thematics within and relationships between texts ranging from the most canonical to the relatively obscure.

The corpus includes a wide range of didactic, heroic, elegiac, and hagiographical texts, of which some have received a great deal of scholarly attention and celebration, while others have been pushed to the margins. Against precedent, this survey will include reference to certain of Ælfric's saints' lives and homiletic texts, which in past scholarship have been considered "rhythmical prose." Following Thomas A. Bredehoft's arguments that the differences between these texts and the traditional poetic canon stem from the former's status as later verse, their inclusion here seems

---

1 Robinson, *"Beowulf" and the Appositive Style*, p. 64.

prudent.[2] Bredehoft's comments on metrics and poetic form have also been influential: "the assertion that the later poetry can be effectively compared to the earlier, or that later poets were, in fact, *trying* to compose verse under the same rules as earlier poets is deeply problematic. The reality is not that the poetic tradition was rigid, but rather that Sievers-Bliss formalism is rigid."[3] Despite the variety of forms, content, and intended audiences, weaving and binding remain prevalent themes throughout much of Old English poetry, both early and late.

The decision to focus the survey on poetry springs not only from necessity – there is simply too much material to permit an exhaustive analysis of the prose as well – but also from a desire to situate the poetic texts within their immediate formulaic environment, something that sets them apart from the prose corpus. Nevertheless, where significant parallels between Old English poetic, prose, and Latin texts exist, the wider tradition will most certainly be addressed.

Similarly, the choice to examine weaving and binding imagery together merits some attention. From a modern standpoint, the weaving of actual or metaphorical fabric and the binding up of a body, thing or abstract concept may appear to have little in common. The link, however, lies in the constructive uses of binding, as John Scheid and Jesper Svenbro's discussion of classical textiles emphasizes: "weaving unites what must be united. To weave is to unite, to interlace, to bind: the act is so straightforward that it requires no explanation."[4] While the constructive nature of weaving and binding is clearly evident in Old English poetry, the Anglo-Saxons were also intensely interested in constrictive binding, which could likewise be linked to textile production. An intriguing example of such a constructive-constrictive nexus relates to the image of the net, which is applied to concepts ranging from dangerous entrapments to pieces of protective armour. These associations likely stem from what Gale R. Owen-Crocker dubs the "symbiosis between cloth and metal" in the medieval period,[5]

---

2   "Ælfric and Late Old English Verse"; *Early English Metre*, pp. 80–98; and *Authors, Audiences, and Old English Verse*, pp. 146–70. See also "Was Ælfric a Poet?"; and Szarmach, "Ælfric's Rhythmical Prose."

3   *Early English Metre*, p. 7. See also his discussion of the lack of scholarly appreciation for poems that do not fit the rules of traditional Old English poetry on p. 70.

4   *Craft of Zeus*, p. 10.

5   Owen-Crocker, Coatsworth and Hayward, eds., *Encyclopedia of Medieval Dress and Textiles*, p. 3.

with similarities between the crafts of textile production and metalwork evident at both linguistic and literary levels. As a result, in the Old English poetic corpus, terms for weaving and binding are frequently invoked together or in similar contexts.

Although many weaving instances relate to construction, while binding occurrences tend to be more concerned with constriction, both sets of terminology and imagery can be and are employed in either context. Rather than seeing them as binary, we may, perhaps, view these constructive and constrictive applications as the poles of a scale, with representations of both weaving and binding existing at various points along it. Interestingly, however, there are certain distinctions between the two sets of imagery; for example, although the Old English poetic corpus contains references to unbinding (or unlocking), no instances of unweaving are extant. Thus, while bonds may be viewed as separate entities even when employed as part of a structure, the threads of woven objects are not perceived in the same way. This difference is likely the result of binding's greater participation in constrictive contexts – the bonds that fetter a body are unlikely to be confused with a part of said body.

The poetic usage of the constructive-constrictive nature of weaving and binding appears, furthermore, to limit this imagery to certain contexts. Nevertheless, this survey will demonstrate the use of weaving and binding diction in a wide variety of situations, whether actual (the weaving of a tapestry or the tying up of a prisoner) or metaphorical (peace-weaving or the binding of the world by winter weather).

The metaphorical application of weaving and binding imagery presents its own unique set of problems, as demonstrated by ongoing debates in metaphor theory. One of the primary divisions that this theory has historically made with regard to metaphor is to distinguish between those that are creative and those that are conceptual. While creative metaphors are the conscious result of literary wordplay, conceptual metaphors are inherent to human thought itself.[6] Thus, because humans understand new things in relation to that which is already familiar, metaphor is essential to both human understanding and communication. Conceptual metaphors, then, are the "metaphors we live by." For example, the metaphor structure

---

6 Lakoff and Johnson, *Metaphors We Live By*, p. 6. The application of conceptual metaphor theory to Anglo-Saxon studies has proven to be a productive methodology: see especially the introductory chapters in Lockett, *Anglo-Saxon Psychologies*; and Wehlau, *Riddle of Creation*.

ARGUMENT IS WAR stands behind language referring to attacking or shooting holes in an argument or winning a disagreement. The equivalence of argument and war supports the understanding of one complex and emotionally-charged concept in terms of another, more physical one.[7]

Any discussion of metaphorical imagery must grapple with this question of consciousness. Creative metaphors may say something about the idea the poet wishes to convey, while conceptual metaphors tell us more about the thought processes lying behind a cultural group's way of thinking. Identifying Anglo-Saxon uses of metaphor is made even more difficult when we take dead metaphors into account, something that is particularly relevant to the study of a language that has undergone so much change. Dead metaphors, or metaphors that are no longer perceived as metaphorical at all, may be defined in opposition to the collections of related metaphors that can be followed through to an underlying structure, and are therefore "idiosyncratic, unsystematic, and isolated."[8] When we discuss a mountain, for example, we may refer to its "foot," but are unlikely to attribute it with a full range of other body parts.[9]

And so we have three types of metaphors to navigate – those in the foreground (creative), those that exercise power over thought processes from their place in the background (conceptual) and those that have undergone such significant semantic change that they are entirely bleached (dead). It is only by looking at sets of imagery together that we can hope to identify the nature of their metaphorical content. If no example in a group of similar images appears either to be highlighted by the poet or to be influencing the poet's thinking, then (and only then) may we have grounds to suggest that the metaphor may be dead. Although I specify "poet" here, this range of metaphor types occurs throughout Old English literature, not only in the poetry that is this survey's main concern. It should be noted that poetic analysis is especially useful where it is not immediately clear that creative metaphor is being invoked. This is because the poet's interaction with the content of the poem can to some extent be determined from the way in which he or she employs poetic and rhetorical devices in order to highlight certain passages. Such highlighting may take the form of stylistic effects, including ornamental alliteration, rhyme, assonance, and formulaic diction.[10]

---

7 Lakoff and Johnson, *Metaphors We Live By*, p. 4.
8 Ibid., p. 55.
9 Ibid.
10 See Orchard, "Artful Alliteration"; and Bredehoft, *Early English Metre*, pp. 63–5, 68, 93, 148–9.

Thus, passages containing weaving and binding references that are considered to be working either concretely or with a semantically bleached sense can be re-examined through the lens of poetics to determine their level of conventionality.

It is in the context of poetic highlighting that the question of expression comes into play. Although metaphors are inherently linked to images and ideas, when we move away from the conceptual aspect to the creative, we find that metaphors may also be consciously expressed for stylistic purposes. Anglo-Saxons writers were, of course, fully capable of employing metaphors in a self-conscious manner. Texts discussing rhetoric and poetics abound in educational contexts, particularly in Anglo-Latin works influenced by classical models.[11] One example in Old English demonstrates the close link between Anglo-Saxon works and their predecessors. Here, the meaning of the Greek *metaphora* as a "transference" is mirrored in the Old English verb *abredgan* (to draw): *Sume sind gebatene* tropi, *þæt sind mislice getacnunga oððe wisan on ledenspræce abrodene of heora agenre getacnunge to oðre gelicnysse*[12] (Some are called figures of speech, which are variously symbols or Latin idioms drawn from their own meaning into another likeness). It is tempting to read this language of carrying over, dragging or even pulling in terms of the yoking together or binding of two concepts. However, it should be noted that the idea of metaphor as binding – useful and relevant as it may be – is not found in Old English.

We need not look far, however, to find indications of bound or woven language. Indeed, material objects like books occasionally stand in for the more abstract enclosures of wisdom for which Old English poetry is famous.[13] A striking example occurs at the beginning of *Solomon and Saturn 1*:

Saturnus cwæð:
Hwæt! Ic iglanda   eallra hæbbe
boca onbyrged   þurh gebregdstafas,
larcræftas onlocen   Libia and Greca,
swylce eac istoriam   Indea rices.   (1–3)[14]

---

11 For more on language, rhetoric and educational texts, see Gneuss, "Study of Language"; and Irvine, *Making of Textual Culture*, pp. 105–6. Irvine especially emphasizes the influence of Donatus' *Ars maior* on discussions of rhetorical tropes in the works of Augustine, Isidore, and Bede.

12 *Ælfrics Grammatik und Glossar*, ed. Zupitza, p. 295, section 26.

13 See chapter 8 and conclusion, pp. 231–50 and 296–302.

14 See also *Solomon and Saturn II* 4b–7a.

(Saturn said: Listen! I have tasted the books of all the islands, through braided letters, unlocked the knowledge of the Libyans and the Greeks, likewise also the stories of the kingdom of India.)

For Saturn, books hold the secrets of other civilizations. This wisdom is so material it can be "tasted" or "consumed," while the intertwined letters that hold the key to knowledge can be unlocked through interpretative skill.[15] The Anglo-Saxon poetic approach to words and the wisdom they convey – whether metaphorical or literal – is closely bound up with the skilful crafting of objects. That *cræft* in Old English signifies not only construction and cunning but also power shows how important the act of interpretation could be.[16]

The skilful control evident in Anglo-Saxon ideas of language and wisdom also ties in nicely with Old English poetry's formulaic nature.[17] Much of the imagery discussed in the following chapters is expressed through formulaic diction, which provides a linguistic framework for conveying

---

15 Although the *DOE* defines *gebregdstafas* as "learning, literally 'astuteness in letters'," the use of *bregdan* in relation to a net of conspiracy in *Beowulf* 2166b–9a implies a possible play on words with a textile/construction term. *DOE*, s.v. *gebrægd-stafas*, *gebregd-stafas*. See also sense 2. of *gebrægd, gebregd*: "astuteness, cunning."

16 See *DOE*, s.v. *cræft*.

17 For the purposes of defining the formula, it should be noted that this study adopts Britt Mize's non-systematic model, according to which variable elements, rather than denoting a larger systematic structure, can be read as part of the formula itself. Mize's example relates to the half-lines *hwitust corna* and *corna caldest*. Despite their evident dissimilarities, these are deemed variations of the same formula, participating as they do in the formulaic template *corna x-st* (Mize uses *q* for the variable element), where *x-st* is the superlative of an adjective describing *corn*. *Traditional Subjectivities*, p. 92 (see also further discussion of this model on pp. 52n44, 89–109). I view the flexibility built into this definition as more in line with recent criticisms of the rigidity of Old English poetic theory. Thus, John Miles Foley understands the formula in terms of "not one but a variety of types of diction: alongside the classical half-line phrase stand single words, whole-line patterns, multi-line patterns, collocations, clusters, and themes." *Traditional Oral Epic*, p. 235. Similarly, Elizabeth M. Tyler advocates for a collocational model that embraces the "range of kinds of formulas which overlap with, and often cannot be separated from, other kinds of more stylistically driven verbal repetitions, on the one hand, and patterns found in everyday linguistic expression, on the other." *Old English Poetics*, p. 101. For more on the history of formulaic theory, see O'Brien O'Keeffe, "Diction, Variation, the Formula"; Orchard, "Oral Tradition"; and Tyler, *Old English Poetics*, pp. 101–22.

both traditional and borrowed knowledge.[18] Rather than static phrasing, this diction should be understood as providing "a vibrant link between language and form," according to which conventional language may act as the source, rather than merely the vehicle, of ideas.[19] With this recognition, the understanding of poetic conventions becomes all the more essential to the examination of Old English poetry, the archaic tendency of which Elizabeth M. Tyler attributes to an Anglo-Saxon desire for familiarity: "[t]he stability of poetic convention amidst the movement of history brings us back to the aesthetics of the familiar, which can both assimilate the new and allow the old to change, because it rests on a two-way relationship between language and ideas: dynamic poetry is created in the space between words (including poetic conventions) and ideas."[20]

An understanding of Old English poetics – of the relationship between the idea/image/metaphor and the conventional (or convention-subverting) language that is used to express and highlight it – is therefore essential to a survey of weaving and binding imagery in the Old English corpus. The fact that this imagery is not inherently tied to only one type of theme, scene or text (indeed, it appears in a series of thus far unrecognized formulas, collocations, themes and type-scenes), speaks to its importance to poetry itself. And so, by looking at the many applications of weaving and binding imagery in the context of poetry at large, we can hope to learn more about the conventional and formulaic nature of Old English poetics. An examination of metaphor and style together can help us determine both what the poet has deemed important enough to emphasize and what

---

18 For the first, see especially John Miles Foley's discussion of traditional referentiality, which "entails the invoking of a context that is enormously larger and more echoic than the text or work itself, that brings the lifeblood of generations of poems and performances to the individual performance or text." *Immanent Art*, p. 7. For the second, see Andy Orchard and Thomas A. Bredehoft's recent exercises in formula-tracking, which have resulted in a new approach to poetry and poetics, known as literate-formulaic analysis. This methodological approach attempts to pinpoint signficant verbal overlaps between particular texts and known poets. As both Orchard and Bredehoft have recently demonstrated, this theory's ramifications are potentially staggering because they promise to offer previously unavailable insights into the use of texts and manuscripts in specific literary communities throughout Anglo-Saxon England. See Orchard, "Computing Cynewulf"; as well as his "Both Style and Substance"; and Bredehoft, *Authors, Audiences, and Old English Verse*.

19 Tyler, *Old English Poetics*, p. 6.

20 Ibid., p. 172.

his or her culture values most highly. Through formulaic analysis, we can begin to interpret Anglo-Saxon poetic constructions of reality.

In approaching the poetry, my immediate focus will be on weaving and binding imagery and diction. Because this imagery and the ideas behind it are my foremost area of interest, the methodology I employ will be primarily inter-textual, with occasional reference to comparative literary traditions – especially Old English prose, Latin, Old Norse and Old Saxon – when texts in these traditions act as specific analogues or sources of the texts at hand. Given that the poetic language and expression that govern this imagery are central to my approach, I will provide close readings of key passages that have been identified by means of a search for specific terms (using the searchable *DOE Corpus*). The specific terms upon which this survey will focus are the verbs -*wefan* and -*webbian* (to weave) and nouns derived from them (*web* (a woven product) and *webba* (weaver)), as well as -*bindan* (to bind) and -*feterian* (to fetter) and their nominal forms (-*bend* (bond) and *feter* (fetter)). Although these terms are common in prose as well as poetry, their rate of alliteration in poetic passages is, notably, very high, which speaks to their stylistic importance.[21] Occasionally it will also be relevant to look at related terms that frequently collocate with the former set. These include -*bregdan* (to braid), -*lucan* (to lock), -*fæstnian* (to fasten), -*hæftan* (to capture/constrain), -*sælan* (to tie), -*windan* (to wind/twist), -*wriþan* (to wrap around/tie), -*clam* (chain), -*loca* (enclosure) and -*teage* (tie). In order to restrict this study to a reasonable scope, this second set of terms will not be surveyed exhaustively.

By looking at all of the contexts in which the above sets of terminology are applied, the following discussions will both detect and analyse the conventional nature of this language – treating situations where it conforms to, reinvents, and subverts convention. For ease of comparison, I have separated my chapter discussions into three main sections, each of which

---

21 See Cronan, "Alliterative Rank in Old English Poetry," p. 150: "the higher frequency of alliteration that is exhibited by the poetic vocabulary indicates that there is a stylistic dimension to alliteration alongside the structural. The restriction of a number of words to poetry has its own stylistic implications, as does the use of words in figurative or extended senses. These words distinguish the language of poetry from the realm of ordinary discourse, and contribute to the creation of a poetic world that is above and beyond the world of everyday life. The stylistic aspects of these words are highlighted by the poets' frequent use of them in alliterating positions. The structure of the verse emphasizes the stylistic dimension of its vocabulary, and thus becomes a stylistic feature itself."

deals with a broad category of weaving and binding imagery. These categories are based on my own observation of similarities and differences in the way the key terms are employed. The main questions I will pose relate to the identification of the conventions relevant to each category of weaving and binding imagery – the broad categories being those covered by sections on: material objects, bondage, and the internal and abstract. In addition to identifying the use of conventional language, I will explore how instances exemplify or play with these categorical and poetic conventions. Furthermore, I will examine the links that can be made between categories, demonstrating the usefulness and necessity of reading all of the instances together. Because the fundamental principles that govern these conventions become apparent from such links, this survey will demonstrate how thematic and stylistic analysis can be used together to reveal new insights into the Anglo-Saxon poetic mindset.

Naturally, some thematic and stylistic analysis has already been undertaken in the general field of this survey. However, as mentioned above, previous scholarship on weaving and binding language and imagery has tended to restrict itself to either passing comments or partial discussion. For example, while numerous intriguing analyses of *The Wanderer* have touched on the poem's emphasis on binding and enclosures,[22] such imagery has either been discussed in relation to this poem alone, or in relation to a select group of texts (frequently elegies). A connection has not before been made between *The Wanderer*'s mental binding and the bonds that hold Grendel's glove together, or the bodily ties and binding afflictions of *Guthlac B* because, at first, they seem to be entirely separate cases. Yet, each may be read in the context of object-construction as well as human construction, implying that they actually have a great deal in common.

Furthermore, where extended discussion has already taken place, it has frequently employed a distinct methodology and exhibited a different focus. Maren Clegg Hyer's doctoral dissertation, "Textiles and Textile Imagery in Old English Literature," examines what poetry can tell us about the history of textiles and textile production in the Anglo-Saxon

---

22 See Clark and Wasserman, "Imagery of *The Wanderer*"; Cook, "*Woriað þa Winsalo*"; Greenfield, "Old English Elegies"; Greentree, "Wanderer's Horizon"; Hait, "Wanderer's Lingering Regret"; Irving, "Image and Meaning"; Johnson, "*Werig* and *Dreorig*"; Klinck, *Old English Elegies*, p. 110; Malmberg, "*Wanderer: waþema gebind*"; Mize, "Representation of the Mind"; Orchard, "Re-Reading *The Wanderer*"; Stanley, "Old English Poetic Diction"; and Wehlau, *Riddle of Creation*, pp. 46–50.

period. Conversely, in rooting my discussion in philology and poetics, this survey's methodology works in the opposite direction: it examines what weaving imagery can tell us about Anglo-Saxon poetry. At the same time, these two surveys' similar interest in textiles – only part of the picture in the case of this survey, which also discusses binding – speaks to a growing interest in the rapidly developing field of textiles history. This emerging research area has gained significant momentum in recent years, through Gale R. Owen-Crocker's pioneering work on interdisciplinary approaches to Anglo-Saxon material culture and literature, and is set to continue expanding since the publication of the *Encyclopedia of Medieval Dress and Textiles of the British Isles, c. 450–1450* (and associated annotated bibliography).

By engaging with weaving imagery alongside that of binding, this survey also addresses the lack of holistic treatment of the constructive and constrictive aspects of such terminology.[23] Ruth Wehlau's monograph *"The Riddle of Creation": Metaphor Structures in Old English Poetry*, though not comprehensive, comes closest to a detailed discussion of binding tropes in Old English poetry. She approaches metaphors of creation through an investigation of architecture and enclosure, arguing that Old English poetry employs these ideas as metaphors in the context of bodily and cosmic order and chaos. Her focus is on the constructive aspect of binding buildings, the body, and the world, and she treats neither the linguistic context of *bindan/bend* words nor their constrictive application. In so doing she addresses a different range of texts than those treated in this survey. Lori Ann Garner, in her recent book, *Structuring Spaces: Oral Poetics and Architecture in Early Medieval England*, focuses, like Hyer, on interrelationships between literature and material culture. While her discussion is intriguing, its specific interest in buildings overlaps only slightly with the current survey's linguistic and poetic foundation.

Overall, this survey's unique goal is to explore the poetic and cultural contexts of the Anglo-Saxon approach to created objects (construction) and bound figures (constriction), which together speak to the poetry's primarily human-centred world view. Each of the survey's three sections is made up of three to four chapters. Part I deals, in particular, with the

---

23 This lack is actually quite surprising considering how common binding is to the majority of types of Old English literature. Indeed, the *DOE* records no less than ca. 675 instances of *(ge)bindan* and its past participle. See the entries for *bindan, gebindan* and *gebunden*.

material context of objects, and so includes discussions of poetic representations of weaving and woven products, as well as the "woven" mail-coat, and the uses of binding in the construction of buildings and objects. In looking at conventional and subversive depictions of objects, this section argues that Old English poetry maintains a focus on status and prestige objects, whose worth is measured in relation to their helpfulness to humans.

Part II examines bondage, with specific discussions of binding in nature, in imprisonment and hell, and slavery and servitude. For the most part, the depictions in this section deal with binding as constriction, with objects, natural forces, and the devil all bound and binding. The emphasis in this section is therefore once again on the human struggle for control over its situation and surroundings, demonstrating the Anglo-Saxon tendency to construct and understand the world in terms of human experience.

Moving on from this context of the bound body, Part III analyses representations of the internal world and abstract concepts. It treats the physical ties of the body, whether structural or destructive, as well as the protective binding of the heart and mind against affliction. The discussion then turns to the use of weaving and binding imagery in relation to language, creation, magic, and fate. Once again abstract forces are imagined in human terms – either because they constrict people or because they are constructed like objects through human processes of manufacture. In addition to these abstract concepts, this section explores imagery of peace-weaving. In my rejection of the peace-weaver as a strictly female role, I look to the formulaic context of the Old English to find that this image is linked to status and prestige (peace being imagined as an object of worth). The final image of the ironic peace-weaver in *Beowulf* offers a perfect example of the Anglo-Saxon poetic construction of the world as a place of both overwhelming bondage and endless opportunity for the regaining of control through creative genius. Thus, Old English poetry, with its distinctly anthropocentric view of the world, reveals that – like humans – all of creation weaves and is woven, binds and is bound.

PART I

Webs and Rings: Experiencing Objects

1 The Material Context of Weaving

Material objects retain a place of great importance in Old English, not just because they are tools for human use, but also because they represent the human skill that went into their construction. Thus, the frequently cited passage from Fred C. Robinson's *"Beowulf" and the Appositive Style* aligns objects with the cultural world, which he sees in binary opposition to the natural world:

> Where nature is malevolent and chaotic, artifice is reassuring, and this, I believe, explains the remarkable accumulation of appositions and compounds for man-made, as opposed to natural, things in *Beowulf*. The man-made wall, the road, the ship, the hall, and human clothing and armor are not only practically useful but also are comforting symbols of the ability of man, through skill and reason, to subdue and control the natural world.[1]

This emphasis on achieving control over one's world through the creation of objects is perhaps less readily apparent in modern, industrialized societies where object-human power dynamics relate more to ownership than construction. In these societies, craftsmanship and the non-industrial creation of objects appear to function less as symbols of collective triumph over nature and more as expressions of personal ability. The focus on skill has shifted from communal to individual. Keeping in mind such differing approaches to the skill of human construction, this chapter will examine

---

1 P. 71. Robinson's approach to objects builds on George Clark's discussion of weapons and armour: "Arms and armor in *Beowulf* are human artifacts, instances of man's creative power and of his control over nature." "Beowulf's Armour," p. 409.

poetic depictions of material weaving, looking first at the contexts in which weaving diction is invoked, before turning to a discussion of the loom and an analysis of *Riddle 56*.

Cloth is an important part of most cultures because of its ability to protect the body, act as currency, and define social status. Given "how readily its appearance and that of its constituent fibers can evoke ideas of connectedness or tying," it is also frequently invoked as a metaphor for society.[2] Because of the importance and universality of cloth in any given culture and because of its aptness as a metaphor for community and social relations, we might very well expect cloth to appear prominently in the Old English poetic corpus. However, in approaching Anglo-Saxon constructions of reality, it becomes apparent that, for the purposes of the poetry at least, cloth was viewed very differently. When cloth does appear it is invariably a prestige object – like swords, halls, and other objects whose status is more readily apparent – invoked in order to indicate wealth or power. Furthermore, when the weaving process, whether material or metaphorical, is treated, it is always in a context that ties together construction, power, and control.

Poetic Representations of Textiles

Extended descriptions of weaving, like those of *Riddle 56* and *Riddle 35* (discussed below and in the following chapter), are few and far between in Old English poetry. Much of our information on textiles and textile-representation comes from brief glimpses in poems largely unconcerned with textiles. The lack of representation of textiles in Old English poetry is due partly to the nature of the poetry which survives – heroic and religious poetry tends not to dwell on domestic contexts – and partly perhaps to the commonness of weaving and textiles. This commonness is, of course, part of what makes them important to our study of their place in culture because anything essential to a cultural group is likely to be embedded in that culture's world view.

One of the references to textiles most commonly invoked by scholars is more of a comment on women's roles in Anglo-Saxon society than a description of cloth production, and it is for this reason that it has received so much attention. This is *Maxims I*'s statement: *Fæmne æt hyre bordan*

---

2 Schneider and Weiner, eds., *Cloth and Human Experience*, p. 2.

geriseð (63b) (a woman belongs at her embroidery).[3] *Maxims I* is one of those texts designated by scholars as "wisdom literature,"[4] the purpose of which is "to convey in a nutshell the full range of spatial and temporal diversity."[5] A wise person is, thus, aware of such diversity, of the changing nature of the world, and the few principles that are stable.[6] Russell G. Poole traces this focus on understanding the world and the place of humanity in it to uncertainty and the desire to guard against misfortune. In doing so, he points towards psychological research that outlines the way in which "unfavourable events are not necessarily distressing so long as one has previously been inducted into the knowledge that they will come and then usually go," with education serving as a method of imparting knowledge to "neutralize" threats.[7] This suggestion that knowledge allows for power over the world and human situation is a common scholarly trend, illustrated by the definition of wisdom literature in terms of its purpose: "to suggest a scheme of life in the broadest sense of the word, to ensure its continuance, to predict its variations and to associate humanity with the fundamental rhythms of nature. It is an attempt to control life by some kind of order, to reduce the area of the unexpected and the sudden."[8] Wisdom literature's interest in patterning, order, and control makes it the ideal place to search for representations of weaving and binding.

What we have in *Maxims I*, however, is a reference not to weaving, but to embroidery.[9] This quite firmly places the context of this passage among the higher levels of society, at court, and in the convent. Indeed, with "no evidence for a parallel 'folk' embroidery tradition," Penelope Walton Rogers concludes that embroidery was likely associated with nobility.[10] Christine Fell notes that while basic tasks such as weaving and spinning may not have had class associations, the production of more expensive

---

3 The importance of textiles to the concept of the "good wife" is also evident in the Bible and comparative European historical contexts. See Proverbs 31:13–24; and Büttner, "Education of Queens," pp. 204–27.

4 Although Thomas D. Hill prefers the term "sapiential" literature; see "Wise Words," p. 166.

5 Poole, *Old English Wisdom Poetry*, p. 18.

6 Ibid., p. 16.

7 Ibid., pp. 10–11.

8 Bloomfield, "Understanding Old English Poetry," p. 71.

9 For more on the surviving Anglo-Saxon embroidery fragments, see Coatsworth, "Stitches in Time."

10 *Cloth and Clothing*, p. 103.

textiles and their often complex ornamentation would be the realm of those with both money and time.[11] It is this more detailed and skilled textile craft of embroidering designs on fine cloth that is linked to noble women, whether they actually performed the work or had it commissioned.

The majority of the remaining references to textiles in Old English poetry do tend to include some element indicating their woven nature; however, these too are high status objects. The terms used in these descriptions may take the form of compounds with *web* as the second element or may simply pay particular attention to the interlinked or braided nature of the object. Such fine cloth often had religious associations, and thus might find its way into Old English poetic texts, as in the case of the temple veil that is rent in two at Christ's crucifixion. This veil is referred to as the *godwebba cyst* (1134b) (best of fine-woven cloths) in *Christ III*. *Godweb*, literally "God-web," is a compound describing cloth of the highest quality. Known as *purpura* in Latin, this heavy silk appeared in a variety of colours, and it would have been in use both for liturgical purposes and in (wealthy) secular contexts.[12] *Godweb* is thus invoked in *Christ III* not to describe everyday fabric, but to point to both the cloth's high value and its importance as a religious symbol. Hence, to the overt context of Christ's crucifixion tearing down what came before and building a new spirituality from its foundations is added another layer in which Christ, even in death, denies the importance of material wealth.[13]

Such a negative context of wealth, integral perhaps to Christian tenets,[14] is repeated elsewhere in Old English poetry, particularly in translations or adaptations of Latin works and biblical accounts. Hence, *godweb* is again invoked in relation to wealth in *The Metres of Boethius (Metre 8)*:

---

11 *Women in Anglo-Saxon England*, p. 40. Fell also reminds us that toward the end of the Anglo-Saxon period, the situation was more complex. By this time, the greater demand for high quality secular and religious garments led to the training of slaves from large households in this work.

12 Owen-Crocker, "Women's Costume," pp. 427–8. See also the section on purple by Owen-Crocker and John Munro, in Owen-Crocker, Coatsworth, and Hayward, eds., *Encyclopedia of Medieval Dress and Textiles*, pp. 436–8.

13 For more on the temple veil in this text, the Vulgate and the Old Saxon *Hêliand* (5664b–70a), see my forthcoming article "Sails, Veils, and Tents."

14 For more on the function of treasure in Old English poetry and its relationship with Christianity, see Tyler, *Old English Poetics*, pp. 24, 36–7.

> nalles win druncon
> scir of steape.   Næs þa scealca nan
> þe mete oðþe drinc   mængan cuðe,
> wæter wið hunige,   ne heora wæda þon ma
> sioloce siowian,   ne hi siarocræftum
> godweb giredon,   ne hi gimreced
> setton searolice,   ac hi simle him
> eallum tidum   ute slepon
> under beamsceade,   druncon burnan wæter,
> calde wyllan.   (20b–29a)

(They did not drink wine, bright from the cup. There was not at all any man then who knew how to mix food or drink, water with honey, nor, moreover, sew their garments with silk, nor did they construct fine-woven cloth with clever skills, nor did they cunningly build bejeweled halls, but they always slept outside at all times under the shade of trees, drank water from the stream, the cold spring.)

This metre appears in the tenth-century C-text of the Old English translation of Book 2, Metre 5 of Boethius's *De consolatione philosophiae*.[15] The B-text, an entirely prose translation into Old English, was copied later, probably from the end of the eleventh or early part of the twelfth century, although it likely represents an older version than the prosimetric C-text.[16] For ease of comparison, the Latin text is printed below on the left and the B-text prose on the right:

Non Bacchica munera norant
liquido confundere melle
nec lucida uellera Serum
Tyrio miscere ueneno.
Somnos dabat herba salubres,
potum quoque lubricus amnis,
umbras altissima pinus. (6–12)[17]

Nalles scir win hi ne druncan, ne nanne wætan hi ne cuþon wið hunige mengan, ne seolocenra hrægla mid mistlicum bleowum hi ne gimdon. Ealne weg hi slepon ute on triowa sceadum. Hlutterra wella wæter hi drincon. (9–12)[18]

---

15 Godden and Irvine, eds., *Old English Boethius*, 1:18.
16 Ibid., 1:9, 46. For more on the relationship between the texts, see ibid., 1:44–9.
17 *De Consolatione Philosophiae*, ed. Moreschini, p. 45.

<table>
<tr>
<td>(They did not know the gifts of Bacchus, to combine liquid with honey, nor to imbue bright Chinese silks with Tyrian dye. The grass gave them pleasant sleep, likewise the flowing river drink, the highest pines shade.)</td>
<td>(Not at all did they drink bright wine, nor did they know how to mix liquid with honey, nor did they desire silk clothing with various colours. They always slept outside in the shade of trees. They drank the water of pure springs.)</td>
</tr>
</table>

All three texts – the Latin original, prose, and poetic translations – similarly invoke the simplicity of the lifestyle practiced by the earth-dwellers from the first age. While the Latin poem focuses to some extent on the innocence of these people (they did not know about later technologies), the Old English prose text implies a sense of moral superiority (they neither knew nor desired later technologies). The prose text relates content similar to that found in the Old English poetic version, but there is no mention of hall-building nor is there any emphasis on the construction of cloth. Yet in focusing on the cloth's colour, the prose more faithfully translates the Latin poem's reference to dyes.

The difference between the three versions is particularly noteworthy because it demonstrates the importance of weaving and binding imagery to the poetics of Old English. Indeed, it is the fine construction of cloth that here represents the more complex technologies of later cultures, which are depicted as increasingly dependent upon material objects as sources of riches and status. The description of cloth is also more extended than in the previous and following examples discussed in this section, with direct reference to the skilful sewing that goes into making cloth in the Anglo-Saxon period. This emphasis can also be seen at the level of poetics, especially in light of Thomas A. Bredehoft's recent discussion of ornamental effects (such as rhyme and secondary alliteration) as "linguistic or poetic interlacing."[19] He particularly notes the use of such effects in cases where the poet wishes to emphasize construction motifs,[20] a context that is especially appropriate in this passage given the reference to

---

18 Godden and Irvine, eds., *Old English Boethius*, 1:271, ch. 15.

19 *Early English Metre*, p. 65.

20 Ibid., pp. 65, 68, 93, 148–9. In particular, Bredehoft cites *Judith*, *The Ruin* and *The Death of Alfred*. Seth Lerer also discusses binding imagery in relation to poetic construction, although he is less concerned with poetic devices; see *Literacy and Power*, pp. 112–25.

textile-production. Here, the poet-translator includes a variety of effects in order to highlight the construction of and the construction in these lines: in addition to an interlinear assonance of short and long "ea" (*scealca/eallum/-sceade* and *steape/beam-*), "æ" (*Næs/mængan/wæter/-cræft/wæda*[21]) and "io" (*sioloce/siowian*), the passage contains a near-rhyme in one half-line (*druncon burnan*), and plays with both "i" and "m" sounds in two consecutive b-verses (*hi gim-* and *hi simle him*). Perhaps most interesting, however, is the interlacing of "s" alliteration, which occurs in three lines in this passage.[22] Given that "s" is the only letter to alliterate more than once in these lines, its multiple use strongly emphasizes the silken textile (*sioloce*), its sewn construction (*siowian*) and the skill that went into said construction (*siarocræftum*), as well as the skilfully bejeweled hall (*setton searolice*).

This context of skilful craft is elided in the other two references to *godweb* in Old English religious poetry, both of which invoke the rich material for its association with wealth and status. Thus, the poetic retelling of *Exodus* depicts fabric as a treasure and links it specifically with gold in the passage describing the Israelites' deliverance from Egypt:

> Heo on riht sceodon
> gold and godweb,   Iosepes gestreon,
> wera wuldorgesteald.   (587b–9a)

(They equally divided the gold and the fine-woven cloth, Joseph's treasure, the glorious riches of men.)

Similarly invoked in the context of spoils of war, Ælfric refers to *godweb* in his description of Judas Machabeus' victory over Antiochus' army, in the saint's life, *Passio Sanctorum Machabeorum*:

> and iudas þa funde þa ða he fram fyrde gecyrde
> gold . and seolfor . godeweb . and purpuran .
> and fela oðre herereaf on þam fyrdwicum.   (358–60)[23]

---

21 Although *wæda* contains a long "æ," paired as it is with *wæter*, the visual similarity makes it notable.

22 Bredehoft notes that late Old English verse allows "sc" and "s" to alliterate with one another; *Authors, Audiences, and Old English Verse*, p. 132.

23 *Lives of Saints*, ed. Skeat, 2:90.

(and then Judas found, when he returned from the undertaking, gold and silver, fine-woven cloth and purple, and many other army-spoils in that military camp.)

The linking of fine fabric and gold in these two passages is not particularly out of place since cloth operates as a form of currency in many cultures.[24] Indeed, cloth could even be woven with threads of gold, a technique that was practiced throughout the Roman Empire, with the archaeological record supporting its use both on the Continent and in England.[25] In most of the finds, the woven thread has disintegrated, leaving only the strips of gold behind, except in one of the brocaded pieces found at Taplow where the warp has survived.[26] A number of bands woven with gold thread have also survived in Anglo-Saxon contexts, and these have been identified as brocaded hair bands and girdles worn by aristocratic women, as well as two examples of women's cuffs or bracelets and two later examples of men's jacket borders and a belt.[27]

Cloth that is ornamented by gold is also referred to in *Beowulf*'s banquet scene, following the fight with Grendel. The hall is described as shining and splendid with what appear to be great tapestries on the walls:

> fela þæra wæs,
> wera ond wifa   þe þæt winreced,
> gestsele gyredon.   Goldfag scinon
> web æfter wagum,   wundorsiona fela
> secga gehwylcum   þara þe on swylc starað.   (992b–6)

---

24 Schneider and Weiner, eds., *Cloth and Human Experience*, p. 2; Owen-Crocker, Coatsworth and Hayward, eds., *Encyclopedia of Medieval Dress and Textiles*, p. 3. See also the section on gold and silver thread by Paul Garside, pp. 237–9.

25 Rogers, *Cloth and Clothing*, p. 96. A similar reference to cloth woven with gold occurs in Ælfric's *Natale Sancte Agnetis, uirginis*, ed. Skeat, 1:172, lines 36–7 (referring to spiritual clothing).

26 Rogers, *Cloth and Clothing*, p. 96. Indeed, this very process of disintegration is described in homily 10, *Þisses Middangeardes Ende Neah Is*, Morris, ed., *Blickling Homilies*, p. 113: *Nu þu miht her geseon moldan dæl & wyrmes lafe, þær þu ær gesawe godweb mid golde gefagod* (Now you can see here a portion of earth and the leavings of worms, where earlier you saw fine-woven cloth dappled with gold).

27 Rogers, *Cloth and Clothing*, p. 96; and Wilson, "Craft and Industry," p. 272.

(there were many men and women who prepared that wine-hall, the guest-hall. Gold-adorned webs shone on the walls, many wonderful sights for each man who looks at such things.)

Here, the linking of gold and woven material draws attention to the lavishness of Heorot. The fine cloth is yet another symbol of the Danes' wealth, but this is wealth of a different kind than the typical treasure-motif of metal weapons passed down as heirlooms. The description of the gold-adorned cloth stands in contrast to the destruction of the hall by Grendel. Indeed the lines directly following this passage return to the fight scene, reminding us that, despite the iron bonds that held it in place structurally, the hall was attacked and broken not long before. The juxtaposition of these two descriptions of the hall implies that, here, the fine, gold-woven cloth acts as a symbol of the community, brought together once again, protected, cleansed and made safe. This implication is further emphasized by the intertwining of "w" and "s" alliteration in alternating lines, which links the people (*wera/wifa/secga*) and their experience of (*starað*) the hall (*winreced/-sele/wagum*) and its woven adornments (*scinon/web/wundor-siona*).

A parallel to these shining, gold-adorned webs also occurs later in *Beowulf*, this time in the form of the banner that Wiglaf finds in the dragon's barrow:

> Swylce he siomian geseah   segn eall gylden
> heah ofer horde,   hondwundra mæst,
> gelocen leoðocræftum;   of ðam leoma stod,
> þæt he þone grundwong   ongitan meahte,
> wrætte giondwlitan.   (2767–71a)

(Likewise he saw an entirely golden banner rising high over the hoard, the greatest of hand-wonders, skilfully interlocked – a light extended from it, so that he was able to make out the ground, to examine the treasure.)

While this banner is not described as woven, a parallel term of construction is employed: *gelocen*, literally "locked," but perhaps more appropriately "interlinked" or "interlocked." This term is often used in the context of interlinked mail, and is fitting here given that the banner is entirely golden – thus it appears to be interwoven metal rather than woven cloth. Working with metals in such an intricate way implies great skill, as does the presence of *-cræft*, which further connects this example to the depiction of complex construction in *The Metres of Boethius*, discussed above. Here, however, the context is arguably a more positive (or at least ambiguous) one, with no overt rejection of material wealth articulated with reference to the banner. Both the skilful construction and the rich materials that went into the making of the banner, furthermore, signal its status as an object of value. As treasures, these woven objects are also strongly associated with power – hence their invocation in contexts of war and victory. Their status therefore, is a reflection of their skilful creators and mighty possessors alike.

The final instance of a tapestry in *Beowulf* has generally been read as one of several references that metaphorically link fate and weaving:[28]

>   Ac him dryhten forgeaf
> wigspeda gewiofu,   Wedera leodum,
> frofor ond fultum,   þæt hie feond heora
> ðurh anes cræft   ealle ofercomon,
> selfes mihtum.
>
> (696b–700a)

(But the lord gave them webs of battle-success, the people of the Weders, comfort and support, so that they completely overcame their enemy through the skill of one, by his own might.)

The *wigspeda gewiofu* have been explained as an example of Christian providence or a fate bestowed by God,[29] although the usual (admittedly controversial) term for fate, *wyrd*, is not employed here. However, as outlined in chapter 9, examples where fate is associated with weaving tend to include the verb *-wefan* rather than the nominal form of the woven object used in this passage. Such an inconsistency of forms indicates that this example may be working differently.

This occurrence is further individuated from fate-weaving references by its similarity to the passage from *Elene* that describes the battle standard Constantine has fashioned in response to his heavenly vision. After the standard brings the Roman army victory, the king asks his advisors:

---

28 See chapter 9, pp. 270–9.
29 Hyer, "Textiles and Textile Imagery in Old English," p. 162.

> þe þis his beacen wæs
> þe me swa leoht oðywde   ond mine leode generede,
> tacna torhtost,   ond me tir forgeaf,
> wigsped wið wraðum,   þurh þæt wlitige treo.   (162b–5)

(whose beacon this was, which appeared to me, so radiantly, and saved my people, the brightest of signs, and gave me glory, battle-success against my foes, through that beautiful tree.)

Here we have a reference to the giving (*forgeaf*) of battle-success (*wigsped*), just as in the *Beowulf* passage. Likewise, the verse structure is mimicked, with *forgeaf* appearing as the last word of the b-verse and *wigsped* as the first word of the following a-verse. The battle-success is also explicitly linked to the use of God's symbol on his standard. Thus, the victory-standard here acts as a metonymy for victory, which is bestowed on people by God. It may well be, then, that when *Beowulf* refers to webs of battle-success it is a reference to the concept of victory, imagined as a visual sign from God, rather than the invoking of a general weaving metaphor to indicate fate. The association turns once again on the importance of treasure, which here, as in the other cases, offers a visual representation of the outcome of conflict.

The Loom and *Riddle 56*[30]

We have already seen that there is a precedent for depicting high status cloth in Old English poetry without a great deal of reference to the production process. There is, however, one riddle among the *Exeter Book*'s collection that appears to describe a weaving loom.[31] This is not unexpected

---

30 An earlier version of this and the following section has been published as "Looming Danger and Dangerous Looms."

31 Other suggested solutions include "lathe," "flail," and "execution." Fry, "Exeter Book Riddle Solutions," p. 24. However, "loom" and "web and loom" retain the most support, especially among editors of the *Exeter Book* and the riddles. See Tupper, *Riddles of the Exeter Book*, pp. 192–3; Krapp and Dobbie, *Exeter Book*, p. 350; Williamson, *Old English Riddles of The Exeter Book*, p. 305; and Muir, *Exeter Anthology of Old English Poetry*, 2:575. Note that Hans Pinsker and Waltraud Ziegler support but do not elaborate upon the solution "lathe" in their edition, *Die altenglischen Rätsel des Exeterbuchs*, pp. 277–8.

since the Old English riddles provide an ideal environment for references
to quotidian life because of their interest in commonplace subject matter
and objects. As John D. Niles notes, in playing with the "bric-a-brac of
daily life," these texts "give life to things that are so often seen that they are
no longer seen."[32] The conventionality of subject matter makes these objects and ideas ideal for riddling, a type of literature that has long fascinated anthropologists because of the way it is "used to demonstrate
control over words and objects and ideas that are central to the life of the
riddling group."[33] It is in this context of play and power that the riddles'
tendency to invert social hierarchies becomes apparent.[34] The riddles' association with control, like wisdom literature's desire for stability, offers
us a way into the imagery of weaving and binding.

The *Exeter Book* loom riddle, which the ASPR numbers *Riddle 56*, reads:

Ic wæs þær inne   þær ic ane geseah
winnende wiht   wido bennegean,
holt hweorfende;   heaþoglemma feng,
deopra dolga.   Daroþas wæron
weo þære wihte,   ond se wudu searwum
fæste gebunden.   Hyre fota wæs
biidfæst oþer,   oþer bisgo dreag,
leolc on lyfte,   hwilum londe neah.
Treow wæs getenge   þam þær torhtan stod
leafum bihongen.   Ic lafe geseah
minum hlaforde,   þær hæleð druncon,
þara flana,   on flet beran.[35]

---

32 *Enigmatic Poems*, p. 52.
33 Abrahams, "Literary Study of the Riddle," p. 182.
34 See Teele, "Heroic Tradition," pp. 202–5.
35 For line 12, the manuscript reads *flan*, which Williamson and Muir emend to *flana*.
    I have adopted this reading here, rather than the ASPR's *flana geweorc*, because
    Williamson's argument that the genitive is governed by *lafe* (which frequently takes
    the genitive in the riddles and thus does not require a parallel accusative noun) both
    accounts for the grammar of the lines and is preferable to supplying whole words. See
    Williamson, *Old English Riddles of The Exeter Book*, p. 307; and Krapp and Dobbie,
    Exeter Book, p. 350.

(I was inside there, where I saw a wooden object wounding a certain struggling creature, the turning wood;[36] it received battle-wounds,[37] deep gashes.
Darts were woeful to that creature, and the wood skilfully bound fast. One
of its feet was held fixed, the other endured affliction, leapt into the air, sometimes near the land. A tree, hung about by leaves, was near to that bright
thing [which] stood there. I saw the leavings of those arrows, carried out onto
the floor to my lord, where the warriors drank.)

The solution "loom" is perhaps more readily understandable if the poem's
historical context – a context in which looms played a much more important role than they do in modern life – is taken into account.

One of the looms in use at this time, with archaeological evidence supporting its existence in Anglo-Saxon contexts, was the vertical, warp-
weighted loom.[38] This type of loom was used in many parts of medieval
Europe, and survived in some areas of modern Scandinavia.[39] Marta
Hoffmann, in surveying the warp-weighted loom's use and distribution,
argues that this type of loom, the oldest known in Europe, was passed

---

36 The syntax of the first two and a half lines is somewhat ambiguous because of the
    nature of the reported vision. Both the subject of the infinitive verb *bennegean* (to
    wound) and the object being wounded are in the accusative. This is further compli-
    cated by the use of apposition, making it unclear which terms refer to the object that is
    wounding and which to that being wounded. Williamson takes *wido* and *holt hweor-
    fende* as appositives, and Bosworth and Toller read these as the subject, making the
    ane and *winnende wiht* the object, as I have attempted to show in my translation. *Old
    English Riddles of The Exeter Book*, p. 306; and *Anglo-Saxon Dictionary*, s.v. *bennian*.
37 The term *heaþuglemm* is a *hapax legomenon*, as is the second component of the
    compound, *glemm*, which appears in Wulfstan's homily, *Her Ongynð be Cristendome*,
    where it refers to the need to hold the Christian church *unwemme* (unblemished) and
    without *glemme*. See *Homilies of Wulfstan*, ed. Bethurum, p. 202, line 45. For *glemm*,
    the *DOE* notes some ambiguity with regard to the definition, offering "? stain, ?
    wound." For *heaþuglemm*, Bosworth and Toller, perhaps because of the first element,
    offer "a wound got in fight" with no reference to difficulties defining the term.
38 See Owen-Crocker, *Dress in Anglo-Saxon England*, p. 287. The two main types of
    looms are horizontal and vertical, which refers to the direction of the warp. The vertical
    loom can also be subdivided into the tapestry loom, in which the warp is attached to
    two beams, and the warp-weighted loom, in which the warp is attached to an upper
    beam and tension is maintained by hanging weights. This was probably the most com-
    mon loom during the period. See Hoffman, *Warp-Weighted Loom*, p. 5; and Rogers,
    Cloth and Clothing, p. 28.
39 Hoffmann, *Warp-Weighted Loom*, p. 6.

down with few modifications from the Neolithic Age.[40] Hoffmann also offers a straightforward description of weaving, in which "two systems of threads cross each other at right angles: one – the warp – is stretched taut, while the other – the weft – is introduced as the work proceeds, and is bound in place by the warp threads."[41] Already, we can see how the stretching of one system of threads and the moving and binding of another relates to the riddle's description of this bound and struggling creature.

In order to fully contextualize this riddle, an explanation of the mechanism of the warp-weighted loom is necessary.[42] This particular loom, depicted in Figure 1, consisted of two uprights with a horizontal beam across the top, and would have rested against the wall or roof so the uprights were tilted. Warp threads were attached to the top beam, and kept taut with weights attached at the bottom. Half of the threads would be pulled in front of and half placed behind the shed rod, a cross bar fixed between the uprights and towards the bottom of the loom.

Sitting in brackets attached to the uprights were the heddle rods, which were movable, attached only to the warp threads at the back of the loom. When a heddle rod was pulled away from the loom, the weaver could move the back threads forward and change the shed, the space between the warp threads through which the weft threads were passed. The warp threads relate to the poem's description of the struggling creature's bound foot and jumping foot: of the two rows of warp threads, one remains in place while the second row moves with the change of shed.[43] The weft threads may have been passed through the warp in a ball or skein,[44] or with the help of a needle or shuttle.[45] While no shuttles survive today, there is a reference to a *hrisil* in *Riddle 35*, which will be discussed in chapter 2. Erika von Erhardt-Siebold argues that the piece of wood wounding the

---

40 Ibid., p. 5.

41 Ibid.

42 The following description relies especially on Owen-Crocker's *Dress in Anglo-Saxon England*, pp. 286–91. For more on Anglo-Saxon loom-types, see Owen-Crocker, Coatsworth, and Hayward, eds., *Encyclopedia of Medieval Dress and Textiles*, pp. 344–7.

43 Erhardt-Siebold, "Old English Loom Riddles," p. 15; and Williamson, ed. *Old English Riddles of The Exeter Book*, p. 307. On the other hand, Maren Clegg Hyer suggests that the stationary foot could be the loom posts, while the moving foot is the heddle rod, in Owen-Crocker, Coatsworth, and Hayward, eds., *Encyclopedia of Medieval Dress and Textiles*, p. 456.

44 Poole, "Textile Inventory," p. 470.

45 Erhardt-Siebold, "Old English Loom Riddles," p. 15.

Figure 1 – Drawing of a Scandinavian warp-weighted loom from the Faroes.[46]

---

46 This illustration of a loom in the Copenhagen Museum is taken from Montelius, *Civilisation of Sweden in Heathen Times*, p. 160, via Roth, *Ancient Egyptian and Greek Looms*, p. 34, as it appears on the Project Gutenberg website.

web in the riddle refers to one of these implements,[47] an assertion that is supported by Craig Williamson[48] and F.H. Whitman.[49]

The threads of the fabric were straightened with bone or wood picks when they clung together and, because the weft would be left loose in order to stop the cloth from contracting, it was beaten upwards with a sword-shaped beater. The fabric picks and sword beater also arguably appear in the riddle, in the reference to the darts that wound the creature.[50] As for the nearby tree, hung about by leaves, this is likely the distaff standing near the loom (see Figure 1), whose wool or flax would have gone in to the making of the web.[51] Finally, the *laf* – the leavings that are carried to the lord in the hall – refers to the finished cloth, the struggling web having now been fully subdued. Looms like these were essential parts of Anglo-Saxon life, since the work of clothing the family through spinning and weaving was frequently performed at the household level.[52] As noted above, the loom is an obvious candidate for the riddling genre because the riddles so often find their subject matter in the commonplace.

---

47 Ibid., pp. 15–16.
48 *Old English Riddles of the Exeter Book*, p. 306.
49 *Old English Riddles*, p. 140.
50 Ibid., and Erhardt-Siebold, "Old English Loom Riddles," p. 15.
51 Erhardt-Siebold, "Old English Loom Riddles," p. 15.
52 Rogers, *Cloth and Clothing*, p. 47. In villages, the work of clothing the family through spinning and weaving was probably done communally on a small-scale level (i.e., for the household and extended family), making the loom an essential part of Anglo-Saxon life. David Wilson suggests that weaving was so common that there was likely to have been a loom in every household, and he argues that, as a standard piece of household equipment, loom finds do not necessarily signify huts devoted entirely to weaving. See "Craft and Industry," p. 271. However, both Owen-Crocker and Rogers support the conception of the Anglo-Saxon village that consists of a main hall surrounded by huts for various crafts including weaving. See "Women's Costume," p. 448; and *Cloth and Clothing*, p. 44. According to Rogers, in later periods spinning and weaving equipment continues to be linked to domestic buildings, and perhaps this is where Wilson's theory fits in. As the Anglo-Saxon period covers several hundred years, it is important to keep in mind the changing cultural climate. Indeed, throughout the age, larger-scale weaving must have taken place in wealthier estates as is evidenced by the textile inventory in *Gerefa*, the late eleventh- or early twelfth-century guide to the role of the reeve or estate manager. See Rogers, *Cloth and Clothing*, pp. 44–6. For an edition of *Gerefa*, see Liebermann, ed., *Die Gesetze der Angelsachsen*, 1:453–5. For a discussion of the changing climate of textile production throughout the Anglo-Saxon period, see Owen-Crocker, Coatsworth, and Hayward, eds., *Encyclopedia of Medieval Dress and Textiles*, pp. 3–4.

Reading *Riddle 56*

For all that the subject matter of *Riddle 56* is commonplace, the approach to this subject is a warlike one. Violence in the riddles is, of course, not a new topic, with many scholarly discussions examining the way commonplace objects are personified and then attacked, bound, mutilated, and/or killed.[53] This violence, which is both carried out by humans and at the same time frequently punctuated by expressions of human empathy for the wounded objects, has been explained as acceptable because it occurs in the safe, playful, and inverted world of the riddle.[54] Indeed, Ruth Wehlau notes that, as with the saints' lives, "[p]art of the pleasure in reading the riddles comes from the idea of violence as spectacle, combined with our knowledge that the violence is confined to the words."[55] The loom riddle is one of these texts, and the violent imagery here is particularly problematic because it characterizes the construction of an object that was beneficial to humans – that is, cloth.

From the perspective of textiles research, this violence is off-putting; cloth is generally conceived of as playing a positive role because it is essential to human culture and is an apt metaphor for society.[56] An approach of construction-through-destruction, however, is wholly appropriate to the world of riddles:

What the riddles prize above all is the way things turn to the welfare of humankind. Rarely is the 'raw' stuff of nature introduced (a deer's antlers, an ox's hide) without its being brought into relation to the 'cooked' elements of culture (a pair of inkwells, a set of leather goods). The riddles thus domesticate the elements of nature and turn them to human use.[57]

---

53 See Bitterli, *Say What I Am Called*; Denno, "Oppression and Voice"; Wehlau, *Riddle of Creation*, pp. 102–5; and Wilcox, "'Tell Me What I Am'."

54 See Irving, "Heroic Experience," p. 199; Nelson, "Four Social Functions"; and Teele, "Heroic Tradition," pp. 205, 226.

55 *Riddle of Creation*, p. 105.

56 Schneider and Weiner, eds., *Cloth and Human Experience*, p. 2.

57 Niles, *Enigmatic Poems*, p. 54. Niles employs the terminology of Claude Lévi-Strauss's *The Raw and the Cooked*, originally published as *Le Cru et le Cuit*. This anthropological study views cooking as a cultural process and outlines the way in which mythological depictions of the raw and the cooked correspond to a nature/culture binary.

Even with the recognition that this raw/cooked or living/dead opposition is part of the riddling tradition, the loom riddle remains a complicated text. Both the loom and the fabric being woven upon it are "cooked," man-made artefacts, indicating that the violence inherent in the construction-from-destruction motif is working differently here. The premise that violence is an important part of the riddling genre has been well established. Consequently, this discussion will not explore why violence is associated with weaving, but rather how this association functions and what this means for our interpretation of the riddle at large.

As riddle theory makes clear, it is the function of riddles to play with the limitations and parameters of the riddler's society.[58] Thus, one of the questions we must address is what aspect of the riddler's society *Riddle 56* is probing. A useful starting point here is gender, a concept with which many domestic riddles play. Given that weaving was women's work in the medieval period,[59] gender is a fairly obvious avenue to take. Thus, some have read this poem as an inversion of two types of work generally divided by gender.[60] With weaving being the work of women and battle the work of men in the Anglo-Saxon period, the fact that these two spheres of work are mapped onto one another is very interesting. However, while this is a valid line of inquiry, it is also important to note that the weavers and their gender are not actually referred to in this text, unlike in some riddles where women are clearly present and involved in domestic labour.

---

58 Wilcox, "'Tell Me What I Am'," p. 58; and Abrahams, "Literary Study of the Riddle," p. 182.

59 The major discussions of Anglo-Saxon weaving all place this activity within the realm of women. While some, like Owen-Crocker and Rogers, are more concerned with the technology and process itself, many discussions of weaving approach this task through the lens of gender studies and women's roles. See Fell, *Women in Anglo-Saxon England*; Chance, *Woman as Hero*; and Hyer, "Textiles and Textile Imagery in Old English," which has a strong focus on the role of women as literal or metaphorical weavers. For an archaeological perspective, see Stoodley's analysis of data from Anglo-Saxon burials, which finds that weaving tools were primarily female grave goods; *Spindle and the Spear*, pp. 31, 33, 75, 136. Notable, however, is the fact that a search of the *DOE Corpus* (s.v. *webba*, *webbe*) yields more references to male weavers than to female ones. The fact that men also played a role in Anglo-Saxon weaving is emphasized by the named weavers in manumission documents. See Craster, "Some Anglo-Saxon Records," p. 190; and Earle, *Hand-Book to the Land Charters*, pp. 257, 259.

60 See, for example, Poole, *Viking Poems*, pp. 138–40.

Notable in this context are *Riddles 25* and *45*, solved as "onion" and "bread dough." In these poems, female figures are presented as fearless sexual aggressors.[61] These women are described in a fair amount of detail, with attention given to their physical appearance, class and personalities. The woman in *Riddle 25*, a *ceorles dohtor* (6b) (free man's daughter), is described as *ful cyrtenu* (6a) (very pretty) and *wundenlocc* (11a) (curly-haired).[62] *Riddle 45* is much shorter and does not refer explicitly to the woman's appearance, but her clothing is signified by the term *hrægle* (4b), which is both a cloth used to cover the bread dough and a garment that hides the sexual encounter. This woman is a *bryd* (3b) (bride) and a *þeodnes dohtor* (5b) (ruler's daughter), with a "proud-minded" or "-hearted" bearing (4a: *hygewlonc*) that echoes her counterpart in *Riddle 25* (7a: *modwlonc*). Both women's actions are also described, with the use of *gripan* (*Riddle 25* 7b) (to grip) and *grapian* (*Riddle 45* 3b) (to seize), focusing attention on the women's hands – a somewhat violent tool of seduction according to the double entendre-reading, or of domestic labour according to the solutions "onion" and "bread dough."[63]

The highly gendered and sexualized approach to women and their work evident in these two riddles could easily have been applied to weaving in *Riddle 56*, and yet it is not.[64] In its approach to the labour of weaving, this poem maintains a greater focus on the construction of the cloth rather than on the weavers. Indeed, this trend can be read across the Old English poetic corpus at large, with all of the references to weaving or woven objects[65]

---

61 Williams, "What's So New about the Sexual Revolution?" p. 48.

62 On the translation of *wundenlocc*, see Cavell, "Old English 'Wundenlocc' Hair."

63 Glenn Davis maintains that hands and touching are often invoked euphemistically in Old English literature. "Exeter Book Riddles and the Place of Sexual Idiom," pp. 44–9. Note, however, that his reading of Beowulf's fight with Grendel's mother is problematic because he fails to note that hands are used thematically (and non-sexually) throughout the poem. See Carens, "Handscóh and Grendel"; and Rosier, "Uses of Association."

64 Indeed, the Old Norse loom riddle from the H-text of the Riddles of Gestumblindi in *Heiðreks saga* does appear to invoke equine sexuality, although this choice may relate more to associations between horses and virility, than between textiles and sex. For the text, see Helgason, ed., *Heiðreks saga*, p. 78; and Tolkien, *Saga of Heidrek the Wise*, p. 81. Tolkien's edition also includes a translation of the first four lines, noting that the final two are corrupt.

65 This statement applies to the production of objects and artifacts. I should emphasize that I am excluding metaphorical weaving because there are several instances where Old English poetry refers to weavers of abstract concepts, which will be dealt with in the following chapters.

focusing upon the object rather than the creator of the object. The same can be said for several Anglo-Latin enigmata that deal with embroidery.[66] Tatwine's personified needle and fabric in *De acu* (on a needle) and *De acu pictili* (on an embroidery needle) both relate the violence done to them, in order that fine cloth may be created. The first is blinded: *Est mirum dictum, cludam ni lumina uultus, / Condere non artis penitus molimina possum* (4–5) (It is strange to say, unless one blocks up the lights of my face [i.e., eyes], I cannot produce by my art the slightest undertaking), while the second's face is pierced: *Quippe meam gracilis faciem iugulauerat hospes, / Nobilior tamen adcrescit decor inde genarum* (4–5) (Of course, a slim stranger has in the past slit my face, yet the beauty of my cheeks grows nobler from then on).[67] These enigmatic texts' emphases on the product rather than the producer distinguish them from other medieval representations of weaving, such as the supernatural women who weave a bloody banner in the Old Norse *Darraðarljóð*, a poem which is often read in conjunction with *Riddle 56*.[68] This is a significant distinction, which problematizes the poem's use as evidence in broader discussions of gender.

In addition to gender, the riddles also frequently probe issues of social class, which provides another possible approach to the use of violent imagery in the poem. Riddles dealing with domestic chores often include imagery of forced servitude, as will be discussed in chapter 6. Another Latin enigma from the seventh/eighth century appears in a collection that

---

66   For more on the Anglo-Latin enigmata, see chapter 2, pp. 55–7.

67   These can be contrasted with the North African Symphosius' *Enigma 55, Acula*, which, rather than a victim of violence, depicts the needle as both a wielder of chains and a restorer of fabric:

> Longa sed exilis, tenui producta metallo,
> Mollia duco leui comitantia uincula ferro;
> Et faciem laesis et nexum reddo solutis.
> (Tall but small, stretched from thin metal, I draw my flexible bonds along with my nimble iron; I restore both beauty to the damaged and binding to the loosened.)

68   The first to make this connection is F. Dietrich in "Die Räthsel des Exeterbuchs," p. 476. For other discussions, see Poole, *Viking Poems*, pp. 138–9; Teele, "Heroic Tradition," p. 153; Hyer, "Textiles and Textile Imagery in Old English," p. 139; and Bek-Pedersen, "Are the Spinning *Nornir* Just a Yarn?"; as well her *Norns in Old Norse Mythology*, pp. 141–2.

was produced on the Continent, but likely shared an insular connection.[69] Bern *Enigma 54*, *De insubulo* (on a weaver's beam) reads:

Duo generantur multo sub numero fratres,
Nomine sub uno diuisus quisque natura.
Pauper atque diues pari labore premuntur;
Pauper semper habet, diuesque saepe requiret.
Caput illis nullum, sed et os cum corpore cingunt,
Nam stantes nihil, iacentes <sed> plurima portant.

(Two brothers are produced out of a large number, each divided by nature, under one name. Poor and rich are oppressed by a like labour; the poor one always has, and the rich one often seeks. Those ones [have] no head, but they encircle mouth with flesh, thus standing they carry nothing, but lying down they carry much.)

Here, what are likely the loom's heddle rods[70] are described as separated by social class, despite sharing a name and similar function. The imagery of oppression (*premuntur*) is to be expected in a domestic context such as this, although the implication that both rich and poor are equally afflicted appears to intentionally jar. We might expect such servitude from the poor, the riddle suggests, but not the rich.

It is notable, given this enigma, that *Riddle 56* maintains a focus on binding and violence without reference to prisoners, the poor or slaves at work. Once again, the focus is seen to be the product rather than the producer. The *Exeter Book* loom riddle does not deal with class or servitude, themes which are more characteristic of agricultural riddles in Old English. The aggressive sexuality attributed to women working in the domestic sphere and the violence of slavery imposed upon objects used in agriculture are both linked, at a fundamental level, with food growth and production. While it would seem to make sense that weaving, as a similarly

---

69 The relationship between the *Bern* riddles and the Old English and Anglo-Latin enigmata is briefly discussed in Williams, "Riddles of Tatwine and Eusebius," p. 12. For more on this tradition, see Andy Orchard, "Enigma Variations," and his forthcoming edition of Anglo-Saxon riddles.

70 According to Maren Clegg Hyer in Owen-Crocker, Coatsworth, and Hayward, eds., *Encyclopedia of Medieval Dress and Textiles* p. 456.

widespread domestic chore, should be associated through shared imagery with food production, and while all of our modern conceptions of medieval women's work would encourage us to see this connection, it is simply not so. The violence in *Riddle 56* has nothing to do with gender or class. Instead, weaving is depicted in terms of battle, torture, and execution, and the association seems to be with heroic literature.

Two of the battle words that link the riddle's imagery to martial violence are the *heaþoglemma* (3b) (battle-wounds) and *deopra dolga* (4a) (deep gashes) caused by the wooden object of line 2. As noted above, these probably refer to the piercings of the shuttle through the web's body, but – as wounds – they are associated with battle. While the term *heaþuglemm* appears only in this riddle, compounds beginning with *heaþu-* are very common in heroic discourse. A search of the *DOE Corpus* leads to sixty-three compounds in poetry with *heaþu-* as the first component, the vast majority of which occur in *Beowulf*. Eight of these are proper names and the rest adjectives or nouns that can be placed within the realm of heroic diction, given their concern with battle.[71]

The wounds described here may, in a poetic context, also hold associations with religious tribulation and martyrdom. There are fifteen other instances of the term *dolg* (wound) (and the related past participle *gedolgod* (wounded)) in Old English poetry, ten of which describe Christ's crucifixion and the torture of saints.[72] Of the remaining five, two of them refer to violence done to evil figures and two refer to battle wounds and medical ailments.[73] The final instance is ambiguous because it occurs in the unsolved *Riddle 53*,[74] in a description of a tree that has been mutilated and enslaved for human use. Several solutions have been offered for the

---

71 The most common second components are *-wielm* (burning): *Elene* 579a, 1305a; *Beowulf* 82b, 2819a; *Andreas* 1542a; *Exodus* 148a; and *Genesis B* 324a; *-rinc* (warrior): *Beowulf* 370a, 2466a; *Judith* 179a, 212b; *Exodus* 241a; and *Metres of Boethius* (*Metre 9*) 45a; and *-rof* (brave): *Beowulf* 381a, 864a, 2191a; *Menologium* 14a; and *Phoenix* 228a. Interestingly, *heaþuwylm* is frequently applied to descriptions of hell, while *heaþurinc* and *heaþurof* are generally more straightforward descriptions of brave fighters.

72 See *Andreas* 942a, 1244a, 1397a, 1406a, 1475a; *Christ III* 1107b, 1206b, 1454a; *Dream of the Rood* 46b; and *Riddle 59* (chalice) 11a.

73 See *Beowulf* 817a; *Judith* 107a; *Riddle 5* (shield) 13a; and the *Metrical Charm, Wið Wæterælfadle* (Against Water-Elf Disease) 12a.

74 Notably alongside binding imagery: *deope gedolgod, dumb in bendum, / wriþen ofer wunda* (6–7a) (deeply wounded, silent in bonds, bound over his wounds).

riddle, including "battering ram,"[75] which would indicate that the connotations are martial ones. However, it has also been solved as "cross" and "gallows,"[76] in which case the use of this term could be a reference to the torture and execution of martyrs and the crucifixion of Christ. The higher quantity of occurrences in religious contexts would seem to suggest that, although the term could be applied to other contexts (and frequently was in prose, of course),[77] as poetic diction, it also commonly carried religious connotations.

Indications of torture may also be read in the description of the weighted warp-threads, one of whose feet is fixed while the other *bisgo dreag* (7b). This phrase can mean either "endured affliction" or "worked busily,"[78] and thus points to a double meaning at work. The "affliction" sense of the term *bysgu* notably appears also in *Juliana* 625b, *Guthlac A* 714b and *Beowulf* 281a, and of course other affliction terms are prevalent in the torture scenes of saints and martyrs in Old English. Obviously affliction can equally be endured in battle, indicating that the imagery here is once again applicable to both war and martyrdom.

Another place where the imagined struggle arguably carries connotations of both warfare and torture is in lines 4b-6a, where *[d]aroþas wæron / weo þære wihte, ond se wudu searwum / fæste gebunden* (darts were woeful to that creature, and the wood skilfully bound fast). As discussed above, these darts seem to be either the fabric picks or possibly the points

---

75 Fry lists other solutions including "spear," "phallus," and "cross," but notes that "battering ram" has the most support. "Exeter Book Riddle Solutions," p. 24. This solution is supported by Krapp and Dobbie, *Exeter Book*, pp. 348–9; and Williamson, *Old English Riddles of the Exeter Book*, p. 297.

76 Whitman solves the riddle as "cross" and Wilcox puts forward a strong case for "gallows." See "Significant Motifs"; and "New Solutions."

77 The simplex, *dolg*, is most common in medical contexts, especially in *Leechbook I*'s *Herbarium* and *Leechbook II*'s remedies. *DOE*, s.v. *dolg*, senses 1.-1.a.ii. and 1.b. It also appears in compounds with -*bot* (remedy), -*drenc* (drink, i.e., medicine), -*sealf* (salve), -*smelt* (bandage) and -*swæþ/swaþu* (scar), as well as in several compounds only appearing in poetry: -*benn* (wound), -*slege* (strike/blow) and -*wund* (wounded). See the respective *DOE* entries.

78 The *DOE* offers the following definitions for *bysgu*: "activity, occupation; work, toil, labour" (sense 1.); and "affliction, trouble, anxiety, care" (sense 2.). For *dreogan*'s connotations of suffering and endurance, see senses A.2.a. and B.2. For its connotations of labour, see senses A.1. and B.1.b.: "*dreogan unstille / bysig* 'to be busy',", which the *DOE* gives as the main sense of this particular passage.

of a toothed weaver's beater.[79] Such beaters were similar to swords in form, and there is at least one find of a beater having been refashioned out of a pattern-welded sword, as well as others possibly fashioned from spear-heads.[80] Thus, the association between the weaver's beater and weapons links the imagery to warfare and the heroic realm. In this particular passage, the wood that is bound fast relates to the bound construction of the loom. Not only is the wood a bound object, but it is also doing the binding, as it holds the creature fast. Hence, both the loom and the fabric are bound in their construction and in their servitude to humans. This multi-layered binding of construction and service is, of course, common in other riddles, and several of the armament riddles employ references to binding to emphasize their situation.[81]

The nature of the riddles makes them some of the most useful Old English poetic texts for discussions of material culture. And, indeed, if we look at other large wooden constructions known to the Anglo-Saxons, the imagery of violence in *Riddle 56* is heightened. Niles draws attention to the loom as a type of *hengen* (cross/rack).[82] He notes "the physical resemblance of a *hengen* that is used to hang or stretch criminals to a *hengen* that is used to support the weaving apparatus of a loom," remarking that Ælfric's homilies join imagery of weaving with that of a torture device.[83] The relevant passage from *Sanctorum Alexandri, Eventii, et Theodoli* reads:

> Ða het Aurelianus on hengenne afæstnien
> Þone halgan wer, and aðenian his lima
> swa swa man webb tyht; ac he nan word ne gecwæð.   (190–2)[84]

(Then Aurelianus commanded that the holy man be fastened to a rack and that his limbs be drawn out just as one stretches the weft; but he did not say a word.)

---

79 Erhardt-Siebold, "Old English Loom Riddles," p. 15.
80 Owen-Crocker, *Dress in Anglo-Saxon England*, p. 276.
81 See chapter 6, pp. 172–84, 190–1.
82 *Enigmatic Poetry*, p. 81.
83 Ibid., pp. 81–2. See also Irvine, "Hanging by a Thread."
84 *Homilies of Ælfric*, ed. Pope, 2:745.

This example lends credence to the torture reading of the loom riddle, as does the description of the harmful wooden object in terms of *holt hweor-fende* (3a) (turning wood), which could imply the stretching out of its victim. Niles also indicates that the Anglo-Saxons clearly had knowledge of the rack because elsewhere Ælfric refers to the rack used to torture St. Vincent as a *hengen*, a structure that is different from the gallows to which he is later moved:[85]

> Ahoð hine on þære hengene, and hetelice astreccað
> ealle his lima, þæt þa liþa him togaan. (99–100)
> [...]
> Dacianus þa het hine gedon of þære hengene,
> and hine eft ahon on heardum gealgan sona. (157–8)[86]

(Hang him on the rack, and violently stretch out all his limbs so that his joints are separated. [...] Dacianus then ordered that he be taken from the rack, and immediately hung again on the cruel gallows.)

The rack's ability to tear limbs as outlined here could be reflected in *Riddle 56*'s description of the struggling creature's wounds.

In addition to the possibility that the poem refers to a torture device, we may equally read the constructed object in the context of a gallows. Andrew Reynolds has shown that execution cemeteries are distinguished by "untidy" and sometimes "excessively violent" deaths either by beheading or by hanging, the latter of which being the most common method of execution.[87] Furthermore, there is archaeological evidence for a two-post gallows at several execution sites, including Sutton Hoo in Suffolk and South Acre in Norfolk,[88] as well as pictorial evidence for such two-post constructions in the Anglo-Saxon illustrated Hexateuch, where the gallows' uprights and crossbeam resemble a warp-weighted loom.[89]

---

85 Niles, *Enigmatic Poetry*, p. 74.

86 *Passio sancti Vincentii martyris*, in *Old English Homilies from MS Bodley 343*, ed. Irvine, pp. 103, 106. Notably, lines 101–3 also associate the *hengen* with the stretching of woven cloth, employing the same formula as above: *swa swa man webb tyht*.

87 "Executions and Hard Anglo-Saxon Justice," pp. 8–9.

88 Ibid., p. 9.

89 Niles, *Enigmatic Poetry*, p. 71. The picture in the Hexateuch (London, British Library, Cotton MSS, Claudius B IV) occurs at folio 59.

The gallows is, of course, also frequently referred to in Old English literature, not least in descriptions of martyrdom. If we read this poem as linked to the torture of religious heroes, as evidenced by the motif of the *miles Christi* (soldier of Christ) and by the above *hengen* passages from Ælfric, then the gallows is a fitting construction to consider. Of course, stoic acceptance in the face of tribulation, imprisonment, and torture are all common elements in the Old English saints' lives. This stoicism is something the saints have in common with other Old English heroes,[90] which suggests parallels between the two genres, as well as between secular warriors and *milites Christi*. Another example commonly drawn upon is the martial diction of *The Dream of the Rood*, as applied to both Christ and the cross, which aligns the religious hero with an undeserved violent death upon the gallows. The cross is referred to as a *gealga* (gallows) on three occasions, twice as a simplex in lines 10b and 40b and once as the first element in the compound, *gealgtreow* (146a) (gallows-tree), and is depicted as taking on the suffering of Christ, who is eager to redeem mankind through his crucifixion. As demonstrated by the violent descriptions of Christ's death on the gallows as well as by archaeological evidence and prose depictions of torture, it is safe to say that Anglo-Saxon writers were certainly aware of the potentially painful outcomes of judicial punishment. Indeed, we need only look at the extant law codes to find a trail of missing fingers, hands, eyes, and noses, which marked the committing of a crime upon the human body.[91]

Thus, the wounds and violence of *Riddle 56* may be situated within a number of contexts – battle, torture, and execution – all linked by their inherent violence. This violence is, furthermore, associated with heroic depictions in Old English poetry, whether of actual fighters or of Christ and his martyrs. Even executions of non-religious figures find their way into heroic poetry: familiar are the lines of *Beowulf* (2444–59) which depict a father lamenting his son who has been hanged as a criminal. Furthermore, references to gallows are found in a long list of violent deaths and maimings in *Fortunes of Men* 33–42. Because that gallows-death is accompanied by a description of the raven, one of the beasts of battle, it is arguably placed in a context of war and battle-related violence, acting as a further reminder that, as Adrien Bonjour put it, "death is foreordained

---

90 Hill, "Unchanging Hero," p. 236.
91 For a detailed discussion of this legal context of mutilation and torture in Old English literature, see O'Brien O'Keeffe, "Body and Law."

for every man on earth."[92] Given this context, we can see that drawing parallels between the common domestic task of weaving and imagery of violence through battle, torture, and execution causes the riddle to transgress boundaries of genre and register, moving it from the quotidian realm to the heroic.

Standing as a bridge between *Riddle 56*'s battle scene and mead-hall is the description of the leafy tree. It does not seem to be a part of the creature's torture, even if the gallows is occasionally referred to as a gallows-tree. Other objects made from the wood of bright trees also find their way into the riddles. Elinor Teele discusses in particular the image of the innocent tree in several poems:

> In *Genesis A*, the tree represents the state of humankind before Adam and Eve sinned; the *Riddles* and the *Dream* extend this metaphor. The fall of humans results in all manmade objects, especially wooden ones, being tainted with sin, since they were not needed in Paradise; in the *Dream* the wooden object is redeemed because it is Christ's cross, in the *Riddles* weapons and their wielders cannot expect to escape censure.[93]

When these examples of trees are paired together, our attention is brought to the pre- and postlapsarian state of humanity. The innocent tree is that of paradise, while the wooden object constructed from a similar tree is relegated to the fallen, human realm. This adds another layer to the living/dead, raw/cooked dimension of living things and the objects made from them. Perhaps the living or raw object can be read as part of a prelapsarian world, while the dead or cooked object belongs to the human world that exists after the fall. Humanity's imperfect attempt to imitate God's creation by binding objects into some semblance of structure is thus evident. However, in *Riddle 56*, the tree's description seems too brief and generic to align it firmly with either the tree of life or cross/gallows motif. It serves a functional purpose here, in that it offers us another clue to the solution of the riddle.

Following the brief interruption in heroic imagery come the final lines, which tie the riddle firmly to the heroic world of lord and retinue: *Ic lafe geseah / minum hlaforde, þær hæleð druncon, / þara flana,*[94] *on flet beran*

---

92 "Beowulf and the Beasts of Battle," p. 566.
93 "Heroic Tradition," p. 76.
94 See above, p. 28n35.

(I saw the leavings of those arrows, carried out on the floor to my lord, where the warriors drank). The images presented in these lines are interspersed, but remain clear examples of heroic diction. Each half-line contains at least one term relevant to heroic poetry, and together they draw a recognizable picture of the hall-setting. *Hlaford* (lord) is common in Old English poetry, occurring sixty-three times in total. It may be employed in religious contexts, as well as in reference to worldly lords; here, in conjunction with the rest of the terms, it is placed within the heroic realm. *Flan* (arrow) rather obviously finds its place in heroic diction because it is a weapon-term, as is *laf* (leavings/remnant), when used of swords – although here it refers to the finished web. *Laf* occurs frequently in verse, either as a simplex or as the second element in a compound. According to Phyllis Portnoy, the two most common uses of *laf* are "survivor," at about 34 per cent of instances, followed by "sword" at 29 per cent.[95] *Beowulf* once again dominates the poetic uses, followed by *Genesis A*.[96]

These weapon terms evoke the hall, as does the formulaic description of men drinking. Line 11b's formulaic *þær hæleð druncon* also occurs in line 1b in *Riddle 55*, the poem directly preceding the loom riddle in *The Exeter Book*.[97] *Riddle 55*, a poem similarly inflected with heroic imagery, is one of the riddles whose solution has not yet achieved scholarly consensus. Suggestions include "mead barrel" or "drinking bowl,"[98] "shield," "scabbard," "harp," "cross," "gallows," "swordrack," "tetraktys," and "swordbox," with "cross" and "swordrack" maintaining the most support.[99] However, Niles also offers a solution that is in line with scholarly

---

95 "Riddle of the Remnant," n.pag.

96 *Beowulf* contains thirteen instances of the term *laf*: 455b, 795b, 1032a, 1488b, 1688a, 2036b, 2191b, 2563b, 2611b, 2628b, 2829b, 2936b, 3160b; while *Genesis A* has five: 1343a, 1496b, 1549b, 2005b, 2019a.

97 *Riddle 55* also includes binding imagery: *wrætlic wudutreow ond wunden gold, / sinc searobunden, ond seolfres dæl* (3–4) (a wondrous forest-tree and wound gold, a skilfully bound treasure, and a portion of silver).

98 Taylor, "Mazers, Mead, and the Wolf's-head-tree," p. 504.

99 Fry, "Exeter Book Riddle Solutions," p. 24. Krapp and Dobbie favour "swordrack." *Exeter Book*, p. 350. Williamson remains uncertain, offering the guess "that the creature is an ornamented sword box and that somehow (either by an unknown wordplay or because of some unknown similarity of function or design) the box is being compared to a gallows or rood in the riddle." *Old English Riddles of the Exeter Book*, pp. 300–1. Tupper argues that it refers to any vertical pole that contains a crossbeam, a solution that simultaneously explains the imagery of the cross, the gallows and the swordrack. *Riddles of the Exeter Book*, p. 189.

trend: **wæpen-hengen* (weapon-rack).[100] If this were a two-post structure, like the warp-weighted loom, then we have both an explanation for
the similarities between the two poems and also the reference to the gallows: when hung with a mail-coat, this object could resemble both.[101]

In addition to the formulaic reference to men drinking in *Riddle 56*, the
term *flet* is consistent with the heroic imagery of the hall. It occurs no less
than fifteen times in *Beowulf*, sometimes as a simplex and sometimes as the
first element of a compound. It occurs frequently in heroic contexts, and
the formula in which it appears here, *on flet beran*, is also repeated in
Riddle 55 2a. These two riddles are, then, further bound together by their
imagery of a person bearing an object onto the hall floor where the warriors drink.

Thus, one set of images – the lord and retinue drinking on the floor of
the mead-hall – appears to be depicted in the positive light of celebration
and camaraderie, as is typical of this sort of scene.[102] However, the second
set of images – the leavings and the work of arrows that are carried out
onto the mead-hall floor – is not as easy to interpret. Is this a victorious
presentation of a defeated foe? Is the *laf*, literally the remains of the struggling creature, a token of battle like the swords so often named by this
term in heroic poetry? Or is this a loss for the war-band? The *laf* could as
easily be referring to a companion, just as Beowulf refers to Wiglaf as the
final remnant of their tribe in his last speech: *Þu eart endelaf usses cynnes,
/ Wægmundinga* (2813–14a) (You are the final remnant of our kin, of the
Wæmundings).[103]

Given this close reading, it is fair to say that the imagery of the loom
riddle is quite clearly concerned with the heroic, and the violence depicted carries associations of battle, torture, and execution. That being
said, this connection is initially surprising given that most of the riddles
describing objects through heroic imagery can be associated with battle in
some way. The obvious example is the sword of *Riddle 20*, but also the
bow of *Riddle 23*, and the horns of *Riddles 14* and *80*. The use of heroic
imagery in all of these is appropriate because the objects are artefacts that
would be used by noble warriors. But the loom is an object used by

---

100 *Enigmatic Poetry*, p. 75.
101 Ibid., p. 84.
102 Magennis, *Images of* Community, pp. 35–103.
103 It is notable that, according to Scheid and Svenbro, dream interpretation aligns fin-
     ished cloth with death. *Craft of Zeus*, pp. 69, 159.

women, and not just noblewomen – its use is universal. The crucial question, then, is why the loom and the act of weaving upon it are so associated with heroic violence.

Situating this poem within the broader context of Old English poetry demonstrates that this association is actually not so strange. As we have seen in the examples of *godweb* above, and as will be further discussed in the context of binding, when construction through weaving and binding is applied to objects, they are invariably objects of high status. Whether religious cloths, like the temple veil that is torn during the crucifixion in *Christ III* 1134b, or tapestries and banners, like those on the walls of Heorot after Beowulf has defeated Grendel, woven objects only gain attention in the poetic corpus if they carry great value. Hence, weaving and binding terms are powerful, and because they are associated with acts of great artistry and with high status, it is appropriate that the poem should present the act of weaving in a heroic register.

A final note of emphasis should be placed on the way in which the loom riddle carves out a space for the creative aspects of a domestic chore within the ethic of the war-band and the mead-hall. The craftsman is just as essential to the lord and to the war-band as he or she is to the household because nobles, like farmers, need to be clothed and armed with the implements of their trade. And, of course, God, as the creator of the world, is the ultimate craftsman, as Wehlau emphasizes: "[t]he supreme architect is God, who is often called *meotod* ("measurer") and *scyppend* ("shaper"). These terms are so commonly used as to be barely noticeable. Nevertheless, they make clear the predominant metaphors underlying Anglo-Saxon concepts of Creation, and these metaphors are concerned with artistic skills."[104] Thus, in creating objects through the weaving and binding together of elements, humans exercise power and control over the world around them – they both emulate God's example and, perhaps more controversially, imagine God in their own image.

---

104 *Riddle of Creation*, p. 16. For more on this, see chapter 6, p. 184 and chapter 9, p. 251.

2 The Woven Mail-Coat

A similar craftsmanship to that of weaving and binding textiles is invoked in a great number of Old English poems that deal with a very different product: the coat of mail. Descriptions of mail-coats abound, particularly in heroic texts, and in them we see another type of high status construction. The prestige associated with armour and weaponry, which are frequently passed on as gifts, is something that Michael Cherniss explores in relation to heroic quality. For him, treasures are "material manifestations or representations of the proven or inherent worthiness of whoever possesses them. We may define the function of treasure as that of a tangible, material symbol of the intangible, abstract qualities of virtue in a warrior."[1] Thus, material objects won in combat or given as rewards for heroic deeds are more than simply wealth or riches according to the world view presented in Old English heroic poetry,[2] they become a representation of the heroic nature.

Among these heroic objects, mail garments feature prominently. In modern translations, they are often described as "woven,"[3] although a number of Old English descriptors are actually employed, including forms of *bregdan* (to braid/intertwine) and *-lucan* (to lock/interlock). Attention

---

1 "Progress of the Hoard," pp. 475–6.

2 Ibid., p. 473.

3 See references to *Beowulf* 552a, 1443b, 1548a and *Elene* 257a in the following editions and translations: Hall, *Beowulf: A Metrical Translation*; Jack, *Beowulf: A Student Edition*; Liuzza, *Beowulf: A New Verse Translation*; Swanton, *Beowulf*; and Kennedy, *Elene*. See also the term's glossary entries in Klaeber Four, p. 357; Mitchell and Robinson, *Beowulf*, p. 248; and Wrenn, *Beowulf with the Finnesburg Fragment*, p. 223.

is frequently drawn to their interlinking iron rings – particularly impressive features, judging by the archaeological evidence. Unfortunately, there are no surviving Anglo-Saxon byrnies, but a well preserved Iron Age mail-coat with over twenty thousand iron rings was recovered from a bog in Vimose, Denmark.[4] The association of interlocked rings with weaving is unsurprising, given the "symbiosis between cloth and metal" during the Middle Ages.[5] It should be noted that modern lexicographers are not the only ones to draw such assocations; the Anglo-Saxon composer and translators of the Latin and Old English mail-coat riddles, discussed below, also consciously engage with the cloth-metal nexus. This chapter will focus on representations of the woven mail-coat, discussing both the broader poetic context and the specific riddle elaborations.

Descriptions of Woven Mail-Coats

There is substantial textual evidence for mail-coats, which appear both on their own and frequently in doublets with *bill* (sword).[6] Their construction is also often invoked, as in the example from *Beowulf* that links the hero's mail-coat and textiles: *on him byrne scan, / searonet seowed smiþes orþancum* (405b–6) (a byrnie shone on him, an armour-net sewn by the skills of the smith). We have already encountered *seowan* above, in the context of *godweb*; it is worth noting that, while its primary definition is "to sew," the verb can also be understood metaphorically as "to knit together, link, unite."[7] It is through this broader, metaphorical sense that construction terms related to sewing, weaving, binding, and interlocking come together. Their overlapping use in similar contexts of warfare and domesticity means that these construction terms often become interchangeable, as demonstrated by the *TOE* entries for binding/fastening, woven material/fabric and mail/iron rings.[8] Such interchangeability makes a joint study of them all the more relevant and necessary.

---

4 Niles, *Enigmatic Poetry*, p. 75.

5 Owen-Crocker, Coatsworth and Hayward, eds., *Encyclopedia of Medieval Dress and Textiles*, p. 3.

6 See *DOE*, s.v. *byrne*, sense 1–1.b.

7 Hall, *Concise Anglo-Saxon Dictionary*, s.v. *seowan*. Bosworth and Toller only include the definition "to sew." *Anglo-Saxon Dictionary*, s.v. *seowian*.

8 See entries 05.05.03, 04.04.05 and 13.02.08.03.01.01.

A glance at the *DOE*'s entries for *(ge)bregdan* reveals the versatility of the verb, which can be used in a number of contexts, including movement and the drawing of weapons, variation and change in appearance and, most relevant here, both weaving and binding. There are a total of nine instances of the verb's past participle *bro(g)den* in three poems. Four of those instances refer to mail-coats in *Beowulf* and *Elene*,[9] three to swords (all as the first element of the compound *bro(g)denmæl*) in the same poems,[10] and the final two to the feathery ring of the fantastic bird and the gem-studded crowns of the heavenly souls in *The Phoenix*.[11] These last two instances arguably employ the verb because of the passages' emphasis on high status craft and artifice.[12]

While as a simplex *(ge)brogden* does not appear in any formulas, it does tend to be used in collocations with *byrne* in lines alliterating on "b." Such collocations emphasize the constructed nature of high status objects like the mail-coat, and may appear in elaborate lists of armour and weaponry, as in *Elene*:

Ðær wæs on eorle   eðgesyne
brogden byrne   ond bill gecost,
geatolic guðscrud,   grimhelm manig,
ænlic eoforcumbul.   (256–9a)

(There was easily seen upon a warrior a woven byrnie and a proven sword, a magnificent battle-shroud, many a visored-helmet, a peerless boar-crest.)

---

9 See lines 552a, 1443b, and 1548a; and 257a.

10 See lines 1616a and 1667a; and 758a.

11 See lines 306b and 602b. These separate passages are clearly linked by collocations of *brogden*, *beag* (ring), *beorht* (bright) and *wundor* (used adjectivally/adverbially to mean "wondrous(ly)"), indicating that we should read the two together. Interestingly, the corresponding images in the Latin sources, Lactantius' *De ave phoenice* and Ambrose's *Hexameron*, refer simply to the phoenix's crown and to the heavenly crown of righteousness (from II Timothy 4.7–8), neither of which are described as braided or woven rings. See the editions of these texts as they appear in the appendices of Blake, *Phoenix*, pp. 91, 93 (from CSEL 32.1, p. 198); and Allen and Calder, *Sources and Analogues*, pp. 117, 119. For more on the relationship between the Old English poem and its Latin sources, see Steen, *Verse and Virtuosity*, pp. 35–70; and Cross, "Conception of the Old English *Phoenix*."

12 See Steen, *Verse and Virtuosity*, pp. 65–7; and Calder, "Vision of Paradise," pp. 174–5, 180.

All of the items listed are accompanied by a modifier, and with the exception of the mail-coat and helmet (whose compound form contains the modifying component *grim* in itself), these tend to be abstract adjectives (*gecost/geatolic/ænlic*). The helmet's accompanying adjective is simply *manig*, a common enough descriptor in such lists, while the mail-coat is described in terms of its construction. Perhaps this different use of adjectives is of little significance, and merely reflects Cynewulf's predilection for double alliteration; yet it is still interesting that the only object described in terms of its construction is the item that can be linked to the traditional and multi-purpose constructing terms of weaving and binding.

The descriptions of woven mail-coats in *Beowulf* are less extended than in *Elene*. In fact, references to the byrnie's construction appear less often in lists of weaponry than in passages focused solely upon the corselet. One example occurs in the famous passage where Beowulf's armour is described not in terms of a passive object used by Beowulf, but as an active comrade in arms who safeguards the life of his lord:

> scolde herebyrne   hondum gebroden,
> sid ond searofah,   sund cunnian,
> seo ðe bancofan   beorgan cuþe,
> þæt him hildegrap   hreþre ne mihte
> eorres inwitfeng,   aldre gesceþðan.   (1443–7)

(the army-corselet woven by hand, wise and skilfully decorated, had to test the sea, that which knew how to protect the bone-chamber so that battle-grips, the malicious grasp of the angry one, might not injure his heart, his life).

With this piece of armour as the focus of attention, the construction of the mail-coat becomes significant. A number of rhetorical techniques highlight that significance, including interlinear assonance ("o": *scolde/hondum/gebroden/-cofan*; "u": *sund/cunnian/cuþe*), an envelope pattern that links the initial and final "sc" sounds (*scolde/gesceþðan*), and cross alliteration between a- and b-verses ("h" and "b": *herebyrne hondum gebroden*; "b" and "c": *bancofan beorgan cuþe*).[13] This cross alliteration, notably, occurs in the line that describes the mail-coat's construction as *gebroden*,

---

13 The presence of "c"-alliteration also links this line to the previous one, which ends in *cunnian*.

where it effectively links the woven *herebyrne* together with the hands that constructed it (*hondum*). Also linked – several lines below in another "h"-alliterating line – are the constrictive grips (*hildegrap*) of a nastier pair of hands, as well as the hero's life itself (*hreþre*). This passage is, thus, clearly foregrounded, both because of the mail-coat's skilful, woven construction and because of the object's overall importance to the hero.

A less ornamented example occurs later during Beowulf's fight with Grendel's mother. This time the *breostnet broden* (1548a) (woven breast-net) carries the alliteration, and, as an essential element in the fight (i.e., it saves Beowulf's life), its well-constructed nature merits attention.[14] The final instance of a woven mail-coat (again carrying the alliteration) in *Beowulf* relates less to the object's protectiveness and more to its loyal service. Beowulf, dying, has asked to see the treasure for which he fought, and Wiglaf

> hyran heaðosiocum,   hringnet beran,
> brogdne beadusercean   under beorges hrof.   (2754–5)

(obeyed the battle-sick one, bore the ring-net, the woven battle-shirt, under the barrow's roof.)

These lines firmly link Wiglaf's actions with the mail-coat itself, a linking visible at the level of ornamental alliteration: the second line inverts the alliterative pattern of the first, so that h h-s h b becomes b b-s b h. Just as the mail-coat has been depicted as a loyal comrade and retainer, here Wiglaf, the bearer of the armour, is a faithful retainer to the end. In *Beowulf*, the construction of the mail-coat is more likely to be highlighted in scenes of extended description rather than in lists. The skilful construction of the corselet signals its strength and protective nature, and is sometimes connected with its personification. It also points to the status of the byrnie as a prestige object, indicating that one who is both wealthy and heroic enough to possess such armour will stand a fair chance in battle.

The imagery of interlocking used to describe the braided mail-coats is prominent elsewhere in the poetry. These references employ the past participle of the verb *-lucan*, providing variation on the image of the *brogden*

---

14 The mail-coat is again referred to as a *-net* in at 1553a, while mention of a similar *breostnet* occurs in *Exodus* 236b.

byrnie.[15] The examples appear in two related formulaic contexts, the first
of which – *heard hondlocen* – is unique to *Beowulf*.[16] One instance of this
formula occurs in a passage that invokes both *-lucan* and *bregdan* to describe the same object:

> þær me wið laðum   licsyrce min
> heard hondlocen   helpe gefremede;
> beadohrægl broden   on breostum læg
> golde gegyrwed.   (550–3a)

(there my life-protection performed help for me, the hard hand-locked material against the hateful ones; the woven battle-garment lay on my breast
adorned with gold.)

As in the passages above, "h" and "b" are again linked here, with the
double "h" alliteration (*heard/hond-/helpe*) carrying over into a third
half-line (*-hrægl*), where the alliteration falls on "b" (*beado-/broden/
breostum*). The emphasis is once again on the mail-coat, a product of human hands and skilful construction, and how it may protect the hero's
life against foes. The construction reference here alludes to the work of
the smith, rather than that of the weaver, but the result is a similar high
status object.

This status is clearly flagged in the second instance of the formula:

>   Guðbyrne scan
> heard hondlocen;   hringiren scir
> song in searwum.   Þa hie to sele furðum
> in hyra gryregeatwum   gangan cwomon,
> setton sæmeþe   side scyldas,
> rondas regnhearde   wið þæs recedes weal.   (321b–6)

(The hard, hand-locked war-byrnie shone; the shining ring-iron sang in the
equipment. When they came walking forth into the hall in their battle-gear,

---

15 *Elene*'s reference to *wriðene wælhlencan* (24b) (twisted slaughter-mail) is also a variation on the braided and interlocked byrnie, likely employed because an alliterating "w"
   was required.
16 See lines 322a and 551a.

the sea-weary ones set their broad boards, wondrously hard shields against the wall of the hall.)

Here, rather than emphasizing the mail-coat's role in protecting the hero, the poet is offering a triumphant display of the troop's wealth and accomplishment. The song of the mail-coats announces the heroes' presence, as well as their intentions.

We may also read the second formulaic context for the past participle of *lucan* – *locene leoðosyrcan* – in light of Beowulf's arrival scene. This formula is applied to Beowulf and his companions as they bear their *hringnet [...], / locene leoðosyrcan* (1889b–90a) (ring-nets, interlocked battle-shirts) to the ship in order to depart from Denmark. The two formulaic contexts thus form an envelope pattern around the hero's arrival and departure. This latter example, however, is not nearly as extended or ceremonial as the arrival scene, although it does point once again to the heroes' status.[17]

The formula *locene leoðosyrcan* occurs a final time in *Beowulf*, used once again in the context of battle:

Grap þa togeanes,   guðrinc gefeng
atolan clommum;   no þy ær in gescod
halan lice;   hring utan ymbbearh,
þæt heo þone fyrdhom   ðurhfon ne mihte,
locene leoðosyrcan   laþan fingrum.   (1501–5)

(She reached then against him, seized the battle-warrior with terrible grips; no sooner for that could she injure the unharmed body within; a ring protected outside, so that she might not pierce the army-coat, the interlocked war-shirt, with hateful fingers.)

This passage, relating yet again to Beowulf's fight with Grendel's mother, is highlighted by its importance to the action of the poem. While the previous passages include references to the skilful hands that constructed the mail-coat, here the only hands mentioned are those of Grendel's mother as she attempts to penetrate Beowulf's armour and seize the body within. Although the emphasis is not on the mail-coat's construction, the use

---

17 As does the final instance of this formula, *gelocen leoðocræftum* (2769a), which relates to the golden tapestry, discussed in chapter 1.

of *locen* does remind us of the term's other formulaic context, invoked less than a hundred lines previously. The byrnie in this passage is described both as constructed of interlocking rings, and as forming a protective ring around Beowulf's whole body – a circle without start or end. Because the mail-coat is constructed from many rings, it is strong as long as the integrity of the circle holds. The failure to hold is, of course, reflected in *The Battle of Maldon*, where the injury of Byrhtnoth's opponent is described: *he wæs on breostum wund/þurh ða hringlocan* (144b–5a) (he was wounded in the breast, through the ring-locked mail). Without the bonds of the byrnie holding firm, the link to life is destroyed and the warrior dies.

The mail-coat itself, outside of verse, may be more appropriately placed in a category between weaving and binding since it is constructed through the interlinking of bound, metal rings. In Old English poetry, however, this object is clearly described in terms of braiding and interlocking, something that we may initially take to be an expression of Anglo-Saxon technological knowledge rather than a metaphor. However, as the following discussion of the mail-coat riddles will demonstrate, this traditional imagery of the woven corselet could be the subject of play and reinterpretation.

The Mail-Coat Riddles: Variants and Context

If the above references to woven and interlocked mail-coats are intriguing insights into how Anglo-Saxon poets and audiences imagined the construction of such a high status item, then the elaborated account in *Exeter Book Riddle 35* (mail-coat) is even more useful. This poem refers to the creation of a byrnie through a series of negations of the craft of textile-weaving, by which process it adamantly denies being created. However, before delving into a discussion of the mail-coat riddle, its wider cultural context merits attention. This is because *Riddle 35* is not the only version of this riddle to come down to us; it is not even the original. There also exists a Northumbrian version (*The Leiden Riddle*), which follows *Riddle 35* closely with a few minor differences.[18] Both of these Old English riddles are, furthermore, translations of Aldhelm's Latin *Enigma 33, De lorica*:

---

18 For more on the relationship between the versions of the riddle, see Dance, "Old English Language," pp. 40–1; Orchard, "Old English and Latin Poetic Traditions," pp. 66–72; Smith, ed., *Three Northumbrian Poems*; and Zandvoort, "Leiden Riddle."

Roscida me genuit gelido de uiscere tellus;
Non sum setigero lanarum uellere facta,
Licia nulla trahunt nec garrula fila resultant
Nec crocea seres taxunt lanugine uermes
Nec radiis carpor duro nec pectine pulsor;
Et tamen en 'uestis' uulgi sermone uocabor.
Spicula non uereor longis exempta faretris.

(The dewy earth brought me forth from its icy innards; I am not made from the bristly fleece of wool; no loom-leashes pull me nor do noisy threads rebound, nor do Chinese worms weave me from their yellow floss; I am not tortured by beams nor beaten by the cruel comb; yet, lo, I am called a coat in common speech. I do not fear arrows drawn from long quivers.)

De lorica appears as part of the one hundred enigmata included in the *Epistola ad Acircium*, a late seventh-century metrical treatise sent to King Aldfrith of Northumbria.[19] The well-connected cleric, Aldhelm, was not only influential in the formation of the Christian church in England, but was also an important Anglo-Latin writer whose verse was studied in schools across early medieval Europe. Furthermore, Aldhelm's influence pervades not only Latin literature, but also Old English, pointing to the inextricable link between these two languages and their literatures within Anglo-Saxon England. Since Latin was the language of learning and

---

19 For more on Aldhelm and this work, see Lapidge, *Anglo-Latin Literature*, pp. 7–10, 247–69. The subject matter of Aldhelm's enigmata is often similar to that of the Old English riddles, mostly concerning natural phenomena and household objects, with a few treating abstract ideas. A number of Aldhelm's enigmata, in addition to those adapted into Old English, include references to weaving and binding. A woven garment is mentioned in *De ariete*, where the ram provides twisted thread (7), while the sling of *De fundibalo* is characterized by the two straps that bind it (3). More notable than these is the bullock of *De iuvenco*, which, after death, binds men in a fashion similar to *Riddle 12* (oxhide) of the *Exeter Book* (5–6), discussed in chapter 6. The silkworm enigma, *De bombicibus*, is also concerned with weaving, and it is linked further to the mail-coat riddle by its mention of fate (4), a motif that is associated with the silkworm in the Old English versions of the mail-coat riddle, but not in the Latin. Finally, the spindle enigma demonstrates that Aldhelm was familiar with the classical tradition of textile-working deities of fate, a tradition significant to the discussion of *wyrd* in chapter 9. In general, however, although Aldhelm employs textile imagery frequently, references specific to weaving and binding are not as prevalent in his enigmata as they are in the Old English riddles.

Christian-Latin poems were the basis of the curriculum, their study influenced Anglo-Saxon tastes, as well as Old English literary form.[20] Anglo-Latin scholarship reminds us time and time again to be aware of this interrelationship: "Anglo-Saxonists need to attend more to the transformation of Latin culture under Germanic imagination, to see what may be seen of the cultural brinkmanship that prevails when two languages, each with its own value-system, artistic tradition, and cultural history, confront each other in one tonsured head."[21]

The merging of these languages and literatures is perfectly exemplified in the riddle tradition. The popularity of riddles in the Middle Ages may derive from any one of a number of factors, including their use in education, a pragmatic one considering that their short length, interesting subject matter, and basic vocabulary made them a useful starting point on the road to more difficult works of literature.[22] Furthermore, their allegorical nature lent itself well to medieval interests, while their subject matter was considered "the first step in an ascending order of knowledge."[23] Regardless of the reasons why this type of literature was so popular, it is clear from the surviving manuscripts that riddles were of interest to scholars writing in both Latin and Old English.[24]

While the link between Anglo-Latin and Old English is overt, the exact nature of interaction between riddles in the two languages is not easy to

---

20 Lapidge, *Anglo-Latin Literature*, p. 4.

21 Davis, "Agon and Gnomon," p. 112. See also Lapidge, *Anglo-Latin Literature*, pp. 4–5; Orchard, "Enigma Variations," p. 300; and McGowan, "Introduction to the Corpus of Anglo-Latin," p. 22.

22 Whitman, *Old English Riddles*, p. 60.

23 Ibid., p. 63.

24 Despite this, scholars occasionally impose a false dichotomy of serious Latin enigmata on the one hand and, by implication, more frivolous Old English riddles on the other. Indeed, Lapidge has argued: "In view of the seriousness of Aldhelm's theme, the term [enigmata] should probably be rendered 'Mysteries' rather than 'Riddles', for Aldhelm set out to reveal the hidden links between all creation – animate and inanimate – and by means of an intricate web of interlocking themes and metaphors to lead the reader to contemplate God's Creation afresh." *Anglo-Latin Literature*, p. 9. However, this same goal of examining links and interlocking themes of God's Creation can be argued of Old English riddles. Such a differentiation between sober Latin works and less serious Old English ones may derive in part from the scholarly trend of discussing vernacular riddles with a focus on play and playfulness. See Abrahams, "Literary Study of the Riddle"; Irving, "Heroic Experience"; Lieber, "Riddles, Cultural Categories, and World View"; Maranda, "Riddles and Riddling"; Niles, *Enigmatic Poetry*; and Wilcox,

pin down.[25] Just as Anglo-Latinists warn us not to become "myopic" in our approach to the Old English riddles,[26] we must also keep in mind that these texts are not simply copies of an earlier Latin tradition; they had developed their own themes, styles, and diction.[27] Of course, both Latin and Old English riddlers may have drawn from the same sources and may have held overlapping though independent ideas about certain subjects, making the original derivation of similar motifs difficult to determine.[28] The most useful approach, then, is one that is conscious of the coexistence of Latin and Old English in Anglo-Saxon England, viewing both the riddles and the enigmata as "unique to their language but founded in a common cultural background."[29]

Within this dual-language tradition, Aldhelm is one of the only poets to have left indisputable evidence for his influence in the form of direct translation of his works.[30] The identity of the writer of the Old English translations of *De lorica* is not clear, but it should be noted that if the West Saxon Aldhelm ever did translate his Latin verse into Old English it is highly unlikely that he would have done so in a Northumbrian dialect. This implies that the older of our two surviving translations is not likely his.[31]

"'Tell Me What I Am'." The real differentiator between seriousness and frivolousness seems to be the presence of sexual imagery in some of the vernacular riddles (especially *Riddles 12* (ox), *20* (sword), *25* (onion), *37* (bellows), *42* (cock and hen), *44* (key), *45* (dough), *46* (Lot and his offspring), *54* (churn), *61* (helmet), *62* (poker), *63* (beaker), *65* (onion), *87* (bellows), and *91* (key)). However, Mercedes Salvador-Bello has recently argued that a number of references in Aldhelm and Tatwine's enigmata may be read as double entendre. See "Sexual Riddle Type." We need to be cautious in permitting a misleading distinction to banish the vernacular riddles from the realm of serious literature. Perhaps a more important difference is that some manuscripts contain solutions for their Latin enigmata while the Old English riddles are recorded unsolved.

25 Teele, "Heroic Tradition," p. 218.

26 Orchard, "Enigma Variations," p. 299.

27 Teele, "Heroic Tradition," p. 221.

28 Williamson, *Old English Riddles of the Exeter Book*, p. 20.

29 Teele, "Heroic Tradition," p. 227.

30 Despite the tentative suggestion that the Old English riddle translations of Aldhelm's enigmata were penned by the man himself (see Smith, *Three Northumbrian Poems*, p. 18), no Old English verse known to be written by Aldhelm survives. Our evidence that he did write poetry in the vernacular comes from William of Malmesbury who claimed that "no less a critic than King Alfred believed Aldhelm to be the finest vernacular poet whose works he knew, and Alfred, if we are to believe Asser, was no mean judge of vernacular verse." Orchard, *Poetic Art of Aldhelm*, p. 5.

The Northumbrian text is known as *The Leiden Riddle*, from the manuscript in which it was found. Historically, scholars have argued that palaeographical evidence points to a ninth-century date for the text,[32] although M.B. Parkes suggests a tenth-century date[33] and both Andy Orchard and Robert D. Fulk maintain an eighth-century date for the original, though not for the manuscript itself.[34] Whatever its date, *The Leiden Riddle* remains fairly faithful to the Latin, and, with both the riddles of Symphosius and Aldhelm preceding it in the manuscript, this closeness to the original is not entirely surprising. As is evident from the text below, the manuscript has suffered some damage and reconstruction was necessary to produce a complete rendering of the poem.[35] Fortunately, given the survival of both the Latin and West Saxon versions, we can look to them for hints when the manuscript fails us. Both texts are given below (*Leiden* in the left-hand column, *Riddle 35* in the right), with variants of words and forms noted in the translation.

Mec se ueta uong, uundrum freorig,	Mec se wæta wong, wundrum freorig,
ob his innaðae aerest cæn[.]æ.	of his innaþe ærist cende.
Ni uaat ic mec biuorthæ uullan fliusum,	Ne wat ic mec beworhtne wulle flysum,
herum ðerh hehcraeft, hygiðonc[.....].	hærum þurh heahcræft, hygeþoncum min.
Uundnae me ni biað ueflæ, ni ic uarp hafæ,	Wundene me ne beoð wefle, ne ic wearp hafu,
ni ðerih ðreatun giðraec ðret me hlimmith,	ne þurh þreata geþræcu þræd me ne hlimmeð,
ne me hrutendu hrisil scelfath,	ne æt me hrutende hrisil scriþeð,
ni mec ouana aam sceal cnyssa.	ne mec ohwonan sceal am cnyssan.
Uyrmas mec ni auefun uyrdi craeftum,	Wyrmas mec ne awæfan wyrda cræftum,
ða ði geolu godueb geatum fraetuath.	þa þe geolo godwebb geatwum frætwað.
Uil mec huethrae suae ðeh uidæ ofaer eorðu	Wile mec mon hwæþre seþeah wide ofer eorþan
hatan mith heliðum hyhtlic giuæde;	hatan for hæleþum hyhtlic gewæde.
ni anoegun ic me aerigfaerae egsan brogum,	Saga soðcwidum, searoþoncum gleaw,
ðeh ði n[...]n siæ niudlicae ob cocrum.	wordum wisfæst, hwæt þis gewæde sy.

---

31 Whitman, *Old English Riddles of the Exeter Book*, p. 126.

32 Anderson, "Aldhelm and the Leiden Riddle," p. 168.

33 "Manuscript of the *Leiden Riddle*," pp. 215–17.

34 Orchard, "Enigma Variations," p. 287; and Fulk, *History of Old English Meter*, p. 405.

35 Zandvoort, "Leiden Riddle," p. 49.

(The wet plain, wonderfully cold, bore me out of its womb. I know in my mind I was not wrought of wool from fleeces, with hair through great skill. I am not wound about with a weft, nor do I have a warp, nor does thread resound in me through the force of blows, nor does a whirring shuttle (*Leiden*:) shake / (*35*:) glide upon me, nor must the beater strike me anywhere. The worms which adorn fine yellow cloth with trappings did not weave me together with the skills of (*Leiden*:) fate / (*35*:) the fates. Nevertheless widely over the earth (*Leiden*:) one / (*35*:) someone calls me a joyful garment for warriors; (final two lines of *Leiden*:) nor do I fear terror from the peril of a flight of arrows, though they be eagerly pulled from the quiver. / (final two lines of *35*:) Say with true words, clever with skilful-thoughts, with very wise words, what this garment is.)

The West Saxon version is among the collection of riddles in *The Exeter Book*. Numbered *Riddle 35* by Krapp and Dobbie, the text's palaeography and grammatical differences suggest that it is probably the youngest of the three variants.[36] Because this riddle follows the Northumbrian text in its deviation from the Latin line order (the lines correspond to the Latin thus: 1–2, 3–4, 5–6, 9–10, 7–8, 11–12), it has been assumed that *Riddle 35* was not a direct translation of the Latin poem, but an adaptation of an already-translated version that was almost identical to *The Leiden Riddle*.[37]

There are a number of differences between the two Old English poems, most notably the conclusion: the *Exeter Book* riddle replaces the final two lines of the Latin poem with a challenge to the audience. The two poems contain various differences in their grammar and phonology, which are inherent to their separate dialects and dates.[38] Important variations occur in line 7, where the singular *wyrdi* becomes plural *wyrda*, and in line 5, where *scripeð* (glides) replaces *scelfath* (shakes). Elsewhere, *aam sceal* is reversed to *sceal am* in line 8 and *mon* is inserted into line 11.

As noted above, both poems also differ from the Latin through their line arrangement. One consequence of this is that Aldhelm's lines about weaving (3, 5) now stand together, with the mention of wool placed before them and the reference to silk after.[39] It has been argued that this deviation in the Old English poems is an improvement on the Latin version: "[b]y

---

36 Smith, *Three Northumbrian Poems*, p. 17.
37 Whitman, *Old English Riddles*, p. 127.
38 Smith, ed., *Three Northumbrian Poems*, p. 9.
39 Zandvoort, "Leiden Riddle," p. 47.

transposing, he binds together in better consecutiveness the references to the actual tools of the weaver,"[40] although this perhaps overlooks the fact that the poem turns on the differences and similarities between multiple types of weaving.

Another difference removes an element of linguistic play and is, therefore, according to Nicholas Howe, detrimental to the Old English version.[41] This occurs in the image of the last line, which in the Latin version hinges upon two alternative meanings for *vestis*:

> Here the allusion to the alternative name *Vestis* serves as the final paradox (*et tamen en*) in the extended metaphor of weaving around which the riddle is framed. Although the object is called *Vestis*, it is not made of wool or cotton or silk, nor is its material spun or combed. In short, when is a garment which is not a coat called a coat? The answer of course is an iron 'coat of mail', as the reference to the earth in line 1 indicates.[42]

The Old English translations call the riddle-object a *hyhtlic gewæde*, meaning "joyful or delightful garment," which Howe claims "is at best a faint approximation of Aldhelm's enigmatic reference to *vestis* [...] By denying that the garment he describes is a woven coat and then insisting that it is commonly called a coat, Aldhelm presents a better riddle than does the Old English version."[43] Of course, the opposite opinion can also be argued, as Thomas Klein does: "[t]he Latin *enigma* turns upon a simple play on names, but in the Old English, a strange, sentient creature suddenly emerges. The iron corselet of Aldhelm's riddle is a dumb thing given a rhetorical voice. The Anglo-Saxon riddle-object by contrast has its own voice and thought."[44] Klein further asserts, in contrast to Howe, that *(ge)wæd* can also refer to a coat of mail,[45] which would mean that the Old English version does retain the final paradox in some form.

Yet another position has been presented by Benjamin Weber who recently suggested that the scholarly preoccupation with this clue misses the

---

40 Anderson, "Aldhelm and the Leiden Riddle," p. 170.
41 "Aldhelm's *Enigmata* and Isidorian Etymology," p. 54.
42 Ibid., p. 53.
43 Ibid., p. 54.
44 "Old English Translation," p. 345.
45 Ibid., p. 346.

point of the riddle.[46] He maintains that the central conceit "is not that the 'lorica' is unwoven, but that it is woven without traditional materials or techniques."[47] His reading is supported not only by the many references to woven and interlocked mail-coats discussed above, but also by Isidore of Seville's definition of *lorica*: *Lorica vocata eo quod loris careat; solis enim circulis ferreis contexta est* (The *lorica* is called thus because it lacks leather ties; for it is woven from entirely iron hoops).[48] The linking of this definition with the descriptions in the Latin and Old English riddles gives us excellent insight into the Anglo-Saxon use of overlapping terminology of weaving, interlocking, and binding for different sorts of construction; the method and material may vary, but the underlying process appears to have been understood as the same.

Reading the Mail-Coat Riddle

The mail-coat riddle is particularly useful to scholars of Anglo-Saxon textile technology because, in the space of fourteen lines, it makes reference to the *wefle* (weft), *wearp* (warp), *þræd* (thread), *hrisil* (shuttle) and *am* (beater), as well as to various materials used to create garments: *wulle* (wool), *flysum* (fleece), and *hærum* (hair). The fine-woven cloth discussed in chapter 1 also makes an appearance here in the reference in line 10 to *godwebb*. These terms, listed all together and placed in a context of their function in textile craft, have allowed scholars to fill in the gaps in our knowledge of Anglo-Saxon weaving. While the existence of the Latin text allows us to identify terms in the Old English poems that may not be evident elsewhere, the phrasing of the Latin poem also contextualizes the information we do have in Old English, such as the simple listing of implements in *Gerefa*.[49]

But the real beauty of *Riddle 35* is the way it uses the double meanings of words and phrases to play upon the distinctions of weaving and war. The famous and controversial half-line *þurh þreata geþræcu* brings this

---

46 "Isidorian Context." He also argues against Janie Steen's reading that the *lorica* being referred to is a figurative, spiritual one in *Verse and Virtuosity*, pp. 91–8. Such an interpretation, Weber asserts, relies on associations with the title, whereas the *Exeter Book* version omits both this and the final line, thus eliminating the only evidence for the metaphor in Aldhelm's enigma. "Isidorian Context," p. 464.
47 "Isidorian Context," p. 460.
48 *Etymologiarum sive Originum libri XX*, 2:XVIII.xiii.1.
49 See chapter 1, p. 32n52.

double set of imagery to the forefront. Like *Riddle 56*'s phrase *bisgo dreag* (endured affliction/worked busily), this half-line has been read both as indicative of the functioning of a loom and as providing associations with martial conflict. The description of loom-leashes that pull the noisy thread in the Latin text is transformed into thread that resounds *þurh þreata geþrǣcu*. Many translations of this phrase have been offered, some aligning more with the function of the loom, as in Erika von Erhardt-Siebold's general "pressing the many,"[50] some bolder, like Eilert Ekwall's "the pressure of weights."[51] These suggestions derive from F.E.C. Dietrich's early discussion of the poem and rely on the rationale that since our knowledge of Old English weaving terminology is incomplete and we do not have a term for loom-weights, this phrase may refer to a part of the loom even if such a definition is not yet recorded.[52] Given *þreat*'s senses of "force" and "oppression," scholars who adopt this position maintain that the term could have developed from merely "pressure" to "something that presses, weight."[53] Johan Gerritsen, however, maintains that the "recorded meanings of *þreat* are not particularly encouraging, being either abstract or collective, which makes it rather hazardous to conjecture that the word could have been applied to an individual clay ring or cone such as we know the contemporary loom-weight to have been."[54] He argues instead that the phrase describes an operation of a weaving implement, rather than the implement itself.[55] Given the context, Gerritsen suggests it is "the system of leashes" that is being referred to here as "the crowded many," with *geþræc* signifying "collected force, collected objects exerting force."[56] Leashes are looped strings used in the loom to lift the warp threads, and they correspond to one of the meanings of the Latin *licia*, a term that is also used of "weft/woof."[57] Therefore, Aldhelm's *Licia nulla trahunt nec garrula fila resultant*, which Gerritsen translates as "no leashes draw, nor do noisy threads spring back," leads to a clearer understanding of the

---

50 "Old English Loom Riddles," p. 14.

51 Review of *Three Northumbrian Poems*, p. 81.

52 *Kynewulfi poetae aetas*, p. 18.

53 Ibid; Ekwall, Review of *Three Northumbrian Poems*, p. 81; and Zandvoort, "Leiden Riddle," p. 48.

54 "Þurh þreata geþrǣcu," p. 261.

55 Ibid., p. 262.

56 Ibid., p. 261–2.

57 Zandvoort, "Leiden Riddle," pp. 45–6.

Old English poem, where the vibration is caused by weights falling into place during the shedding operation of a warp-weighted loom.[58] This noise could apply to either the context of weaving with a heavy, wooden loom whose threads are under constant pressure, or to the very different clashes of the battlefield.

Of course, *þurh þreata geþræcu* has also been read more literally, with such translations as "through the force of strokes," through the "violence of blows," "with violent pressure"[59] and through "the pressing of multitudes" or "the force of many strokes."[60] A.H. Smith recognizes both literal and figurative readings of this half-line: "[t]aken literally, the sentence would mean 'there is no thread in me which can resound through the onrush of troops' (i.e., in battle); but it may have a more figurative sense 'through the violence of its blows' in allusion to the passing of the thread backwards and forwards in the loom."[61] This reading provides a double meaning, which may be closer to what the Old English riddler had in mind, pointing as it does to the physicality involved in both weaving and warfare, as well as to the mail-coat's dual nature as an object woven, not of wool but of metal, and worn, not at home but into battle.

Klein also disagrees with associating this half-line with any one loom part or operation, maintaining that the poetic link between *þreat* and groups of warriors or angels makes it more appropriate to associate this line's reference with the sound of battle. [62] His reading of lines 6–8 characterizes the middle of the poem as "a miniature battle, carried out on the loom itself," as evidenced by the association between three of the key verbs and warfare: *hlimman* (to resound/clang), *hrutan* (to whiz) and *cnyssan* (to strike/overcome).[63] While the whirring and resounding of the shuttle and thread can be explained in the context of the craft of weaving, as Erhardt-Siebold does,[64] the grouping together of such verbs with multiple meanings

---

58 "Þurh þreata geþræcu," p. 260.
59 Zandvoort, "Leiden Riddle," p. 47.
60 Tupper, ed., *Riddles of the Exeter Book*, p. 152.
61 *Three Northumbrian Poems*, p. 45.
62 "Translation of Aldhelm's Riddle *Lorica*," p. 348.
63 Ibid.
64 She argues that the moving shuttle "in striking the taut warp-threads, cause[s] them to vibrate and produce low notes, a sort of irregular humming or buzzing." "Old English Loom Riddles," p. 11.

and associations, explicable in both the contexts of weaving and warfare, cannot be accidental.

Furthermore, the Latin riddle's technique of focusing on negation allows the Old English riddler to play with the imagery in the translation, as Klein maintains: "The list of things that do not 'clang' or 'whiz', 'slide towards' or 'strike' the object calls to mind the things that do. The translator has so infused the riddle with his imagination that, even in describing what the object is not, he begins to hint at the corselet's true environment."[65] When we consider that the object that does not strike the mail-coat could be a sword-beater, the weaving and warfare layers begin to merge even further into one fascinating set of images.

The form and style of the short riddle have also been marshalled to support the battle imagery of the poem. Onomatopoeia is present in certain places: "*hrutende* suggests the ring of the shuttle shot through the weft threads and *þurh þreata geþræcu þræd* reproduces the sound and vibration it describes."[66] In addition, the *Exeter Book* version rearranges the word order of line 8b to invoke the "clashing" metre of Sievers' Type C, bringing together "[s]ound and sense" in the process.[67] While previous analyses of the riddle's rhetorical and metrical techniques have thus far focused on the poem's associations with battle, it is also notable that the translator's use of ornamental devices amounts to Bredehoft's "poetic interlacing," which points particularly to the construction of the mail-coat. Thus, not only are the keywords *searo* and *cræft* present, but poetic highlighting is also provided by formulas and collocations (*wordum wisfæst*;[68] *searoþoncum gleaw*[69]). It is especially intriguing that "w" alliterates so frequently, appearing six times in total (spaced apart every two to four lines) and providing an alliterative weave throughout the poem.

---

65 "Translation of Aldhelm's Riddle *Lorica*," pp. 348–9.

66 Ibid., p. 348.

67 Ibid.

68 This formula also appears at *Precepts* 3a, while a variation with inverted word order appears at *Andreas* 1167 and *Beowulf* 626a. The three elements also collocate elsewhere: *Andreas* 1648; *Christ I* 64; *Elene* 314; *Paris Psalter (Psalm 102)* 52; *(Psalm 106)* 54; *(Psalm 118)* 43–4; and *(Psalm 145)* 17–18.

69 This formula appears in *Andreas* (817b: *hygeþances gleaw*) and *Fates of the Apostles* (96b: *foreþances gleaw*). The three elements collocate elsewhere: *Christ I* 220; and *Metrical Preface to Cura Pastoralis* 6–7. *Gleaw* and *þonc* also collocate independently of *searo*: *Andreas* 557a; *Azarias* 190–1; *Daniel* 742b; *Elene* 806b; *Genesis A* 1078b; *Guthlac B* 914a; *Judith* 13b; and *Phoenix* 144a.

The weaving *wyrmas* (worms) of line 9, though not particularly related to battle, are also interesting to a study of Anglo-Saxon textile craft because they depict an imported material.[70] Silkworms, called *seres uermes* (Chinese worms) in line 4 of the Latin version, were farmed in China from an early date, where their cocoons' filaments were used to create silk threads for fine-quality textiles. Erhardt-Siebold notes the debate surrounding knowledge of sericulture in western Europe in her discussion of Aldhelm's well-informed description of the silkworm's annual cycle, seen in *Enigma 12, De bombicibus:*[71]

Annua dum redeunt texendi tempora telas,
Lurida setigeris redundant uiscera filis,
Moxque genestarum frondosa cacumina scando,
Vt globulos fabricans tum fati sorte quiescam.[72]

(When the annual times for weaving cloths return, my yellowing innards overflow with silky threads, and soon I mount the leafy summits of broom, so that, having fashioned tiny orbs, I may then rest according to fate's lot.)

While the image of the silkworm in this poem offers a fairly factual account of the creature's life cycle, the worms of the mail-coat riddles are personified to become the weavers themselves.[73]

These worms are, furthermore, somehow connected to fate. Klein has suggested that the phrase *wyrda cræftum* (with the skills of fates) indicates "with the skills accorded to them by providence (or nature)," drawing on the final line of *De bombicibus* in comparison.[74] The Latin version of the mail-coat riddle does not include a reference to fate or fates, however, and the number of fates is different (singular rather than plural) in *The Leiden*

---

70 Silk was imported to Anglo-Saxon England from the beginning of its Christianization. Owen-Crocker, "Women's Costume," p. 453. See also Rebecca Woodward Wendelkin's discussion of silk in Owen-Crocker, Coatsworth, and Hayward, eds., *Encyclopedia of Medieval Dress and Textiles*, pp. 515–20.

71 "Aldhelm in Possession of the Secrets," pp. 384–6.

72 The Bern collection also contains what appears to be a silkworm riddle, *Enigma 43, De uermibus bombycibus serica uestes formantibus.*

73 Note also the use of "t"-alliteration to highlight the cloth in the first line. In at least one manuscript witness, *telas* is glossed by Old English *webb*. See Stork, *Through a Gloss Darkly*, p. 113.

74 "Translation of Aldhelm's Riddle *Lorica*," p. 349.

Riddle. Reference to the classical fates and their association with textiles is clear in Aldhelm's spindle enigma, as noted above,[75] so a reading of the phrase *wyrda cræftum* (with the skills of the fates) or *uyrdi craeftum* (with the skills of fate) could rely on that sense.[76]

As for the nature of the garment (produced by none of the methods described in the riddle), one sentence does offer a hint: *Wile mec mon hwæþre seþeah wide ofer eorþan / hatan for hæleþum hyhtlic gewæde* (Nevertheless widely over the earth someone calls me a joyful garment for warriors). Since *hæleþ* refers to a "warrior" (although it can be generalized to a "man" in poetry), this description indicates the object's connection with the battlefield where it acts as an implement of helpfulness and protection. And while *(ge)wæd* often functions as a generic term for garment, its use as a battle-garment is attested in heroic poetry,[77] and it is this use, as mentioned above, that Klein insists upon.[78]

While *The Leiden Riddle* and the Latin original end in a very concrete return to battle imagery, with a reference to the riddle-object's lack of fear in the face of a flight of arrows, *Riddle 35* instead challenges the audience's wisdom in naming the object. Zandvoort maintains that this new conclusion represents the removal of a clue,[79] but Klein argues quite the opposite. According to his reading of *searoþoncum gleaw* (clever with skilful-thoughts), the last lines provide a pun: "As a separate word, *searo* has several competing senses. It may designate either a 'device' or the intellectual power that created such a device. But more specifically, *searo* can mean 'armour' – so the pun reads, 'clever with thoughts of armour'."[80] The ambiguity inherent in *searo*'s multiple associations is something that we shall see time and time again,[81] in particular in the shared use of weaving and binding in the positive imagery of construction and the negative imagery of constriction.

---

75 See p. 55n19. For a more in-depth discussion of *wyrd*, see chapter 9, pp. 270–8.

76 See also Weber, "Isidorian Context," p. 465.

77 See in particular *Beowulf*'s use of the term in compounds indicating war-, warrior-, army- or breast-garments: for example, *heaðuwæd* (39b); *guðgewæde* (227a, 2617b, 2623b, 2730a, 2851a, 2871b); *eorlgewæde* (1442a); *herewæd* (1897a); and *breostgewæde* (1211a, 2162a). It also appears on its own in the doublet *wæpen ond gewædu* (292a) (weapons and armour).

78 "Translation of Aldhelm's Riddle *Lorica*," p. 346.

79 "Leiden Riddle," p. 47.

80 "Translation of Aldhelm's Riddle *Lorica*," p. 349.

81 See also chapter 6, pp. 181–3 and chapter 8, pp. 249–50.

Thus, the double meanings, ambiguity, and references to both weaving and warfare link these texts with *Riddle 56*. While the loom riddle depicts an implement of weaving described in relation to war and violence, the mail-coat riddles present an object of war described in relation to the domestic task of textile-weaving, a connection that the narrative voice both plays upon and emphatically denies. This refusal to accept the metaphor – a metaphor traditionally associated with mail-coats in Old English poetry – runs contrary to the usual riddling form, which in its very nature requires the embracing of metaphoric style. Although we have no way of knowing for certain whether the formulaic language describing mail-coats as woven or interlocked led to the mail-coat riddle or whether the thinking expressed in the riddle later became a poetic convention, the negation in *Riddle 35* would seem to imply that there already existed a strong association between weaving and the construction of armour in Anglo-Saxon England.[82] Thus, as flip sides of each other, the loom and mail-coat riddles are useful texts for gaining insights into the way in which Anglo-Saxon poets linked the destructive nature of warfare and violence with the constructive nature of weaving and binding. Put plainly, construction was not imagined as a wholly positive process, but as a violent struggle for control.

---

82 As, indeed, Weber has noted. See above, pp. 60–1.

3 The Material Context of Structural Binding

While the creation of mail-coats involves fitting together metal links to create an interlocked garment, iron rings are also depicted alongside wood and other materials used for constructing objects. Old English poetry frequently refers to objects in terms of the pieces of iron that bind the wood together and hold the structure firm. Earl R. Anderson emphasizes these rings in his discussion of technological descriptions in Old English poetry, applying H.W. Burris, Jr's anthropological theory of the "carpentered world"[1] to Anglo-Saxon contexts:

> To borrow a term from cultural anthropology, the world of Old English poetry is 'uncarpentered', a world 'where manmade structures are a small portion of the visual environment and where such structures are constructed without benefit of carpenter's tools … Straight lines and precise right angles are a rarity.' In consequence, if geometrical figures are named they will tend to be curved rather than angular, such as are predominant in the environment.[2]

According to this hypothesis, geometric terms across languages evolve according to five stages, the first having no terms, the second having terms for circles or curves, the third including squares or angularity, the fourth triangles and the fifth rectangles.[3] Anderson argues that the language used

---

1 "Geometric Figure Terms."
2 "Uncarpentered World," p. 67.
3 Ibid.

in Old English poetry places it in the second stage, while Old English prose texts demonstrate transition from this stage to the next.[4] He draws attention to the fact that *beag* and *hring* are core vocabulary terms, both of which relate to circles or curves, and claims that the lack of Old English geometric terms means that poetic buildings are often described with reference to their height, size, and internal construction, but not their shape.[5]

This theory helps to explain the emphasis placed upon iron rings in Old English poetic descriptions of construction, especially given Rosemary Cramp's discussion of the scant evidence for the use of iron clamps or bands in Anglo-Saxon material culture.[6] She refers to the iron bands of the hall in *Beowulf* as "an enigma," and notes that only Yeavering gives evidence of this sort of construction material (at the time of her study, at any rate).[7] The emphasis on circularity and bonds, therefore, speaks to the "cultural archaism" of a poetry that utilizes only certain geometric terms when describing the built landscape.[8]

The interlocking of rings also provides a point of connection between weaving and binding. As Karen Bek-Pedersen notes, textile production and blacksmithing correspond to one another by "giving shape to that which has no shape."[9] Indeed, the idea that fire *stricta solvit, soluta restringit* (loosens bound things, binds loosened things), expressed in Isidore's description of blacksmithing,[10] points to the importance of discussing the constructive aspects of binding in medieval literature. In Old English in particular, the generality of binding made available a rich world of formulaic language, metaphor, and imagery that continually arises in the poetry. This chapter will explore the conventional descriptions of bound constructions, which range from large-scale objects (such as buildings and ships) to small-scale ones (such as domestic and agricultural implements, and weapons), but all with an eye to how binding is employed on a structural level.

---

4 Ibid., 68.
5 Ibid.
6 "Hall in *Beowulf* and in Archaeology."
7 Ibid., 341.
8 Anderson, "Uncarpentered World," pp. 65, 80.
9 *Norns in Old Norse*, p. 120n77.
10 *Etymologiarum sive Originum libri XX*, 2:XIX.vi.3.

Large-Scale Constructions

The bound objects that make up the largest group in Old English poetry
are buildings. Although archaeological evidence points to a number of different construction methods available to the Anglo-Saxons – involving
stone (both native and salvaged from Roman ruins), as well as timbers –
Lori Ann Garner has recently argued for an Anglo-Saxon preference for
vertical wooden structures.[11] She maintains that both dynamically changing techniques and innovations distinct from those taking place elsewhere
in Europe indicate that "the use of wood was not merely a mindless exercise in imitation, but a genuine preference."[12] That this method of building
arose not from necessity but from choice is further implied by certain
stone constructions that have been decorated to appear wood-like, as well
as by the descriptions of idealized halls appearing in the poetry.[13] The attention that the poetry lavishes on buildings is likely due to the nature of
the hall as the centre of social life in heroic literature:[14]

> What the poems celebrate is, of course, not simply the hall as a building but
> the social system associated with it. Though assumptions about halls were
> never elaborated into an articulated social philosophy, any reader can deduce
> from incidental comments that the hall was pictured, for poetic purposes, as
> a circle of light and peace enclosed by darkness, discomfort and danger.[15]

This symbolism is a contributing factor to the poetic representation of
the building's construction. Given that the hall encapsulates "what was
best in life,"[16] poetic emphases upon not only its grandiose scale and decoration, but also its security and stability are easily explained. This stability is often articulated by means of binding terminology, which, as the
following chapters will demonstrate, is applied to myriad constructive
and constrictive contexts.

Binding imagery appearing in relation to poetic depictions of halls often
employs the formula *x-bendum fæst*, which *Beowulf* employs no less than

---

11 *Structuring Spaces*, pp. 32–5.
12 Ibid., p. 33.
13 Ibid., pp. 32, 35.
14 Hume, "Ruin Motif," pp. 356–7.
15 Hume, "Concept of the Hall," p. 64.
16 Hume, "Ruin Motif," p. 357.

six times.[17] In addition to this formulaic context, *bend* or *bindan* are also frequently found in collocation with *fæst*, indicating the conventional nature of this diction. It is the iron bonds, which are mentioned in *Beowulf* three times in conjunction with Heorot, that point to the hall's ability to hold firm despite the danger within and without. The first reference to Heorot's metal bonds occurs when Grendel arrives at the hall and bursts through the doors: *Duru sona onarn / fyrbendum fæst, syþðan he hire folmum (æt)hran* (721b–2) (The doors sprang open at once, fast in fire-forged bonds, after he touched them with his hands). Here, the doors are specifically described as constructed with metal bonds that hold them securely in place. When Grendel touches them, the doors do not merely open, but "spring" open, implying that despite their strength they cannot hold against the monster's powerful hands. Wehlau notes that this scene's focus on opening the door is due to the emphasis placed upon Grendel's "breaking of the barrier."[18] If the bonds of the hall door cannot keep the monster at bay, then the humans inside also run the risk of being bound and enclosed in Grendel's grasp. Garner further connects the hall's construction with constrictive bonds, noting: "[w]hen under attack a protective hall can quickly become a prison, a transformation even more easily achieved since in the Anglo-Saxon world prisons *were* usually buildings such as halls or churches that were more typically employed for other purposes."[19] The desecration of the hall is, thus, all the worse for the fact that Grendel – an outsider – is the prison-keeper, while the owners of the hall are the imprisoned victims.

It is perhaps for this reason that a reminder of the hall's cleansing is invoked during the gift-giving scene, with the hall again depicted as both broken and strong in its bonds. The description of the banquet and the ornate golden webs adorning the walls is interrupted by a flashback to the

---

17 See lines 722a, 998b, 1878b, 1918a, 2086b, and 3072b. *Guthlac B* also makes use of this formula in relation to the bonds of the body at line 955b. Indeed, there are many similarities between the structural binding of the objects addressed here and of the body, which is discussed in chapter 7.

18 *Riddle of Creation*, p. 83. Garner also notes that "doors typically receive special mention in poetry only when there is a threat from outside or within, most frequently in the contexts of hell or prisons. Thus, while the presence of doors as an architectural feature is of course not noteworthy in itself, the explicit mention of the doors is connotatively potent in idiomatically marking danger." *Structuring Spaces*, p. 85.

19 *Structuring Spaces*, pp. 87–8. For more on imprisonment, see chapter 5.

damage caused by the monster-fight. The evoking of a violent memory during the middle of the banquet is of course appropriate because it reminds us that Grendel's mother is due to arrive. This digression reads:

> Wæs þæt beorhte bold   tobrocen swiðe,
> eal inneweard   irenbendum fæst,
> heorras tohlidene;   hrof ana genæs,
> ealles ansund.   (997–1000a)

(That bright hall was very broken up, within entirely fast with iron-forged bonds, the hinges split apart; the roof alone survived entirely sound.)

The formula *x-bendum fæst* is once again invoked, using *iren* to alliteratively bind the formula to the previous half-line's reference to the inside of the hall (*inneweard*). The bonds that strengthen the hall are, furthermore, depicted as having undergone strain. While the hall is again described as *fæst* with iron bonds, the splitting apart of the hinges and the assertion that only the roof survived completely intact points to a partial failure of these bonds. And yet Heorot is still standing securely enough to hold a feast inside it, so it would seem that the superb construction of the hall has held it firm.

The final instance of hall-bonds in *Beowulf*, also a collocation of *iren-bend* and *fæst*, depicts the hall's stability in a more positive light. During Beowulf and Grendel's fight, the poet refers back to the hall:

> Þa wæs wundor micel   þæt se winsele
> wiðhæfde heaþodeorum,   þæt he on hrusan ne feol,
> fæger foldbold;   ac he þæs fæste wæs
> innan ond utan   irenbendum
> searoþoncum besmiþod.   (771–5a)

(That was a great wonder, that the wine-hall withstood the battle-brave ones, that it did not fall to the earth, the fair building; but it was so fast within and without by iron bonds, skilfully forged.)

Like the passage above, these lines make reference to the hall's interior (*innan*), which is lauded for remaining intact. This success is, interestingly, attributed to the skill (*searo*) of the smith rather than the architect or builder – to the metal bonds, that is, rather than the timbers that make up the majority of the structure. The bonds are also mirrored poetically by

means of assonance ("æ": -*hæfde*/*fæger*/*fæste*; "o": *fold*-/-*bold*; "e": *iren*-/
-*bend*; "ea": *heaþo*-/*searo*-) and double alliteration in all lines but the
first.[20] Furthermore, the compounds *heaþodeorum* and *searoþoncum* share
consonance of "þ" and homeoteleuton (which the latter shares with the
half-line preceding it: *irenbendum*). The focus on the skilful construction
of the hall thus evokes the skilful construction of the poem itself.

These lines' careful composition and their emphasis on the hall's stability speak to the need to reassert control over the recently violated social
space. In his discussion of the Finnsburh Fragment, Hugh Magennis in-
vestigates acts of violence that occur within the hall. There, he argues, the
confined nature of the space adds excitement, but also signals something
deeper: "for the fact that the fight in this poem is an attack on a hall, which
should be a place of security and of harmonious social interaction [...],
gives an added dimension of gravity to the conflict."[21] The above passage
from *Beowulf* indicates a similar intent. The violent parody of feasting that
has occurred in the hall under the regime of the man-eating Grendel cannot be tolerated in a healthy society. Indeed, this sort of intensely antisocial behaviour undermines the community at large: "Grendel's revenge
takes the form of attacking the community of the hall. He does this not
only by eating the Danes, individually, but by causing such fear that the
men will not sleep in the hall. In this way he attacks the social body as
well."[22] Thus, the concern of the poet with the security of the hall and the
breaking of such boundaries explains the emphasis placed upon the bound
construction of the hall. The passage makes it clear that it is entirely due to
the iron bonds that the hall remains stable when it is being attacked from
within, and were the hall made from less-securely fastened timbers, it
would likely fall to pieces.

These references in *Beowulf* are the only descriptions of entire buildings
having been constructed through binding; however, there are also mentions of bound walls in the poetic corpus. *The Ruin* refers to the binder of
such walls:

---

20 Andy Orchard notes that the negligibility of the relatively low frequency of double
    alliteration in *Beowulf* (49 per cent, according to Hutcheson, *Old English Poetic Metre*,
    p. 271) is counteracted by the poet's tendency to employ it in irregular clusters, which
    produces a highlighting effect. *Critical Companion*, pp. 60–1.
21 *Images of Community*, p. 47.
22 Wehlau, *Riddle of Creation*, p. 82.

..........]g orþonc   ærsceaft [.........
...........]g[..]   lamrindum beag
mod mo[........]yne swiftne gebrægd
hwætred in hringas,   hygerof gebond
weallwalan wirum   wundrum togædre. (16b–20)

(... cunning ancient creation ... ring ... with layers of clay ... mind ... braided
... swift, ingenious in rings, one renowned in thought wondrously bound
together the wall-ridge with wires.)

The damage to the manuscript makes a full translation of the text impossible, although key words related to attributes of the building (*ærsceaft/
lamrindum/beag*), as well as to the wisdom and skill of its creator (*orþonc/
mod/swiftne*) are evident in the partially reconstructed lines. For the purposes of this survey, the main verb here is *gebond*, although the use of
-bregdan as a construction verb pointing to weaving and interlocking has
also been discussed in chapter 2. This interpretation of *-bregdan* diverges
from the previous ones alluded to in the *DOE* entry: "in a passage in *The
Ruin* where MS damage makes it impossible to ascertain the subject or its
exact sense; proposed translations attempt to capture the quick movement
of the mind: ? to stimulate ? to prompt ? to make active."[23] A reading that
acknowledges *-bregdan*'s constructive use – whether it is here applied to
the mind or the building itself – is strongly supported by the clear reference to the twisted metal wires that hold the walls together. Indeed, they
are reminiscent of the interwoven links of the *(ge)brogden* mail-coat.

These rings may also speak to us of the "uncarpentered" nature of Old
English poetry, which William C. Johnson echoes in his discussion of the
organic nature of language that "stresses not the squaring of distances and
the erecting of linear parts, but a weaving and tying together of sinuous
wires and rings."[24] Weaving is also evident on a poetic level in the two intact lines. These lines, which notably contain cross alliteration ("h" and
"r": *hwætred in hringas, hygerof gebond*), as well as triple "w"-alliteration,
contribute to Bredehoft's argument that the ornamental alliteration "pow-
erfully supports the image of the braided thoughts and encircling wires

---

23 s.v. *gebregdan*, sense 4. See also Muir, *Exeter Anthology*, 2:702; and Klinck, *Old English
     Elegies*, p. 104.
24 "Ruin as Body-City Riddle," p. 405.

which together gave the structure its strength. Throughout *The Ruin*, in fact, the use of both rhyme and secondary alliteration patterns serves to present the poem itself as a marvel of careful construction and functional beauty."[25] The careful construction of the poem is, of course, at odds with the content – a depiction of a ruined building. However, when we recall the importance of the hall and its associations with human power, it is not difficult to see that what was once considered a separate "ruin motif" is actually an "emotional and poetic response" to the motif-complex of the hall.[26]

In addition to these halls and walls, there is also one instance of a door described as bound.[27] This is none other than the golden gate of paradise, which is bound and wound about with metal according to the prophet Isaiah's speech in *Christ I*:

> Eal wæs gebunden
> deoran since   duru ormæte,
> wundurclommum bewriþen.   (308b–310a)

(The huge door was entirely bound with precious treasure, wrapped around by wondrous chains.)

Here, both the splendour and the strength of the door seem to be the focal point. Not only are the gates ornamented with gold and treasure, but they are also entwined with chains that hold them secure. From all of these examples of bound buildings or parts of buildings, we can see that Old English poetry is particularly interested in constructions that are mighty or symbolic. Whether they are the walls of a hall or the gates of heaven, these bound constructions are associated with (literal or spiritual) power and prestige.

So too is a second large-scale object whose construction is depicted in Old English poetry: the ship, which is, notably, a holder of people like the hall. Yet, despite the importance of the ship and the frequency with which

---

25 *Early English Metre*, p. 68.

26 Hume, "Ruin Motif," p. 356. See also Garner's discussion of buildings as elegiac symbols of abstract concepts such as transience and loss. *Structuring Spaces*, p. 154.

27 That this door is metaphorically associated with Mary bringing Christ into the world in lines 328–31 provides a link between structural and bodily binding, discussed in chapter 7. For more on the context of the lines noted here, see Clarke, *Writing Power in Anglo-Saxon England*, pp. 118–21.

it is mentioned (in *Beowulf* in particular), ships are more generally described by adjectives and kennings implying their speed or grace on the water than in terms of their construction.[28] One reference in *Beowulf* to the ship's build occurs when Beowulf and his men are leaving Denmark to return home:

> no þær wegflotan   wind ofer yðum
> siðes getwæfde;   sægenga for,
> fleat famigheals   forð ofer yðe,
> bundenstefna   ofer brimstreamas.   (1907–10)[29]

(by no means did the wind over the waves deprive the wave-glider of its journey; the sea-goer, the foamy-necked ship, floated forth over the waves, the bound-prowed boat over the sea-streams.)

According to Klaeber Four's notes to this passage, the compound *bundenstefna* likely implies that the prow is bound to the ship, not that the ship is particularly well built or "properly joined."[30] However, given how frequently this general sort of binding occurs in Old English poetry and in *Beowulf* in particular, ruling it out may be unwise. At the start of Beowulf's initial voyage, for example, the ship is simply *wudu bundenne* (216b) (bound wood). Since early techniques for constructing ships were similar to those used for buildings, often involving the sewing together of planks by lacing thongs or ropes through drilled holes,[31] this may be the method of binding wood referred to in *Beowulf*. Similarly, the poet may have chosen to refer to "bound wood" simply because of the conventional and universal nature of binding terminology, which can be used to describe so many different processes.

A further reference to a ship occurs in *Maxims I*, although there the craft is described as "nailed": *Scip sceal genægled, scyld gebunden, / leoht linden bord* (93–4a) (A ship must be nailed, a shield bound, the light linden board). Mike McCarthy has recently discussed in detail the clinker

---

28 See in particular the extended passages describing Beowulf's sea voyage to and from Denmark at lines 198b–224a and 1903b–1919.

29 The prow is also referred to as *wundenhals* (293a) (wound-necked) during the coastguard's speech.

30 P. 221.

31 Hodges, *Artifacts*, p. 118; McCarthy, *Ships' Fastenings*, pp. 11–29.

shipbuilding that was prevalent in early medieval Europe.[32] This process involves overlapping planks that are held together by nails or rivets. Interestingly, in this poetic passage, paratactic phrasing juxtaposes the nailed ship to the bound shield. That the construction of shields also involved fastening planks and fittings with metal rivets and leather bindings[33] points to the similarity of these two objects. Indeed, it could be argued that *Maxims I*'s juxtaposition of ship and shield deliberately highlights this comparison:[34] both ship and shield are wooden objects that have been bound firmly into structures that must remain stable in order to protect the lives of the people for whom they have been constructed. Richard MacGregor Dawson notes that the juxtaposition may arise from "a comparison of the two methods of fastening wood together" or from an association between the studs on a shield and the nails on the ship,[35] although it is possible that the two verbs were fairly interchangeable in this context.[36] Whatever the reason for the juxtaposition, the objects are certainly linked in that they are both man-made constructions that speak to their owners' status and power.

In addition to the structural binding of ships, there is also one instance in *Beowulf* where binding relates to the constriction of a ship.[37] This constriction occurs in a passage describing Beowulf's arrival home to Geatland:

---

32 *Ships' Fastenings*, pp. 52–62.

33 Arnold, *Archaeology of the Early Anglo-Saxon Kingdoms*, pp. 77–9.

34 There has been much comment on whether or not the *Maxims* poems contain an internal structure, or whether they are merely strings of random gnomic statements, as suggested by Krapp and Dobbie, *Exeter Book*, pp. xlvi–vii. Some argue that the poems are deliberately and structurally associative: Dawson, "Structure of Old English Gnomic Poems"; and Barley, "Structure in the Cotton Gnomes." Others are slightly more cautious in their suggestion that the works hint at connectivity: Cavill, *Maxims in Old English Poetry*, p. 159; Larrington, *Store of Common Sense*, p. 220; and Shippey, *Poems of Wisdom and Learning*, p. 18. Nicholas Howe, on the other hand, rejects any idea of structure, stating: "a maxim cannot serve two masters at once: it cannot easily remain a valid, self-contained statement while simultaneously contributing to the structure of a poem," and concluding that these "forms of short statement have their own logic and their own structure." *Old English Catalogue Poems*, p. 165.

35 "Structure of Old English Gnomic Poems," p. 18.

36 Indeed, nails and bonds appear in apposition in the Old Saxon *Hêliand* 5536a–8a, which further implies their similarity.

37 See also *The Whale*'s reference to *oncyrrap* (14b) (anchor-rope).

> sælde to sande   sidfæþme scip
> oncerbendum fæst,   þy læs hym yþa ðrym
> wudu wynsuman   forwrecan meahte.   (1917–19)

(the broad-beamed ship sailed up to the sand, fast with anchor-bonds, lest the force of the waves might drive it out, the joyful wood.)

Again we have the formula *x-bendum fæst*, but here it does not apply to construction, as it did in the case of the hall that was held fast from within. This differing use of the same formula indicates a close connection between construction and constriction in the Anglo-Saxon poetic imagination. Indeed, construction itself may be seen as a constricting force, whether internal (i.e., halls are bound fast from within) or external (i.e., objects held together by binding two or more elements). The difference is that while most constriction is depicted negatively, the structural importance of the constriction employed in the creation of objects makes constriction a positive factor benefiting human civilization. Here, again, the importance of power and control is made manifest – even in the positive light of construction, these objects are viewed through the lens of the control maintained by their creators and owners.

Small-Scale Constructions

The binding of smaller objects is also common, particularly in relation to metalwork where the term's versatility means it is used in many different contexts. One such object associated with binding is the sword, *bunden golde* (1900b) (bound with gold), which Beowulf gives to his ship-guard. This description seems to refer to ornamental gold adorning the weapon, perhaps in strips around the hilt like the gold thread that adorns braiding and tapestries in the literary and archaeological record.[38] *Beowulf* contains other references to a *heoru bunden* (1285a) (bound sword) and one bound by wires:

---

38 See chapter 1, pp. 24–7. For a discussion of the Anglo-Saxon twisted sword grip, see Davidson, *Sword in Anglo-Saxon England*, pp. 58–62. For recent analyses of the sword and other weapons in material culture, see Owen-Crocker, "Seldom ... does the deadly spear rest for long," pp. 210–15.

> wearp ða wundenmæl   wrættum gebunden
> yrre oretta,   þæt hit on eorðan læg,
> stið ond stylecg.   (1531–3b)

(The angry warrior threw down that twisted/wound-ornament, bound about by wires, so that it lay on the earth, strong and steel-edged.)

This particular blade is the same ancient weapon with which Beowulf defeats Grendel's mother, and the binding here indicates that the sword is not only structurally wound, but also encircled by wires that bind it.[39] Descriptions of blades as braided or wound appear elsewhere in *Beowulf*[40] and *Elene*,[41] and have been read as referring to pattern-welding, the process of creating swords by twisting together bars of iron and beating them flat and into shape.[42] Thus, the *DOE* defines *brogden-mæl* as a "sword (or part of sword) with woven patterns (cf. *bregdan* sense 2.c); has also been taken as a compound adjective with the sense 'patterned'." Hilda Roderick Ellis Davidson points to several parallels in the description of sword construction, including an Arabic comparison of pattern-welded blades and woven cloth, as well as several Old Norse terms that link sword blades to the weft, and blood and inner organs to the warp.[43] In addition to these cross-cultural links to textiles, *Beowulf* 1030–1 appears to link wound-about wires (*wirum bewunden*) to the structure of armour. Roberta Frank's discussion of the helmet's *wala* (ridge) emphasizes the term's connection to architecture: "[it] suggests a vault, an overhanging, protecting roof that shielded the man within from the showers raining down upon him."[44] The repeated invocation of bound, wound, and braided swords and helmets, then, marks out such diction as traditional language, something that comes as little surprise given the mail-coat's use of similar terminology.

The next bound object presents a great many problems because it occurs in a riddle whose solution has not achieved scholarly consensus.

---

39 Davidson, *Sword in Anglo-Saxon England*, p. 134.
40 See lines 1531a, 1616a, and 1667a.
41 See line 758a.
42 See Wilson, "Craft and Industry," p. 265; Davidson, *Sword in Anglo-Saxon England*, pp. 23–33, 122–3.
43 See *Sword in Anglo-Saxon England*, pp. 122–3.
44 "*Beowulf* and Sutton Hoo," p. 55. See also Ælfric's homily, *De falsis diis*, in *Homilies of Ælfric*, 2:687, for a reference to idols *mid leade gebundene* (194–6) (bound with lead).

Riddle 4 has been solved as "bell," "millstone," "necromancy," "flail," "lock," "handmill," "pen," and "phallus," with "bell" having the most supporters at the time of Fry's survey of riddle solutions.[45] Since then, further suggestions have been proposed: "(watch-)dog,"[46] "devil,"[47] and perhaps most intriguingly "plough team,"[48] "bucket of water"[49] and "bucket on a chain or rope in a cistern or well."[50]

There are two relevant passages in the poem that describe the object as bound, the initial one reading:

Ic sceal þragbysig   þegne minum,
hringum hæfted,   hyran georne,
min bed brecan,   breahtme cyþan
þæt me halswriþan   hlaford sealde.   (1–4)

(At times busy, bound by rings, I must eagerly obey my servant, break my bed, proclaim with a cry that my lord gave me a neck-ring.)

The references to rings, both confining and adorning, continue a few lines later in lines 7b–8: *Wearm lim / gebundenne bæg hwilum bersteð* (sometimes a warm limb bursts the bound ring). The fettering rings at the beginning and this "bound ring" seem to be different objects with which the poet plays.

Let us first examine the riddle according to the "bucket" reading. There is a great deal of archaeological evidence for buckets made of wooden staves that were bound together by metal hoops.[51] It is this sort of binding to which *Riddle 4* refers, according to both Ann Harleman Stewart and A.N. Doane.[52] Stewart maintains that the neck-ring in line 4 signifies ice,[53] while Doane offers several compelling interpretations for the type of

---

45 "Exeter Book Riddle Solutions," p. 22.
46 Tigges, "Signs and Solutions"; and Brown, "Exeter Book's Riddle 2."
47 Heyworth, "Devil's in the Detail."
48 Cochran, "Plough's the Thing."
49 Stewart, "Solution to Old English Riddle 4."
50 Doane, "Three Old English Implement Riddles," pp. 244–9.
51 Wilson, "Craft and Industry," p. 254; and Stewart, "Solution to Old English Riddle 4," p. 54.
52 "Solution to Old English Riddle 4," p. 55; and "Three Old English Implement Riddles," p. 247.
53 "Solution to Old English Riddle 4," p. 55.

fitting – a hoop handle, an attached chain made from interlocked rings, or a twisted rope[54] – all of which fit the bucket solution. This reading implies that the neck-ring and the rings that bind the bucket are a part of its structure, the iron bonds maintaining the shape of the wood.

The singular bound ring of line 8, however, seems to be unconnected to the previous set of plural rings because the breaking of this ring is pleasing to the personified object.[55] Furthermore, the use of *hwilum* (sometimes) indicates that the bursting of the ring is only occasionally associated with using the object, while the transitive use of *berstan* may imply a more explosive breaking than the sort linked to metal rings.[56] This leads to the conclusion that, as in Stewart's reading, "[t]he *bundenne bæg* that the servant "sometimes" bursts is the weak layer of ice in the bucket present only on cold mornings: that is, the servant *always*, every morning, draws the water (hence *þragbysig*) and causes the bucket to "break its bed," but he only breaks the ring of ice *hwilum*, when it is cold enough for ice to form."[57]

The binding, according to this reading of the riddle, refers to the structure of the bucket as an object bound together, and also to the structure of a circle of ice as bound water. Perhaps it is the ice here that elicits the use of binding – that is, it is water in solid, bound form – a prominent motif in the many winter references discussed in chapter 4. Or, perhaps it is the circular shape of the ice that makes it "bound," harking back to Anderson's discussion of the Anglo-Saxon awareness of shape and poetic geometrical terms being limited to curves and circles.[58] The bound nature of the bucket, interestingly, runs contrary to other instances where weaving and binding are reserved for high status constructions. However, given that other riddles play with the difference between slavery and elevated servitude,[59] the use of lord and servant imagery here could be a reference to that inversion.

Such an inversion is similarly present if the riddle is solved as "bell." Patrick J. Murphy's recent discussion of the *Exeter Book* riddles and their comparative context retains this widely accepted solution on the grounds

---

54 "Three Old English Implement Riddles," p. 248.
55 Ibid., p. 247.
56 Ibid.
57 Ibid., 248.
58 "Uncarpentered World." See above, pp. 68–9.
59 See chapter 6.

that the poem "produces a chain of ring-related puns," which point to the sound and shape of the bell.[60] If we maintain the manuscript reading of line 2a, as Williamson does, *hringum hæfted* becomes *hringan hæfted*,[61] which Murphy claims is a verbal form that indicates the bell's ringing (and acts as a play on the *hring*-shape of the bell's mouth).[62] The multiple references to rings (*halswriþan/beag*) and the bound nature of the object therefore refer to this circularity, as well as to the servantile status of the bell, bound as it is to carry out its prescribed action. For Murphy, furthermore, the experience of the bell being awoken is then playfully transferred to the sleeping servant (as in Tatwine's bell enigma), causing a further play on the verb *hyran*, which can mean both "to obey" and "to hear."[63] Murphy also points out that this duality of meaning is present in other Anglo-Saxon texts, with *belle* frequently being governed by *hyran*.[64] The poem's punning references to shape and sound help to support the bell reading, although it is notable that the round, metal links of the mail-coat are also depicted as producing a ringing sound in Old English poetry.[65] Moving from the metal links of armour to those of chains, we see that the bucket reading – with its fetters and hoops – is still a possibility.

Cochran's solution "plough team" offers an equally interesting reading. For her, the *halswriþa* is the yoke around the neck of the oxen,[66] while *hringum hæfted* implies that the oxen are bound *to* rings, rather than *by* them.[67] She reads these, as well as the *gebundenne bæg*, as wheels,[68] although they could equally refer to the plough harness, and thus retain the sound associated with clinking metal rings. Similarly, the poem may refer to both "bell" and "plough team" simultaneously if the oxen are imagined as wearing bells around their necks.[69] Indeed, *Riddle 21*, which presents a similarly fettered plough, supports Cochran's solution:

---

60 *Unriddling the Exeter Riddles*, p. 72.

61 *Old English Riddles of the Exeter Book*, pp. 70, 143. Williamson notes that the plural ending, *-an*, may be a late West Saxon form.

62 *Unriddling the Exeter Riddles*, p. 72.

63 Ibid., pp. 73–4.

64 Ibid., p. 73.

65 See *Beowulf* 327b; and *Solomon and Saturn II* 89b.

66 "Plough's the Thing," p. 305.

67 Ibid., p. 304.

68 Ibid., pp. 304, 306.

69 For evidence that oxen wore bells in Anglo-Saxon England, see *Hundredgemot's* reference to an *hryðeres belle* (ox's bell), in Liebermann, *Die Gesetze der Angelsachsen*, 1:194, section 8.

> Ic snyþige forð,
> brungen of bearwe,   bunden cræfte,
> wegen on wægne,   hæbbe wundra fela.   (6b–8)

(I go nose forwards, brought from the wood, skilfully bound, borne on a wagon, I have many marvels/horrors.)

The nature of the binding in this passage is complex because it appears to speak to both construction and constriction. While objects are often personified as bound, enslaved figures in the riddles,[70] the presence of *cræfte* (skilfully) also implies that the binding refers to the object's creation – at least on a literal level. Edith Whitehurst Williams specifically aligns this craft reference with the smith: "The plough must have been a heavy and unwieldy implement. The ploughshare itself was wooden, but the coulter was iron, bound by *cræft*, that is, the mysterious craft of smiths who worked wonders with fire – hence the sharp weapons, one pushed through his back and the other through his head."[71] The forced labour evident in this poem is tied to the function of the object in question, so, as in the bucket, bell or plough team riddle, we have something commonplace imagined as a slave because it lacks prestige status. The ambiguity with regard to the object's binding (as both constructive and constrictive) is likely purposeful on the part of the poet, who plays with his or her power over the object.

Grendel's Glove

A final object whose bound nature similarly straddles constructive and constrictive purposes is described by Beowulf in the tale he recounts after returning to Geatland. This tale, which contains information supplementary to events just recounted in the poem, presents us with a particularly knotty passage:

> Þær wæs Hondscio   hild onsæge,
> feorhbealu fægum;   fyrmest læg,
> gyrded cempa;   him Grendel wearð,
> mærum maguþegne   to muðbonan,
> leofes mannes   lic eall forswealg.

---

70 Irving, "Heroic Experience," pp. 207–8. See also chapter 6.
71 "Annals of the Poor," p. 77.

> No ðy ær ut ða gen   idelhende
> bona blodigtoð,   bealewa gemyndig,
> of ðam goldsele gongan wolde,
> ac he mægnes rof   min costode,
> grapode gearofolm.   Glof hangode
> sid ond syllic,   searobendum fæst;
> sio wæs orðoncum   eall gegyrwed
> deofles cræftum   ond dracan fellum
> He mec þær on innan   unsynnigne,
> dior dædfruma,   gedon wolde
> manigra sumne.   (2076–91a)

(There the battle was fatal for Hondscio, deadly-evil for the doomed one; he fell first, the girded champion; Grendel was for him, the famous retainer, a mouth-slayer; he swallowed up the entire body of the beloved man. Then no sooner for that, still empty-handed, the bloody-toothed slayer, mindful of evils, wanted to go out from the gold-hall, but the strong one tested my strength, he grasped ready-handed. A glove hung, vast and strange, fast with cunning bonds, it was entirely adorned with skilful work, with the devil's arts and with dragons' skins. He, the brave doer of deeds, wanted to put me, guiltless, inside there – one of many.)

The reference to Grendel's glove in this passage has received a great deal of comment, and at the same time very little. Most of the discussions of this object occur in the form of notes, references in companions or footnotes in editions, with very few (by the standards of *Beowulf*-scholarship!) full-length articles devoted to this puzzling object.

The trends in the treatment of this passage can be loosely categorized thus: first, the oldest camp interprets the glove as a remnant of Old Norse mythology, linking it to Thor's encounter with the giant Skrýmir, his house-glove and craftily-tied food bag.[72] A second group emphasizes the

---

72 This includes Laborde, "Grendel's Glove"; Whitbread, "*Beowulf* and Archaeology"; Davis, *Beowulf and the Demise of Germanic Legend*, pp. 137–8; Taylor, *Sharing Story*, p. 128; and Rosier, "Uses of Association." There are also countless comments in editions and companions which refer to this reading, the initial ones coming from ten Brink, *Beowulf: Untersuchungen*, p. 123; and Hoops, *Beowulfstudien*, p. 118; but also Klaeber Four, p. 233; Dobbie, *Beowulf and Judith*, p. 225; Jack, *Beowulf*, p. 150; Mitchell and Robinson, *Beowulf*, p. 119; Swanton, *Beowulf*, p. 201; Wrenn, *Beowulf with the Finnesburg Fragment*, p. 124; and Orchard, *Critical Companion*, p. 122.

connection between the name of the slain Geat warrior, Hondscio, and the glove, *Handschuh* being the word for "glove" in German.[73] The object is then usually interpreted as a type of bag, which is invoked for the sake of wordplay. A third group insists that *glof*, and even *hondscio* in some instances, simply refers to Grendel's hand, reaching for his victim in the darkness.[74] This latter theory has been rejected because several of the descriptors quite clearly carry connotations of material objects, and because of the reference to Grendel wanting to place his victim inside his *glof*, which does not make sense if the word is read as "hand."[75]

Following these initial readings, scholarly approaches diverge. Some individuals focus less on what the *glof* is than on why it is invoked so suddenly. Kenneth Sisam, for example, suggests that Beowulf includes the glove and Hondscio's name in order to provide realistic detail and embellishment in his retelling.[76] Niles, on the other hand, argues that the glove is described not for the sake of realism, but rather because it is a truncated motif, "a motif that is introduced, often with some fanfare, only to lead to no narrative consequences," something that is common in oral traditional literature.[77] Owen-Crocker's analysis of parallels between passages links this section to Hama (a traitorous foil for the loyal Hondscio), whose name she argues may refer to "snake-skin."[78] Owen-Crocker's argument that these careful correlations are essential to *Beowulf*'s style runs contrary to Lapidge's assertion that the passage displays intentional nonlinearity, which points to the mental processes of understanding and perception.[79] For Lapidge, Grendel's glove or sack is evidence that these lines "represent

---

73 There is some overlap with the previous set of scholars (ten Brink, *Beowulf: Untersuchungen*, p. 123; Whitbread, "*Beowulf* and Archaeology," p. 28; and Orchard, *Critical Companion*, p. 122), but also some new contenders, including Chickering, *Beowulf: A Dual-Language Edition*, p. 353; and Sisam, *Structure of Beowulf*, p. 47.

74 W.W. Skeat claims this when he argues that Grendel is actually a bear. See "On the Signification of the Monster Grendel," pp. 126–8. Similarly, P.G. Thomas argues the *glof* is Grendel's hand: "the hard texture of which reminded the poet of devil's craft and dragon skins: it hung pendent as Grendel advanced." "'Beowulf,' lines 1604–5, 2085–91," p. 64.

75 See especially ten Brink, pp. 122–3, who also points out that *hangode* carries the opposite connotations of the stretched out or groping hand that Skeat proposes. See also Hoops, p. 118; Dobbie, *Beowulf and Judith*, p. 225; and Klaeber, "Beowulfiana," p. 212.

76 *Structure of Beowulf*, p. 47.

77 *Beowulf: The Poem and its Tradition*, pp. 172–3.

78 *Four Funerals*, pp. 159–60.

79 "*Beowulf* and Perception," p. 63.

Beowulf's own perception of his experiences in Denmark, and the poet clearly expected the audience retroactively to compare Beowulf's account of events with the narrator's."[80] Beowulf has, of course, now had a great deal of time to reflect on his fights with Grendel and his mother (whom he did not know existed when he fought Grendel), so the suggestion that the object, whose purpose may not have initially struck him, only later makes sense to him is an interesting one.

Additional interpretations of this passage have been offered in several longer studies. Earl R. Anderson claims that the glove may have been inspired in part by the Roman practice of the *culleus*, that is, the leather bag in which parricides were tied before being drowned.[81] Seth Lerer, on the other hand, connects this passage to "an older myth about heroic escape from the belly of the beast – a belly playfully defined as the enormous glove."[82] For him, the glove is a metaphor for dismemberment and ingestion. Andrew M. Pfrenger's article builds on this idea, arguing that the glove is a literal belly referent.[83] According to Pfrenger, "the term *glof* here [functions] figuratively as a continuation of clever word play on hands describing the monster's swollen bag of a belly as a pun for a kind of "glove." His mouth, then, becomes the gaping mouth of the glove, and his belly the body into which he greedily stuffs his victims with his own hand."[84] If this is so, he argues, then we also have a physical description of Grendel,[85] with the phrase *searobendum fæst* indicating either that Grendel is wearing a mail-coat or that he has very strange skin.[86]

Pfrenger's argument is intriguing, but Lerer's metaphorical reading of the glove is perhaps more balanced. There are a number of points that cast doubt on the idea that the glove is a literal belly. First, the phrases *grapode geareofolm* (he grasped ready-handed) and *[g]lof hangode* (a glove hung) occur in the same line, linked together by alliteration, which implies that the glove is hanging from his grasping hand. Second, the only other things that hang at all in *Beowulf* are the old sword hanging on the wall in the Finnsburh Episode,[87] and the son's dead body, which hangs from the

---

80 Ibid., p. 70.
81 "Grendel's *Glof* (*Beowulf* 2085b–88) and Various Latin Analogues."
82 "Grendel's Glove," p. 725.
83 "Grendel's *Glof*: *Beowulf* line 2085 Reconsidered," p. 210.
84 Ibid., p. 222.
85 Ibid., p. 224.
86 Ibid., pp. 224–6.
87 See lines 1662b–3a.

gallows-tree in the Father's Lament.[88] These are both things that hang from other things, rather than a part of something that sags, such as the belly of Pfrenger's reading. This trend is carried out in the larger context of Old English literature, wherein bodies frequently hang from things, but again never with this connotation of sagging.[89] Thus, while interpretation of the glove as the belly of the beast is an interesting new avenue to pursue, it seems to work only metaphorically. On a literal level, the glove appears to be something that Grendel is holding.

This leads to an obvious question: *what* is he holding? There is a case to be made for a type of bag or pouch – the presence of the dragon skins (*dracan fellum*) certainly implies a cloth element. If this is a primitive bag made of animal skins, then it is the only such instance in the entire poetic corpus. As discussed in chapter 1, poetry tends to refer only to fabrics if they are of high quality and can thus indicate the value of the object they adorn. More primitive garments made of animal hides, not considered worthy of the elevated poetic content, are uncommon in poetic contexts. Of the few references to animal skins that do occur in the poetry,[90] only this one would refer to a bag fashioned from them.

That being said, animal hides and leather do crop up in Old English poetry within a more war-like setting and outside the context of cloth and garments; they are used to create fetters, which will be discussed in chapters 5 and 6. Fetters would, of course, tie in nicely with the *searobendum* (cunning bonds) of this passage since collocations of *searo* and *bend* refer to captivity and constraint elsewhere.[91] This leads to a potential solution to the problem of Grendel's *glof*; rather than simply a bag, it could refer to

---

88 See line 2447b.

89 A search of the *DOE Corpus* yields a total of forty poetic instances and 253 prose instances of forms of the verbs -*hangian* and -*hon* (to hang) as well as nouns and adjectives derived from them. The vast majority of these occurrences refer to Christ's crucifixion.

90 The term *fell* (skin/hide) has five other occurrences in Old English poetry. Three of these, quite unsurprisingly, describe objects in the riddles: *Riddle 13* (ten chickens) 3b; *77* (oyster) 5b; and *82* (harrow) 4a; one describes the saint's lack of injury (despite having been thrust into boiling lead) in *Juliana* 591a; and one refers to the location of the injury in the *Metrical Charm, Wið Færstice* (Against a Sudden Stitch) 18a.

91 There are three poetic collocations of these terms: *Andreas* 107b–9 and 1395b–7a; and *Riddle 56* (4b–6a). Interestingly, *searo* is also compounded with the past participle of *bindan* in *Riddle 55*'s description of the *sinc searobunden* (4a) (skilfully bound treasure), noted in chapter 1, p. 44n97. If we accept Niles' reading of the poem, the context highlights both the craftsmanship and violence associated with weapons.

a device that Grendel uses to contain his victims. After all, one of the meanings of both *searo* and *orðanc* is "device" or "mechanical art,"[92] with further implications of an object of *cræft* being something that is skilfully wrought. There is a parallel containing the terms *cræft*, *orðanc*, and a reference to fetters in *Solomon and Saturn I*. In that poem, we seem to have a fairly concrete – or at least a much more detailed – description of a confining device, which only God is capable of destroying:

> He mæg ða saule   of siennihte
> gefeccan under foldan,   næfre hie se feond to ðæs niðer
> feterum gefæstnað;   ðeah he hie mid fiftigum
> clusum beclemme,   he ðone cræft briceð
> ond ða orðancas   ealle tosliteð.   (68–72)[93]

(He may fetch the soul from eternal night under the earth, the fiend never fastens it with fetters too deeply; though he enclose it with fifty locks, he will break that handiwork, and tear the skilful device apart entirely.)

By comparing the two, we see that the Grendel's *glof* passage actually contains the formulaic diction of constraint, in addition to the terminology of constructed objects. This is, of course, entirely appropriate, given the nature of the glove as a constructed object that fits tightly around the hand. That hand is itself a powerful body part of constraint, as implied by references to Grendel's grasping and Beowulf's *mundgrip* (380b, 753a, 965a, 1534a) (hand-grip).[94]

Given that the object in question is referred to as a *glof*, the context of other Old English gloves may also provide insight. For the most part, Old English references to gloves simply point to fabric coverings for the hands.[95] However, there are also other types of gloves, such as the hawking

---

92 Bosworth and Toller, *Anglo-Saxon Dictionary*, s.v.; Hall, *Concise Anglo-Saxon Dictionary*, s.v.

93 This reference is from Cambridge, Corpus Christi College 422. Anlezark's edition also includes the poem as it appears in Cambridge, Corpus Christi College 41, which, apart from orthographical differences, is identical.

94 For more on the uses of hand-terminology in *Beowulf*, see Carens, "Handscóh and Grendel"; and Rosier, "Uses of Association."

95 Prose references to gloves occur in chapter 4 of *The Life of St. Guthlac*, in Gonser, *Das angelsächsische Prosa-Leben des heiligen Guthlac*, p. 144, lines 9, 17; the law tract, *Rectitudines Singularum Personarum*, in Liebermann, *Die Gesetze der Angelsachsen*, 1:450, nos. 10, 12; chapter 17 of the monastic list of signs, *Monasterialia indicia*,

glove mentioned in *Maxims II* 17a–18b, which is, interestingly, the only other poetic instance of the term.[96] That falconry was particularly associated with the nobility is evident from Anglo-Saxon prose, as well as from references in *Battle of Maldon* 7–8a, *Fortunes of Men* 85–7a and *Gifts of Men* 80b–1a.[97] Although the bird in *Maldon* is not tied, the one in *Fortunes* is in the process of being tamed, and thus is described as fettered. Furthermore, several scholars consider "falconry" to be a possible solution for *Riddle 20* (sword), which will be discussed in chapter 6.[98] Thus, Eric G. Stanley reads the phrase *bende legde* (30a) (laid bonds) as a reference to the trained birds' jess and varvel.[99] With the image of fetters and binding being applied to both the hawking glove and to Grendel's glove, it is not such a stretch to imagine this particular enigmatic object as one used for hunting, capture, and containment. This would, of course, be an inversion on the part of the poet. Rather than a nobleman, we have the anti-hero Grendel, a terrifying monster with a grotesque version of an object commonly associated with heroic life.

Finally, one more image to be considered, related to the term *glof*, is the manacle. According to the *DOE*, there is one instance where Old English *glof* glosses Latin *manicula* and indicates "manacle, (pair of) handcuffs,"[100] as well as two where it glosses *manica* (from *manicae*, commonly "sleeve" or "glove," but also "manacle"[101]).[102] Because the description of Grendel's glove includes references to imagery of containment, the definition

---

in Kluge, "Zur Geschichte der Zeichensprache," p. 108; and the monastic guide to the use of forms of service, *Ordo ad visitandum et unguendum infirmum*, in Fehr, "Altenglische Ritualtexte für Krankenbesuch, heilige Ölung und Begräbnis," p. 60: L-text nos. 82, 86, C-text nos. 54, 56. For more on gloves, see Owen(-Crocker), "Anglo-Saxon Costume," 2:614–18; and Owen-Crocker, Coatsworth and Hayward, *Encyclopedia of Medieval Dress and Textiles*, pp. 236–7.

96 For more on Anglo-Saxon falconry, see Oggins, *Kings and Their Hawks*, pp. 36–49.

97 Falconry is also alluded to in the runes of *Riddles 19* and *64*.

98 "Heroic Aspects," p. 207.

99 These are the straps fastened to the hawks' legs and the ring about which a leash could be tied.

100 Sense 2. Gloss number 3920 in Stryker, "Latin-Old English Glossary in MS. Cotton Cleopatra A.III," 2:296.

101 Lewis and Short, *Latin Dictionary*, s.v.

102 Gloss number 631 (spelled *gloob* in the Epinal Manuscript and *glob* in the Erfurt Manuscript) in Pheifer, *Old English Glosses in the Épinal-Erfurt Glossary*, p. 34; and gloss number 36 in Ker, "Grammatical and Glossarial Fragments," p. 471.

"manacle" may lend credence to the idea that the object being described in *Beowulf* is some sort of device used to contain victims.

The exact object indicated by Grendel's *glof* may not be clear.[103] However, it is clear that the poet once again employs imagery of structural binding in connection to constriction and constraint. If material objects are meant to comfort and control, as Robinson has suggested,[104] then Grendel's *glof* is an exception to this rule. Indeed, Lerer notes that

> as a work of *deofles cræftum*, made with dragon skin, Grendel's glove presents a counter-instance of the works of artifice that fill the world of men. It stands as a lone exception to the social norm [...]. For here, we have a grim work of horrific craft, a thing whose *orðonc* exemplifies neither the ingenuities of men nor the inherent artistry of God's Creation.[105]

Hence, the marginal figure and boundary-pusher that is Grendel gains part of his terrifying aspect from this inversion. This passage serves to emphasize his evil (in that he knows the arts of the devil), his strength (in that he or his kin have killed a dragon, skinned it, and fashioned clothing out of it!) and his uncanny intelligence (in that he possesses similar powers of creation and construction to humans). Through Grendel's *glof*, the poet plays with questions of power and control related to human construction. It is only when Beowulf defeats his monstrous opponent that this question is laid to rest.

The struggle for power and control that marks this passage and all of the above descriptions of bound objects will be further developed in the following chapters' examination of fettering. While this chapter and those preceding it have focused on material construction, they have also outlined the way in which that construction is ultimately tied to constriction in Old English poetry. These poems, especially *Beowulf* and the riddles, provide us with valuable information about how the Anglo-Saxons constructed ideas of construction, and how they interpreted and translated material objects into words.

---

103 This ambiguity may be intentional, given that Beowulf describes it as *syllic* (strange).
104 *"Beowulf" and the Appositive Style*, pp. 71–4, as noted in chapter 1, p. 17.
105 *Literacy and Power*, pp. 185–6.

The violence inherent in so many of these depictions emphasizes the importance of craft and creation as useful tools in the human war against instability and change. This worldly instability, when mapped onto material contexts, has been usefully read in terms of a theory of raw and cooked; but perhaps it would be more appropriate to read the poetry in terms of materials that are (often violently) woven or bound into new forms. By taking materials from nature and weaving or binding (rather than cooking) them, the Anglo-Saxons yielded for themselves useful objects. Furthermore, because of their link to all types of connecting, weaving and binding become multi-purpose terms for many methods of construction in the Anglo-Saxon period. It is this multi-purpose nature that allows them to permeate so fully the poetic corpus, with few types of poetry that do not allude to weaving, binding or interlocking at some point.

PART II

Fetters and Chains: Experiencing Bondage

4 Binding in Nature

Anglo-Saxon conceptions of the natural world were to a great extent characterized by all that was alien to humanity, and, because of this, depictions of nature commonly demonstrate fear and defensiveness.[1] From literary references to the natural world, Jennifer Neville concludes that "the Anglo-Saxons viewed their society both as a necessary defence for individuals and as a fragile structure always under attack, one that required a God-like founder and defender to maintain it."[2] This defensiveness feeds into the Anglo-Saxon tendency to value things only in relation to what they can do for humanity (as seen in Part I's discussion of constructed objects), resulting in an approach to the natural world that is for the most part concerned with how that world affects humanity. Indeed, Neville notes that representations of nature are never an end in and of themselves, instead acting "as a literary device, used to define what were apparently more important issues: the state of humanity and its position in the universe, the establishment and maintenance of society, the power of extraordinary individuals, the proximity of the deity to creation, and the ability of the written word to control and limit information."[3]

Because of this anthropocentric concern, nature is frequently depicted in the poetic corpus as bound or imprisoned. Like binding in the construction of objects, this constrictive fettering keeps elements in place, though this time on a much larger scale. The fact that the object of this binding must be fettered or imprisoned also speaks to its ultimate power: fear of

---

1 Neville, *Representations of the Natural World*, p. 7.
2 Ibid., p. 88.
3 Ibid., p. 18.

the bound person or entity creates the need for the binding in the first place. The desire to control nature is clearly seen in poetic depictions of the bound natural world; however, nature's power itself is also imagined in terms of binding. In fact, the dangerous aspects of nature and thus the reason that it must be bound relate to its function not merely as an afflicter, but more specifically as a binder, of humans. This chapter will discuss both nature as bound and nature as binder, especially with regard to water and winter.

Controlling the Natural World

God is frequently depicted as governing and controlling the natural world because, according to Anglo-Saxon Christianity, he is the only one with sufficient power to take on such disorder. This divine ordering occurs in relation to his binding of the sea in the religious poems *Genesis A*, *Andreas*, *Paris Psalter (Psalm 65)* and *Christ III*. The example from *Genesis A* depicts the creation of the world, on the third day of which,

> Frea engla heht
> þurh his word wesan   wæter gemæne,
> þa nu under roderum   heora ryne healdað,
> stowe gestefnde.   (157b–60a)

(The lord of angels commanded through his word that the waters should be gathered together, which now hold their course under the heavens, their place regulated.)

The poem further reads:

> Gesette yðum heora
> onrihtne ryne,   rumum flode,
> and gefetero ...[4]   (167b–9)

(He assigned the proper course for the waves and for the wide ocean, and fettered ...)

---

4 The *DOE* assumes that the verb form here should be *gefeterode* at the point where the manuscript breaks off. s.v. *gefeterian*.

Unfortunately, the text cuts off at the end of this passage and the next several pages are missing. We can imagine, however, that it is the waters that are fettered, as in the first part of the passage describing the holding in place of water, and as in the descriptions below of the binding of the elements. In addition to the imagery of imprisonment suggested by the fettering of the waters, the language here is strongly related to governance. God commands (*heht*) and regulates (*gestefnde*) his followers and his creation, as well as assigning roles for them (*gesette*) according to what is proper (*onrihtne*). This God is a powerful king in addition to being the supreme architect of Creation.[5] By regulating the unstable world of nature and by binding various elements of it into place, he displays his power over great forces – forces that are powerful in their own right.

The example from *Andreas* builds on this depiction of the order of the world and its ultimate connection to binding. Here, we catch a glimpse of the sort of language that may have been lost in the missing pages of *Genesis A*. The description of the bound sea occurs when God, disguised as a sailor, speaks to Andreas about the nature of storms and their relation to divine power:

> Flodwylm ne mæg
> manna ænigne   ofer meotudes eśt
> lungre gelettan;   ah him lifes geweald,
> se ðe brimu bindeð,   brune yða
> ðyð ond þreatað.   He þeodum sceal
> racian mid rihte,   se ðe rodor ahof
> ond gefæstnode   folmum sinum,
> worhte ond wreðede,   wuldras fylde
> beorhtne boldwelan.   (516a–24a)

(The welling ocean is not able to suddenly oppress any men without God's consent: he has for himself control of life, he who binds the seas, curbs and censures the glimmering waves. He must by right rule humanity, he who raised up heaven and fastened it with his own hands, wrought and tied it, filled it with glory, that bright dwelling.)

---

5 See chapter 6, p. 184 and chapter 9, p. 251.

Again we have two metaphors – that of the imprisoned oceans and that of God as a divine architect. The move from one to the other is perhaps in part dictated by the binding language, which could, as we have already seen, be used in both constructive and constrictive contexts. The first image is one of God as guardian and ruler of the world and of the *human* world in particular. The ocean is not able *gelettan* (to oppress) *manna ænige* (any men) unless God gives it his permission. God's *geweald* (power/rule/control) over the world manifests in terms of his ability to bind the sea and hold the waves in check. Unlike the imagery in *The Metres of Boethius* (discussed in chapter 6 below), where the portrayal of the elements emphasizes the need to keep them apart, the description here shows God as sometimes allowing those bonds to be released. Thus the seas are kept in check when God wishes them to be; we must assume that when storms occur God has some purpose in allowing them, if only to demonstrate that *He þeodum sceal / racian mid rihte* (He must by right rule humanity). This knowledge that the world is under the control of God, if not of humanity, is more comforting than the idea that disaster occurs at random.

God's incredible power over the ocean is seen elsewhere in Old English poetry, perhaps most notably in *Psalm 65* of *The Paris Psalter*. The poems of the *Paris Psalter* are rarely looked to for their innovation and are generally thought to contain little in the way of traditional poetic diction.[6] However, the passage that praises God's power significantly expands the *Vulgate* psalm, verse 6 of which reads: *convertit mare in aridam in flumine pertransibunt pede ibi laetabimur in eo* (he changes the sea into dry land; they will pass through the river on foot; there we will rejoice in him). The Old English translation, on the other hand, reads:

He mæg onwendan   wætera ðryðe,
þæt þas deopan sæ   drige weorðað,
and þa strangan mæg   streamas swylce
gefeterian,   þæt þu mid fote miht
on treddian   eorðan gelice.   (17–21)

---

6 Griffith, "Poetic Language." For more on the poems' translation style, see Toswell, "Translation Techniques"; and "Awended on Engliscum Gereorde."

(He is able to change the power of the water so that the deep sea becomes dry, and he is likewise able to fetter the strong streams so that you might walk by foot on them as though on the earth.)

Here, into a fairly straightforward reference to God turning the water to land during the flight of the Israelites, is added a much more vivid description of the water. Its depth (*deopan*), power (*ðryðe*), and strength (*strangan*) all signal it as a force to be reckoned with. God, however, is able to mediate this power, with the polyptoton that links the fettering (*gefeterian*) of the sea to the walking upon it by human feet (*fote*) emphasizing his power over the movements of all his subjects, human and environmental alike.[7]

There is, however, one instance during Christ's crucifixion in *Christ III* where God's control of the world seems in question, at least momentarily. The veil in the temple is torn, the earth trembles and the sea breaks its bonds:

> ond se brada sæ
> cyðde cræftes meaht   ond of clomme bræc
> up yrringa   on eorþan fæðm.   (1144b–6)

(and the broad sea made known the might of its strength and angrily broke from its bonds up onto the lap of the land.)

The imprisonment imagery is quite clear, one of *clam*'s primary definitions being "bond, fetter; prison, restraining bound."[8] It can also be employed figuratively or to indicate the grasp or clutches of a creature,[9] with all of its uses related through the underlying notion of restraint. In total, the term appears as a simplex or the second component of a compound thirty-seven times in poetry, often in the dative plural. It is frequently invoked to describe hell(-like) imprisonment in religious poems.[10] Here, *clam* participates

---

7 The etymology of "fetter" from "foot" appears to originate in Indo-European, as indicated by the variety of cognates, including Latin *pes* (foot) and *pedica* (fetter). See the *OED* entry for "fetter, n."; and Holthausen, *Altenglisches etymologisches Wörterbuch*, p. 103.

8 *DOE*, s.v. *clam*, sense 1.a.

9 Ibid., sense 1.a.i., 1.b.

10 See chapter 5, pp. 125–56.

in a line whose content is reflected by its sound, with the repetition of velar plosives at the beginning or end of most stressed words emphasizing the breaking of the sea's chains.

The chains described in this passage were created by God to hold the sea in place, but with the death of Christ comes a brief return to chaos, as Ruth Wehlau emphasizes in her discussion of Noah's flood: "The elements, once released, return the cosmos to chaos by mixing together, and this mixing is the opposite of binding. Where binding is constructive, maintaining the separate identities of substances, while joining them together, mixing means the breakdown of distinctions and boundaries."[11] Thus, the Old English interpretation of the scene depicts some ambiguity on the part of God's control over the imprisoned elements. Indeed, if God has ordered this sea-storm, the poem does not say so,[12] and the overt reference to the breaking of chains implies quite strongly that the waters have broken free, not that they have been released by God.

Another instance of nature imprisoned – here much more surrealistic than in the case of the elements – occurs in *Solomon and Saturn II*. The passage describes a bird-like creature called the *Vasa Mortis*, which was caught by Solomon and guarded by the Philistines:[13]

Ligeð lonnum fæst,   locað unhiere,
swiðe swingeð   ond his searo hringeð,
gilleð geomorlice   ond his gyrn sefað,
wylleð hine on ðam wite,   wunað unlustum,
singgeð syllice;   seldum æfre
his leoma licggað.

(88–93b)

---

11 *Riddle of Creation*, p. 67.

12 Note that *The Hêliand*'s description of the same events does refer to them as *uundartêcan* (miraculous signs) at line 5660a.

13 According to Daniel Anlezark, this poem is part of a wider dialogue tradition spanning from biblical times to the early modern period, in which Solomon becomes associated with magical power over demons. This and the other dialogues include many references that scholars have found difficult to contextualize, with this one "rank[ing] as one of the most obscure in Old English." Anlezark points to several parallel traditions of strange and powerful birds in Irish and Indian traditions. *Dialogues of Solomon and Saturn*, pp. 12, 21–3, 123.

(It lies fast in fetters, looks fiercely, beats [its wings] violently and clashes its trappings, it calls out miserably and mourns its misfortune, it fumes in that punishment, it dwells unhappily, sings wondrously; its limbs seldom lie still.)

The fetters (*lonnum*)[14] that hold the creature are a torment (*wite*) to it, and the description of the Philistines' attempt to hold it in place is punctuated by images of frantic movement and instability. The creature's constant efforts to break free are not mirrored elsewhere in descriptions of bound nature, humans, animals, or objects, except perhaps in the shaking of the wind trapped underground in *Riddle 3*.[15] This is not a slave resigned to its fate, nor a conquered element serving its master. The description also diverges from depictions of humans in prison, discussed in the following chapter, because again such figures and settings are not represented in terms of frenzied motion.

Due to the creature's unchanging desire for freedom, binding becomes all the more essential. Solomon describes his role in the following terms:

ond hine ða gebindan het   ofer brad wæter,
ðæt hine se modega heht   Melotes bearn
Filistina fruma,   fæste gebindan,
lonnum belucan   wið leodgryre.   (98–101)

(and over the wide water I ordered that it be bound, so that the bold son of Melot, ruler of the Philistines, ordered that it be bound fast, locked in fetters against the people's terror.)

The terror (*-gryre*) residing in the release of the bird is due to its link to the apocalypse. Like the elements, whose mixing causes a return to chaos, the *Vasa Mortis* must be kept bound and imprisoned in order to ward off the destruction of the world and of the human race. Kathryn Powell discusses the significance of the connection between the *Vasa Mortis* and its location among the Philistines in the East, arguing that this passage "enacts on a literal level the process whereby the ephemerality of the world is ejected into and loosely confined within the space of the Other."[16] While suffering may be confined to the East, to the relief of the Christian English, the

---

14 The term *lann* occurs only twice in Old English, both times in this poem.
15 See chapter 6, pp. 187–9.
16 "Orientalist Fantasy," p. 136.

threat to civilization remains, making necessary "constant vigilance to ward off disaster."[17] The *Vasa Mortis* is, thus, more than simply a bound bird. It represents the chaos that the natural world is capable of, and the binding of it by humans puts them on a par with God, who binds the world. Hence, the imprisonment of nature does not take place on a literal level in Old English poetry; rather, these terms and metaphors are employed in order to make clear the power structure, showing who rules and controls whom and what. The binding of nature is generally the province of God, whose power is described in human terms. He is a lord, master, and prison-guard, something humans can try to emulate, but ultimately only with his permission.

The Natural World as Binder

Neville's opposition of human versus nature holds true for many descriptions of the bound natural world; however, it is notable that God is not the only one to bind the world. Indeed, nasty weather is frequently depicted as a binding force, making aspects of nature both the binder and the bound victim in Old English poetry. These descriptions demonstrate Anglo-Saxon poetic attempts to pin down the natural world in order to enable understanding and acceptance of the human lot in life. In attempting to access this understanding, a world that is frequently viewed as opposed to humanity is also described using human-centred terminology. Thus, by imagining both the natural world and humanity as binder and bound, a link between the two opposing forces is forged, adding, in the process, another level to Neville's opposition.

These bonds of nature are generally invoked in relation to winter, with imagery of freezing weather laying fetters upon the land and its vegetation.[18] Eric G. Stanley points out that this imagery is stock poetic diction, arguing that a "good example of the difficulty the modern reader has in evaluating the extent of OE poetic diction is provided by "the fetters of frost." He has no means of establishing if what seems to him so imaginative an example of imagery was not a scientific fact to the Anglo-Saxons; for how else is the solidifying of water to be explained?"[19] Stanley raises a

---

17 Ibid.

18 See also Paul Langeslag's discussion of the bonds of winter in his dissertation, "Seasonal Setting and the Human Domain," pp. 137–45.

19 "Old English Poetic Diction," pp. 474–5.

valid point, especially when we read these poetic depictions in light of Isidore's description of the ability of frost (*gelus*) to constrict the earth (*eo stringatur tellus*).[20] The link between frost and binding certainly appears to be a widespread association in the medieval world, which may well indicate scientific understanding. Thus here, as in the case of metaphors that are presumed to be dead, stylistic analysis becomes important in determining the use to which the poet is putting such imagery. Extended metaphorical treatment of winter binding and the use of ornamental poetic techniques are the key to understanding the passages discussed below.

Whether scientific interpretation or imaginative metaphor, descriptions of frozen fetters riddle Old English poetry, and are frequently found among related sets of imagery. Cold is associated with misery, both are linked to the sea, and of course to darkness, "for they combine to assail man in his misery."[21] The combination of darkness and fetters also evokes the imagery of hell, which was represented as a place of extreme winter weather in Anglo-Saxon writing.[22] Finally, since the hall is imagined to be the centre of warmth and light in an Anglo-Saxon community, being victim to severe weather can be associated with exile: "To wander alone in a scene of wintery desolation is to feel all the misery there can be on earth. Whoever finds himself there, cold and without shelter against the blasts of wind, may well remember the joyous feasting in the wine-hall and the king, the gold-giving friend of men, sharing out treasure by the hearth."[23] As stock poetic diction, the fetters of frost and binding of winter mesh well with many other sets of formulaic language employed by the Anglo-Saxon poet.

However, as suggested by Isidore's explanation of frost, these fetters are not restricted to Old English poetry, but are frequently present in closely connected Latin literature.[24] Examples include Symphosius' *Enigma 10, Glacies*, which describes ice as *rigidi caeli duris connexa catenis* (2) (bound by the harsh chains of fixed heaven),[25] Alcuin's *Disputatio Pippini cum Albino*, which refers to frost as the *vinculum terrae* (binding of the earth),[26]

---

20 *Etymologiarum sive Originum libri XX*, 2:XIII.x.7.

21 Stanley, "Old English Poetic Diction," p. 478.

22 Ibid., p. 479.

23 Ibid., p. 482.

24 Martin, "Aspects of Winter," pp. 380–4.

25 Ice is also described as bound in Bern *Enigma 42, De glacie*.

26 Daly and Suchier, *Altercatio Hadriani Augusti et Epicteti Philosophi*, p. 140, no. 62.

and Eusebius' *Enigma 23, De aequore*, which depicts the sea's immunity to wintry afflictions: *Nix neque me tegit, aut grando premit, aut gelu uincit* (3) (snow does not cover me, nor does hail oppress me, nor does frost bind me). B.K. Martin discusses the use of such imagery in both Latin and Old English, arguing that descriptions of winter binding, locking, and bridging the land were not chance usages, but "artistic and conventional diction for amplifying the topic of winter or cold" in both languages.[27] Part of their function, he maintains, is to emphasize "the hardships of a solitary man by setting him in a frostbound wintry landscape."[28] By linking the binding of the earth by winter to misery, exile, loneliness, and hell, the poets link said wintry bondage to everything in life that is unpleasant. Thus it comes as no surprise to find that the loosening of winter's grasp and the melting of the fetters of frost are associated with God's order and governance.[29]

Such a point of view is evident, for example, in *The Menologium*'s description of the coming of winter. This poem, which has been largely overlooked in poetic scholarship, directly precedes *Maxims II* and the C-text of the *Anglo-Saxon Chronicle*.[30] Thomas A. Bredehoft argues that contextual evidence suggests *The Menologium*, along with several other *Chronicle*-poems, may be associated with Æthelwold and Winchester.[31] The poem itself outlines the major religious feast days of the Anglo-Saxon calendar and provides detailed seasonal information about when they occur:

> Syþþan wintres dæg   wide gangeð
> on syx nihtum,   sigelbeortne genimð
> hærfest mid herige   hrimes and snawes,
> forste gefeterad,   be frean hæse,
> þæt us wunian ne moton   wangas grene,
> foldan frætuwe.   (202–7a)

(After six nights, winter's day walks widely; it receives the sun-bright harvest with an army of rime and snow, fettered with frost, by the lord's bidding, so that we might not dwell in green plains, adorned lands.)

---

27 "Aspects of Winter," pp. 380–3.
28 Ibid., p. 379.
29 Ibid.
30 Ed. O'Brien O'Keeffe, 5:3–10. The text quoted here is from the ASPR.
31 *Authors, Audience, and Old English Verse*, p. 116.

The harvest, which is characterized as *sigelbeortne* (sun-bright), the green plains (*wangas grene*), and adorned lands (*foldan frætuwe*) are juxtaposed to the desolation of ice and snow. This desolation is metaphorically linked to the damage caused by a hostile army. Indeed, winter is quite clearly personified here: it walks (*gangeð*) and sends its army (*herige*) of bad weather against the human world. Such a personification indicates that the invocation of frost's fettering is likely metaphorical here; whether or not the concept derives from scientific knowledge, its use alongside other martial imagery indicates that it is acting in an unconventional way. Interestingly, the line's alliteration also associates *forste gefeterad* with the term *frea* (lord), making manifest the connection between the binding of the earth and God's supreme power; it is *be frean hæse* (by the lord's bidding) that the earth is fettered by winter. Understanding this is essential because it reminds the Anglo-Saxon audience that God is in control. Because God is the commander of the natural world, it might seem that the poem contradicts the idea that the natural world is an opponent to humanity. However, this is not problematic for the Anglo-Saxons, who are willing to accept both a malignant world and a benign yet omnipotent God. Indeed, as Neville points out, Old English literature's varying depictions of the natural world ultimately lead to the assertion that "[i]nstead of a cosmological system ordained by a God who directs the natural world with a constant plan, the focus is on defining the power of a God who *can* make order out of chaos, who *can* wield, focus and transform the hostile power of the natural world into good as he did in Creation, but does not always do so."[32] That is to say, God's plan may not be clear to humanity, but it is to him.

Although concern with God and his creation are of importance throughout the Old English corpus, we may link these concerns especially to *The Menologium*'s place in the canon of wisdom literature. Its list-like repetitions are, thus, not employed in order to emphasize "the events themselves, the manifest subject matter of the poem, but instead the formal structure that contains them, the connections and systematic computations with which human beings mark and reckon the passing of time and thereby make a meaningful order out of experience."[33] In

---

32 *Representations of the Natural World*, p. 177.
33 Hansen, *Solomon Complex*, p. 117.

celebrating wisdom, the poem further reflects the anthropocentric perspective of this type of literature and its focus on humans "as the special goal and concern of divine thought and action."[34]

The importance assigned to understanding the way in which the world was ordered is, of course, found in other wisdom poetry, such as *Solomon and Saturn II*:

> Ac forwhon fealleð se snaw,   foldan behydeð,
> bewrihð wyrta cið,   wæstmas getigeð,
> geðyð hie ond geðreatað,   ðæt hie ðrage beoð
> cealde geclungne?   (124–7a)

(But why does the snow fall, it conceals the land, winds around the shoots of plants, ties up growing things, oppresses and attacks them, so that for a time they are diminished by cold?)

Here we have even more elaborated imagery, with repetition and variation occurring in line 125a and b. Not only does the snow hide or conceal (*behydeð*) the land, but it also winds about or encloses (*bewrihð*) plants and ties or binds (*getigeð*) things that grow. It is characterized by verbs of attack and oppression, and the plants are noticeably weakened by it (*geclungne*). Unfortunately we do not have the beginning of Solomon's response, although if we compare other answers to cosmological questions in this poem, we see that many of them refer to God's ultimate power[35] – something that is knowable for the Anglo-Saxons, even if it may not be understandable.

Turning to the elegies, we see that they too employ imagery of winter, but this time with direct and metaphorical relation to humanity, rather than only to the land and the crops that sustain humanity. This shift in focus is, of course, unsurprising, given the elegies' concentration upon human struggle. *The Seafarer*, for example, contains two references to the bound earth, both sharing imagery of darkness, night, and misery in addition to cold. One reads:

---

34 Ibid., p. 119.
35 See references to God's might at lines 51b, 144a, 151a, 160–1, and 278b–97.

Nap nihtscua,   norþan sniwde,
hrim hrusan bond,   hægl feol on eorþan,
corna caldast.   (31–3a)

(The shadow of night darkened, it snowed from the north, frost bound the ground, hail fell on the earth, coldest of grains.)

The snow comes from the north, a place associated with further cold and hell,[36] while the hail that binds the earth is referred to as *corna caldast*.[37] This phrase initially appears to be a creative metaphor; however, when read alongside Isidore's explanation of hail, its use is placed in a wider context: *Grando appellata quod forma eius granorum similtudinem habeat. Haec autem ventorum rigore durantur in nube, ac solidantur in nivem, ruptoque aere solvuntur.*[38] (Hail is named because it has the same shape as grains. Moreover, these are hardened in the cloud by the coldness of the winds, and made solid into snow, and released when the cloud is broken.) This link between *grando* (hail) and *granum* (grain), then, may stem from a medieval observation and understanding of the world rooted in Latin, rather than a poetic coining on the part of the Old English composer. Nevertheless, the invocation of both binding and grain in *The Seafarer* also connects it to the harvest attacked by snow and ice in *The Menologium*. Thus, an association based on shape and abundance becomes an ironic inversion, where hail is aligned with nourishment. Of course, this grain will not feed those who reap it, being rather more likely to afflict them.

The second example makes mention of the seafarer himself:

Calde geþrungen
wæron mine fet,   forste gebunden,
caldum clommum,   þær þa ceare seofedun
hat ymb heortan.   (8b–11a)

(Constricted by cold were my feet, bound by frost, with cold chains, while cares seethed hot about my heart.)

---

36 See St. Paul's vision in homily 17, *To Sanctae Michaheles Mæssan*, where the frozen wasteland of hell is clearly situated to the north. Morris, *Blickling Homilies*, p. 209.

37 See also *Rune Poem* 25a: *hægl byþ hwitust corna* (hail is the whitest of grains).

38 *Etymologiarum sive Originum libri XX*, 2:XIII.x.5.

Now it is not only the earth that is bound by frost, but also the body, which is fettered by the cold chains associated with prison and hell.[39] This prison imagery, heightened by the passage's use of near-rhyme and homeoteleuton (*geþrungen/gebunden*; *caldum/clommum*), makes explicit the trapped state of humanity, which is the central focus of so much of this binding imagery.

The seafarer is in a metaphorical prison,[40] but his body is also a prison for the hot misery that wells up inside him. In her recent work on Anglo-Saxon psychologies, Leslie Lockett maintains that the Anglo-Saxons conceptualized the mind as a hydraulic system in which cardiocentric boiling and heat are often associated with negative emotions.[41] She describes this hydraulic model as

> a loose psycho-physiological pattern, in which psychological disturbances are associated with dynamic changes of pressure and temperature in the chest cavity. These physical changes resemble the behaviour of a fluid in a closed container, which expands and presses outward against the walls of the container when heated, threatening either to boil over or to burst the container if too much heat is applied. When the moment of intense emotion or distress passes, the contents of the chest cavity cool off and are no longer subject to excess pressure, just as if a heat source were removed from a container of boiling liquid.[42]

Lockett further links this Anglo-Saxon psychology to a holistic approach to the mind/body, in which types of physical and mental experience (which are often intimately connected) are not conceived of as separate, as they would be in post-Cartesian thinking.[43] This is something that Michael Matto initially seems to support when he points out that, though

---

39 See chapter 5. *Forst* appears in collocations with binding and fettering in three other Old English poems discussed here: *Beowulf* 1609a; *Maxims I* 75a; and *Menologium* 205a.

40 Peter Clemoes has linked the body of the seafarer to a prison, arguing that the flight described in lines 58–64a refers to the soul escaping from the body. "*Mens Absentia Cogitans*," p. 64. Similarly, F.N.M. Diekstra maintains that the flight of the soul is not one of death, "but is achieved by interiorisation, by which man's celestial nature, the soul, raises itself above its baser nature, the body." "*The Seafarer* 58–66a," p. 440.

41 *Anglo-Saxon Psychologies*, pp. 59–62.

42 Ibid., p. 5.

43 Ibid., pp. 150–78.

tormented through separate afflictions, the mind and body in this poem "suffer together, which suggests a unity of experience."[44] However, he goes on to argue that "the primary opposition of heat and cold [...] also suggests that the body and the *mod*, though they suffer together, might also be opposed in a fundamental way," as we see later in the poem when the seafarer's spirit leaves his body.[45] The differentiation made between cold and hot afflictions here may imply that the cold is aligned with the physical, while the hot is associated with mental affliction – something that both the hydraulic model of the mind and the metaphor of sin as poison seem to bear out. However, we need only look to the literal seething poison that strikes down Beowulf[46] or the heat of Guthlac's disease[47] to recall instances where physical afflictions are described in terms of heat. A better differentiation might then be between external suffering (cold attacks the outside of the body) and internal suffering (heat attacks the organs and the mind). Both extremes, hot and cold, victimize through binding.

The Wanderer, which will be discussed further in chapter 7, contains a passage so similar to *The Seafarer* that the two must be read alongside one another. Here, the poet similarly invokes darkness, night, and storms that descend from the north:

> Eorlas fornoman   asca þryþe,
> wæpen wælgifru,   wyrd seo mære,
> ond þas stanhleoþu   stormas cnyssað,
> hrið hreosende   hrusan bindeð,
> wintres woma,   þonne won cymeð,
> nipeð nihtscua,   norþan onsendeð
> hreo hæglfare   hæleþum on andan.   (99–105)[48]

---

44 "True Confessions," p. 167.

45 Ibid.

46 See chapter 7, n46: p. 211.

47 See chapter 7, n47: pp. 210–11.

48 See also the formula *ofer waþema gebind* (over the binding of the waves) in lines 24, 57. It has been discussed as a kenning (Stanley, "Old English Poetic Diction," p. 475; and Greenfield, "Esthetics and Meaning," p. 106), a natural feature (Klinck, *Old English Elegies*, p. 110), and a metaphor (Malmberg, "*The Wanderer: waþema gebind*," p. 98; and "Literal-Figurative Identity of the *Wanderer*," p. 367).

(The might of ash spears has seized the warriors, weapons eager for slaughter, renowned fate, and storms beat against the stony slopes; falling snow binds the ground, the tumult of winter, when darkness comes, the shadow of night darkens, sends forth from the north fierce hailstorms in malice against men.)

Here we have a collocation of *bindan* and *hruse* similar to that found in *The Seafarer*, in which *hrim hrusan bond* (32a) (frost bound the ground). These examples can both be linked to the opening of *Riddle 3* (wind/ storm), in which the earth acts as prison-keeper for the wind that God has bound.[49] While most poetic examples of bad weather involve storms binding the earth, *Riddle 3* depicts the earth as the binder and the wind as the victim, inverting the poetic convention that poems like *The Wanderer* serve to entrench.

In addition to using verbs of binding, beating, and falling to describe winter weather, *The Wanderer* contains martial imagery. This is not just a storm, but a storm with purpose: a storm with a malicious intent towards humanity. The only other poetic instance in which storms and arrows are collocated occurs in *Beowulf*. *The Wanderer* inverts the *Beowulf*-passage, in which the hero is eulogized as having endured many a *stræla storm* (3117a) (storm of arrows). That storms and battle scenes are placed alongside one another is clearly appropriate given the Anglo-Saxon conception of the natural world's hostility towards humanity. Passages such as these, with their expanded descriptions of winter as an aggressive, personified opponent and binder indicate that the fetters of frost are more than an aspect of scientific interpretation. If indeed they did originally result from such interpretation – which seems likely given Isidore's explanation of frost – the metaphorical content inherent in them does not appear to have been lost on poets of Old English, who used them here and elsewhere to their fullest potential.

Another instance of wintry binding that is most certainly metaphorical occurs in *Beowulf*. There, *isgebinde* (icy bonds) are mentioned in the Finnsburh Episode, at the point when Hengest, having just come to an uneasy peace settlement with Finn, is stranded in Finnsburh over winter:

---

49 See chapter 6, pp. 187–90.

> Hengest ða gyt
> wælfagne[50] winter   wunode mid Finne;
> h[e] unhlitme[51]   eard gemunde,
> þeah þe ne[52] meahte   on mere drifan
> hringedstefnan   – holm storme weol,
> won wið winde,   winter yþe beleac
> isgebinde –   oþ ðæt oþer come
> gear in geardas,   swa nu gyt deð,
> þa ðe syngales   sele bewitiað,
> wuldortorhtan weder.   Ða wæs winter scacen,
> fæger foldan bearm.   (1127b–37a)

(Hengest then remained with Finn for the slaughter-stained winter; he earnestly remembered his homeland, although he was not able to drive his ring-prowed ship upon the sea – the ocean welled with a storm, contended against the wind, winter locked the waves in icy bonds – until another year came into the courtyards, as it now still does, the gloriously-bright weather, which always observes the seasons. Then winter was shaken/put to flight, fair the bosom of the earth.)

When faced with determining whether or not this terminology is indeed metaphor or scientific interpretation, it is important to note the use of poetic techniques that highlight the passage. Thus, cross alliteration occurs in a key line ("h" and "s": *hringedstefnan – holm storme weol*), along with a great deal of assonance throughout ("ea": *eard/þeah/meahte/-leac/gear/*

---

50 If the "æ" in *wæl-* is long, then this compound may be read as "hostile-water." See Klaeber Four, p. 187.

51 This term is a *hapax legomenon*. Bosworth and Toller define it as "an ill-sharing(?)," translating this phrase as Finn's "lot was not a happy one." *Anglo-Saxon Dictionary*, s.v. *unhlytm*. Hall similarly defines it as "very unhappily [...] (or ? = unflitme)." *Concise Anglo-Saxon Dictionary*, s.v. *unhlitme*. *Unflitme* is also a *hapax* occurring in this episode (1097a). Bosworth and Toller define it as "without dispute," while Hall includes only "unreservedly?" The editors of Klaeber Four accept the emendation to *unhlitme*, maintaining that it means "not reluctantly," "eagerly," "fondly" or "earnestly." See pp. 187–8, 449.

52 The MS reading is *he* rather than *ne*. The editors of Klaeber Four point out that some have argued *gemunde* and *þeah* should be read together as "he considered whether." They counter that "[t]he construction is dubitable" and "without the emendation the following description of winter seems ill integrated with what precedes." See p. 188.

geardas; "o": *holm/storme/won/com/-torhtan/foldan*;[53] "i": *hringed-/ wið/winde/winter/-binde*). There is also ornamental alliteration continuing between certain lines (1129b–30: *gemunde/meahte/mere*; 1131b–2: *weol/won/wið/winde/winter*; 1135b–6: *-witiað/wuldor-/weder/winter*), and a repeated alliterative pattern of h/w/vowel in lines 1127–9 and 1131–3. The binding together of these lines thus invokes the binding together of the icy water.

This passage's use of personification also serves to highlight the poetic quality of the lines, implying the careful selection of imagery. Thus, the ocean is painted as an entity that contends against the winds during a storm, arguably supporting a similar reading of winter as a personified figure that binds the natural world. It is also significant that here the natural world is at variance with itself, rather than with humanity. The two contenders are the ocean and winter, the latter of which here constricts and restrains the waters in an interesting nature versus nature dynamic. One might argue that the ocean is represented as a sympathetic figure because of its impotence; if indeed this is the case, the reason it is depicted so sympathetically is likely because it is Hengest's only means of returning to the homeland for which he yearns.

The final lines of this passage are also interesting because they convey similar wisdom to that discussed above in relation to *The Menologium* and *Solomon and Saturn II*. Although there is no explicit reference to God as controller of cosmic order, there is a depiction of the orderly passing of time and seasons. While in *The Menologium* the autumn harvest was *sigelbeortne* (sun-bright), here brightness is associated with spring. This draws a distinction between the fruitful, sunny seasons and the darkness of winter – darkness, again, being associated with prison and hell.[54] Furthermore, the bright weather of spring is given agency as an entity that observes the correct order of things, coming and going when it is right to do so.

Equally intriguing is the half-line *Ða wæs winter scacen*, which again implies agency on the part of the seasons. Although *wæs scacen* can be translated simply as "was gone" or "departed," there seems to be more of a sense of defeat here. Henry Cecil Wyld notes the verb's associations with

---

53 Arguably, the use of *oþ* and *oþer* alongside *com* invokes an aural similarity, despite the long "o" of the first two words.
54 See chapter 5.

agitated movement, arguing that its use in *Beowulf* retains the sense of shaking.[55] This more dynamic understanding of *scacan* is strengthened by the fact that it also appears only twelve lines before in the half-line *wæs hira blæd scacen* (1124b) (their glory was shaken/put to flight), a phrase that refers to the dead on either side of the battle. While this case is a negative image, a loss for humanity, the "shaking" of winter is positive because it indicates the return of good weather, and with it, prosperity.

Similar to the icy bonds of the Finnsburh Episode is a passage that comes later in the poem. After Beowulf has killed Grendel's mother and decapitated her son's dead body, the ancient sword he used to perform both deeds melts:

> Þa þæt sweord ongan
> æfter heaþoswate   hildegicelum,
> wigbil wanian;   þæt wæs wundra sum
> þæt hit eal gemealt   ise gelicost,
> ðonne forstes bend   fæder onlæteð,
> onwindeð wælrapas,   se geweald hafað
> sæla ond mæla;   þæt is soð metod.   (1605b–11)

(Then the sword, the battle-blade, began to dissolve into battle-icicles from the war-blood; it was a wonder that it melted entirely, most like ice, when the father loosens the bonds of frost, unwinds the flood-ropes, he who has power over seasons and times; that is the true creator.)

This passage is also heightened by poetic techniques, such as rhyme (*sæla* and *mæla*) and assonance within individual half-lines ("i": *hilde-/-gicelum*; *ise/gelicost*; "ea": *eal/gemealt*; "u": *wundra/sum*). The collocation of *forst* and *bend* is also not unlike that of *forst* and *bindan* in *The Seafarer*. Indeed, both of these can also be linked to collocations of *forst* and *feter* in *Maxims I* and *forst* and *feterian* in *The Menologium*[56] through similar semantic content and formulaic phrasing. At a literal level, this simile refers to the melting of the sword in terms of the melting of a frozen body of water. A link between the sword and seasonal change may imply the passing of

---

55 "Diction and Imagery," pp. 85, 87.
56 See *DOE*, s.v. *forst*, sense 1.b.–c.

Grendel and his mother's regime,[57] or it may simply be a simile, which naturally arose out of the traditional collocation between *forst* and fetters or bonds.

The fact that the melting of the sword is depicted in positive terms does indicate a certain amount of tension within the context of heroic literature. This passage would seem to indicate that heroic values are no longer guiding the poem, and that a rejection of violence is now deemed valuable. That this passage is an overtly Christian one, with the unwinding and loosening of bonds and ropes being clearly linked to God's power over the earth and its seasons, supports the assertion that the sword in this passage cannot be read in the same context as the other swords that appear throughout *Beowulf* and associated heroic texts.

Thomas D. Hill's reading of the imagery of winter in Old English poetry points out that cold is frequently related to sin and heat to charity in patristic texts.[58] Since Gregory's *Moralia in Job* treats conversion in relation to the melting of "the ice of wickedness," and since ice and cold are "among the traditional torments of hell,"[59] Hill reasons that the passage from *Beowulf* contains elements of this motif. Thus, for him, the simile "may allude to the conception of the ice of evil being melted away," something that is supported both by its clear Christian context and the fact that it occurs after the evil of Grendel and his mother has been vanquished.[60] However, despite the prevalence of such an opposition of heat and cold in patristic sources, Old English poetry seems to follow a different pattern; although cold is usually a negative and thus may perhaps be aligned with sin, heat is also frequently negative, arising as it does in descriptions of hell, poison, and turbulent emotions,[61] none of which are related to charity. Other contexts for heat in *Beowulf* include battle and blood,[62] the dragon,[63] and the funeral pyre upon which Hildeburh's kinsmen are laid in the Finnsburh Episode.[64] Thus, heat and cold appear to be working less as

---

57 S. Viswanathan argues for a direct link between this episode and the reference to the sword-hilt's depiction of the flood by which God sweeps away the race of the giants in lines 1688–90. "On the Melting of the Sword," pp. 361–2.

58 "Tropological Context of Heat and Cold," p. 523.

59 Ibid., p. 524.

60 Ibid.

61 See chapters 5 and 7.

62 See lines 849, 1422–3a, 1667b–8a, 2558a, and 2691a.

63 See lines 897b, 2296a, 2522, 2546b–7a, 2604b–5, 2781a, 2819a, and 3148a.

64 See lines 1107–24.

oppositions than as negative extremes, a usage also discussed above in relation to *The Seafarer*.

On perhaps the opposite end of the religious spectrum is Paul Beekman Taylor's reading of this passage. He discusses the melting of the sword in the context of magic, pointing to *gemeltan*'s use in relation to the dragon that Sigemund slays in *Beowulf* 897b, the waters that fall upon the Egyptians in *Exodus* 485, and the piece of iron that afflicts the recipient of the charm known as *Wið Færstice* (Against a Sudden Stitch).[65] However, Taylor's search for magic in Old English goes too far; perhaps more appropriate would be a discussion of these various instances of melting in the context of the miraculous or the supernatural. The charm is the only instance of actual magical agency, while the melting waters in *Exodus* are a miracle (having gone from liquid to solid to liquid again). The other two instances – the melting of the sword and of the dragon – can be linked to a physical, albeit supernatural, cause: that is, the hot blood of the slain monsters. In fact, another incident of melting occurs in *Beowulf*, in the funeral pyre scene of the Finnsburh Episode where the heads of the slain soldiers *multon* (1120b), suggesting that the association in *Beowulf* at least seems to be with heat rather than magic. According to Taylor, the charm *Wið Færstice* "applies equally well to the heroic context of a wound made by iron; but even in its domestic form it solicits the same power as God's magic to melt ice and release waters."[66] Here again, perhaps "magic" is the wrong word to describe the powers of God. God does seem to have cosmic control over (un)binding natural phenomena, but this power does not result from practicing magic or speaking incantations.

The powers of God are invoked in one other significant passage, found in *Maxims I*. Like the other wisdom poems that touch on the passing of the seasons, this text celebrates the proper order of the world:

Forst sceal freosan,   fyr wudu meltan,
eorþe growan,   is brycgian,
wæter helm wegan,   wundrum lucan
eorþan ciþas.   An sceal inbindan
forstes fetre   felameahtig god.   (71–5)

---

65 *Sharing Story*, p. 85.
66 Ibid.

(Frost will freeze, fire melt wood, the earth flourish, ice build bridges, the water wear a helmet, wondrously lock up the shoots of the earth. One will unbind the fetters of frost, God, the most mighty.)

As in the lines cited previously from *Solomon and Saturn II*, which also refer to plants' shoots, this passage similarly describes the locking up of plant-life. The dominant image here is that of winter, with the two instances of *forst* creating an envelope pattern that traces the cyclical process of the freezing of nature through to its release by God. The introduction of icy water also provides variation through the concepts of the ice building bridges and the water wearing a helmet. The latter appears to be a metaphor, with martial connotations similar to those of *The Wanderer*'s battle-storm – although here the ice is protective armour rather than an attacker. As for the former, the half-line *is brycgian* is a formula, occurring also at *Andreas* 1261b. This conception of ice as a bridge-builder appears only in poetry,[67] indicating that it may be metaphorical. However, since ice can literally form a walkway over bodies of water, it may also stem from scientific interpretation of a natural phenomenon. Regardless, its formulaic use certainly indicates its importance to poetic convention.

The ice-bridge motif invoked in *Andreas* is far more elegiac in tone:

>   Snaw eorðan band
> wintergeworpum.   Weder coledon
> heardum hægelscurum,   swylce hrim ond forst,
> hare hildstapan,   hæleða eðel
> lucon, leoda gesetu.   Land wæron freorig
> cealdum cylegicelum,   clang wæteres þrym
> ofer eastreamas,   is brycgade
> blæce brimrade.   (1255b–62a)

(Snow bound the earth in winter-storms. The weather cooled with harsh hail-showers, likewise rime and frost, grey warriors, locked up the homeland of men and the people's dwelling. The lands were frozen with cold icicles, the water's might diminished in the river-streams, ice bridged the dark sea-road.)

---

67 *DOE*, s.v. *brycgian*, sense 1.a.–1.a.ii. See also Martin, "Aspects of Winter" for Latin depictions of ice bridges.

The ocean is here characterized as *blæc*, which commonly signifies a black or dark colour, although the *DOE* notes that *blæc* (or *blac*) frequently overlaps with *blāc*, a mainly poetic usage meaning "bright" or "shining."[68] This term often refers to "naturally luminous substances or objects such as light, the sun, the moon, and fire."[69] Despite this overlap, the *DOE* editors place the *Andreas* instance in the first group (*blæc*) among examples "with connotations of gloom, mourning, or misery."[70] Together, the cold, binding, locking, and (possibly) darkness may be read as part of the *Andreas*-poet's use of the prison theme, the imagery of which is common throughout the poem.[71] Constriction is further emphasized by the reference to the ocean as a *brimrade* (sea-road); having been covered in ice and therefore rendered impassable, its effectiveness as a "road" is diminished. As for the imagery of binding and locking up the earth, we can be fairly certain that these are creative metaphors because the *hrim* and *forst* that are responsible for the binding, are personified as *hare hildstapan* (grey warriors).

This scene is also a particularly good example of stock poetic diction and formulaic motif because the cold weather is distinctly out of place with regard to geography. As Stanley notes, none of the sources of the poem, be they Old English prose, Greek or Latin, include such a winter scene.[72] Furthermore, Mermedonia appears to be identified as Ethiopia, which causes obvious problems for the logic of such winter weather, as R.E. Diamond argues: "It seems likely that the poet, in detailing the sufferings of the imprisoned saint, added cold to the list of torments and was carried away by the theme."[73] He also points out the high number of formulas employed in the passage, with ten of the fourteen half-lines being formulaic, including three instances of formulas that are repeated verbatim elsewhere in the poetic corpus.[74] The result is that we cannot deny the formulaic nature of such winter imagery, depicted as it is in a variety of poetic texts throughout the genres, manuscripts, and audience traditions.[75]

---

68 s.v. *blāc*, sense 1.

69 Ibid., sense 1.a.

70 Sense c.

71 See chapter 5, pp. 128–36.

72 "Old English Poetic Diction," p. 482.

73 "Theme as Ornament," p. 468.

74 Ibid.

75 Bredehoft uses several techniques, including analysis of literate-formulaic composition, to identify a number of Anglo-Saxon audiences. The "local audience tradition" refers to the audience of texts not intended to be widely disseminated (this applies to many of

The *Andreas* passage is, then, particularly good evidence for the existence of a type-scene in which the miseries of winter – including freezing cold (with ice, snow, hail, and frost figuring prominently), darkness, battle-storms and the binding and locking of the earth and water – are described, sometimes with reference to the passing of the seasons.

And yet, the formulaic nature of this imagery and diction does not mean that we are dealing with dead metaphors or static poetic devices. Rather, the build-up of formulaic language, apposition, variation, and personification serves to highlight this passage. The fact that the *Andreas*-poet would actually include a winter scene in a location where it is out of place suggests the popularity of the motif in Old English, but it also indicates that the poet was linking this section to other sets of binding imagery, the bondage element being integral to the poem as a whole. Neville touches upon this aspect when she argues that the wintry passage emphasizes both the binding of nature and of humans, with this immobilization being particularly threatening in a tradition that depicts both heroic life and its opposition in terms of motion.[76] For Neville, human helplessness in the face of nature is "an extension of the depiction of Andreas's confinement, and Andreas fulfills the 'ideal' of heroic endurance to its fullest extent, remaining cheerfully steadfast despite nature's cold grip and his other bonds and wounds."[77] In recognizing the bound nature of the world, and in accepting this, Andreas demonstrates the ultimate in heroic and saintly resolve. Unlike many figures depicted in Old English poetry, Andreas does not struggle against his bonds, nor does he attempt to bind others. He understands that God controls the world and surrenders himself to the power of his lord.

As a figure, Andreas is rather exceptional in his relation to bondage and the natural world. A typical Anglo-Saxon could not be expected to remain so cool in the face of torments. The wisdom texts and elegies discussed above all share a similar approach to the bound world, one that is also reflected in *Andreas*. These poems frequently depict the natural world as bound and binding, and since the function of wisdom literature is to

---

the Old English poems most celebrated in modern scholarship), while another tradition was characterized by an authorial voice, necessary given the texts' multiple copying and distant audience (this applies especially to the works of Bede, Alfred and Ælfric, among others). See *Authors, Audiences, and Old English Verse*, pp. 39–64.

76 *Representations of the Natural World*, p. 46.

77 Ibid. See also Mize's discussion of Andreas' positivity in the face of wintry affliction. *Traditional Subjectivities*, pp. 8–9.

disseminate received wisdom,[78] they thus provide an image of the world as one in which humans simply have to make do with what they get, much like Andreas does.

The texts, however, are also in themselves attempts to order the world through knowledge, and they ultimately hinge upon issues of control. Control is, of course, a concept integral to the roles of poet and scribe who make decisions about which images to include and how to depict events, concepts, and characters. This issue of personal choice speaks to the variety of depictions of the natural world, which, as Neville points out, "means nothing in itself, but can be used to mean almost anything."[79] Just as the natural world becomes a device for Old English poetry, so too does the language of binding and weaving. Its importance is highlighted by the way it plays a role in so many formulaic contexts and type-scenes, which together demonstrate an Anglo-Saxon poetic obsession with the bound nature of the human condition, an obsession which is translated onto every aspect of their lives.

---

78 See chapter 1, p. 19.
79 *Representations of the Natural World*, p. 204.

5 Imprisonment and Hell

Imprisonment, like the examples of bound nature, relates to the restraining of another's power. This bound condition is not only metaphorical, as in the case of the personified slaves discussed in the following chapter. There are also concrete instances of imprisonment as binding. It is necessary to note, however, contrary to what Old English depictions of slavery might lead us to believe, slaves in Anglo-Saxon England likely worked and lived unfettered and were constrained only for the purposes of punishment or detention.[1] Fettering was not for everyday use, but was a method employed to control movements in certain circumstances.

The most notable of these circumstances is the detaining of criminals and other prisoners. Although there is no archaeological evidence for Anglo-Saxon prisons, references to imprisonment in the law codes may provide some additional context.[2] From these and other texts, Lori Ann Garner establishes not only that imprisonment was a lesser punishment, but also that the Anglo-Saxons did not have separate prisons, using instead existing structures such as churches, residences, and yards or stocks to hold perpetrators of certain crimes.[3] Linguistic evidence similarly speaks to an absence of dedicated prisons, with the main Old English prison term *carcern* being a late borrowing from Latin *carcer* compounded with the native *ærn* (building).[4] In *Andreas*, the frequent description of prison by

---

1 Pelteret, *Slavery in Early Mediaeval England*, p. 58.

2 Garner, *Structuring Spaces*, pp. 69–72.

3 Ibid., p. 70.

4 Ibid., p. 73; Pugh, *Imprisonment in Medieval England*, pp. 1–3. For more on the borrowing of building terms and technology, see Biggam, "*Grund* to *Hrof*," p. 114.

way of its characteristics – using terms that are not extant in the poem's analogues – is an indicator that the poet anticipates the audience's unfamiliarity with the concept.[5]

Given the absence of prisons in Anglo-Saxon culture, evidence for imprisonment paraphernalia becomes all the more important. The texts discussed below make mention of leather fetters made from animal hides and of metal chains. Notable in this context are the eleventh-century shackles with locks found at Winchester, only recently discovered to have been human shackles rather than horse fetters, as was previously assumed.[6] Other useful evidence from a comparative context is found in Symphosius' Latin chain riddle, *Enigma 5, Catena*:

> Nexa ligor ferro, multos habitura ligatos;
> Vincior ipsa prius, sed uincio uincta uicissim;
> Exsolui multos, nec sum tamen ipsa solute.

> (Fastened with iron, I am bound, I shall keep many in bonds; I myself am bound first, but bound I bind in turn; I have loosed many, yet am not myself loosed.)

This riddle in particular speaks to the representation of something or someone as both binder and bound, a paradox that is central to the Anglo-Saxon understanding of the human condition and the nature of the devil. In a discussion of imagery relating to binding and imprisonment, this chapter will focus on conquest, religious heroes, and hell.

Conquest and Fettering

Thus far this survey has explored construction and constriction in relation to objects and the natural world, both of which were frequently personified in Old English poetry. This use of personification demonstrates that binding was first and foremost associated with people, something that can be seen in the literal instances of human captivity and imprisonment that Old English poetry records. Imagery of imprisonment and fettering as a result of war most frequently occurs in descriptions of historical events,

---

5 Garner, *Structuring Spaces*, p. 73.
6 Pelteret, *Slavery in Early Mediaeval England*, pp. 58–9.

and this is the case for both of the instances discussed below which appear in the *Anglo-Saxon Chronicle*.[7] It should come as no surprise that a culture frequently embroiled in fighting and warfare employs terminology of binding in depictions of such conflicts. Indeed, the vast majority of instances of binding referred to in the Anglo-Saxon law codes describe cases where it is unlawful to bind another human being,[8] which only implies that the trussing up of people, either as a result of a conflict or in order to sell them into slavery, was common enough to merit attention in the laws.

The first example of binding imagery in a historical context examined here occurs in *The Capture of the Five Boroughs*. This poem, entered under year 942 of the *Chronicle*,[9] describes King Edmund's victory against the Vikings and the restoration of the Five Boroughs of the Danelaw to English rule.[10] Before the coming of Edmund, the Danes were

under Norðmannum   nyde gebegde
on hæþenra   hæfteclommum
lange þrage.   (9–11a)

(under the Northmen, forcefully surrounded by the fetter-chains of the heathens for a long while.)

---

7 A third, brief example appears in *Beowulf* 419–24a.

8 References to the illegal binding of freemen occur in *Laws of Æthelberht*, in Attenborough, *Laws of the Earliest English Kings*, p. 6, section 24; *Laws of Alfred*, in Attenborough, p. 78, section 35; and *Laws of Canute II*, in Robertson, *Laws of the Kings of England*, p. 204, section 60. References to the illegal binding of priests also occur in *Laws of Canute II*, in Robertson, p. 196, section 42. That it was illegal to bind another man's servant is demonstrated in *Laws of Æthelberht*, in Attenborough, p. 16, section 88; as was the binding of a man who took asylum in a monastery according to *Laws of Alfred*, in Attenborough, p. 64, section 2.1. The only reference to binding in a lawful context occurs in *Laws of Alfred*, in Attenborough, p. 62, section 1.4, regarding a man who refuses to submit after reneging upon an oath.

9 It appears in four manuscripts: Cambridge, Corpus Christi College, MS 173 (A), London, British Library, MS Cotton Tiberius A.vi (B), MS Cotton Tiberius B.i (C), and MS Cotton Tiberius B.iv (D). Dobbie uses the A-text as the basis for his edition of this poem. *Exeter Book*, p. xxxvii. The other versions of the poem contain only minor spelling variations for these lines. See *Anglo-Saxon Chronicle: MS A*, ed. Bately, 3:73; *MS B*, ed. Taylor, 4:53; *MS C*, ed. O'Brien O'Keeffe, 5:79; and *MS D*, ed. Cubbin, 6:43.

10 Dobbie, *Minor Poems*, p. xli.

We may read this passage as a poetic elaboration upon one of the senses of *bend*: "in custody,"[11] with connotations of being under the control of someone or something. An example of this context occurs in the *Laws of Ine*, where the thief who is *on cyninges bende* (under the control/in the custody of the king) is unable to clear himself by oath.[12] Thus, the Danes in this poem are described as having been subject to the Norwegians through imagery of physical bondage.

A second, more elaborate example of binding in warfare occurs in *The Death of Alfred*, a slightly longer poem entered at year 1036 of the *Chronicle*,[13] which describes the traitorous acts of Godwine. After the death of Cnut in 1035, Alfred, the son of Queen Emma and her first husband, the deceased King Æthelred, returns to England from Normandy only to be attacked by Godwine who has his own ideas about the succession.[14] In the poetic depiction of this encounter, binding is invoked twice: first in a list of the ways Godwine treats Alfred's companions:

Ac Godwine hine þa gelette   and hine on hæft sette,
and his geferan he todraf,   and sume mislice ofsloh;
sume hi man wið feo sealde,   sume hreowlice acwealde,
sume hi man bende,   sume hi man blende,
sume hamelode,   sume hættode.   (6–10)

(But Godwine captured him and put him in prison, and he drove off his companions, and some he slew in various ways; some he sold for money, some cruelly killed, some he had bound, some he had blinded, some he hamstrung, some he scalped.)

---

11 *DOE*, s.v., sense 1.a.iii.

12 Attenborough, *Laws of the Earliest English Kings*, p. 40, section 15.2.

13 This text, which does not regularly alliterate and is partly prose, partly rhymed verse, appears only in the C- and D-text, the first of which Dobbie uses as a basis for his edition. *Minor Poems*, pp. xxxii and xxxvii. See also *Anglo-Saxon Chronicle: MS C*, ed. O'Brien O'Keeffe, 5:106. The poem in the D-text does not include Godwine's name, the verb *gelettan*, the reference to hamstringing and occasional adverbs and pronouns. The content is not significantly altered by these differences, although the absence of two rhyming verbs changes the poetics. See *Anglo-Saxon Chronicle: MS D*, ed. Cubbin, 6:65.

14 O'Brien O'Keeffe, "Body and Law," p. 213.

The binding here occurs as though it were simply one among many crimes listed in order to demonstrate Godwine's bad character. However, it is also reflected at the metrical level, with the initial two-stress half-lines of 7b–10's *sume*-catalogue giving way to one-stress verse units in lines 9 and 10.[15] Furthermore, most of the final stressed elements in the catalogue rhyme across a- and b-verses, while the final instances both rhyme and alliterate, prompting Thomas A. Bredehoft to argue that "the linking devices become progressively more effective, while the lines and verses themselves grow shorter. It is hard not to read this as a formal 'tightening' of verses, lines, and links, providing a nice formal parallel to the tightening bonds and other tortures dispensed by Godwine and his men."[16]

At the level of content, this passage's descriptions of crimes carried out upon innocent men echo the laws, which accord various types of compensation to victims of physical violence. Generally speaking, more obviously apparent injuries demanded higher compensation.[17] Katherine O'Brien O'Keeffe argues that the poet's emphasis upon the innocence of Alfred and his men shows concern that their mutilation would be read "in the context of the forensic exactments of the law codes of the two fathers, Æthelred and Cnut. To view those eyeless, noseless faces, those scalpless heads, arms without hands, legs without feet is to read upon their bodies the legal exactment of punishment for crimes."[18] However, the poet quite clearly marks Alfred and his party out as guiltless, something that makes Godwine's acts all the more horrifying.

Later in the poem, Alfred shares the fate of his men and is described as being bound:

Se æþeling lyfode þa gyt;   ælc yfel man him gehet,
oðþæt man gerædde   þæt man hine lædde
to Eligbyrig   swa gebundenne.
Sona swa he lende,   on scype man hine blende,
and hine swa blindne   brohte to ðam munecon,
and he þar wunode   ða hwile þe he lyfode.   (16–21)

---

15 Bredehoft, *Early English Metre*, p. 93.
16 Ibid.
17 O'Brien O'Keeffe, "Body and Law," p. 215.
18 Ibid., pp. 214–15.

(The nobleman still lived then; [despite] every evil commanded for him, until it was ruled that he should be bound and led to Ely. As soon as he arrived, he was blinded on the ship, and brought thus blind to the monks, and he remained there for as long as he lived.)

These lines are once again poetically heightened, with an envelope pattern (indicated by repetitions of the verb *lyfode*) marking the fact that the man's life hangs in the balance. Rhyme and near-rhyme also occur in several lines (*gyt/gehet*; *gerædde/lædde*; *lende/blende*; *wunode/lyfode*), as does alliterative and assonantal sound-play between certain half-lines (*lyfode/ yfel*; *blende/blinde*; *munecon/wunode*). Ornamental alliteration also links *-byrig*, *gebundenne*, *blende*, *blindne* and *brohte*, indicating an emphasis on Alfred's lack of control over himself while in the power of his enemies. Ultimately, Alfred is blinded in order to make him ineligible for succession;[19] however his mutilated body also marks Godwine's guilt and corruption of justice.[20] O'Brien O'Keeffe further notes that the "metaphor could cut both ways, for the discourse of the mutilated body could equally point to the guilt of the sufferer. This, the chronicler contests by pious prayers for the dead men and by pointed and detailed mention of the honourable resting place of Alfred's body."[21] Thus, the binding described in these passages is a marker of a criminal attack, with the *Chronicle* scribe using poetry to highlight both this fact and the innocence of the dead prince.

Binding Religious Heroes

The war-like setting that frames the binding of political figures can also be mapped onto the poetic saints' lives, and extended to the broader category of religious poetry and prose. Like the riddles discussed in Part I, hagiographical texts demonstrate a fascination with binding and fettering bodies; however, here the frequent reference to binding and loosing has "precise theological implications," stemming as it does from biblical and patristic sources.[22] These sources indicate a common approach to understanding sin and the human condition: "In Old English religious poetry, bondage is a pervasive image for man's fallen condition, and deliverance from bondage

---

19 Ibid., p. 214.
20 Ibid., p. 228.
21 Ibid.
22 Rendall, "Bondage and Freeing from Bondage," pp. 498–500.

is the primary metaphor by which Christ's salvation of man is expressed."[23] This metaphor in part derives from Matthew 16:19 and 18:18, in which Christ bestows upon his disciples the ability to bind and loose sinners on earth and in heaven. While loosing involves the power to forgive sins, binding refers to divine judgment over unrepentant sinners.[24]

This binding is also understood far more concretely, however, as Helen Foxhall Forbes demonstrates in her analysis of the chains of sin depicted in Latin and Old English religious documents. Rather than being wholly metaphorical, she determines that "[t]hese chains were both metaphorical and physical, and helped to make the terrifying and unknown prospect of the afterlife somewhat easier to understand."[25] Such a focus on physicality is likewise attested in the Old Saxon translation of the biblical verses from *The Hêliand*,[26] which recent analyses have established was known and likely fairly influential in Anglo-Saxon England.[27] There, the translator rearranges the biblical wording, and, in doing so, "interprets the biblical power of legally "binding and loosing" more physically than in Scripture, envisioning Peter as having the authority to make prisoners of souls and/or to let them go free."[28] Given this focus on physical binding in Old English and Latin religious prose and the Old Saxon verse gospel, it comes as little surprise that the imprisonment of souls is a wide-ranging motif in Old English poetry.

While the bound nature of humanity is a favoured trope in Old English poetry, the only non-Ælfrician saint who demonstrates the ability to bind human sinners is Elene.[29] In order to punish Judas and force him to reveal the whereabouts of Christ's cross, the heroine orders that he be incarcerated:

---

23 Ibid., p. 512

24 Ibid., p. 498.

25 "Power of Binding and Loosing," p. 64. This corporealization of the soul and its suffering is also something that Lockett touches on in *Anglo-Saxon Psychology*, pp. 383–8.

26 See lines 3071b–82a.

27 For more on the relationship between Old English and Old Saxon written traditions, see Bredehoft, "Old English and Old Saxon"; and *Authors, Audiences, and Old English Verse*, pp. 68–72.

28 Murphy, *Heliand*, p. 101n141. See also p. 100n140.

29 Saints exhibiting such powers in later Ælfrician texts also tend to be more concerned with loosing. See *Vita S. Martini episcopi et confessoris Anglicae*, in *Lives of Saints*, 2:290–2, lines 1143–77; *Sancti Benedicti abbatis*, in *Catholic Homilies: Second Series*, ed. Godden, p. 105, lines 450–60; and *Dominica XII post Pentecosten*, in *Homilies of Ælfric: Supplementary*, 2:765–8, lines 72–133.

Heht þa swa cwicne   corðre lædan,
scufan scyldigne   (scealcas ne gældon)
in drygne seað,   þær he duguða leas
siomode in sorgum   VII nihta fyrst
under hearmlocan   hungre geþreatod,
clommum beclungen.   (691–6a)

(Then she ordered the one to be led away, still living, by a troop, the guilty
one to be shoved (the servants did not delay) into a dry pit, where he stayed
companionless in sorrows for the span of seven nights in the prison, harassed
by hunger, surrounded by chains.)

The narrow confines of the *seað* (pit) resemble a prison, something that is
further indicated by the presence of the term *hearmlocan*, which is extant
four times in Old English religious poems. The term is used once of hell at
Genesis B 91a and twice of earthly prisons at *Andreas* 95a and 1029b, while
-loca is a frequent element in other terms for confined and enclosed spaces.
A notable parallel occurs in *Christ and Satan*'s *fyrloca* (58a) (fiery-prison)
of hell. In the description of Judas' punishment, the point is made that the
prison is also equipped with chains (*clommum*), an essential tool for fettering and binding, as has already been noted.

Despite the fact that the binding and loosing of human sinners was an
important activity ascribed to the followers of Christ,[30] Old English poetry focuses less on this type of constriction and more on the fettering of
saints by earthly enemies. The physical binding of these devout heroes, as
well as their ability to overcome such affliction through their spirituality,
echoes the passion of Christ.[31] References to the binding of holy figures
occur repeatedly in Ælfric's homilies and saints' lives, where they appear
to be a rite of passage for those on the road to sainthood.[32] However,

---

30 As will be discussed below, saints and God are also frequently depicted as embroiled in
a war against demons and the devil, which often results in religious heroes binding their
supernatural foes or demonic binding of humans.

31 See my article, "Binding of Religious Heroes."

32 See the following examples from *Lives of Saints*: *Passio sancti Eadmundi regis et martyris*, 2:318, 320, 322, 328, 330, lines 70, 100, 106–11, 207, 213; *Passio sancti Sebastianus
martyris*, 1:144, lines 421–4; *Passio sancti Ivliani et sponse eivs Basilisse*, 1:100, lines
181–6; *Vita S. Martini episcopi et confessoris Anglicae*, 2:230, lines 155–6; *De sancta
Lucia, virgine*, 2:216, lines 100–2 (the saint later binds her oppressor in lines 139–45);
Natalis sanctorum Abdon et Sennes, 2:54, lines 8–14; *Passio Chrisanti et Dariae sponse
eivs*, 2:386, lines 164–8; and *Passio sancti Thomae apostoli*, 2:406, lines 116–19. See also
Passio sancti Vincentii martyris, in *Old English Homilies from MS. Bodley 343*, p. 101,

despite the proliferation of saint-binding in these later texts, nowhere is this theme more concentrated than in *Andreas*, which will thus be central to the present discussion.[33] This poem, in particular, has been read as a typology of Christ,[34] with some scholars maintaining that past criticism's focus on similarities between the voyage to Mermedonia and Beowulf's journey to Denmark misses the point: "it seems likely that what the poet really wanted his audience to be reminded of by Andreas' divinely commanded journey is the coming of Christ to the world to free mankind from the bondage of the devil."[35] Indeed, imprisonment, fetters, and binding are one of the most pervasive sets of imagery in *Andreas*, while they are not nearly as prevalent in the poem's analogues.[36] The poem depicts the binding of Matthew, Andreas, prisoners in general, a Mermedonian, and even Christ himself. Due to the extent of binding imagery in *Andreas*, I shall discuss the occurrences in clusters except where they are particularly unique or poignant.

One such cluster of images relates to the actual binding of the body. When the Mermedonians take Matthew captive, their first step is to bind his hands:

---

lines 46–53; and *Natale sancti Iacobi apostoli*, in *Catholic Homilies: Second Series*, ed. Godden, pp. 242–3, lines 29–75. Because many of these examples follow their source material fairly closely, they will not be the focus of discussion here.

33 See also Jagger, "Body, Text and Self," pp. 258–74.

34 See Rendall, "Bondage and Freeing from Bondage," pp. 509–12; Bjork, *Old English Verse Saints' Lives*, pp. 110–24; Hermann, *Allegories of War*, pp. 119–49; and Hieatt, "Harrowing of Mermedonia." For other typological readings of the poem, see Hill, "Figural Narrative"; and Walsh, "Baptismal Flood."

35 Rendall, "Bondage and Freeing from Bondage," p. 512. However, the literate-formulaic composition style of the *Andreas*-poet does point to liberal borrowing from *Beowulf*. See Riedinger, "Formulaic Relationship"; and Powell, "Traditional Art," pp. 105–67.

36 There is no extant source of *Andreas*, although it clearly stems from the apocryphal *Acts of Andrew and Matthew in the City of the Cannibals*. This narrative exists in several Greek and Latin recensions, as well as in two Old English prose versions (in Cambridge, Corpus Christi College MS 198 and *Blickling Homily* 19). Considered to be the closest analogues are the twelfth-century Latin *Recensio Casanatensis*, and the ninth-/tenth-century Greek *Praxeis Andreou kai Matheian eis ten Polin ton Anthropophagon*. For the Latin and Greek texts, see Blatt, *Die lateinischen Bearbeitungen der Acta Andreae et Matthiae apud anthropophagos*. For the Old English prose texts, see Bright, *Anglo-Saxon Reader*, pp. 113–28; and Morris, *Blickling Homilies*, pp. 228–49. English translations are available in Boenig, *Acts of Andrew in the Country of the Cannibals*; and Allen and Calder, *Sources and Analogues*, pp. 15–34. For discussion of textual relationships, see Friesen, "Visions and Revisions."

Hie þam halgan þær   handa gebundon
ond fæstnodon   feondes cræfte,
hæleð hellfuse,   ond his heafdes segl
abreoton mid billes ecge.   Hwæðre he in breostum þa git
herede in heortan   heofonrices weard,
þeah ðe he atres drync   atulne onfenge.   (48–53)

(There they bound the holy one's hands and secured them with the cunning
of the devil, the hell-eager men, and they destroyed the orbs of his head with
the edge of a sword. However, he still praised in his heart the guardian of the
heavenly kingdom, although he took the terrible drink of poison.)

This passage is highlighted by the use of assonance in addition to alliteration in nearly every verse, occasionally carrying on to the following half-line ("æ": *fæstnodon/cræfte/hæleð*; "e": *hell-/segl*; long "eo": *abreotan/breostum*; short "eo": *heortan/heofon-*). Interestingly, the pattern of long "a"/short "a" that opens the passage (*halgan/handa*) also closes it (*atres/atulne*), forming an aural envelope pattern that is only heightened by the alternation of "h"-alliteration in every other line. Poetic highlighting is also furthered by the heavy use of formulas throughout the passage; indeed the entire first line is repeated later in the poem at line 1222.[37] Other formulas include: *feondes cræfte*,[38] *herede in heortan*,[39] and *heofonrices weard*.[40]

---

37 *Handa* and *gebunden* also collocate in *Genesis B* 379b–8a. See also *Genesis A*'s reference to the fettering of Isaac's hands and feet at lines 2902–4a, which corresponds to Genesis 22.9's description of Abraham binding his son. Notably, the *Vulgate* does not refer to the boy's limbs, mentioning only a general binding (*conligare*).

38 See *Andreas* 1196b and *Genesis B* 449b. The formula is preceded by *þurh* in *Andreas* 1294b and *Genesis B* 453b. The two terms also frequently collocate: *Beowulf* 698b–9a, 982b–4a, 2289–90a; *Exodus* 30b–2a; *Guthlac A* 141b–2a, 184–6a, 566b–8; *Juliana* 14, 573b–5; as well as in several of Ælfric's *Lives of Saints*: *Natale Sancte Agnetis, uirginis*, 1:180, line 183; *Vita sancti Martini episcopi et confessoris Anglicae*, 2:270, line 823; and *Passio Chrisanti et Dariae sponse eius*, 2:388, line 174.

39 See *Juliana* 239a.

40 See *Andreas* 56a; *Daniel* 12a, 26a, 457a (*halig heofonrices weard*); *Dream of the Rood* 91b; *Elene* 197b, 445b, 718b; *Exodus* 486b; *Genesis A* 1363b, 1484a, 1744b, 2073a; *Guthlac A* 611b, 789b; *Judgement Day II* 70a; *Juliana* 212b; *Menologium* 4b; *Paris Psalter (Psalm 90)* 2b; *(Psalm 91)* 23b; and *(Psalm 98)* 34b.

As for the content of these lines, they paint a strikingly similar picture to that of *The Death of Alfred*. The victim is bound, leaving his enemies free to mutilate and blind him. While the blinding of Alfred left him an unsuitable ruler and eliminated him as a threat to the succession, Matthew's own blinding plunges him into the darkness of a symbolic prison. He is, of course, literally imprisoned, but this passage's reference to the holy man's faith and the diabolic nature of his enemies equally points to this prison as an allegorical hell. The fact that the Mermedonians use *feondes cræfte* (the cunning of the devil) in order to secure (*fæstnodon*) him also links the language of this passage to the terrifying device of Grendel's *glof*.[41]

The mystical and evil nature of the Mermedonians' ability to capture people is frequently referred to in *Andreas*. Matthew again alludes to their dark skill in a prayer to God: *Hu me elþeodige inwitwrasne / searonet se-owað!*[42] (63–4a) (Oh, how these alien men sew/weave for me a malicious fetter, a skilful net!). This is the only reference to a textile metaphor used to describe binding in the poem. The term *inwit* carries connotations of deceit in addition to evil,[43] and these fetters, along with the skilful nature of the net, speak to the Mermedonians' association with magic and the devil. Instead of weaving fishing nets, the Mermedonians sew metaphorical nets in order to ensnare human victims. This seems to be a perversion of Christ's invitation to Simon Peter to follow him and become a fisher of men in Matthew 4:19–20: *Et ait illis venite post me faciam vos fieri piscatores hominem. at illi continuo relictis retibus secuti sunt eum* (And he said to them, "come after me [and] I will make you fishers of men." And they, leaving their nets behind, followed him at once).[44] Obviously, Christ was not encouraging cannibalism, but was using the net as a metaphor for his teachings, and the fishing image to portray the drawing in of more followers. However, in Matthew's attempt to do just this and to spread the word of Christ, he becomes ensnared by treachery.

The initial image of Matthew's binding is echoed later in the poem when Andreas is similarly incarcerated and tortured by the Mermedonians. As

---

41 See chapter 3, pp. 83–90.
42 The phrase *elþeodige inwitwrasne* is invoked later in *Andreas* at line 946 when God commands the hero to free the bound Matthew.
43 Bosworth and Toller, *Anglo-Saxon Dictionary*, s.v. *inwid*.
44 See also the parable of the dragnet in Matthew 13:47–50, in which Christ compares the separation of good and evil souls at Judgment Day to the separation of a catch of fish.

noted above, the poet repeats line 48 while describing the binding of Andreas' hands at 1222. However, rather than being blinded, Andreas is wounded in a manner that alludes to Christ's crucifixion:

> Wæs se halga wer
> sare geswungen,   searwum gebunden,
> dolgbennum þurhdrifen.   (1395b–7a)

(The holy man was sorely afflicted, skilfully bound, driven through with wounds.)

Although the nails of the cross are never explicitly mentioned, the use of the verb *þurhdrifan* certainly brings them to mind.

Matthew and Andreas are also similarly depicted in terms of their bonds and imprisonment. When God initially commands Andreas to free Matthew, he describes the imprisoned saint as *mid þam burgwarum bendum fæstne* (184) (bound fast among the inhabitants of that city). Likewise, while Andreas is in prison, the demons afflicting him describe his bound state:

> Utan gangan eft,
> þæt we bysmrigen   bendum fæstne,
> oðwitan him his wræcsið.   (1356b–8a)

(Let us go back, so that we might mock him, bound fast, taunt him in his misery.)

While the formula *x-bendum fæst* is attested in relation to architectural binding,[45] the shorter, related formula *bendum fæstne* is common in contexts of human fettering. This formula appears in *Andreas*,[46] *Juliana*,[47] and *Riddle 52* (flail),[48] where it refers to both construction and constriction. Unlike bonds applied to buildings and objects, bonds applied to a body serve to weaken it rather than strengthen it; yet, ironically, it is in Andreas' weakened and bound state that he demonstrates a great deal of

---

45 See chapter 3, pp. 69–76.
46 See lines 184b, 962b, 1038b.
47 See line 535b, with an echo of it in 625a.
48 See line 7b.

power. Indeed, the demons' desire to ridicule the hero stems from their inability to physically harm him due to God's intervention. In his protection of Andreas, God turns the saint's body into a fortress under siege,[49] with the bonds that confine Andreas's body becoming the bonds that hold a fortress firm – hence the architectural echoes invoked through formulaic diction.

Matthew and Andreas are not the only ones to be forcefully held by the Mermedonians. Other prisoners are referred to as bound and incarcerated, literally, here, though perhaps also symbolically by their sins, as Rendall's analysis of binding and loosing would suggest. A description of the binding of these prisoners occurs when Andreas frees them:

> ond þa gelædde   of leoðobendum
> fram þam fæstenne   on frið dryhtnes
> tu ond hundteontig   geteled rime,
> swylce feowertig,
> generede fram niðe,   (þær he nænigne forlet
> under burglocan   bennum[50] fæstne).   (1033–8)

(and he then led two hundred and forty people out of their limb-bonds from that fortress into the protection of the lord, saved them from strife (he abandoned none there, bound fast in the city-enclosure).)

The formulaic half-line *bennum fæstne* once again echoes Matthew and Andreas's binding, while the bonds are also invoked in collocation with prison terms. Thus, *fæstenne* and *burglocan* refer to prisons as well as fortresses, indicating once again that the absence of dedicated prison-buildings made these "a foreign concept for most early medieval English audiences."[51] However, the multi-purpose nature of such structures also adds to the poem's besieged fortress motif, since the evil ones' sinful campaign against human souls is inverted by Andreas' one-man campaign against the fortress-prison.

------

49 The concept of the soul as a fortress is a common one in Christian tradition, and one that will be further discussed in the context of *Juliana* below.

50 Despite its irregular form, the *DOE* treats this instance as an error for *bend*. S.v. *bend*, sense 1. See also *Juliana* 519b, which Krapp and Dobbie similarly read as a variant spelling of *bend*, *Exeter Book*, p. 285.

51 Garner, *Structuring Spaces*, p. 69.

The prison itself is characterized in terms of the types of fetters it employs, which form an overlapping group of images. Thus, the poem invokes the compound *leoðubend* (limb-bond) five times[52] and *witebend* (torture-bond) twice,[53] the latter term appearing only in this poem. *Leoðubend* also occurs in *Genesis B*'s description of hell,[54] as well as in *The Hêliand*, where it is only used of Christ.[55] Given that *Genesis B* is a translation from an Old Saxon original,[56] and given *The Hêliand*'s constant reference to the binding of Christ[57] – an elaboration that is not extant elsewhere – it is possible that the *Andreas*-poet, a known borrower of formulaic diction,[58] employs the compound, *leoðubend*, in order to allude directly to this Germanic portrayal of Christ. Previous discussions of Andreas' suffering have linked the hero to Christ, but also argued that the Old English poet develops the bondage theme on his own:

> Seizing upon and developing these hints, however, he made Andreas' *imitatio Christi* something much more meaningful than it was in his source. By a stress upon the bondage motif not found in either the original *Acts* or the Old English prose version of this saint's life, the *Andreas* poet is able to parallel Andreas' rescue of his fellow missionary Matthias with Christ's salvation of man.[59]

---

52 See lines 100b, 164a, 1033b, 1373b, 1564b.

53 See lines 108b, 1561a.

54 See line 382a.

55 See lines 3797a, 4927a, and 5268b. A collocation of *liðo* and *bend* does occur once in relation to John the Baptist at lines 2723b–4a.

56 Eduard Sievers argued for this relationship based on metrical and stylistic comparisons of *The Hêliand* and *Genesis B* in 1875 (in *Heliand und die angelsächsische Genesis*), a hypothesis that was confirmed by the discovery of Old Saxon fragments in 1894. See Doane, *Saxon Genesis*, pp. 7–8, 55–64; and Timmer, *Later Genesis*, pp. 45–50.

57 See lines 3526b–7a, 3796b–7a, 4791a, 4822a, 4869a, 4917–18a, 4927–8, 4947a, 4959a, 4984b–5a, 5050b, 5054a, 5113a, 5117b–20a, 5122a, 5171b, 5234b, 5260–3a, 5268b, 5299b, 5354a, 5412–13, 5431b, 5488b–9a, 5535b–8a, 5578b, and 5659a. See my article "Binding of Religious Heroes."

58 In addition to liberal borrowing from *Beowulf* (see above, p. 128n35), there are also direct links between *Andreas* and the works of Cynewulf. See Orchard, "Both Style and Substance"; Powell, "Verbal Parallels," pp. 168–232, 283–99; as well as Orchard's "Computing Cynewulf," pp. 76–7; and Bredehoft, *Authors, Audiences, and Old English Verse*, p. 87.

59 Rendall, "Bondage and Freeing from Bondage," p. 510.

Analysis of overlapping terminology in *Andreas* and *The Hêliand* suggests, however, that the poet of the former may well have found inspiration for the motif in the influential Old Saxon gospel.

In addition to the poem's use of *leoðubendas*, *Andreas* also frequently invokes chains, with *clam* appearing five times.[60] Twice the term alliterates with *carcern*[61] (prison) and twice it appears in the formula *clamme belegde/ clommum belegdon*.[62] Two of these instances of *clam* describe not an earthly prison, but Satan's imprisonment in hell,[63] indicating a link between both of the settings at the level of diction. In these passages, Andreas reminds Satan, who has come to taunt him, that God locked him in hell and bound him with tortures. Similar tortures are also in store for the Mermedonians, as *Andreas*'s reference to the *feter-wrasen* (fetter-bond) indicates. This unique compound is applied to the victim who is chosen from among the Mermedonians themselves: *Hraðe siððan wearð / fetor-wrasnum fæst, feores orwena* (1106b–7) (After he quickly became fast in fetter-bonds, despairing of life). The fact that the cannibals are willing to bind, kill, and eat humans is bad enough, but that they would do this to one of their own nation demonstrates the treacherous depths to which they are willing to sink.

Happily for the audience of *Andreas*, not all fettering and imprisonment in the poem are depicted as final. Indeed, many of the other depictions of bound humans are hopeful because they refer to God's power to loose prisoners from their physical and metaphorical imprisonment. Thus, we already know the answer when Satan taunts the imprisoned Andreas, asking:

Hwylc is þæs mihtig   ofer middangeard,
þæt he þe alyse   of leoðubendum,
manna cynnes,   ofer mine est?   (1372–4)

(Who is there on earth, of humankind, so mighty that he may release you from your limb-bonds against my consent?)

---

60 See lines 130b, 1192b, 1212a, 1378b, and 1560b.
61 See lines 130 and 1560.
62 See lines 1192b and 1560b.
63 See lines 1192b and 1378b.

That is because a line almost identical to 1373 has occurred over a thousand lines earlier at the beginning of the poem, when God vows to free Matthew:

> Ic þe mid wunige
> ond þe alyse   of þyssum leoðubendum,
> ond ealle þa menigo   þe þe mid wuniað
> on nearonedum.   (99b–102a)
>
> …
>
> Geþola þeoda þrea!   Nis seo þrah micel
> þæt þe wærlogan   witebendum,
> synnige ðurh searocræft,   swencan motan.   (107–9)

(I will remain with you and loose you from these limb-bonds, and all of the many who remain with you in confinement. [...] Endure the abuse of the people! It is not for a great amount of time that the sinful oath-breakers may afflict you with torment-bonds, through their cunning trick.)[64]

Both the *leoðubend* and *witebend* fetter-types discussed above appear here, as does a reference to imprisonment as *nearonedum*, both "confinement" and "sore need."[65] The Mermedonians are again associated with diabolic evil and deceit through their use of a *searocræft* (cunning trick).

Finally, a notable reference to binding and loosing occurs when a penitent Mermedonian, who recognizes that they have done wrong to bind the saint, begs that they loose him:

> Nu ge magon sylfe   soð gecnawan,
> þæt we mid unrihte   ellþeodigne
> on carcerne   clommum belegdon,
> witebendum.   Us seo wyrd scyðeð,
> heard ond hetegrim.   Þæt is her swa cuð,
> is hit mycle selre,   þæs þe ic soð talige,
> þæt we hine alysan   of leoðobendum,
> ealle anmode,   (ofost is selost),
> ond us þone halgan   helpe biddan,
> geoce ond frofre.   (1558–67a)

---

64 God also commands Andreas to loose Matthew at lines 943b–7a.
65 Bosworth and Toller, *Anglo-Saxon Dictionary*, s.v. *nearu-nid*.

(Now you may recognize the truth for yourselves, that we unjustly surrounded the foreigner with chains, with torment-bonds, in prison. Fate oppresses
us, hard and cruel. It is evident here that it is much better, as I reckon the
truth [to be], that we loose him from the limb-bonds, all of us unanimously,
(haste is best), and ask the holy one for help, support, and consolation.)

The poet employs a great deal of conventional prison imagery here, invoking limb-bonds (*leoðobendum*), torture-bonds (*witebendum*), chains (*clommum*), and the prison itself (*carcerne*). There is also a note of hope in the
penitent sinner's desire to make right his people's wrong. Because he has
repented, he emulates the examples of the saints and of God by loosing
prisoners. This repentance and act of good faith means that only the evil
Mermedonians are cast into an abyss beneath the flood that God calls
down upon the city, an epic ending with resonances of the apocalypse.[66]
Were this the apocalypse, of course, it would already be too late for the
people of Mermedonia. Indeed, if *Andreas* has one thing to offer, it is that
immediate repentance and a voluntary life of service to God are the keys
to an afterlife free from binding and imprisonment.

The conventional nature of this imagery of binding further implies that
we are dealing with an Old English type-scene in which prison is imagined
in relation to its confined space, fettering and chains, darkness and torments.[67] Although *Andreas* provides us with the greatest number of examples showing the formulaic nature of binding as employed in this type-scene,
examples of bound religious figures do occur elsewhere. One prominent
instance is the passage from *Azarias*, which describes Nebuchadnezzar's
speech about the three youths who survive his religious persecution:

> Þæt ic geare wiste,
> þæt we III hæfdon,   þeoda wisa,
> geonge cniehtas,   for gæstlufan
> gebunden to bæle   in byrnendes
> fyres leoman.   (170b–4a)

---

66 A time when prisoners may be unbound by God, as evident in *Judgement Day II*
46b–8.

67 The conventionality of these depictions is, of course, demonstrated by the lack of actual
Anglo-Saxon prisons, as Garner notes. *Structuring Spaces*, pp. 82–3.

(I, leader of the nations, knew well that we had three young boys bound on a pyre in the glare of burning fire because of spiritual love.)

The formulaic nature of the half-line *gebunden to bæle* is made clear when we read the corresponding lines from *Daniel*:

> Þæt eower fela geseah,
> þeode mine,   þæt we þry sendon,
> geboden to bæle   in byrnende
> fyres leoman   (411b–14a)

(Many of you saw that, my lords, that we sent three, commanded to [be burnt on] the pyre, into burning, the light of the fire.)

Rather than binding the three youths, the *Daniel*-passage's version of the formula refers to Nebuchadnezzar's ordering of the deed (*geboden to bæle*). This is not, however, a poem that shies away from binding, since elsewhere it describes the warlord's symbolic dream of a shackled tree and the burning away of the three youths' fetters.[68] Burning is closely tied to binding in depictions of hell discussed below, being linked by alliteration;[69] it is even described as having the agency to bind in *Christ III*: *ac se bryne bindeð bidfæstne here, / feoð firena bearn* (1597–8a) (but the burning will bind the motionless army, persecute the children of criminals). The fact that *Azarias* uses the past participle of *bindan* rather than *beodan* in this passage may relate to the conventional nature of binding terminology as part of the poetic vocabulary, the implication being that the *Azarias*-poet selected *bunden* rather than *geboden* because of the former's formulaic resonances.[70]

The last victim of binding with which this section deals is the ultimate Christian hero: Christ himself. Christ, as both human and god, undergoes all of the suffering to which mankind is subject, while at the same time

---

68 See lines 227b–8, 434–5, 518–22.

69 See *Christ III* 1621.

70 For more on the relationship between and exemplars of *Daniel* and *Azarias*, see Remley, *Old English Biblical Verse*, pp. 334–434; Farrell, *Daniel and Azarias*, pp. 38–45; and Jones, "*Daniel and Azarias* as Evidence." Note also that the *Vulgate* account in Daniel 3:20–2 includes both references to binding and commanding (*iussit/ligatis/vincti/ iussio*).

possessing the power to stop it. The binding of Christ is thus all the more important because it is voluntary. Although *The Hêliand* contains numerous references to Christ's binding, there are only a few such instances in Old English poetry. The first occurs in *Judgement Day I*:

Hyht wæs a in heofonum,   siþþan user hælend wæs,
middangeardes meotud,   þurh þa mæstan gesceaft
on ful blacne beam   bunden fæste
cearian clomme.   (64–7a)

(There was exultation always in heaven, after our saviour, the lord of the earth, according to that greatest prophecy, was bound fast on a vile, dark beam with a painful chain.)

Even though this passage describes Christ's crucifixion, the imagery is that of imprisonment. He is tied to the tree, *bunden fæste* and held in place with a *cearian clomme*. However, Christ is not depicted as fettered and bound for the same reasons as human sinners; while imprisonment may act as a metaphor for sin, in this case it is the demonstration of saintly spirituality with which Christ is aligned. According to early Christian doctrine, Satan's attempt to bind the innocent Christ was the misstep that caused the loosing of the bonds of sin and death for mankind.[71]

A second instance of Christ's binding occurs in *Andreas*. Here, Christ advises the hero to remember his own suffering: *me bysmredon bennum fæstne / weras wansælige* (962–3a) (unhappy men mocked me, bound fast). The formula *bennum fæstne* once again carries echoes of the binding of Andreas, Matthew, and the other prisoners, who are all described in this way. Interestingly, it appears to be the Germanic Christ's shackles, rather than the doctrinal bonds of sin and death, that influence the *Andreas*-poet most. Thus, although the poem frequently makes reference to the physical bondage and imprisonment of humans, Andreas and Matthew's imitation of Christ is perhaps most emphasized through binding imagery. This indicates a dark fascination with all manner of binding and fettering, torture and mutilation, as well as a focus on the idea that, in order to imitate Christ's good works, one must suffer in his image.

---

71 Rendall, "Bondage and Freeing from Bondage," p. 500.

Not only bound to the cross, Christ is also bound by the crown of thorns, as in the passage from *Christ and Satan* where Simon Peter asks:

Eart þu þis, drihten,   dome gewurðad?
We ðe gesawon   æt sumum cyrre,
þec gelegdon   on laðne bend
hæþene mid hondum.   (535–8a)

(Is this you, lord, adorned with glory? We saw you at a certain time, the heathens laid a hateful bond/crown on you with their hands.)

The key term, *bend*, may mean either a "bond, cord, especially referring to restraining fetters" or a "crown."[72] It seems to be the crown of thorns that is invoked here, but it is important to keep this parallelism in mind because elsewhere the laying (*lecgan*) of bonds is clearly depicted in light of constriction.[73] The crown of thorns is elsewhere described as a *beag* (ring),[74] indicating that it is both a bound object, and one that contributes to the binding of Christ. Worse than a fetter, this crown is meant to torture and ridicule Christ's human body by inverting the nature of the crown as a prestige object. However, when Christ ultimately proves to be divine, the crown of thorns achieves supreme prestige status because of its relation to him and his martyrdom. Thus, although Christ's binding and crucifixion depict a struggle for control not unlike that between human beings, the lack of fight exhibited by him and by those who act in his image adds a new layer to the question of power and status. The irony of the binding of Christ is, of course, that God is the ultimate binder of enemies and unbinder of followers.

Hell and Demonic Binding

If God is the ultimate binder, whether constructively (in that he created the world by joining materials together) or constrictively (in that he holds all aspects of that creation strictly in place), then it may seem logical for his adversary and opponent to be the ultimate unbinder – the lord of chaos

---

72 *DOE*, s.v., senses 1, 2.a.
73 See chapter 6, pp. 176–7, 187–8.
74 See *Christ II* 1125–7a and *Christ III* 1443b–5.

and destruction. This is, of course, true in Old English poetry, as in a myriad of other cultures' approaches to Christianity; however, Old English poetry does not leave us with as tidy a binary as we might like. The poems presenting us with images of Satan and his demonic followers do not depict God the binder and builder of creation versus Satan the unbinder and destroyer. They depict, rather, a Satan who also binds, but this time with bonds of pain and torture.

The portrayal of Satan is complicated in the Old English tradition because of his split nature as terrifying demon and comedic weakling, the first a device aimed at frightening followers into behaving, the second a folkloric attempt to relieve fear.[75] These two approaches to the devil may be further aligned with binding, in that Satan is both a powerful and terrifying binder and a disempowered, bound victim. In his discussion of Satan, Peter Dendle points to this contradiction as fundamental to the Anglo-Saxon view of the demonic: "The devil consistently exhibits a fluidity, an elasticity, that allows him to bleed over into overlapping regions of time and space, of heart and world, of history and allegory. The contested grounds debated by saint and demon are the paradoxes of the devil's simultaneous binding and liberty, his strength and impotence, his omnipresence and his nothingness."[76] The devil's ability to defy boundaries of categorization makes him an important figure to the study of binding in Old English poetry because this unclassifiability points to the danger he poses in a culture and poetics so concerned with order.

Therefore, when we think of hell as a place of binding, it is important to remember that Satan himself is its original occupant. Not only are humans bound in hell, but Satan and the other fallen angels are also repeatedly described as punished by hellish torments. Here, the binder is God (or his followers), and the order that he imposes is seen as positive. Because the examples of such descriptions are numerous, only a selection of extended passages will be discussed.

The most elaborate descriptions of the binding of Satan in hell occur in *Genesis B* and *Christ and Satan*. Both treat the treachery of Satan and the fallen angels, and describe hell in great detail. This first passage from *Genesis B* focuses on the binding itself:

---

75 Russell, *Lucifer*, p. 63.
76 *Satan Unbound*, p. 8.

Ac licgað me ymbe   irenbenda,
rideð racentan sal.   Ic eom rices leas;
habbað me swa hearde   helle clommas
fæste befangen.   Her is fyr micel,
ufan and neoðone.   Ic a ne geseah
laðran landscipe.   Lig ne aswamað,
hat ofer helle.   Me habbað hringa gespong,
sliðhearda sal   siðes amyrred,
afyrred me min feðe;   fet synt gebundene,
handa gehæfte.   Synt þissa heldora
wegas forworhte,   swa ic mid wihte ne mæg
of þissum lioðobendum.   Licgað me ymbe
heardes irenes   hate geslægene
grindlas greate.   Mid þy me god hafað
gehæfted be þam healse,   swa ic wat he minne hige cuðe;
and þæt wiste eac   weroda drihten,
þæt sceolde unc Adame   yfele gewurðan
ymb þæt heofonrice,   þær ic ahte minra handa geweald.   (371–88)

(But iron-bonds lie about me, a halter of chain rides me. I am powerless; such harsh hell chains have firmly taken hold of me. Here there is great fire, above and below. I have never seen a landscape more hostile. The flame does not cease, hot over hell. Clasps of rings, an excessively cruel halter, have obstructed my departure, taken my motion from me; my feet are bound, my hands constrained. The paths through these hell-doors are barred, so I may not at all [go] from these limb-bonds. Thick bolts of hard iron, forged in heat, lie about me. With them God has tied me by the neck, so I know he recognized my intention; and the lord of hosts also knew that it should end up badly with me and Adam regarding that heavenly kingdom, if I had control of my hands.)

The emphasis here is on the prison-like constriction imposed on Satan.[77] As with *Andreas*, various types of bonds and chains are described through the terms *irenbend*, *racente*, *sal*, *clam*, *leoðubend*, *iren*, and *grindel*. Many of these terms have been discussed above, but it is worth pointing out that *grindel* (bolt/bar) appears only here.[78] A search of the *DOE Corpus*, in

---

77 Garner also notes the similarity of hell and prison imagery. See *Structuring Spaces*,
    pp. 83–8.
78 *DOE*, s.v.

contrast, yields six poetic occurrences of *racente*[79] and eighteen of its compound form, *racenteag*;[80] both forms are much more common in prose. This passage also points to Satan's imprisonment through terms such as *fæste* (fast/firmly) and *hæftan* (to capture/constrain), the latter being repeated twice. In fact, the majority of elements beginning with "h" are repeated two or more times: *habban* (373a, 377b, 384b), *hel-* (373b, 377a, 380b, as well as in 389a, the line directly following this passage), *-heard* (373a, 378a, 383a), *hat* (377a, 383b; the noun, *hæt*, also appears in 389b), *hand* (380a, 388b) and *gehæftan* (380a, 385a).[81] This repetition of "h"-terms highlights the interesting pattern of alliteration: "h" governs the alliteration six times in this passage, alternating every two to four lines.

In addition to conventional prison imagery, the obstruction of motion is also emphasized here. Not only are the paths through the gates of hell barred (*wegas forworhte*), but Satan's journey or departure is also impeded (*siðes amyrred*) and his motion (*feðe*) is specifically referred to as having been taken from him (*afyrred*). Furthermore, the *sal* is not only a "tie" or "bond," but also a "rein,"[82] implying that Satan has lost control over his movements within hell. This is further emphasized by Satan's statement that he would attack Adam if he had *geweald* (control) over his hands.[83]

Descriptions of constriction and deprivation of motion would seem to be typical of prison imagery. Hell, however, has added layers of torment.[84]

---

79 See *Genesis B* 434a; *Metres of Boethius (Metre 13)* 8a, 29a; *(Metre 25)* 37a; and *(Metre 26)* 78a.

80 This figure includes certain homilies and saints' lives by Ælfric, which the *DOE Corpus* classifies as prose. *Racenteag* also appears in *Solomon and Saturn II* 116a. The second element, *teag* (tie), occurs as a simplex three times. It is part of the formula *fyrnum teagum* in *Christ II* 733b and *The Panther* 60b, where it refers to Satan's imprisonment in hell (which is also described by *fyrnum clommum* (ancient chains) in *Andreas* 1378b). The third occurrence is at line 11a of the *Metrical Charm, Wið Dweorh* (Against a Dwarf/Fever). There, it refers either to the fetters with which the creature ties the neck of the suffering patient, or to the disease-agent's own fettering. See chapter 9, pp. 261–5.

81 There are only four "h"-terms that are not repeated: *hring, heals, hyge,* and *heofon-*.

82 Bosworth and Toller, *Anglo-Saxon Dictionary*, s.v.

83 Note that line 388b marks the end of an envelope pattern, with the same formula opening it at line 368b.

84 M.E. Bridges discusses the many torments of hell and particularly notes the association between hell-bonds, torture and flames, as well as the "[p]rivation of joy or glory" which marks out Satan's fall; *Generic Contrast*, p. 247. With a greater focus on poetic style and diction, Hildegard Tristram outlines the pattern where *þær is* is followed by an "enumeration of nouns indicating various kinds of pain, suffering, or, inversely, joy or physical benefit" in order to describe heaven or hell; "Stock Descriptions of Heaven and Hell," p. 102.

Not only is hell a place of bondage, it is also the home to fire (*fyr*), flame (*lig*), and heat (*hat*). *Hat* and *hell* conveniently alliterate, which may explain why they appear so frequently in collocation with one another. Indeed, there are seventeen poetic collocations occurring for the most part in *Genesis B* and *Christ and Satan*,[85] several instances of which are formulaic half-lines: *on þa(s) hatan hell(e)*[86] and *hat x helle*, where *x* is the preposition *ofer*, *on* or *in*.[87]

Although the fire and flame present in the above passage imply that hell would be alight, hell is a lightless land, the opposite of the illuminated heavens:

> Forþon hie leng ne magon
> healdan heofonrice,   ac hie to helle sculon
> on þone sweartan sið.   Swa þu his sorge ne þearft
> beran on þinum breostum,   þær þu gebunden ligst,
> murnan on mode,   þæt her men bun
> þone hean heofon,   þeah wit hearmas nu,
> þreaweorc þoliað,   and þystre land,
> and þurh þin micle mod   monig forleton
> on heofonrice   heahgetimbro,
> godlice geardas.   (*Genesis B* 731b–40a)

(Therefore they may no longer hold the heavenly kingdom but they shall go on the dark journey to hell. Thus you do not have to bear the sorrow of it in your breast, where you lie bound, mourn in your mind, that humans dwell here in high heaven, yet now we two suffer harms, painful work, and a land of darkness, and through your great pride we have given up many lofty buildings, fair courts, in the heavenly kingdom.)

Echoing the darkness of prisons – something that may not have reflected reality[88] – the journey to hell is a dark one (*sweartan*) and the land itself is covered in darkness (*þystre*). The evocation of prison-like binding is now

---

85 *Genesis B* 324, 331a, 362a, 377a, 439a; *Christ and Satan* 97–8, 131–2, 158a, 192, 280a, 340b, 454a, 483; *Andreas* 1187a; *Christ III* 1426a, 1619; *Judgement Day II* 193. There are also sixteen prose collocations, most occurring in homiletic texts.

86 *Genesis B* 331a, 439a.

87 *Genesis B* 377a; *Christ and Satan* 158a, 280a; *Andreas* 1187a.

88 As Garner notes, given that prisons were not buildings separate from those in everyday use, the emphasis on darkness was likely conventional. In fact, the earlier laws indicate that prisoners were often kept outdoors; *Structuring Spaces*, pp. 82–3.

associated with additional miseries, harm, and painful work. The contrast of hell to heaven is also made explicit in the final lines of the passage, and it is this deprivation of the joys of the homeland that frequently marks out Satan as an exile.

Rosemary Woolf maintains that the devil is the most fitting figure in Christian story to occur in Old English heroic depictions because of the similarity between his betrayal of God and the disobedience of a retainer to his lord.[89] Furthermore, the devil's banishment from heaven "was a fate of which the exile of a *þegn* from his natural place in his lord's hall might well appear the earthly shadow."[90] Leonard Frey similarly argues that the devil can be aligned with an elegiac mood, maintaining that *Christ and Satan* is the Old English Christian narrative most evocative of "exile-elegiac conditions."[91] *Christ and Satan* combines all of the above motifs in its own elaborate description of hell, which is voiced by Satan himself:

> Þis is ðeostræ ham,   ðearle gebunden
> fæstum fyrclommum;   flor is on welme
> attre onæled.   Nis nu ende feor
> þæt we sceolun ætsomne   susel þrowian,
> wean and wergu,   nalles wuldres blæd
> habban in heofnum,   hehselda wyn.
> Hwæt, we for dryhtene iu   dreamas hefdon,
> song on swegle   selrum tidum,
> þær nu ymb ðone æcan   æðele stondað,
> heleð ymb hehseld,   herigað drihten
> wordum and wercum,   and ic in wite sceal
> bidan in bendum,   and me bættran ham
> for oferhygdum   æfre ne wene.   (38–50)

(This home is dark, severely bound by firm chains of fire; the floor is welling with ignited poison. There is not now a remote end, so that we must suffer torment together, woes and wretched things, not at all have the prosperity of glory in the heavens, the joy of high thrones. Listen, formerly we had joys

---

89 "Devil in Old English Poetry," pp. 1–2.
90 Ibid., p. 2.
91 "Exile and Elegy," p. 299.

before the lord, singing in heaven in better times, where now the noble ones stand about the eternal one, heroes about the high throne, they worship the lord in words and works, and I must remain in bonds, in punishment, and not expect a better home for myself because of pride.)

Darkness is again emphasized – hell is a *ðeostræ ham* – while torment (*susel*), woe (*wean*), suffering (*þrowian*), and punishment (*wite*) all make an appearance, as does the typical binding terminology (*gebunden/in bendum*). The firm (*fæstum*) chains described here are chains of fire (*fyrclommum*), and the burning (*welme/onæled*) is not only due to flames, but also to poison (*attre*). The poison here likely refers to snake venom, since we know from other passages in this poem that there was a tradition associating hell with serpents.[92] The deprivation of heavenly joys is reiterated following the enumeration of hell's evils; thus, the memories of the good things that the fallen angels have given up serve to heighten their punishment.

A later depiction in *Christ and Satan* including all of these motifs occurs when the narrator emphasizes God's victory over the inhabitants of hell:[93]

Let þa up faran   ece drihten;
wuldre hæfde   wites clomma
feondum oðfæsted,   and heo furðor sceaf
in þæt neowle genip,   nearwe gebeged,
þær nu Satanus   swearte þingað,
earm aglæca,   and þa atolan mid him,
witum werige.   Nalles wuldres leoht
habban moton,   ah in helle grund,
ne hi edcerres   æfre moton
wenan seoððan.   Him wæs drihten god
wrað geworden,   sealde him wites clom,
atole to æhte,   and egsan gryre,
dimne and deorcne   deaðes scuwan,
hatne helle grund,   hinsiðgryre.   (441–54)

---

92 See lines 101b–2a, 134b–5a, 334–6, as well as *Judith* 115a. The association is an obvious one given the guise of Satan as he tempts Eve in the Garden of Eden. Bonds and burning are evoked by Eve herself in *Christ and Satan* 411–13 where she speaks of the serpent's malice.

93 *Guthlac A* also contains several references to divine victory over minor demons at lines 596–8 and 696–7.

(Then the eternal lord let them go up; he had gloriously inflicted chains of punishment on the fiends, and shoved them further into that deep darkness, crushed tightly, where Satan, miserable adversary, and the terrible ones with him, restrained with punishments, now evilly speak. Not at all may they possess the light of glory, but the depths of hell, nor may they ever afterwards expect a reversal. The lord God had become angry with them, gave them, the terrible ones, the chain of punishment, as an inheritance, and the terror of fear, the dim and dark shadow of death, the hot depths of hell, the fear of dying.)

Here, the punitive nature of God's action is the focus, with *wite* appearing twice in collocation with *clam* and once on its own.[94] God is described as having shoved (*sceaf*) them *in þæt neowle genip, nearwe gebeged* (into that deep darkness, crushed them tightly), with the same verb used of Elene's punishment of Judas in a pit.[95] Hell is depicted as hot (*hatne*) and full of constriction (*nearwe*), and again we have darkness and shadows (*genip/ dimne and deorcne/scuwan*), directly contrasted with the light of heaven (*wuldres leoht*). Twice the place is referred to as *helle grund* (the depths of hell),[96] implying that hell is deep underground, an abyss of horrible torments in contrast to the lofty joys of heaven. The joys of heaven are clearly lost forever, since these lines point to the permanence of the situation, there being no chance of a reversal (*edcerres*), nor any point in hoping or expecting (*wenan*) one. Finally, the emphasis on death (*deaðes*) and the fear of dying (*hinsiðgryre*) ties the passage in with humanity's lot. In case the Anglo-Saxon audience of *Christ and Satan* was tempted to take any hope from the fact that the horrors of hell described here are for Satan and his followers, the poet drives home the idea that all humans must suffer death, the implication being that sinners will join Satan in his bound state in hell.

---

94 Terms such as these frequently collocate in passing references to the horrors of hell. This particular collocation occurs in *Andreas* 1560–1; *Daniel* 519–22; *Christ and Satan* 102b, 156b, 635–6. Directly following *Christ and Satan* 102b is the formula *feste gebunden*, which which also appears at lines 58b and 323b, with an echo of it in *Solomon and Saturn II* 280b: *heht hine ðær fæste gebindan* (he commanded him to be bound fast there).

95 See line 692a.

96 *Grund* is also applied to hell in *Juliana* 328b–37a and *Christ III* 1593–8a, both of which are discussed below. *The Panther* contains a description of hell, which, though far less elaborated than the instances here, includes many of the same motifs; see lines 58b–61a.

All of this formulaic diction implies that, like prison, hell is part of a related type-scene. It is marked by imprisonment imagery (chains, bonds, torment, punishment), depth and darkness, fire and poison, the deprivation of joy, and its eternality. A passage from *Christ II* is especially interesting in light of this context because it describes the bondage, torment, and fire of hell with reference to Christ's "leaps" and the feats he performs. The fifth of these, the harrowing of hell, refers to him binding Satan:

> Wæs se fifta hlyp
> þa he hellwarena   heap forbygde
> in cwicsusle,   cyning inne gebond,
> feonda foresprecan,   fyrnum teagum,
> gromhydigne,   þær he gen ligeð
> in carcerne   clommum gefæstnad,
> synnum gesæled. (730b–6a)

(The fifth leap was when he humbled the host of hell-dwellers in living torment, bound the king inside with ancient bonds, the advocate of the fiends, the fierce-thinker, he still lies there in prison, fastened with chains, tied by his sins.)

The fact that Satan had already been bound by God does not seem to be a problem for the poet. Dendle links this to difficulties in defining and confining the devil on the part of hagiographers who, despite commonly ending "on positive notes of encouragement through repeated claims that the devil was bound a long time ago, is bound now, and will be bound again in times to come (mutually conflicting claims that betray the unease fueling them)," also continue to cultivate the denial of his containment.[97] In doing so, "[t]hey never cease to grant him the dynamically charged unspecificity that is the source of his strength, struggling to contain him by defining him, yet at the same time allowing him to resist absolute containment or definition."[98] It is partly because of this attempt to contain and define Satan that hell becomes a type-scene in Old English poetry. By codifying its depiction, the horrors of hell are made more palatable and easier to relay. The existence of the type-scene itself speaks to hell's overwhelming

---

97 *Satan Unbound*, p. 121.
98 Ibid. See also Doane, *Saxon Genesis*, pp. 135–7.

importance to the Anglo-Saxon mindset, while the constant and repeated binding of Satan demonstrates not only that evil, the devil, and hell were hard to define, but also that binding was essential to hell's formulaic depiction.

As the original occupant of hell, Satan does not lack company. Despite being bound and punished, Satan and his followers are frequently depicted binding humans in hell. This is a popular topic in Old English poetry, with references to humans in hell-bonds occurring in nine passages.[99] Since binding is part of a greater set of formulaic hell diction, there are, of course, many other passages describing the torments of hell not included in this statistic.

One of the most poignant extended passages describing humans who have been bound in hell occurs in *The Descent into Hell*. Here, John greets Christ who has come to rescue the Old Testament patriarchs from their hell-ish captivity:

Þe þæs þonc sie,   þeoden user,
þæt þu us... ...ige   secan woldest,
nu we on þissum bendum   bidan ......
þonne monige bindeð   broþorleasne
wræccan ......   (he bið wide fah),
ne bið he no þæs nearwe   under niðloc ...
þæs bitre gebunden   under bealuclommum,
þæt he þy yð ne mæge   ellen habban,
þonne he his hlafordes   hyldo gelyfeð,
þæt hine of þam bendum   bicgan wille.   (59–68)[100]

(Thanks be to you, our leader, that you were willing to seek us out, while we waited in these bonds where one binds many a brotherless exile (he is guilty far and wide), he is not bound so tightly by hostile locks, so bitterly by baleful

---

99 This statistic refers only to passages including all three elements of binding, hell and humans: *Descent into Hell* 59–68, 86b–8a; *Beowulf* 3069–75; *Christ I* 363–5a; *Christ III* 1593–8a, 1615b–22; *Genesis B* 407b–9a; *Judith* 111b–21; *Solomon and Saturn I* 68–72.

100 There are several parallel passages describing bonds in the context of Christ's powers of loosing, including those that afflicted humanity before the coming of Christ. See *Christ I* 66b–9a and 146b–8a. Neither of these passages refers directly to hell, rather they gesture toward a general, unspecified bond of suffering which is broken by Christ's arrival. In these descriptions of pre-Christian bonds, the promise of relief is always evident.

chains, that he may not obtain courage easily when he trusts in the protection
of his lord, that he will redeem him from those bonds.)

Despite the damage to the manuscript, it is possible to make out much of
the same imagery described in the above discussions of *Andreas* and Satan:
bonds and binding (*bendum/bindeð/gebunden*), confinement (*nearwe*),
hostile locks (*niðloc*) and baleful chains (*bealuclommum*). This imagery is
restated in brief later in the poem, but always with the emphasis on the
expected release from hell-bonds that Christ's coming promises. Thus, not
only is God a binder of the world, he is also a looser of the bonds laid by
the devil upon undeserving humans.[101]

The passage from *Solomon and Saturn I*, examined in relation to
Grendel's *glof* in chapter 3,[102] takes the theme of Christ's loosing powers
one step further. In that depiction of hellish confinement, the soul is described as fastened with fetters by the devil (70a: *feterum gefæstnað*), and
held by fifty locks (71a: *clusum*). The poem makes it clear that God is able
to break *ðone cræft* (71b) (that handiwork) and destroy *ða orðancas* (72a)
(the skilful device). This is not the general binding of most Old English
poetic descriptions, but rather an extended metaphor in which hell and
prison are concretely conflated. The *clusum* can be read as either locks or
bolts on a prison cell or, on a larger scale, an entire cell or enclosure.[103]
Whether we read the skilful device as a hellish object of binding or as the
place of binding – hell itself – it is clear that God's powers outstrip those
of the devil, even on his own turf. While the concrete language draws our
attention to the manner of binding, the focus is not just on the terrors of
being bound in hell, but also on the rescue from hell, and on relief from its
constrictions. In comparing this passage to the actions of Andreas, his imitation of Christ becomes all the more clear.[104]

Of course, this theme of loosing appears only in relation to pious souls.
Those who do not deserve rescue are also described as bound in hell, but

---

101 This context is alluded to in *Guthlac A* 571b–98, when demons threaten the saint with
     hell-bonds and he counters that his treatment rests in the hands of Christ who had
     already driven the demons into captivity.
102 See pp. 83–90.
103 *DOE*, s.v. *cluse*, sense 1.–2.
104 Constance B. Hieatt reads Andreas's trip to Mermedonia as a harrowing of hell. See
     "Harrowing of Mermedonia."

with no hope for relief. Among those characters clearly deserving of their hell-bonds, we may include Holofernes in *Judith*:

>   Næs ða dead þa gyt,
> ealles orsawle.   Sloh ða eornoste
> ides ellenrof   (oð)re siðe
> þone hæðenan hund,   þæt him þæt heafod wand
> forð on ða flore.   Læg se fula leap
> gesne beæftan,   gæst ellor hwearf
> under neowelne næs   ond ðær genyðerad wæs,
> susle gesæled   syððan æfre,
> wyrmum bewunden,   witum gebunden,
> hearde gehæfted   in helle bryne
> æfter hinsiðe.   Ne ðearf he hopian no,
> þystrum forðylmed,   þæt he ðonan mote
> of ðam wyrmsele,   ac ðær wunian sceal
> awa to aldre   butan ende forð
> in ðam heolstran ham,   hyhtwynna leas.   (107b–21)

(He was not yet dead, entirely lifeless. Then the highly courageous lady earnestly struck the heathen hound a second time, so that his head rolled forth onto the floor. The foul corpse lay behind, lifeless, the spirit turned elsewhere under the deep earth and was oppressed there, tied by torment forever afterward, wound about by serpents, bound by punishments, fiercely constrained in hell-burning after the journey hence. Not at all did he need to hope, encompassed by shadows, that he might [go] from the serpent-hall, but there he had to dwell always and forever without an end in the dark home, without the joys of hope.)

As Bredehoft notes, this passage is highlighted through the concentrated use of poetic effects: it contains cross alliteration (vowels and "s": *ealles/orsawle/Sloh/eornoste*; "g" and vowels: *gesne/beæftan/gæst/ellor*), secondary alliteration ("l": *Læg/leap*) and the repetition of alliterating sounds across verses (vowels: *ealles/eornoste/ides/ellenrof/(oð)re*; "h": *hearde/gehæfted/helle/ hinsiðe/hopian*), which he argues "may well contribute a bracketing effect to this passage."[105] Formulaic diction also

---

105 *Early English Metre*, p. 64.

pervades both the slaying of Holofernes and the description of hell,[106] with formulas such as: *ides ellenrof*,[107] *oðre siðe*,[108] *syððan æfre*,[109] *witum gebunden*,[110] *hearde gehæfted*,[111] *æfter hinsiðe*,[112] *awa to aldre*,[113] and *butan ende forð*.[114] Many of the half-lines that are not direct formulas pair commonly collocating words: *gæst* and *ellor*,[115] *neowol* and *-næs*,[116] *susl* and *-sælan*,[117] *hell* and *bryne*,[118] *heolstor* and *ham*,[119] and *hyht, wynn* and *leas*.[120] In addition to the use of formulas, rhyme is employed in lines 113 (*næs/wæs*) and 115 (*bewunden/gebunden*).[121] Interestingly, *-bunden* and *-wunden* only collocate in three other poetic instances, and never in prose. In *Riddle 28*, where the object described is tortured during manufacture, the two past participles occur within the same half-line,[122] while

---

106 Andy Orchard notes the formulaic connection between *Judith* and poems of the Cynewulf canon, especially *Elene*. See "Computing Cynewulf."

107 See *Judith* 146a, as well as the collocation of *ides* and *ellen* in line 133. *Genesis A* 1875 also collocates *ides* and the compound, *ellenrof*.

108 *Andreas* 706b, 808b, 1675b, 1700b; *Beowulf* 2670b, 3101b; *Christ and Satan* 75b; *Genesis A* 1878b (right after *ides* and *ellenrof* collocate), 2395b, 2630b.

109 *Elene* 507b; *Paris Psalter (Psalm 57)* 23b.

110 *Andreas* 580b. *Wite* and *-binden* also collocate in *Christ III* 1621–2; *Christ and Satan* 102b–3a; *Elene* 770–1; *Guthlac B* 885–6; *Soul and Body I* 31–2; *Soul and Body II* 28–9; Ælfric's *Passio Sancti Iuliani et sponse eius Basilisse*, in *Lives of Saints*, 1:100, lines 181–3.

111 *Metres of Boethius (Metre 25)* 49a. *Heard-* also collocates with *-hæft* and *-hæftan* in *Andreas* 1399a, 1470; *Christ I* 260; *Elene* 703b–4; *Genesis B* 373–85 (twice); *Paris Psalter (Psalm 123)* 17; *Soul and Body I* 31–2; and *Soul and Body II* 28–9. The *Soul and Body* lines also collocate *wite* and *gebindan*.

112 *Whale* 68a.

113 *Beowulf* 955a; *Christ and Satan* 312a (also collocates *wunian* and *butan ende*); *Exodus* 425a; *Order of the World* 32a; *Seafarer* 79a.

114 *Judgement Day II* 306b.

115 *Beowulf* 86a, 807b. *Beowulf* also collocates *ellor* and *hwearf* at 55b.

116 *Beowulf* 1411a.

117 *Daniel* 520; *Panther* 59.

118 *Christ and Satan* 25–7 (also collocates *ham, næs* and *neowol*); *Guthlac A* 572–3.

119 *Christ and Satan* 99–100 (also collocates *hell, neowol, wyrm, wite* and *gebunden*); and *Guthlac A* 83a.

120 *Hyht* and *wynn* collocate in *Andreas* 1113–14; *Phoenix* 480b; *Riming Poem* 81b–3a. Other occurrences of the formula *x wynna leas* can be found in *Resignation* 90a; *Wife's Lament* 32a. *Hyht* and *leas* collocate in *Guthlac A* 925a, and *Juliana* 682a, as well as in *Christ and Satan* 155, where they appear in the related formula *hyht-x leas*.

121 Bredehoft, *Early English Metre*, p. 64.

122 See line 5a.

in *Beowulf*[123] and *Riddle 55*[124] the terms are used in apposition to describe high status objects with twisted gold decoration. Thus, the two descriptors seem to share a mutual applicability to both constructive and constrictive contexts. The context here is clearly a constrictive one, since Holofernes's binding is one of his many hellish torments.

Other descriptions of hell make reference to its depth (*neowelne*), shadowy darkness (*þystrum, heolstran*), and eternal nature (*butan ende*). Bredehoft also notes that the off-rhyme (*hund/wand*) of line 110 alludes to both Judith's *hand* and Holofernes *wund*:

> As the passage insists, this crucial moment of separation (Judith from Holofernes; head – and soul – from body) is simultaneously a moment of binding (Holofernes's soul is bound in hell), and the use of rhyme and secondary alliteration serves to emphasize the binding aspects of the passage through a kind of linguistic or poetic interlacing. The effect is strengthened by the repeated use of the same specific verse type [...] in three consecutive half-lines: 115a–16a (and see 114a, as well); one can almost feel the bonds tightening.[125]

The ornamentation of this passage, therefore, demonstrates the importance of hell-bonds, which are invoked both at the level of imagery and poetics.

The concept of binding is also invoked in the metaphorical context of sin in *An Exhortation to Christian Living*:

> Gif þu wilt þa upplican   eardwic ceosan,
> þænne scealt þu hit on eorðan   ær geþencan,
> and þu þe sylfne   swiðe gebindan
> and þa unþeawas   ealle forlætan
> þe þu on þis life ær   lufedest and feddest.   (78–82)

(If you wish to choose the heavenly dwelling-place, then you must think upon it beforehand on earth, and you [must] greatly bind yourself and give up all the evil practices that you loved and sustained earlier in this life.)

---

123   See line 1531.
124   See lines 3b–4a.
125   *Early English Metre*, p. 65.

This is not, however, the biblical binding and loosing of Christ and his disciples. Rather, the binding of the self against sin described here is similar to *The Wanderer*'s expression of heroic composure, in which he binds his heart and mind against powerful emotions.[126] The protective nature of this binding may relate it to constructive depictions of bound and encircling armour or to the tradition of psychomachia, featured prominently in *Juliana*, where the martyr protects her body and soul as a fortress against sin.[127] This sort of positive constriction against a penetrating evil is yet another use of binding in Old English poetry.

If *Andreas* is the archetypal example of binding and prison imagery in Old English poetry, then *Juliana* is the archetypal example of binding and demonic imagery. There are all manner of binding descriptions in *Juliana*, which expands greatly upon its Latin source, the *Passio S. Iulianae* from Bibliothèque Nationale de France, lat. 10861.[128] One example of such an expansion occurs in a passage where the demon afflicting Juliana describes how Satan binds his own men:

> Ne biþ us frea milde,
> egesful ealdor,   gif we yfles noht
> gedon habbaþ;   ne durran we siþþan
> for his onsyne   ower geferan.
> Þonne he onsendeð   geond sidne grund
> þegnas of þystrum,   hateð þræce ræran,
> gif we gemette sin   on moldwege,
> oþþe feor oþþe neah   fundne weorþen,
> þæt hi usic binden   ond in bælwylme
> suslum swingen.   (328b–37a)

(He is not a gentle lord to us, the terrifying chieftain, if we have not done evil; we do not dare to go anywhere in his sight after. Then he sends forth throughout the wide world his retainers from the darkness, orders them to

---

126 See chapter 7, pp. 227–30.

127 See Anderson, *Cynewulf*, p. 90; Irvine, "Cynewulf's Use of Psychomachia Allegory"; Wehlau, *Riddle of Creation*, pp. 41–6; and Hermann, "Recurrent Motifs of Spiritual Warfare," pp. 14–16, as well as his "Some Varieties of Psychomachia"; see also his *Allegories of War*, pp. 7–52.

128 See Lapidge's edition in the appendix to "Cynewulf and the *Passio S. Iulianae*," pp. 156–65.

raise an attack, if we are discovered on earth or are found far or near, that they should bind us and scourge us with torments in a surge of fire.)

The emphasis here is on Satan's role as a deficient lord. Unlike God who protects and encourages his flock, Satan is more than willing to send some of his followers to torture others should they not perform to the standard he expects. They undergo punishments similar to those inflicted on human sinners: binding, torment and fire, the use of which implies they are slaves as opposed to retainers. As Woolf argues, because Satan has nothing valuable to give his followers, "all that he can dispense is evil, and he therefore becomes *morþres brytta*, not the familiar *sinces brytta*. [...] The clear implication is that punishment in hell is not restricted to men who have failed to satisfy God, but is also inflicted on devils who have failed to satisfy Satan."[129]

Binding imagery in *Juliana* is also linked to warfare through Juliana's use of martial imagery in the battle for her soul. There are, of course, many precedents for this association in early Christian literature. It is found not infrequently in the Latin female saints' lives, which acted as a model for Cynewulf's poem.[130] The imagery is also exploited in the writings of Gregory the Great, which depict "the world as a battleground in which we, as soldiers of Christ, stand continually in the front lines. If at any moment we withdraw our attention, the demons will swarm across the battlefield and seize us."[131] Although the binding of and by demons has been depicted as evil, Juliana's own action of binding is seen more favourably. While Juliana successfully defends her faith from attack, she also acts offensively by grappling with and defeating a demon who has come to her prison to tempt her in the guise of an angel. The struggle between Juliana and the demon appears in the Latin source where it is the text's most extended description of binding: *Tunc sancta Iuliana ligauit eum postergum manibus et posuit super terram et adpraehendens unum de uinculis de quibus ipsa fuerat ligata, cedebat ipsum daemonem*[132] (Then Saint Juliana bound him with his hands behind his back and put him on the ground and, taking one of the chains by which she herself had been bound, she subdued the demon). Unfortunately, the Old English manuscript leaf

---

129   "Devil in Old English Poetry," p. 8.
130   Damon, *Soldier Saints*, p. 99.
131   Russell, *Lucifer*, p. 100.
132   Lapidge, "Cynewulf and the *Passio S. Iulianae*," p. 161, section 10.

depicting this scene is lost. The lines that do remain, however, outline the
heavenly command that Juliana should seize the demon and the narrator's
assertion that she does so; thus it is safe to assume that the poem originally depicted this struggle in detail.[133] Later, the demon complains of
his binding:

> Ða cwom semninga
> hean helle gæst,   hearmleoð agol,
> earm ond unlæd,   þone heo ær gebond
> awyrgedne   ond mid witum swong,
> cleopade þa for corþre,   ceargealdra full:
> "Gyldað nu mid gyrne,   þæt heo goda ussa
> meaht forhogde,   ond mec swiþast
> geminsade,   þæt ic to meldan wearð.
> Lætað hy laþra   leana hleotan
> þurh wæpnes spor,   wrecað ealdne nið,
> synne gesohte.   Ic þa sorge gemon,
> hu ic bendum fæst   bisga unrim
> on anre niht   earfeða dreag,
> yfel ormætu."
>
> (614b–27a)[134]

(Then suddenly a lowly hell-spirit came, sang a sorrowful song, wretched
and unhappy, he who, accursed, she had earlier bound and scourged with
punishments, called out then in front of the company, full of sorrowful incantations: "Earnestly repay her now, that she scorned the might of our gods,
and weakened me so much that I became an informant. Let her obtain hateful
rewards through the weapon's mark, avenge the old enmity, beset with sin.
I remember that sorrow, how I, fast in bonds, endured countless tortures in
one night, miseries, immense evil.")

This passage in particular expands upon the source's depiction of the demon's complaints, which in the Latin culminate only in the statement:
Patrem meum superasti; me uinxisti (You conquered my father; you bound
me).[135] In the Old English, on the other hand, binding is invoked twice

---

133 See lines 284–8. A leaf is missing after these lines, with the text picking up mid-
sentence on the next folio. Krapp and Dobbie, *Exeter Book*, p. 282.
134 See also lines 430b–4a and 534b–6a.
135 Lapidge, "Cynewulf and the *Passio S. Iulianae*," p. 162, section 12.

(*gebond/bendum*), along with the suffering of misery and torture (*bisga unrim/earfeða dreag/yfel ormætu*). Taken together, this imagery indicates that the prison has come to symbolize hell for the demon, with Juliana imitating God and Christ,[136] while the demon imitates the bound Satan. However, the demon's language is slippery, and his reference to avenging Juliana's *ealdne nið* (old enmity) echoes descriptions of Satan as *se ealda feond* (the old enemy),[137] thus implying that the demon sees the prison as a hell for Juliana. However, Juliana's ability to take control over her surroundings is evident in her rewriting of the scene: not only does she bind when she should be bound, but she also relishes the idea of martyrdom and death rather than passively fearing it. As John Edward Damon emphasizes, *Juliana* embodies "the trope of the victim becoming victor,"[138] something that is particularly evident in her approach to binding.

In reading this poem, scholars frequently place an emphasis on Juliana's stability and lack of movement.[139] Steadfastness in the face of worldly instability indicates wisdom; thus it is through their calm persistence that the tortured saints exercise their God-given power. And yet, it is not the binding or bound-ness that marks good people in Old English poetry, since a diverse range of figures, including God, Christ, the saints, kings, and even Satan and his demons, are portrayed in relation to such constriction. Instead, what all these imprisoned figures have in common is a power that threatens their enemies and must therefore be contained. Those who are lauded as heroes manage to persevere despite affliction, indicating that value lies in the approach one takes to the human condition and the binding that accompanies it. This makes the human/divine Christ an excellent subject for study since, through his ultimate sacrifice, he engages with two sorts of bonds: he is delivered from suffering and fetters, and yet enters into other bonds as he becomes the divine lord for his earthly retainers. These bonds of servitude will be explored further in the following chapter.

---

136 Whether God with his initial binding of Satan or Christ at the harrowing of hell, as suggested by Wittig, "Figural Narrative," pp. 44–5.

137 See *Christ II* 567a; *Elene* 207b; and *Panther* 58b.

138 *Soldier Saints*, p. 98.

139 See, for example, Dendle, *Satan Unbound*, p. 80; and Wehlau, *Riddle of Creation*, p. 42.

6 Slavery and Servitude

Slavery appears as a common motif in Old English riddles. The concept was well known in the Anglo-Saxon world, as the large body of vocabulary associated with the practice demonstrates.[1] David Pelteret maintains that early Christian writers, influenced by the prevalence of slaves in both the Old and New Testaments, helped to perpetuate slavery by applying its terminology to descriptions of human relations with both God and the devil.[2] With over forty words pointing to slavery and freedom appearing in translations of religious works, this vocabulary became entrenched in Old English, which made it, Pelteret argues, "virtually impossible for an Anglo-Saxon to see slavery as being other than inherent in the human condition."[3]

As an ever present economic institution, slavery needed to continually replenish itself; thus, the making of free people into slaves was integral to its survival. Throughout this period, people were born into slavery or purchased and sold through the slave trade.[4] There were a number of ways new slaves could be acquired, but in the early Anglo-Saxon period the greatest proportion of the slave population were victims of warfare and foreign conquest.[5] The prevalence of this method of slave acquisition is evident at the level of vocabulary, with the term *wealh* carrying an original

---

1 *Slavery in Early Mediaeval England*, p. 48. See the *TOE* for a list of words indicating servants/attendants (12.01.01.08.01), bondage/slavery (12.01.01.09), freedom/being free (12.01.01.10) and freeing/manumission (12.01.01.10.01).
2 Pelteret, *Slavery in Early Mediaeval England*, p. 41.
3 Ibid., p. 47.
4 Williams, "Annals of the Poor," p. 70.
5 Pelteret, *Slavery in Early Mediaeval England*, p. 43.

meaning of "foreigner," frequently "a foreigner of British origin," and transforming into "a Celtic slave" or simply "slave."[6] In the later Anglo-Saxon period, debt, crime, and poverty became the most frequent reasons for enslavement.[7]

These various methods of enslaving free people translate well onto the raw/cooked or wild/bound riddle content. Thus, many of the riddle creatures can be said to be victims of social or economic failure or foreign conquest who are forced into servitude. It is because the riddles are the only poems to deal with these everyday images that we see any references to slavery in the traditional Old English poetic canon. It is to be noted that they all occur in personifications rather than in reference to actual human beings.[8] Here in this "different side of the Anglo-Saxon world,"[9] we find domestic life, agricultural economy, and other quotidian aspects that are so central to a discussion of binding and weaving.

One of the problems that arises in the reading of Old English poetry relates to the differentiation between slavery and servitude. The latter may describe the condition of those in the lowest ranks of the social order or reflect the formal position of the esteemed retainers of the lord's war-band. Since this survey is interested in all forms of binding, the high status "bond" between lord and retainer is also relevant here. When it comes to human lordship, the ruler and retainer arguably inhabit one of the most important social relationships in Anglo-Saxon England. Discussions of

---

6 Ibid.

7 Ibid., p. 248.

8 Outside of these poems, there is little slavery to be found, with the possible exception of the cup-thief in *Beowulf*, who is a *þe(o) nathwylces* (2223b) (slave/servant of an unknown person). Most editions including Klaeber Four, pp. 76, 237, retain the proposed emendation of "slave," despite Theodore M. Anderson's suggestion that the manuscript may actually read *þeof nathwylces* (thief of something). "Thief in *Beowulf*," p. 495. Pelteret also argues for the thief reading, maintaining that it would be highly irregular for Beowulf's death to stem from a slave's action in a poem that espouses aristocratic values. *Slavery in Early Mediaeval England*, p. 53. Slavery is, however, mentioned in later Ælfrician texts, with several examples from the *Natale sancti Swyðuni, episcopi* describing Saint Swithun's freeing of slaves and criminals who are bound for petty infractions. See *Ælfric's Lives of Saints*, 1:452, 466, lines 166–77, 414–23. The presence of slavery in the saints' lives comes as no surprise given the texts' more instructive aims directed to a broader audience than that of traditional Old English poetry.

9 Wehlau, *Riddle of Creation*, p. 93.

this relationship in literature frequently begin with reference to the war-band (sometimes dubbed the *comitatus* by scholars), which was associated with a set of ideals deemed to be "heroic."[10] The scholarly conception of this group relates to its voluntary nature (setting it apart from the kin group), as well as its "newly constructed – cultural – relationship."[11] This constructed relationship is frequently articulated in terms of a lord-retainer "bond." Engaging with issues of definition, this chapter will discuss how binding imagery is invoked in relation to slavery and servitude in agricultural, heroic, and religious contexts.

Agricultural Slaves

There are three closely related Old English riddles that depict animals in the context of slavery and binding. These are the ox/bull riddles – *12*, *38*, and *72* – a group of poems with similar motifs and a long tradition, as demonstrated by the number of Anglo-Latin exemplars and analogues.[12] *Exeter Book Riddles 12* and *38*, in particular, appear to be part of a group that focuses on the cycle of "bull-to-leather."[13] The first to constrast the living creature with the dead is Symphosius' *Enigma 56*, *Caliga*, which describes a boot in relation to the source of its leather:

Maior eram longe quondam, dum uita manebat;
At nunc exanimis, lacerata, ligata, reuulsa;
Dedita sum terrae, tumulo sed condita non sum.

(I was once far larger, while life continued; but now without life, mangled, bound and torn, I am delivered to the earth, but I am not buried in a tomb.)

---

10 Discussions of the war-band are numerous, but for a literary context see Fanning, "Tacitus, *Beowulf*, and the *Comitatus*"; Anderson, "Roman Idea of a Comitatus"; O'Brien O'Keeffe, "Heroic Values"; Tanke, "Bachelor-Warrior"; Bazelmans, *By Weapons Made Worthy*; and Enright, *Lady with a Mead Cup*; as well as his "Warband Context of the Unferth Episode." For a problematization of past scholarship's focus on retainer loyalties, see Hill, *Anglo-Saxon Warrior Ethic*, pp. 5–10 of which outlines the history of scholarly interest in heroic poetry.

11 Bazelmans, *By Weapons Made Worthy*, p. 13.

12 See Tupper, *Riddles of the Exeter Book*, p. 93; and Dieter Bitterli, *Say What I Am Called*, pp. 26–34.

13 Whitman, *Old English Riddles*, p. 128.

This contrast is something that both *Riddles 12* and *38* invoke, albeit in combination with the motif of leather-as-binder-of-humans found in Aldhelm's *Enigma 83, De iuvenco*:

> Arida spumosis dissoluens faucibus ora
> Bis binis bibulus potum de fontibus hausi.
> Viuens nam terrae glebas cum stirpibus imis
> Nisu uirtutis ualidae disrumpo feraces;
> At uero linquit dum spiritus algida membra,
> Nexibus horrendis homines constringere possum.

> (Liberating my dry mouth with frothy jaws, I, thirsty, drank a draft from four springs. While alive, through powerful strength, I break apart the fertile soil of the earth by rooting up the deepest plants; but truly, when life leaves my cold limbs, I am able to constrict people with terrible bonds.)

The influence of Aldhelm's poem is clear in the Anglo-Latin tradition, with Eusebius' *Enigma 37, De vitulo*, Lorsch *Enigma 11, De tauro*, and the pseudo-Bedan *Collectanea* referring to the living creature's four springs of milk and breaking of the earth, as well as the dead creature's binding.[14] Old English *Riddles 12* and *38* also clearly follow in this tradition, and so their references to binding will be discussed together.

The only mention of binding in *Riddle 12* occurs in lines 3–4: *Gif me feorh losað, fæste binde / swearte Wealas, hwilum sellan men* (If I lose my life, I bind fast dark Celts/slaves, sometimes better men). Here we see the reference to slavery quite clearly in the choice of vocabulary, *Wealas* referring to foreigners, Celts or slaves, as noted above. While the riddle creature itself is not directly called a slave, it is clearly being manipulated by its human owners – alive, it works the plough, dead, it is turned into leather fetters used to bind other slaves and captives like its Anglo-Latin counterparts. Dieter Bitterli argues that the dark Celts "represent the enslaved labourers and underdogs of Anglo-Saxon society" who are referred to as *swearte* (dark) in order to contrast them with light-haired aristocrats.[15] Pelteret embellishes upon this point, noting that blond hair is used to

---

14 Bayless and Lapidge, *Collectanea Pseudo-Bedae*, p. 144, no. 194. Eusebius' collection also contains further enigmata with similar solutions, including *Enigma 12, De bove* and *13, De vacca*, although these do not refer to binding.
15 *Say What I Am Called*, p. 31.

signal high status in other Old English riddles, while the term, *wonfeax* (dark-haired), used of a Celt in line 8, implies an equally low status.[16] He argues for a comparison in lines 3–4 between Celts with dark hair and Anglo-Saxons with blond hair, suggesting that the *sellan* (better) men signify Anglo-Saxons.[17] Since such a reference is not likely to have been applied to criminals, the implication is that these are slaves taken in battle, either with the Celts or sometimes (*hwilum*) between different Anglo-Saxon groups.[18] The majority of slaves in the Old English riddles are depicted as Celts, either by the term *wealh* or through their darkness, so this glimpse of possible Anglo-Saxon captives is unique among depictions of slavery in the poetic corpus.

As for the reference to binding, because hide or leather bonds occur frequently in both the Old English and Latin riddle traditions, the conclusion that this was an actual use of animal hides in the early medieval period is strongly supported.[19] The description of the riddle creature's usefulness to its owner is repeated later in *Riddle 12*:

> Saga hwæt ic hatte,
> þe ic lifgende   lond reafige
> ond æfter deaþe   dryhtum þeowige.   (13b–15)

(Say what I am called, I who living ravage the land and after death serve men.)

While there is now no depiction of binding, the ox is said to serve (*þeowian*) after its death. That this service is leather's use for fettering is implied by the previous description and by the analogues, but it also metonymically gestures towards the forced service of those it binds. The final lines of *Riddle 38* show a similar picture of the ox's living/dead jobs: *Seo wiht, gif hio gedygeð, duna briceð;/gif he tobirsteð, bindeð cwice* (6–7) (That creature, if he survives, breaks the hills; if he dies, binds the living). *Toberstan*, of course, means literally "to burst asunder,"[20] indicating that it

---

16 *Slavery in Early Mediaeval England*, p. 52.
17 Ibid., p. 53.
18 Ibid.
19 For more on the history and uses of leather, see Cherry, "Leather"; and Cameron and Mould, "Devil's Crafts and Dragon's Skins?" The latter in particular notes the diverse nature of leather objects in Anglo-Saxon England and the use of leather in everyday life.
20 Bosworth and Toller, *Anglo-Saxon Dictionary*, s.v.

is not the dead animal that binds the living, but pieces of that animal –
strips of leather. Bitterli discusses these lines in relation to the "double
contrast of living/dead and breaking/binding," which he also argues *toberstan* emphasizes: "alive and yoked to the plough, the ox rends the earth,
but when rent itself, it paradoxically binds the living."[21] It is, furthermore,
not only the binding of humans that is described here, but by implication
the binding back together of a broken body. This is similar to the use of
binding in the plough riddle,[22] where the plough is described as a bound
object, but through the metaphor of a fettered creature or slave.

Advancing beyond the influence of the Anglo-Latin enigmata, *Riddle
72* presents a similar picture of the ox as an enslaved creature – this time
without the living/dead antithesis. The riddle is worth quoting at length
because it presents a more unified and elaborated depiction of binding
than the previous two riddles. Unfortunately, *Riddle 72* is fragmentary,
and little in the way of continuous phrasing can be made of the first several lines:

> oft ic feower teah
> swæse broþor,   þara onsundran gehwylc
> dægtidum me   drincan sealde
> þurh þyrel þearle.   Ic þæh on lust,
> oþþæt ic wæs yldra   ond þæt an forlet
> sweartum hyrde,   siþade widdor,
> mearcpaþas Walas træd,   moras pæðde,
> bunden under beame,   beag hæfde on healse,
> wean on laste   weorc þrowade,
> earfoða dæl.   Oft mec isern scod
> sare on sidan;   ic swigade,
> næfre meldade   monna ængum
> gif me ordstæpe   egle wæron.   (6b–18)

(often I pulled four sweet brothers, each of which separately gave me a drink
throughout the day through the heavy hole. I grew there in happiness, until
I was older and relinquished all of that to the dark herdsman, I journeyed
more widely, trod foreign/Celtic border-trails, traversed moors, bound under
beam, I had a ring on my neck, misery on the track, I endured work/pain, a

---

21 *Say What I Am Called*, pp. 29–30.
22 See chapter 3, pp. 82–3.

portion of hardship. Often the iron injured me, sore on my sides; I kept silent, never proclaimed to anyone if the spear-stabs were painful to me.)

Initially, this poem invokes the Anglo-Latin enigmata by referring to the drinking of milk in order to depict the happy, plentiful childhood that is snatched away by the *hirde* (herdsman). Again the humans involved with the ox are described as *sweart* (dark), giving us a hint as to the class of the *hirde*, a term which can also be employed metaphorically to mean "keeper" or "guardian," and thus is not necessarily a mark of social status in itself. The ox's life now turns to exile, indicated by the appositive references to wandering paths.[23] Edward B. Irving, Jr notes that these paths and tracks represent a play on words, since ploughing oxen are "famous for their treading and track-making."[24]

The poem's exile motif is quickly turned into one of slavery, when we discover that the riddle creature is *bunden under beame*. His labour is described as hard and painful, and, unlike in any of the other ox/bull riddles or enigmata, the animal itself is clearly the one that is bound. This difference significantly sets *Riddle 72* apart from the tradition, something that is highlighted by the half-rhyme of *bunden* and *under*, as well as the assonance that surrounds it, both in the previous lines and in those following ("ea": *sweartum/mearc-/beam/beag/wean/earfoða*; "æ": *træd/pæðde/hæfde*). The presence of the *beag* around the ox's neck also serves double duty – it is both a ring and an adornment, like that of a warrior (or exiled warrior in this instance), and an iron fetter, which binds the ox-slave to the plough.[25] Irving concludes that the "stoic and silent enduring of the stabs of the sharp iron goad" offers a sympathetic reading of the ox as "slave-victim."[26] In the alternative, play-world of the riddles, the suffering of a slave is recognized, something which is carefully overlooked by the aristocratic impulse of the majority of Old English poetry.

This riddling interest in the lives of slaves speaks moreover to the poem's connection with the plough. As mentioned in chapter 3, the plough riddle also depicts an enslaved creature, bound and fettered in order to

---

23 Stanley B. Greenfield outlines the four aspects of exile upon which the Old English poet focused: status, deprivation, state of mind, and movement in or into exile; "Formulaic Expression of the Theme of 'Exile'."
24 "Heroic Experience," p. 208.
25 This ring is not unlike that of *Riddle 4*. See chapter 3, pp. 79–83.
26 "Heroic Experience," p. 208.

perform labour for its master. The fact that these Old English riddling descriptions of the plough describe the implement in terms of slavery may be in part because ploughing was, or so the evidence of the Domesday Book indicates, the most common role for a slave in Anglo-Saxon England.[27] Ælfric's *Colloquy* also describes the struggle of the unfree ploughman: *Hig! Hig! micel gedeorf ys hyt. / Geleof, micel gedeorf hit ys, forþam ic neom freoh*[28] (34–5) (Oh! Oh! The labour is great. Yes, the labour is great, because I am not free). Pelteret argues for the importance of this passage, noting that Ælfric's portrayal does not merely describe the ploughman's work but allows him to directly relate his personal experience in a powerful and moving way.[29] That this instance of slavery in Anglo-Saxon culture, expressed through the words and mindset of a human slave, is unique in the literature is indicative of the social separation between the producers of Anglo-Saxon literature and their slaves.[30] Excluding these and a few other personified, riddling examples, the slave is a silent figure in Anglo-Saxon history, as the last lines of *Riddle 72* demonstrate: *ic swigade* (I kept silent) and *næfre meldade* (never proclaimed).[31] The question of silence in *Riddle 72* may relate to the unspoken nature of slavery in Anglo-Saxon England, and yet it also speaks to Old English poetry's emphasis on power and control. Just as the animal's body is bound and controlled by his slave-master, so too is his voice usurped and manipulated by those who copied it into and subsequently used the manuscript (a further animal by-product). If, on the other hand, this were meant to be a subversive and revolutionary text, its existence in the highly treasured *Exeter Book* poses a great many questions.

The depiction of slavery in *Riddle 52* again raises questions of interpretation. This riddle's solution is probably "flail," although Fry notes alternate suggestions, including "buckets," "broom," and "yoked oxen."[32] The poem reads:

---

27 Pelteret, *Slavery in Early Mediaeval England*, pp. 117, 194.

28 P. 21. The Latin reads: *O! O! magnus labor. etiam, magnus labor est, quia non sum liber.*

29 *Slavery in Early Mediaeval England*, p. 65.

30 Ibid.

31 For more on the paradox of the first-person speakers speaking of their very inability to speak, see Denno, "Oppression and Voice"; and Nelson, "Paradox of Silent Speech."

32 "Exeter Book Riddle Solutions," p. 24.

Ic seah ræpingas   in ræced fergan
under hrof sales   hearde twegen,
þa wæron genamnan,   nearwum bendum
gefeterade   fæste togædre;
þara oþrum wæs   an getenge
wonfah Wale,   seo weold hyra
bega siþe   bendum fæstra.

(I saw two violent prisoners carried into the hall, under the hall's roof, they
were seized, fettered firmly together with tight bonds; near to one of them
was a dark-haired Celt/slave, she ruled the movements of both, fast in their
bonds.)

Again we see an interaction between the riddle object and a dark-haired
Celt/slave (*wonfah Wale*), a ready sign that this is an object of domestic or
agricultural labour, as opposed to one of higher social esteem. The depiction of the slave woman's role here is one of inverted power; although she
is a slave herself, she has control over the riddle object, whose movements
she rules (*weold*) by means of their bonds.

The poem itself is almost entirely taken up with the image of the object
in bonds. Employing the verb *gefeterian* (which only appears in poetry),
the middle lines emphasize not only that the two elements of the object are
gefeterade fæste togædre (fettered firmly together), but also the means by
which they are fettered: *nearwum bendum* (with tight bonds). Again we
see in the final line that the companions being manipulated by the slave
woman are *bendum fæstra* (fast in their bonds). The nature of the bonds
and fetters in this case seems to differ from that of the ox and plough.
While this is also clearly a tool for human use, there is an emphasis on the
aggressive nature of the elements that make up the object. These are a
hearde twegen (violent/bold two), with our translation of the adjective
relying on how we interpret the noun, *ræpingas*. Irving maintains that
these two "seem to be war-captives [...] who are dangerous enough to be
held under elaborate restraint."[33] However, *ræpingas* may equally imply
that they are criminals.[34] Accordingly, if they were taken in war, then we
may read *hearde* as "bold" – a common descriptor for warriors in Old
English heroic literature. If we read them as criminals, the seizing of whom

---

33 "Heroic Experience," p. 207.
34 Bosworth and Toller, *Anglo-Saxon Dictionary*, s.v. *ræpling*.

was also a means of acquiring new slaves,[35] then the description is more likely to read "violent." This ambiguity may well be deliberate, since the taking of slaves in war and as a result of criminal activity were both active practices in Anglo-Saxon England. Together with the *wonfah Wale* – a foreign slave – we see several possible sources of slave-making depicted in one poem.

This poem also raises the question of what an outdoor, agricultural implement is doing in a hall setting. The fact that the riddle object has been led inside, and into a hall more precisely, is clearly emphasized, with two appositives in the first two lines: *in ræced fergan* (carried into the hall) and *under hrof sales* (under the hall's roof). This is perhaps where the reading of the riddle as "broom" gains the most momentum. Indeed, there is a Latin analogue to such a solution in the form of Symphosius' *Enigma 80*, *Scopa*:

Mundi magna parens, laqueo conexa tenaci,
Vincta solo plano, manibus conpressa duabus
Ducor ubique sequens et me quoque cuncta sequuntur.

(Great parent of the world/cleanliness, tied together by a restraining snare, bound to the flat ground, pressed by two hands; following, I am led everywhere and likewise all things follow me.)

Although a hall setting is not mentioned in Symphosius' enigma, the reference to the object as bound together and restrained provides an interesting overlap. Of course, the Latin poem's emphasis on the object's position on the ground and as a follower is not mirrored in *Riddle 52*, which refers to the object as carried. The high status location of the Old English riddle is not necessarily a significant indicator of the solution, since the riddler may once again be playing with levels of the social order. We have already seen that a slave woman is given power and control over the captives, something made evident through the use of the verb *wealdan*, which is commonly associated with kings and God. It is not inappropriate that an agricultural tool should be bound in a hall environment, the reference to which may be a clue for an agricultural building or storehouse. If the *ræpingas* refer to violent criminals, then allowing them into this apparent space of social

---

35 Pelteret, *Slavery in Early Mediaeval England*, p. 73.

order without firm bonds would be foolish (as we have seen from Grendel's attack on the hall). The function of the firm bonds may thus reassure us that these criminals are kept in order.[36] On the other hand, I would argue that the presence of the hall setting implies that the *ræpingas* are more likely to be bold war-captives. Due to the riddler's play with levels, we have a scene where female slaves walk free and wield power over noble captives who are fettered, enslaved, and bound to work in an anti-hall. While this disruption to the social hierarchy of master and slave would be occasion for concern in any other form of Old English poetry, the fact that it occurs in a riddle makes it acceptable – even expected.

The final riddle to be discussed in this section is a highly problematic one. *Riddle 28* has been variously solved as "John Barleycorn," "wine cask," "beer," "ale," "harp," "stringed instrument," "tortoise lyre," "malt liquor," "barrow," "trial of soul," "yew horn," and "damascened sword," with the first having the most supporters.[37] There is no consensus even among the major editors of *The Exeter Book* and the riddles: Krapp and Dobbie offer "Beer/Ale,"[38] Williamson "Yew-Horn?"[39] while Muir remains uncertain.[40] Most of the proposed solutions break down into the broad categories of "alcohol" and "musical instrument," but there are a few divergent readings, which are of interest. One that is particularly persuasive is Bitterli's suggestion that the riddle deals with the process of book-making, describing the creation of a holy book in terms of martyrdom.[41] The riddle itself reads:

Biþ foldan dæl   fægre gegierwed
mid þy heardestan   ond mid þy scearpestan
ond mid þy grymmestan   gumena gestreona,
corfen, sworfen,   cyrred, þyrred,
bunden, wunden,   blæced, wæced,
frætwed, geatwed,   feorran læded
to durum dryhta.   Dream bið in innan
cwicra wihta,   clengeð, lengeð,

---

36 See Garner, *Structuring Spaces*, p. 140, where this riddle is addressed in relation to the use of existing buildings as places to hold prisoners.

37 Fry, "Exeter Book Riddle Solutions," p. 23.

38 *Exeter Book*, p. 337.

39 *Old English Riddles of the Exeter Book*, pp. 218–24.

40 *Exeter Anthology*, p. 595.

41 *Say What I Am Called*, p. 189.

þara þe ær lifgende   longe hwile
wilna bruceð   ond no wið spriceð,
ond þonne æfter deaþe   deman onginneð,
meldan mislice.   Micel is to hycganne
wisfæstum menn,   hwæt seo wiht sy.

(A portion of the earth is garnished beautifully with the hardest and sharpest and fiercest of treasures of men, cut, filed, turned, dried, bound, wound, bleached, weakened, adorned, equipped, led far to the doors of men. The joy of living beings is within it, it remains, it lasts, that which, while alive, enjoys itself for a long time and does not speak against their wishes, and then, after death, it begins to praise, to declare in various ways. Great is it to think, for wisdom-fast men, [to say] what the creature is.)

If the actions that are described in emphatic, rhyming fashion are carried out upon a living creature, then what we have here is not so much slavery as it is torture. However, the object seems to be put to a use by humans, as the phrases *gumena gestreona* (treasures of men) and *Dream [...] cwicra wihta* (joy of living beings) imply, making a discussion of it within the confines of fettered servitude appropriate. Binding is mentioned in passing, among the many other tortures to which the object is submitted, with *bunden* and *wunden* alluding to the manufacturing process of whatever riddle-object this poem denotes.

If this poem does refer to the production of alcohol, then the torture here may well be that of John Barleycorn. This solution was first suggested by Thomas Wright who noted that an echo of the famous ballad hero provides an example of "how certain ideas run through the popular literature of different nations at all periods," citing a French fabliau, which described a similar situation.[42] Other scholars initially accepted this solution, with A.J. Wyatt listing it under the column "Solutions Accepted or Favoured" in his 1912 edition of the riddles,[43] and W.S. Mackie including it under the heading "Solutions certain or very probable" in his 1934 edition of *The Exeter Book*.[44] Tupper, supporting the related solution "ale,"

---

42 *Biographia Britannica Literaria*, 1:79. See also Bern *Enigma 13, De uine*'s description
    of itself: *Lacrimis infecta plura per uincula nector* (3) (Stained by tears I am bound by
    many chains).
43 *Old English Riddles*, p. ix.
44 P. 241.

notes that the poem demonstrates "its effects upon man, here good and joyous rather than bad," the bad effects being depicted in the riddle that precedes this one in the manuscript.[45]

The alcohol-related solutions have not received as much elaboration as have the arguments for a musical instrument, an idea prompted by the reference to *[d]ream* (joy/song) and by lines 11–12a, which depict the riddle object itself as being the one who is able to praise (*deman*) and declare (*meldan*), as opposed to the alcohol-induced men. Indeed, Laurence K. Shook took up Trautmann's 1894 suggestion, "harp," and argued that the riddle described the process of killing a tortoise and using its hollowed shell as an instrument.[46] However, Heidi Göbel and Rüdiger Göbel question whether or not such an instrument was ever used in England in their own discussion of the riddle as a "pattern-welded sword."[47] Their reading is interesting, but equally unprovable due to the riddle's vague descriptors, which could point to any number of manufacturing processes. More recently, Waltraud Ziegler has noted the riddle's similarities to a number of Latin enigmata, which result in his solution "parchment."[48]

Parchment enigmata are included in the collections of Tatwine and Eusebius, as well as the Bern riddles. Eusebius' *Enigma 32, De membrano*, in particular, emphasizes the words on the manuscript page using a living/dead motif similar to that of the ox/bull riddles: *Viua nihil loquimur, responsum mortua famur* (4) (Living we say nothing, but dead we speak a response). It makes a great deal of sense, of course, for the ox/bull riddles to be linked to those dealing with an object constructed from animal skin. Thus, Eusebius' reference to *Candida ... arua* (white fields) in line 3 is matched by Tatwine's reference to irrigating furrows in his *Enigma 5, De membrano*: *Frugiferos cultor sulcos mox irrigat undis;/Omnigenam nardi messem mea prata rependunt* (4–5) (A cultivator soon irrigates fertile furrows with waves; my meadows render a harvest of balsam of every kind).[49] However, perhaps most relevant, given this survey's focus on binding imagery, is Bern *Enigma 24, De membrana*:

---

45 *Riddles of the Exeter Book*, p. 135.
46 "Old-English Riddle 28."
47 "Solution of an Old English Riddle," p. 187.
48 "Ein neuer Losungsversuch."
49 Tatwine repeats this agricultural motif in the following poem, *Enigma 6, De penna*, which describes the pen that must furrow fields with its tears.

Lucrum uiua manens toto nam confero mundo
Et defuncta mirum praesto de corpore quaestum.
Vestibus exuta multoque uinculo tensa,
Gladio sic mihi desecta uiscera pendent.
Manibus me postquam reges et uisu mirantur,
Miliaque porto nullo sub pondere multa.

(Remaining alive, I provide profit for the entire world, and dead I furnish remarkable gain from my body. Deprived of garments and pressed by many chains, cut by a sword my innards hang down. Afterward kings admire me with hands and sight, and I carry many thousands with no weight.)

This poem moves from parchment-making to book-making, as Bitterli points out.[50] Building on Ziegler's suggestion, Bitterli argues that the Old English riddle may be solved as a "Biblical codex." He analyzes the poem and argues that the appositive past participles depict the steps involved in making first parchment and then a book.[51] Thus, *corfen* (cut), *sworfen* (rubbed) and *cyrred* (turned) relate to the preparation of the animal skin in a lime bath and *þyrred* (dried) and *bunden* (bound) relate to its mounting on a frame where it is stretched (*wunden*).[52] The skin is then *blæced* (bleached) and *wæced* (softened), and the parchment is *frætwed* (adorned) with writing and illumination and *geatwed* (equipped) with its binding.[53] The use of torture in an account of the making of a holy book is, furthermore, not as out of place as it might at first appear. Such affliction, as mentioned in chapter 1,[54] is an important component of martyr tales, "with their often drastic accounts of the physical harassments and grisly tortures."[55] Bitterli argues that this context should be mapped onto *Riddle 28*, whose subject "first endures a series of painful physical attacks and bodily tortures and yet afterwards carries the 'sound of living beings' inside."[56] In this way, what has before been considered the voice of John Barleycorn or the song of a musical instrument, becomes the word of God as conveyed through a holy book.

---

50 *Say What I Am Called*, p. 182.
51 Ibid., p. 184.
52 Ibid.
53 Ibid.
54 See pp. 38–9.
55 Bitterli, *Say What I Am Called*, p. 178.
56 Ibid., p. 181.

For our purposes, I might also point out that the tendency to depict holy people as servants of God lends further support to the reading of this riddle as "martyr/holy book." The holy book – produced by and therefore servant of humankind – would be nothing if it did not contain within it stories of people whose servitude to God set them apart from the everyday individual. Thus the portrayal of this mute object, which is able to offer praise (*deman*) and declare (*meldan*) after its death, can be linked to the other riddles that depict slavery and silence. In this case, because of the content of the codex, that silence is overthrown, and yet the riddle object never actually says a word.

In Elinor Teele's discussion of the *Exeter Book* riddles, she notes the tension caused by personifying objects and granting them speech when there remains an emphasis on their interaction with humans.[57] Because Old English poetry is fascinated by human experience, the natural world holds no meaning unless it is in contact with humans: "Within the hierarchy of usefulness, humans are placed in a position of power above the inanimate and animals, not only due to the fact that they were made in the image of God and possess the faculty of reason, but because they possess *cræft*."[58] The tendency of human beings to manipulate the world around them, according to the example of God, the creator, is presented differently in the riddles than in other Old English poetic texts. In the riddles, the exploitation of this power is often emphasized, and humans are shown to be in danger of having the objects they have created turn on them.[59] This uneasy power relationship is perhaps one of the reasons that the domestic and commonly used items depicted as riddle objects are firmly bound and controlled. These objects must be enslaved because, when granted voices and given the ability to express their point of view, they become dangerous to the human order, not unlike the imprisoned captives discussed in the previous chapter.

Elaine Tuttle Hansen's reading of the riddles similarly highlights this human focus, asserting that empathy with the riddle-object results in the understanding that "categorical distinctions between human and nonhuman, subject and object, self and other [are] perhaps flawed."[60] Such a questioning of identity ultimately leads to a rethinking of the place of

---

57 "Heroic Tradition," p. 202.
58 Ibid.
59 Ibid., p. 203.
60 *Solomon Complex*, p. 139.

humans in the social order and the world at large, while the recognition of the power of objects breaks down the categories of master/servant and victimizer/victim.[61] The fact that these representations of slaves depict them as independent from their masters, at least at an emotional level, is ironic considering the lack of independence that characterized the life of a slave in Anglo-Saxon England. If the riddles "teach that by manipulating objects in the phenomenal world, [...] human beings run the risk of having the powers they unleash turn against them,"[62] we have further reason to expect binding imagery to be present. In a poetic corpus that taps into human concern with its own instability and the instability of nature, the concept of binding offers some hope of security and protection. And yet, while poetic humans try and often succeed in binding, tying, and holding in place non-human animals, objects, and other people, the reality for the Anglo-Saxon world is that only God can effectively and permanently bind or unbind.

Servants in the Hall

Closely connected to the physical binding of enslaved figures in Old English poetry is the bond between lord and retainer. This relationship plays a key role in scholarly discussions of martial themes, and it is frequently articulated through the terminology of binding. Thus, Katherine O'Brien O'Keeffe's discussion of heroic literature emphasizes the relationship between lord and retainer with reference to loyalty as its "binding virtue."[63] Such loyalty is facilitated by gift-giving, a process that "created, symbolized, and confirmed the relationship between a man and his lord. The offer of a gift and its acceptance established a social relationship; the recipient of the largess placed himself in the debt of the donor and morally obliged[64] himself to requite the favor."[65] Gift-giving was, furthermore, not concerned with rewarding specific, one-time services; rather, it acted as "a challenge to match munificence and avoid shame by further service. Kings [...] depend on the potential wound charity can inflict to tighten the bonds of loyalty and fellowship."[66]

---

61 Ibid., p. 140.
62 Ibid.
63 "Heroic Values," p. 107.
64 The term "obligation," of course, derives from Latin *ligare* (to bind).
65 Abels, *Lordship and Military Obligation*, p. 31.
66 Berger and Leicester, "Social Structure as Doom," p. 47.

Reading these quotations, it is easy to see how the modern conceptual metaphor of social relationships as "bonds" may come to colour our interpretation of Old English poetry. Because this metaphorical sense of "bond" is conceptual – underlying not only our language but also our thought processes – critics must take extra care when looking at Old English equivalents. Thus, Stanley B. Greenfield's analysis of *The Wanderer* interprets the poem's use of binding imagery directly in relation to the lord-retainer relationship, which is also treated in the poem: "Instead of the bonds of the *comitatus*, the speaker enjoins the binding of thoughts (lines 13b, 18, 19–21); he finds that only sorrow and sleep *oft gebindaþ* (line 40b) the poor wretch, and that only the wintry waves are truly bound each to each: *ofer waþema gebind* (lines 24b–57a)."[67] This statement does not question that the lord-retainer relationship was imagined as a "bond" in the poetry, assuming instead that the Old English terminology directly reflects the modern sense. Greenfield is not alone here. Rosemary Greentree similarly invokes this social bond in her discussion of the phrase, *ofer waþema gebind*: "The idea of being bound within the encircling waves enhances the affecting paradox of the lonely exile, at liberty because he is bereft of the bonds of kinship and loyalty, an outcast enclosed in the limitless expanse of the sea."[68] Likewise, Irving refers to social bonds in his discussion of this poem: "The great bonds that hold society together and the self-discipline of the isolated individual are both associated with protective walls and enclosures."[69] Certainly the hall is bound in other texts[70] and the individual is bound by self-discipline here and elsewhere,[71] but does *The Wanderer* ever actually refer to such societal "bonds" between lord and retainer? Indeed, does any Old English poetry refer to this relationship as a "bond"? This question will be addressed below, in relation to several poems that both depict the lord-retainer relationship and employ the Old English terms, *bend* and *bindan*. In doing so, I argue that the sense of this diction is far more concrete and physical than the modern English usage,[72] indicating that the application of this metaphor to Old English poetic contexts represents a fundamental misunderstanding.

---

67 "Old English Elegies," p. 148.
68 "The Wanderer's Horizon," p. 309.
69 "Image and Meaning," p. 163.
70 See chapter 3, pp. 70–3.
71 See chapter 7, pp. 224–30.
72 See also the discussion of the physicality of binding and loosing sinners in chapter 5, pp. 125–7.

Excluding *The Wanderer*, which will be discussed in chapter 7, there are four poems that employ binding terminology in a lord-retainer context, each of which is fairly problematic: *Riddle 20* (sword), *Riddle 23* (bow), *The Metres of Boethius*, and *Riddle 3* (wind).[73] Given the playfulness of the genre, it is not surprising that most of these ambiguous instances occur in riddles. It is also not surprising that two of the three riddling instances of this possible binding/bond-play occur in descriptions of weapons, the most basic heroic implement.

Riddle 20's play with imagery of reproduction and violence means that it is best solved as *wæpen*, a term indicating both "sword" and "phallus."[74] However, for the sake of clarity and to differentiate it from other weapon riddles, I shall refer to the poem's solution as "sword." The opening of the poem reads:

> Ic eom wunderlicu wiht,   on gewin sceapen,
> frean minum leof,   fægre gegyrwed.
> Byrne is min bleofag,   swylce beorht seomað
> wir ymb þone wælgim   þe me waldend geaf,
> se me widgalum   wisað hwilum
> sylfum to sace.   Þonne ic sinc wege
> þurh hlutterne dæg,   hondweorc smiþa,
> gold ofer geardas.   Oft ic gæstberend
> cwelle compwæpnum.   Cyning mec gyrweð
> since ond seolfre   ond mec on sele weorþað;
> ne wyrneð wordlofes,   wisan mæneð
> mine for mengo,   þær hy meodu drincað,
> healdeð mec on heaþore,   hwilum læteð eft
> radwerigne   on gerum sceacan,
> orlegfromne.   (1–15a)

(I am a marvellous creature, shaped in conflict, dear to my lord, beautifully clothed. My mail-coat is variegated, likewise bright wire stands about the

---

73 Notably, *Beowulf*, the archetype of Old English heroic poetry, contains no instances of binding of this sort.

74 *Riddle 20* has also been solved as "falcon," "hawk," and "phallus," but "sword" maintains the most support. Fry, "Exeter Book Riddle Solutions," p. 23. Patrick Murphy argues that *wæpen*'s double meaning solves the problem of the woman's anger at the end of the poem. See *Unriddling the Exeter Riddles*, p. 214; as well as Niles, *Enigmatic Poetry*, pp. 137–9; Wehlau, *Riddle of Creation*, pp. 112–13; and Tanke, "Bachelor-Warrior," p. 413.

slaughter-gem that my ruler gave me, he who sometimes instructs me to go into a fight proudly. Then I carry treasure, throughout the clear day, the handiwork of smiths, gold in the courtyards. Often I kill soul-bearers with battle-weapons. The king clothes me with treasure and silver and honours me in the hall; he does not withhold words of praise, proclaims my nature to the company, where men drink mead, he holds me in confinement, again sometimes he allows me, travel-weary, to hasten in armour, battle-eager.)

The sword is clearly portrayed as a human companion to its owner through descriptions of its clothing and adornment: it is *fægre gegyrwed* (beautifully clothed) and carries treasure (*sinc wege*), *gold ofer geardas* (gold in the courtyards). Its lord is also explicitly stated as clothing it with *since ond seolfre* (treasure and silver), although, of course, the verb *gyrwan* used here and in line 2b carries multiple definitions. The sense "to adorn, ornament (something)"[75] is likely present here, as well as "to dress, clothe,"[76] with the text playing on the personified solution's object-status. In addition to clothing and adornment, the sword is also given other gifts by its lord: a *wælgim* (slaughter-gem) and the usual gift of rings at line 23b (*þe me hringas geaf*). These physical gifts are not all that the sword's lord bestows upon it; it also receives plenty of praise: *Cyning [...] mec on sele weorþað;/ne wyrneð wordlofes* (The king honours me in the hall; he does not withhold words of praise). Indeed, the weapon does appear to be *frean [sinum] leof* (dear [to his] lord). Thus, the lord is depicted as a gift-giver, and the sword is the retainer who receives the gifts.

The relationship that accompanies those gifts is also indicated in the poem, with a number of phrases outlining the sword's obedience to the lord and the lord's ability to dictate the actions of the sword. Thus, the sword's ruler sometimes *wisað* (instructs) it to fight proudly and later *læteð* (allows) it to fight. Furthermore, the middle of the poem reflects the sword's conundrum: if it continues to obey (*hyre*) its lord as it has done in the past, then it will be unable to have children:

> Ic me wenan ne þearf
> þæt me bearn wræce   on bonan feore,
> gif me gromra hwylc   guþe genægeð;
> ne weorþeð sio mægburg   gemicledu

---

75 *DOE*, s.v., sense 5.
76 Ibid., sense 2.

eaforan minum   þe ic æfter woc,
nymþe ic hlafordleas   hweorfan mote
from þam healdende   þe me hringas geaf.
Me bið forð witod,   gif ic frean hyre,
guþe fremme,   swa ic gien dyde
minum þeodne on þonc,   þæt ic þolian sceal
bearngestreona.   Ic wiþ bryde ne mot
hæmed habban,   ac me þæs hyhtplegan
geno wyrneð,   se mec geara on
bende legde;   forþon ic brucan sceal
on hagostealde   hæleþa gestreona.   (17b–31)

(I do not need to expect that a son should avenge me on the life of my killer if
an enemy should attack me in battle, nor will the race into which I was born
become increased by my children unless I must turn lord-less from the protector who gave me rings. Hence it is certain for me, if I obey my lord, take
part in battle, as I have already done with the thanks of my lord, then I must
forfeit the wealth of descendants. I must not have intercourse with a bride,
but he refuses me the pleasant play now, he who earlier laid bonds upon me;
therefore I must enjoy the treasure of warriors in celibacy.)

The children that the sword must forfeit are here depicted as another form
of wealth (*bearngestreona*) in a pun on the "treasure" and "offspring" senses
of *(ge)streon*,[77] as well as the "sword" and "phallus" senses of *wæpen*.
   It is in this discussion of the sword's inability to have children that language of binding is directly invoked. The sword is depicted as unable to
take a bride due to the command of its lord, *se mec geara on / bende legde*
(who earlier laid bonds upon me). At first glance, this passage appears to
be excellent evidence for the use of binding terminology in describing the
lord-retainer relationship: the sword-retainer is bound to serve the lord
who lays bonds upon him. Those bonds could easily refer to social ties
between lord and retainer.[78] This certainly appears to be how Irving reads
the phrase:

---

77 Bosworth and Toller, *Anglo-Saxon Dictionary*, s.v.
78 As mentioned in chapter 3, p. 89, several scholars read this passage as a possible refer-
    ence to falconry. See Shook, "Old English Riddle No. 20"; Nelson, "Old English

Sword's only relationship, and a very close one, is with his lord, who protects and controls him and who is apparently the one who first laid bonds on him long ago. This intense lord-retainer relationship is of course incessantly celebrated in heroic poetry, but here the poet seems to be pointing to its weaknesses and to what it does not provide. It is a bond forged only for the purpose of applying violence; the lord may keep such violence under his control, but he also preserves it for his occasional use. The bond allows no sexual life and no family.[79]

However, after consulting the other poetic collocations of *lecgan* (to lay) and *bend*, it becomes clear that every other case signals a physical binding. These collocations occur in *Christ and Satan* 536–8a (in which "heathens" lay the crown of thorns upon Christ), *Andreas* 1558–61a (which addresses Andreas' unjust imprisonment), *Deor* 4b–6 (in which Weland is burdened with constraints) and *Juliana* 518b–19 (in which the demon laments his binding at the hands of the saint).[80] Each of these examples demonstrates that bonds laid upon someone in Old English poetry carry connotations of physical confinement. This context is also significant because the collocation of *lecgan* and *bend* is restricted to poetry; bonds are never laid upon people in Old English prose. There are prose and gloss instances where binding is invoked in relation to rules,[81] obligation[82] or peace[83] but

---

Riddle 18 (20)"; and Stanley, "Heroic Aspects," p. 207. This solution involves a similar complex relationship of both service and ownership to "sword," and thus works equally well with the current reading.

79 "Heroic Experience," p. 206.

80 A final example from *Riddle 3* 10b–16 is treated below.

81 See *DOE*, s.v. *bend*, sense 1.b.ii.–b.

82 See *DOE*, s.v. *gebindan*, sense C.7.; and s.v. *bindan*, sense D.5.

83 See *DOE*, s.v. *gebindan*, sense A.6.-: "*gebindan tosomne* 'to join (people *acc.*) together (in harmony)'." Two instances that associate binding and peace occur in the Old English translation of Gregory's *Cura Pastoralis*. One is a quotation from Ephesians 4:3–4, invoking the *vinculum pacis* (bond of peace), and the second translates *ligare* to refer to God's love as a binding force. See *King Alfred's West-Saxon Version of Gregory's Pastoral Care*, 2:345, section 46, lines 17–19 and 1:253, section 36, lines 17–23. Two Ælfrician examples also build on this association, invoking *ðone bend þære soðan sibbe* (the bond of true peace) and the *broþerlican bend [...] þæt is þa soþan sibbe* (brotherly bond [...], which is true peace). See *Ælfric's Catholic Homilies, Second Series*, ed. Godden, p. 157, lines 242–4; and *First Series*, ed. Clemoes, p. 327, lines 47–9. This is the only Old English reference to social relationships as bonds not directly translated from a Latin text.

these are, notably, strongly influenced by Latin. Some of these examples, furthermore, demonstrate that the use of Old English binding words to translate Latin terms of obligation may stem from the sense of ensnarement and constraint present in these Latin texts.[84]

Returning to the sword riddle, such physical connotations are equally invoked in a similar statement of the lord's power to restrain the sword at line 13a: *healdeð mec on heaþore* (he holds me in confinement). Hence, it appears that the sword's binding does not work as evidence for the false trail (retainer) of the riddle, but rather as evidence for the solution (sword). Moving from a description of a retainer to a statement that implies this retainer has been tied up by his lord is *meant* to jar. It is meant to jar precisely because good lords do not tie up their retainers. And so this passage asks the question: What sort of retainer *do* you tie up? The answer is a sword.

Furthermore, because the lord in the poem has adorned the retainer with treasure and rings, the poem could be playing with the double meaning of *bend*, which can also translate as "band," "ribbon" or "ornament."[85] In doing so, the poem depicts both the literal physical ties of constraint (i.e., the sheathing of a sword or the tying of the sword onto a belt) and the adornment of precious metalwork. Thus, while this passage may seem ambiguous to a modern reader, the evidence from other Old English poetry indicates that the language of restraint here invoked should be taken fairly concretely. The poem depicts a relationship of respect, but also one of ownership. The fact that the owner of a sword can tie up his weapon, but a lord cannot do so to his retainer is key to reading the binding language in this poem. Hence, while there is some grey area – in that a relationship between lord and retainer is certainly being playfully invoked in this poem – the poem does not refer to the laying of a bond in

---

84 See *DOE*, s.v. *gebindan*, sense C.5.: "to oblige, bind (someone *acc.* by a confession, declaration, *mid* and *dat.*)." The example given is from Gregory's *Cura Pastoralis* (in which *gebindan* translates *ligare*); it relates to the holy Nathan's desire to trap King David with his own confession. *King Alfred's West-Saxon Version of Gregory's Pastoral Care*, 1:184/5, section 26, lines 21–4. See also *DOE*, s.v. *bend*, sense 1.b.i.c.i.: "glossing *obligatio* 'ensnaring, entangling' here, 'an evil device'." The example given is from Psalm 124:5 of the *Lambeth Psalter*, in which *on gebundennesse* and *to bændum* translate *obligationes* in the context of the evils done by *wyrcendum unrihtwisnesse* (workers of injustice). See Lindelöf, *Der Lambeth-Psalter*, p. 207.

85 Bosworth and Toller, *Anglo-Saxon Dictionary*, s.v. *bend*.

the modern metaphorical sense of a social tie. Indeed, it is not *a* bond, but bond*s* – in the plural – that are laid upon this retainer.

A similar binding is also invoked in *Riddle 23*, which has been solved quite conclusively as "bow."[86] This shorter, sixteen-line riddle reads:

Agof is min noma   eft onhwyrfed;
ic eom wrætlic wiht   on gewin sceapen.
Þonne ic onbuge,   ond me of bosme fareð
ætren onga,   ic beom eallgearo
þæt ic me þæt feorhbealo   feor aswape.
Siþþan me se waldend,   se me þæt wite gescop,
leoþo forlæteð,   ic beo lengre þonne ær,
oþþæt ic spæte,   spilde geblonden,
ealfelo attor   þæt ic ær geap.
Ne togongeð þæs   gumena hwylcum,
ænigum eaþe   þæt ic þær ymb sprice,
gif hine hrineð   þæt me of hrife fleogeð,
þæt þone mandrinc   mægne geceapaþ,
fullwered fæste   feore sine.
Nelle ic unbunden   ænigum hyran
nymþe searosæled.   Saga hwæt ic hatte.

(Wob is my name turned back; I am a wondrous creature, shaped in conflict. When I bend, and a poisonous sting travels from my bosom, I am very ready so that I send that deadly evil far away from me. When my ruler, he who arranged that torture, looses my limbs, I am longer than before, until I spit, corrupted by destruction, the terrible poison that I took in before. What I speak about here does not abate easily for each of men, if that which flies from my belly strikes him, so that he buys that evil drink with his strength, [pays] full compensation quickly with his life.[87] Unbound I will not obey anyone unless skilfully tied. Say what I am called.)

---

86 Fry, "Exeter Book Riddle Solutions," p. 23.

87 The term *full-wer* is a contested form. The *DOE* offers two readings of these lines depending on whether we take it to be a compound (meaning "compensation") or two separate words: "so that he pays for that evil drink with his strength, [pays] full compensation at once with his life," or, if the subject is *wer* (man) and *full* (cup) is the object of *geceapaþ*: "the man pays for that evil drink with his strength, [for] the cup at once with his life."

Riddle 23 has a beginning similar to *Riddle 20*, with the object declaring itself a wondrous creature *on gewin sceapen* (shaped in conflict), the same formulaic half-line whose only other poetic instance is line 1b of the sword riddle. However, this riddle focuses more on the bow's battle tactics than on the lord-retainer relationship; the bow is twice described as poisonous (*ætren/attor*) and three times as being involved in a terrible practice, the key terms being: *feorhbealo* (deadly evil), *wite* (torture) and *mandrinc* (evil drink). The poisonous nature of the bow may stem from the fact that yew is a poisonous plant. Indeed, Aldhelm's *Enigma 69, De taxo* describes yew as *pestiferam* (5) (deadly) and *venenatus* (6) (poisonous), implying that the plant was known to be dangerous in Anglo-Saxon England. This may come as a surprise, given Lenore Abraham's discussion of the bow and arrow's use in warfare as foreign to the Anglo-Saxons because yew was hard to come by.[88] According to Abraham, the foreign nature of yew led to the bow and arrow's association with the devil and with invaders like the Vikings.[89] Given that this particular weapon lacked the sword's association with heroic companionship, it is perhaps not out of place for *Riddle 23* to describe the bow in terms of the evil drinking and spewing of poison.[90]

Another Latin link to *Riddle 23* comes in the form of Tatwine's quiver-riddle, *Enigma 34, De faretra*, which associates the bow with fiery flames:

Omnes enim diris complent mea uiscera flammae
Nam me flamma ferox stimulis deuastat acerius
Vt pacis pia mox truculenter foedera frangam
Non tamen oblectat me sponte subire duellum.

(Flames, terrible indeed, fill all my insides, for a bold fire lays waste to me with sharp spurs so that, wildly, I soon break faithful/holy agreements of peace; nevertheless it does not delight me in myself to go to war.)

---

88 "Devil, the Yew Bow, and the Saxon Archer."

89 Ibid., 3, 9.

90 The bow, when used in heroic contexts, is generally described straightforwardly and without the extended metaphor that accompanies the sword. This may be due, in part, not only to the bow's rare use in martial contexts, but also to the nature of the two forms of combat. Because the sword is used in close combat, it is less likely to fail the warrior. However, arrows shot from afar may accidently go awry, as in *Beowulf* 2037–40b's reference to Hæðcyn shooting his brother. This practical concern exists in addition to the demonic association of arrows in Old English. See Hermann, "Varieties of Psychomachia," pp. 211–17; as well as *Andreas* 1048a, 1189b, 1331a; *Beowulf* 1741–7; *Christ II* 762–5; *Juliana* 384a, 404a; and *Solomon and Saturn I* 129–30.

The similarity between Tatwine's quiver of arrows and *Riddle 23*'s bow is interesting, although the association between the weapon and fire or poison may stem from any number of shared traditions. A notable difference, however, is the Latin poem's reluctance towards its use in war. Such reluctance is not present in *Riddle 23*'s eager weapon, even if it is in service to a lord who could not be more different from the benevolent owner of *Riddle 20*'s sword.

Indeed, the bow's lord is only explicitly referred to once in the poem: *Siþþan me se waldend, se me þæt wite gescop, / leoþo forlæteð* (6–7a) (When my ruler, he who arranged that torture, looses my limbs). This manipulation of the bow by its lord parallels the descriptions of the way the weapon was allowed or instructed to act in the sword riddle. Furthermore, the verb *scieppan* indicates not only that the torture or punishment has been arranged by the bow's lord, but also that the bow itself is a created or "shaped" object. As noted above (see chapter 3), binding is frequently invoked in contexts of construction in the Old English poetic corpus; by binding one thing into a new shape (often through a painful process in the riddles), humans demonstrate their ability as skilled creators. Here, the poem seems to refer not only to the object's shaping, but also to the shaping of the outcome of its use. And this outcome (torture/death) is linked to the opposite of binding, i.e., loosing. We have already seen how this pair is invoked in the context of the binding of the devil and the loosing of God and his followers;[91] however, in the present context, it is important to note that the connotations of loosing are somewhat ambiguous. The loosing of the creature's limbs seems to be a positive outcome for the bow, which is no longer constrained. Yet this loosing also leads to violence and torture, with the bow being a tool in the hands of a lord who puts it to a violent purpose. The poet is playing with the connotations of the pair, and, if loosing is both positive and negative in this case, the same ambiguity can be expected of binding.

In employing this imagery of binding, the poet reminds his/her audience that the riddle-solution does not refer to a human but to an object made by craft and skill. The final lines of the poem present us with a pun: *Nelle ic unbunden ænigum hyran / nymþe searosæled* (Unbound I will not obey anyone unless skilfully tied). At a literal level, the phrase refers to the actual stringing of a bow, which must be bound in order to shoot. However, it also indicates a relationship between the bow and its lord: the bow must

---

91 See chapter 5, pp. 125–56.

be bound for it to obey its lord. As with the sword riddle, these lines initially appear to be evidence for a lord-retainer "bond": the bow-warrior seems to be saying that it must form a metaphorical social bond with its lord in order to serve him properly.

With closer scrutiny, however, it becomes clear that this is more an image of enslavement than of the servitude of a retainer, not least because the bow's service is not matched by gifts from its lord. The bow's retainer status is also called into question by the descriptor *spilde geblonden* (corrupted by destruction), which is hardly a trait of the heroic warrior. Furthermore, the bow's lord is also only referred to once as *se waldend* (the ruler). This term, while often applied to God and lordly rulers, carries connotations of power and control, stemming as it does from *wealdan* (to rule/control/command). Although the bow is clearly invoked as an object of service, the negative connotations running throughout the poem would seem to indicate a master-slave relationship – and thus one of more physical bondage – rather than a lord-retainer one. This assertion is further supported by the implication that torture is involved.

As discussed above, riddle objects are frequently described as painfully enslaved and in bonds. Prime examples include the plough of *Riddle 21*, and the components of *Riddle 52*'s flail. These and other riddles demonstrate once again John D. Niles's application of "raw" nature and "cooked" culture to the riddles.[92] Because the raw is the free, wild creature in nature, and the cooked is the enslaved, bound, and often mutilated product, riddles lend themselves well to metaphors of slavery.

The fact that the bow is *searosæled* (skilfully tied) also indicates a power-relationship rather than a reciprocal one. *Searo* appears in myriad contexts, with definitions ranging from: "art," "skill," and "contrivance" to "device," "snare," and treachery," as well as "that which is contrived with art," "machine," "engine [of war]," and "armour," "equipment" or "arms."[93] When compounded with forms of *bend* or *bindan*, it often refers to both an "artistic clasp" and an object that is "cunningly fastened."[94] *Searo* also appears frequently in collocations with *bend* and *bindan*, as in *Andreas* 107b–9 and 1395b–7a (in which Matthew and Andreas are described as having been cunningly entrapped by the Mermedonians),[95] in

---

92 See chapter 1, p. 33.
93 Bosworth and Toller, *Anglo-Saxon Dictionary*, s.v.
94 Hall, *Concise Anglo-Saxon Dictionary*, s.v. *searobend, searobunden*.
95 See chapter 5, pp. 131, 135.

Daniel 434–5 (in which the wise counselors bound by Nebuchadnezzar are freed), and *Riddle 56* (loom) 4b–6a (in which the violent loom is skilfully bound).[96] In each of these cases, the collocation of *searo* and *bindan/bend* indicates an environment of physical torture, punishment, and constriction.

There are a further three collocations of *bend/bindan* and *searo* which refer to the construction of objects. The contexts are the bound treasure in *Riddle 55*,[97] *Beowulf*'s description of Heorot's bonds,[98] and Grendel's skilfully bound *glof*.[99] In all three cases, the use of *searo* indicates great or mysterious craftsmanship, with an implied power-relationship of creator-object similar to that of owner-object discussed in relation to the sword riddle above. Furthermore, these three examples arguably all direct our attention to violence, if we accept Niles's reading of the riddle as "sword-rack," Lori Ann Garner's point about Heorot becoming a prison under Grendel's reign, and my reading of Grendel's *glof* as a device for constraining his victims.

As for *sælan*, "to fasten with a cord," "restrain," or "confine,"[100] and *asælan*, "to bind, fetter, ensnare,"[101] these verbs appear in collocations with *searo* in two other poems: *Exodus* 469b–71a (in which the Egyptians' might is skilfully bound and fettered in death) and *Beowulf* 2763b–4a (in which Wiglaf sees the twisted gold arm-rings in the dragon's hoard). Elsewhere, *asælan* is used to indicate the bonds of sorrow and sin.[102]

Overall, when *bend/bindan/-sælan* and *searo* are invoked together there are two sets of connotations: that of hostile bondage, and that of cleverness and artistic skill in constructing material objects. Both of these connotations are present in the bow riddle and both are appropriate. What is not appropriate here is the lord-retainer bond. Rather than an example of such a metaphorical social bond, *Riddle 23* represents an instance of what Irving describes as a "draftee riddle."[103] His example is a harmless tree, which is felled and turned into a weapon: "It must then go through a stage of being terribly wounded and bound as a captive, before

---

96 See chapter 1, pp. 27–46.
97 See lines 3–4, and chapter 1, pp. 44–5
98 See lines 771–5a, and chapter 3, pp. 71–3.
99 See lines 2085b–88, and chapter 3, pp. 83–90.
100 Bosworth and Toller, *Anglo-Saxon Dictionary*, s.v. *sælan*.
101 *DOE*, s.v. *asælan*.
102 See *Elene* 1242b–4; *Genesis A* 2196b–7a.
103 "Heroic Experience," p. 207.

it can become the cause of fear to others."[104] While the origin of the bow is not made explicit in this riddle, its use certainly sets it alongside the other draftee riddles.

Finally, the evocation of both binding and artistic skill points towards the poet's own artistry in constructing the riddle. As Teele argues, the reference "to the skilful twining might also be the poet's self-congratulation on creating a riddle with so many ancillary allusions. The skill, therefore, is not in the Bow, but in the poet. It is also a direct challenge to the audience: can any unbind this skilfully twined riddle?"[105] The poem, therefore, seems more concerned with craft than companionship, while its wordplay indicates an overlap between the language of binding present in descriptions of constructed objects and that of the physical binding of slavery.

In turning from the sword and bow riddles to *The Metres of Boethius* and *Riddle 3* (wind/storm), we are presented with a very different context. Here, human relationships are mimicked, but through references to the elements and the creation of the cosmos, recalling the personifications of nature discussed in chapter 4. In these examples, Old English poetry seizes upon the biblical tradition of depicting God as an architect who binds and joins elements together,[106] and emphasizes also God's ability to tame, restrain, and rule the cosmos. Through this representation of God as a ruler, the heavenly lord appears to parallel the earthly lord.

Metre 20, in particular, demonstrates this playing out of the lord-retainer relationship with regard to God and the elements:

> Habbað þeah þa feower   frumstol hiora,
> æghwilc hiora   agenne stede,
> þeah anra hwilc   wið oðer sie
> miclum gemenged   and mid mægne eac
> fæder ælmihtiges   fæste gebunden,

---

104 Ibid.

105 "Heroic Tradition," p. 90.

106 Wehlau touches on this idea in relation to her discussion of Creation as a binding or synthesis. She argues that Genesis 1:6–7's description of separating elements "is not as far removed from binding as it might appear since the elements once separated must be restrained or bound in order to keep them from returning to a chaotic mixture." See her *Riddle of Creation*, p. 33. See also the following biblical passages: Psalm 101:26, Proverbs 8:27, Job 38:4–6, as well as the Old English poetic depictions of God building the universe in *Genesis A* 144b–50a and *Caedmon's Hymn* 5–6.

gesiblice,   softe togædre
mid bebode þine,   bilewit fæder,
þætte heora ænig   oðres ne dorste
mearce ofergangan   for metodes ege,
ac [geþweorod] sint   ðegnas togædre,
cyninges cempan,   cele wið hæto,
wæt wið drygum,   winnað hwæðre.   (63–74)

(Nevertheless each of the four have their proper station, their own place, although each of them may be greatly mixed with the other and also, by the might of the almighty father, bound fast, peaceably, gently together by your decree, merciful father, so that none of them dared to go over the other's boundary because of fear of the lord, but the thanes are made to agree, the champions of the king, cold with heat, wet with dry, yet they compete.)

These lines expand significantly upon both the Old English prose version and the Latin of Book 3, Metre 9:

Ælcum þara þu gesettest his agene sunderstowe, and þeah ælc is wið oðre [gemenged] and sibsumlice gebunden mid þinum bebode, swa þæt heora nan oðres mearce ne ofereode, and se cile [geþwærode] wið ða hæto and þæt wæt wið þam drygium. (166–70)[107]

(For each of them you established its own separate place, and nevertheless each is mixed with the others and peaceably bound by your decree, so that none of them went over the other's boundary, and the cold was made to agree with the heat and the wet with the dry.)

Tu numeris elementa ligas, ut frigora flammis,
arida conveniant liquidis, ne purior ignis
evolet aut mersas deducant pondera terras.   (10–12)[108]

(You bind the elements to [their] positions, so that the cold places may come together with flames, the dry lands with liquids, in case purer fire should fly away or weights draw down the immersed lands.)

---

107 The metre is equivalent to the second half of the B-text's prose chapter 33, in Godden and Irvine, *Old English Boethius*, 1:315–16.
108 *De Consolatione Philosophiae*, p. 80.

Perhaps the most striking difference between these three versions is the Old English poetic reference to the elements as the king's *ðegnas* (thanes) and *cempan* (champions), implying fairly explicitly that they are God's retainers. However, the relationship between God and the elements is again a relationship of power and control, something that is indicated by the language of restraint and the imagery of imprisonment. The elements are *fæste gebunden* (bound fast), a common description of imprisonment, *þætte heora ænig oðres ne dorste/mearce ofergangan for metodes ege* (so that none of them dared to cross the other's boundary out of fear of the creator). The sense of binding is physical here – they are held apart and in place by God, the cosmic ruler. The implication may be that the elements are prisoners of war, something that a further reference in the *Metres of Boethius* implies.

This second reference to the binding of the elements occurs later in *Metre 20*, this time in the context of fire alone:

Hafað fæder engla   fyr gebunden
efne to þon fæste   þæt hit fiolan ne mæg
eft æt his eðle   þær þæt oðer fyr
up ofer eall þis   eardfæst wunað.   (153–6)

(The father of angels has bound fire precisely so fast that it may not return to its homeland where that other fire, above all this, remains firmly fixed.)

Although the diction differs, the prose describes a similar binding: *Þu gebunde þæt fyr mid swiðe unanbindenlicum racentum þæt hit ne mæg cuman to his agenum earde, þæt is to þam mæstan fyre ðe ofer us is, þy læs hit forlæte þa eorðan* (206–9)[109] (You bound that fire with exceedingly unloosable chains, so that it may not come to its own land, that is, to the greatest fire which is over us, in order that it should not forsake the earth). Interestingly, the prose and poetic passages both represent an expansion of the Latin, which only mentions binding once in the context discussed above. The fire that is singled out for binding here is once again invoked in relation to imprisonment, with the implication being that fire desires

---

109 Godden and Irvine, *Old English Boethius*, p. 317.

escape but is unable to effect it.[110] Furthermore, the fact that fire's *eðle* (homeland) is not the place where it is bound carries implications of foreign conquest, and with that, slavery. Thus, fire is in some sense a prisoner of God, while at the same time his retainer. Fire, like the bow, is a draftee.

Mixed metaphors relating to prisoners and retainers also appear in *Riddle 3*.[111] This riddle has a variety of proposed solutions, but "wind" and "storm" are both the most popular and those supported by Krapp and Dobbie, Williamson, and Muir.[112] The riddle is lengthy, but it is the opening passage that relates to binding and imprisonment:

> Hwilum mec min frea   fæste genearwað,
> sendeð þonne   under salwonges
> bearm þone bradan,   ond on bid wriceð,
> þrafað on þystrum   þrymma sumne,
> hæste on enge,   þær me heord siteð
> hruse on hrycge.   Nah ic hwyrftweges
> of þam aglace,   ac ic eþelstol
> hæleþa hrere;   hornsalu wagiað,
> wera wicstede,   weallas beofiað,
> steape ofer stiwitum.   Stille þynceð
> lyft ofer londe   ond lagu swige,
> oþþæt ic of enge   up aþringe,
> efne swa mec wisaþ   se mec wræde on
> æt frumsceafte   furþum legde,
> bende ond clomme,   þæt ic onbugan ne mot
> of þæs gewealde   þe me wegas tæcneð.   (1–16)

---

110 Interestingly, *Riddle 50* (fire) contains a reference that could be construed as binding: *Forstrangne oft / wif hine wrið* (4b–5a) (a woman often wraps around/ties him, the very strong one).

111 The third section of *Riddle 1*, according to Williamson's numbering. See also Bern *Enigma 41*, *De vento*, which depicts the wind as unbindable.

112 *Exeter Book*, p. 321; *Old English Riddles of the Exeter Book*, p. 127; and *Exeter Anthology*, p. 574. Other solutions include "sun," "hurricane," "atmosphere," "apocalyptic storm," "cross," "revenant," "spirit," "supernatural force," "land earthquake," "storm at sea," and "thunderstorm"; see Fry, "Exeter Book Riddle Solutions," p. 22. The majority of the solutions accept that this riddle is concerned with a powerful element of nature. Indeed, Michael Lapidge goes as far as to link the first three riddles with the Stoic conception of *pneuma* or cosmic breath described in Seneca's *Naturales quaestiones*, a work that he maintains would have been familiar to many learned Anglo-Saxons. See "Stoic Cosmology," p. 15.

(Sometimes my lord confines me firmly, drives me under the broad lap of the fertile plains, and pushes me to a halt, he restrains some of my power in darkness, violently in confinement, where my keeper, earth, sits on my back. I have no escape from that oppression, but I shake the dwelling place of men; the gabled halls wobble, the homes of men, the walls quake, steep over the householders. The air over the land seems still and the ocean is silent, until I burst forth from my confinement, even as he instructs me, he who first laid fetters upon me at creation, bonds and chains, so that I might not bend from the power that shows me my path.)

Here again we have the laying of bonds in a collocation of *lecgan* and *bend*. These bonds are clearly physical ones, since *bend* appears alongside *clam* (chain), with *wræd* (fetter) occurring two lines above.

In this poem, the lord, God, makes a prisoner of wind, with the implication that, should it be released, it will wreak havoc upon humanity. After a description of a storm later in the poem, the wind refers to itself as: *meahtum gemagnad mines frean* (66) (subdued by the might of my lord) – *min frea* also being the term used to denote God in line 1a – and as a *þrymful þeow* (67a) (powerful servant/slave). Thus, the wind, like the elements in *The Metres of Boethius*, seems to be under the command of God, although whether as a retainer or as a slave is not made explicit. The confinement to which the wind is consigned is, however, described through characteristic prison terminology. Twice the riddle subject speaks of being *on enge* (5a, 12a) (in confinement), the adjectival form of which (*engu*) frequently describes narrowness and confined spaces, and hell in particular.[113] Likewise, *-nearwian*, along with its nominal, adjectival, and adverbial forms, is also a typical descriptor of prisons and hell, and carries the meanings "to narrow, straiten, constrain, confine, oppress, afflict."[114] This confining is done *fæste* (firmly), a term that often accompanies binding terminology, whether it be in relation to the construction of a building or the holding of a creature in chains. Together, this diction demonstrates that the wind's prison is narrow, tight, and the element's oppression (*aglace*) is firmly maintained.

Another characteristic of this narrow prison is its darkness, which makes prisons and hell so oppressive. God is depicted as restraining (*þrafað*) the

---

113 *DOE*, s.v. *enge*, sense 1.a.i.
114 Bosworth and Toller, *Anglo-Saxon Dictionary*, s.v. *ge-nearwian*.

wind's power (*þrymma*) *on þystrum* (in darkness). This term is frequently used in Old English religious poetry and prose; a search of the *DOE Corpus* yields 299 instances of *ðeostru* (darkness) and related adjectives and adverbs, the vast majority of which occur in Christian contexts.[115] This instance, however, does not describe an actual prison, but reveals the riddling tendency to play with language and boundaries. The narrow confines and dark spaces of the wind's imprisonment are natural ones: *me heord siteð / hruse on hrycge* (my keeper, earth, sits on my back). Given that the prison-guard is earth, both the darkness and the narrowness are explained: the wind is trapped under the ground.

Teele associates the wind's imprisonment with slavery and argues that the imagery "evoke[s] both Satan and also the general theme of bondage that runs through the *Riddles*."[116] She notes that the "devilish" are not the only ones to be constricted like this, maintaining that there is an indication in the poem that "the poet sympathises with the Wind/Storm's position, as in its elegiac lament: *Nah ic hwyrftweges / of þam aglace*, 'I have no escape from that misery.'"[117] As the examples from *The Metres of Boethius* demonstrate, the cosmic nature of the elements means that descriptions of them and their relation to God often switch back and forth between imagery of lord and retainers, master and slaves, keeper and prisoners. The inability or unwillingness of Old English poets to capture the elements using one metaphorical tradition only speaks to their great power – one that is above human control.

In a human world obsessed with, but unable to attain, stability and safe boundaries, it is important to acknowledge that "the elements in their natural state are constantly battling, and are only restrained by God. When free to follow their natural courses, a chaotic mixing occurs."[118] Storms, as

---

115 There are four instances in poetic passages that are not overtly Christian, including descriptions of a thief in the darkness (*Maxims II* 42a; and *Riddle 47* 4a) – although the thief in the night is also a common Biblical motif (noted examples include 1 Thessalonians 5:2, 2 Peter 3:10, Revelation 3:3, Luke 12:39, and Job 24:14). The term is also used once in relation to Grendel waiting in the darkness (87b) and once of Beowulf's dark thoughts (2332a), yet even here we may read Grendel as an enemy of God (as is emphasized throughout the poem) and the dark thoughts in relation to the idea that Beowulf has offended God, which is mentioned in the lines above this statement (2329–31a).

116 "Heroic Tradition," p. 117.

117 Ibid.

118 Wehlau, *Riddle of Creation*, p. 67.

an embodiment of disorder, represent this chaos in that they unbind works of human construction.[119] It is because of their ability to unbind that the elements must themselves be bound, although God, of course, has the power to unleash them when he chooses to. *Riddle 3* is the only riddle instance where nature is depicted as bound in order to keep it confined, rather than to harness its power for human purposes. This may reflect the fact that, while the riddles generally depict binding in terms of slavery or servitude, wind and storms were not harvested for any human purposes, and thus did not bear an association to the downtrodden slave. Rather, wind's exceptional power makes it both the noble servant and unwilling prisoner of God. The binding of the elements in both *Riddle 3* and *Metre 20* is thus a method of creating order out of chaos. However, the ability of God's creation to return to chaos is an ever-present concern: "Just as the cosmos is the supreme structure, so the broken cosmos is the supreme ruin, the return to the disorder of primordial chaos."[120] The relationship between God and his creation is thus a much more powerful and controlling one than that between a human lord and retainer or owner and object.

Taken as a whole, the weapon riddles and poetic descriptions of elements outlined above refer to relationships between two figures, one powerful and the other in service to the first. In this, they gesture towards the relationship between lords and retainers. However, in their use of binding terminology, the poems refer to the concretely negative bonds of slavery and imprisonment or the concretely positive bonds of construction. In other words, they refer to actual, physical bonds, but not to metaphorical social bonds. We can relate this back to the formulaic language of binding in the type-scenes discussed in previous chapters. Indeed, imagery of slavery and servitude gestures towards the conventionally constrictive binding applied elsewhere to prison, hell, and even winter. Thus, binding is recognized as integral to the structure and content of Old English poetry, which speaks to an Anglo-Saxon fascination with control and (in)stability.

The significance of the physicality of binding in contexts of servitude is that, despite the emphasis placed upon the lord-retainer bond in scholarship, the poetry does not actually refer to such relationships using this

---

119 Ibid., p. 53.
120 Ibid., p. 54.

metaphor. Although in modern English the metaphorical connotations have taken over when we refer to a social "bond," Old English binding terminology was much more physically grounded. Indeed, it is possible that *bend* and *bindan* had not yet developed the same semantic range that our modern equivalents possess. Hence, while in modern English we may refer to the "bond" that existed between lord and retainer, Old English poetry does not. And if we continue to allow our conceptions of what constitutes a "bond" to dictate our readings of Old English texts, significant insights into Anglo-Saxon constructions of the world run the risk of being lost in translation.

PART III

Patterns and Nets: Experiencing the Internal and the Abstract

7 The Body and Mind

Given the anthropocentric view of the world that the preceding analyses of object-construction and physical constriction have made evident, it is unsurprising that such imagery is also applied to the internal ties governing human life. Like objects whose structural bonds hold them together, the body itself is imagined as an interwoven entity in Old English. Never simply a lump of flesh, bodies are depicted as systems of connected muscles, joints, and bones, prompting Raymond P. Tripp, Jr to coin the term "knot-body."[1] Tripp addresses the multiple ways in which bonds and binding are applied within *Beowulf*, evoking the work of Mircea Eliade whose symbolist approach focuses on the magico-religious aspects of binding in archaic literature and culture.[2]

One of Eliade's most relevant contributions is his demonstration of the conflicting uses of magico-religious bonds and knots, which functioned as both benefit and detriment to humans.[3] Thus, knots both cause illness and death and protect against them, with the essential aspect of magico-medical rituals being "the orientation that they give to the power that resides in any kind of binding, in every act of 'tying.'"[4] This is a useful analogy to the multiple and sometimes opposing approaches to binding in Old English poetry, where similar formulaic diction is applied to both construction and constriction. However, we need not read the idea of the "knot-body" as stemming from magic or ritual. Given both the martial economy that is

1 Tripp, "Language, Archaic Symbolism, and the Poetic Structure of *Beowulf*," p. 9.
2 *Images and Symbols.*
3 Ibid., p. 112.
4 Ibid.

espoused in a fair number of texts, as well as the rich vocabulary of wounds and wounding in Old English,[5] it is safe to say that the Anglo-Saxons were familiar with bodily injury – a familiarity which could well have led to a conventional way of speaking about the inner workings of the body based on observation of its mechanics. Indeed, although amputation was likely fairly rare,[6] witnesses to deep wounds or loss of limb (whether in warfare, as a punitive measure or by accident) would be exposed to the fibrous nature of human tissue. Furthermore, given that wounds and injuries require wrapping and binding,[7] wordplay with the positive and negative extremes of both external and internal binding is unsurprising. This chapter in particular looks not to the external binding of the body by those who wish to harm it, but to the way it functions as an entity whose internal connections are essential to human life.

These internal connections are, in turn, vulnerable to afflictions whose description frequently makes use of a set of diction similar to that which describes the bonds that hold the "knot-body" together. If those bonds were constructive, then the afflicting bonds are constrictive, echoing the negative depictions of slavery and imprisonment. The afflictions that commonly invoke similar binding imagery include disease, poverty, hunger, sleep, sorrow, alcohol, old age, and death. These metaphorical fetters participate in several formulas and collocations, indicating their interchangeability, especially in a system that views the body and mind holistically. This chapter will address first constructive bodily bonds, before turning to discussions of disease and other common bodily and mental constrictions.

---

5 See *TOE* 02.08.04.01 (a wound). Common to poetry are simplexes and compounds utilizing the nominal forms: *benn, bite, dolg, sar, wund.*

6 Cameron, *Anglo-Saxon Medicine*, p. 173.

7 Binding verbs occur frequently in this context in prose medical texts. See *DOE*, s.v. *bindan*, senses B.2., B.3., C.2; s.v. *gebindan*, senses A.3., B.2.-B.2.a.; s.v. *gebunden*, sense B.1.b. References to *-wriðan* (to wrap around/tie) are also common in medical texts, with a search of the *DOE Corpus* yielding over sixty occurrences. References to medical binding are less prolific in poetry, but see *Beowulf* 2982; Ælfric's *Natale sanctorum quadraginta militum*, in *Lives of Saints*, 1:252, line 222; as well as his *Vita sancti Martini episcopi et confessoris Anglicae*, in *Lives of Saints*, 2:256, lines 569–73; *Depositio sancti Cuthberhti episcopi*, in *Catholic Homilies, Second Series*, ed. Godden, p. 82, line 42; and his homily, *Nativitas sanctae Mariae virginis*, in *Angelsächsische Homilien und Heiligenleben*, p. 47, line 558.

Sinew-bonds

There is a certain degree of overlap between terms used for sinews, ligaments, and tendons in Old English poetry.[8] Of the two terms invoked in
poetry, *æder* appears more often in prose.[9] *Seonu*, however, has a higher
poetic profile,[10] with eight references – all of which are focused on illness
or loss of life caused by injury to the body. These sinew terms frequently
collocate with semantically related verbs indicating unlocking, breaking or
loosing,[11] slitting,[12] and bursting.[13]

The instance of *seonu* occurring in *Deor* is particularly controversial,
not least because the poem itself has proven hard to interpret.[14] The poem's first stanza, which has caused a great deal of scholarly debate due to
the inexact definition of several key terms, reads as follows:

> Welund him be wurman   wræces cunnade,
> anhydig eorl   earfoþa dreag,
> hæfde him to gesiþþe   sorge ond longaþ,
> wintercealde wræce;   wean oft onfond,
> siþþan hine Niðhad on   nede legde,
> swoncre seonobende   on syllan monn.   (1–6)

---

8 According to the *TOE* (02.04.05.06), sinews, tendons and ligaments can be referred
   to by *seono* (commonly appearing in both poetry and prose), as well as *æder* (with the
   DOE citing ca. 150 occurrences taking on a variety of related and unrelated meanings,
   including "veins"). Less common and restricted to prose are: *cnyttels, streng, wælt* and
   wealdweaxe.

9 Poetic instances where *æder* refers to "veins" occur in *Beowulf* 742b; *Juliana* 478a;
   and Ælfric's *Vita sancti Martini episcopi et confessoris Anglicae*, in *Lives of Saints*, 2:278,
   line 962.

10 *Andreas* 1406a, 1425a; *Beowulf* 817b; *Deor* 6a; *Fortunes of Men* 19a; and *Soul and Body
   II* 57a, 68a, and 105a (every instance of which collocates with *-slitan*). *Æder* has only
   two poetic occurrences in *Beowulf* 743b and *Juliana* 478a.

11 *Tolucan* and *gebrecan*: *Andreas* 1404; *toslupan*: *Andreas* 1425a.

12 *-Slitan*: *Soul and Body II* 57a, 68a, and 104b.

13 *Onspringan*: *Beowulf* 817b.

14 *Deor* has been discussed as an elegy, an incantation or charm, a self-reflexive work
   of poetry, and a survival of a different, Germanic poetic form. For work on the
   form, thematic stock, and genre of *Deor*, see Bloomfield, "Form of *Deor*"; Tuggle,
   "Structure of 'Deor'"; Condren, "Deor's Artistic Triumph"; Frankis, "*Deor* and *Wulf
   and Eadwacer*"; and Klinck, *Old English Elegies*, pp. 43–4. The content of the stanzas
   themselves is as disputed as the form and function of the poem because it refers to
   mythological and legendary figures, some of whose traditions have been lost.

(Weland knew misery among snakes, the resolute hero endured hardships, had sorrow and longing as his companions, winter-cold misery; often he received woe, since Niðhad laid constraints upon him, supple sinew-bonds on the better man.)

The description here is of the legendary, lame smith, Weland, who is bound both literally and metaphorically when he is taken into King Niðhad's service. The key image for this study is that of the *seonobende* (sinew-bonds), with which Weland is constrained. In the past this compound has been emended to *seonobenne* (sinew-wounds), a form that is attested in *Fortunes of Men* 19a. However, L. Whitbread makes a good case for the retention of the manuscript form on phonological grounds.[15] There is also a contextual argument for retaining this form because, as we have seen in chapter 6, collocations of *lecgan* and *bend* are attested elsewhere. An interesting parallel also occurs in *Riddle 12*'s reference to binding *sellan men* (4b) (better men), which likely refers to slaves taken in conquest.[16] Indeed, it is tempting to read this reference in *Deor* as an allusion to the ox/bull riddle (which appears not far after it in *The Exeter Book*), with Weland representing precisely the sort of enslaved *syllan monn* referred to in that riddle – part of a tradition with a demonstrably wide circulation.[17]

Yet retaining the manuscript reading poses the problem of just what these sinew-bonds are: actual fetters or a metaphor for Weland's hamstringing? One scholar argues that they represent fetters made from animal sinews, which are used to bind Weland.[18] Taking *nede* as abstract "constraints" rather than concrete "fetters," he maintains that the "interpretation of *seonobende* as 'sinew-bonds, i.e. cut sinews' depends for its viability on the reading of *nede* 'fetters', and once this is arrived at it becomes a metaphorical variation of a concrete statement. But if *nede* is taken in an abstract sense, *seonobende* must be understood in a concrete sense instead: that is, 'bonds made of sinew'."[19] What this reading fails to take into account is the tendency for words to work on multiple levels in Old

---

15 "Binding of Weland," p. 17.

16 See chapter 6, pp. 160–1.

17 Ibid., pp. 159–65.

18 Stephens, "Weland and a Little Restraint." Others read the compound as referring to fetters that are applied to Weland's sinews; see Klinck, *Old English Elegies*, p. 159; Whitbread, "Binding of Weland," p. 18.

19 Stephens, "Weland and a Little Restraint," pp. 373–4.

English poetry. The *nede* could well be both literal and metaphorical bonds, as could the *seonobende*.

Reading this compound as a reference to the metaphorical shackling of Weland's movement through hamstringing – a well-known part of the myth – is not uncommon, an interpretation supported by its portrayal both in the Old Norse *Völundarkviða* and in the depiction of Weland on the Franks Casket.[20] Anne L. Klinck approaches this suggestion tentatively, noting that, while the motif of the lame smith is ancient, the Old English poem does not explicitly refer to such an injury.[21] However, Whitbread embraces it enthusiastically, arguing that mere fettering is not a drastic enough form of imprisonment: "A much more severe and remarkable device was used. By the severing of tendons in one of his legs, Weland was made on the spot a permanent captive, who still had the use of his skilled arms which had made him so desirable a prisoner."[22] He argues further that the lasting nature and inescapability of laming is what provides the "seemingly colossal element of difficulty" that is so thematically central to the poem.[23]

There is certainly traditional evidence for the hamstringing of this legendary figure, and the poetic artistry of *Deor* allows for the possibility that the poet may be employing the metaphor of physical bonds to indicate the severed tendons of the hero, and thus his permanent disabling. As noted above, *seonu* was commonly associated with severing in the poetry. If such is the case here, the text provides an excellent example of the "knot-body," which is here bound together by sinews and fettered by their improper functioning. However, the metaphor is even more complicated than at first glance because what it entails is the binding – thus, the tying, constricting, and ultimately connecting – of the body through the severing and disconnecting of part of it. Like the final lines of *Wulf and Eadwacer*, what should have been joined is torn apart. This is not an untying or loosing of a bond but rather a shearing through, which acts to bind the body precisely because it is no longer bound by the sinews that should hold it together. Of course, the poet could well be attempting to invoke both the

---

20 Whitbread, "Binding of Weland," pp. 18–19. This approach is maintained by Condren who argues that the "sinewy designs on his artifacts (cf. *be wurman*) match the carved sinews of his legs (cf. *swoncre seonobende*)"; "Deor's Artistic Triumph," p. 66.
21 *Old English Elegies*, pp. 159–60.
22 "Binding of Weland," p. 18.
23 Ibid.

literal and metaphorical bodily bonds of fettering and hamstringing simultaneously through clever wordplay. However, even if the *seonobende* are Weland's sinews, bound by fetters, rather than metaphorical bondage of hamstringing, the importance of the interwoven nature of the body is still evident here. This reference shows that by targeting the sinews, the entire body may be controlled.

Binding and Disease

If *Deor*'s *seonobende* are indeed the bonds that hold the body together, then they offer an interesting counterpoint to the imagery of illness damaging internal bodily bonds. Representations of disease are particularly interesting because they participate in two different but related sets of formulaic diction. One refers conventionally to the binding of the body with pain and suffering, while the second turns convention on its head by referring to disease's attack on the body as the unlocking of a hoard.[24] Other formulaic uses relate to hoards of speech and knowledge that are unlocked by a human or divine agent. Yet, in *Guthlac B*, the agent of disease unlocks not knowledge, but the life-hoard, thus having the profoundly negative effect of unbinding and killing the body. This section will focus on these two quite different, even contradictory, approaches to disease – essentially as *both* binder *and* looser.

Most scholarly discussions of disease in Anglo-Saxon England do not relate to the sorts of descriptions evident in the poetic corpus. Certain causes, symptoms, and cures are available for critical analysis because of the excellent array of vernacular and Latin medical literature that survives from the period, most of which is prose.[25] Yet, for the most part (with the exception of the *Metrical Charms*), descriptions of disease in poetry tend to be vague; they do not generally refer to specific symptoms, causes or theories of illness, and, since the cures mentioned are often miracles, the passages that do touch upon disease usually focus on something other than the physical. We can draw a parallel here with the discussion of

---

24 See Jagger, "Body, Text and Self," pp. 175–81.
25 For more information on Anglo-Saxon views of illness, see Barley, "Anglo-Saxon Magico-Medicine"; Cameron, *Anglo-Saxon Medicine*; Lee, "Body and Soul"; Meaney, "Anglo-Saxon View of the Causes of Illness"; and Neville, *Representations of the Natural World*, p. 119.

material weaving in chapter 1, where the commonness of weaving meant that it was not generally mentioned in poetry unless the woven product was of particularly high status. Thus, because of poetry's separate focus, its references to disease have not been particularly useful to scholars of the history of medicine, and so have frequently fallen by the wayside. But when it comes to poetic language and formula, these vague depictions of disease are very interesting in and of themselves.

Most poetic depictions of disease and binding can be quite firmly placed in a formulaic context where disease and the pain that it causes bind the body, much like chapter 5's bonds of prison and hell. This linking of the imagery of prison, hell, and disease through the same formula is noteworthy, not least because it has not been treated before in the scholarly literature. The formula, which nearly always occurs in the b-verse, is *x gebunden*, with *x* generally being a dative noun, although there are also examples of dative adjectives or adverbs, such as *searwum gebunden* (skilfully bound)[26] and *fæste gebunden* (bound fast/firmly).[27] Frequently, this formula invokes terms for torment or punishments (*susle gebunden*;[28] *witum gebunden*[29]), flame or fire (*lege gebundne*;[30] *fyr gebunden*[31]), fetters (*fetrum gebunde*),[32] and evil (*bealuwe gebundene*).[33] It is also present in the context of myriad other physical and mental afflictions, such as hunger (*hungre gebunde*),[34] sorrow (*sorgum gebunden*),[35] sleep (*slæpe gebundne*),[36] frost (*forste gebunden*),[37] old age (*eldo gebunden*),[38] and labour/

---

26 *Andreas* 1396b.

27 *Christ and Satan* 58b, 103a, and 323b; *Metres of Boethius (Metre 20)* 67b; and *Riddle 56* 6a.

28 *Andreas* 1379b; and *Elene* 771b.

29 *Andreas* 580b; and *Judith* 114b.

30 *Christ III* 1538b.

31 *Metres of Boethius (Metre 20)* 153b.

32 *Juliana* 433b.

33 *Andreas* 947a.

34 *Soul and Body I* 31b; and *Soul and Body II* 28b.

35 *Deor* 24b; and *Metres of Boethius (Metre 26)* 96b. See also *sorgum asæled* in *Genesis A* 2197a, and the collocation of *sorg, asælan* and *gebindan* in *Elene* 1243–4.

36 *Christ III* 873b.

37 *The Seafarer* 8b.

38 *Beowulf* 2111b.

toil (*bisgum gebunden*[39]).[40] These are all aspects of the fallen world,[41] and so it is unsurprising that this formula often occurs in a hellish context, with some eight to nine of the variations just mentioned describing hell, demons, and Satan.[42] This accounts for over half of the fourteen violent prison references (i.e., not including the more general mental and physical afflictions).

Less obvious than the association between prison, hell, and binding is that between disease and binding. Our first example of the binding nature of disease emphasized through this formula occurs in *Andreas*, where it describes Christ's many miracles:

> Sealde he dumbum gesprec,   deafe gehyrdon,
> healtum ond hreofum   hyge blissode,
> ða þe limseoce   lange wæron,
> werige, wanhale,   witum gebundene
> æfter burhstedum   blinde gesegon.   (577–81)

(He gave speech to the mute, the deaf heard, he made joyful the spirit of the lame and the leprous, who were for a long time limb-sick, weary, weak, bound by torments, throughout the cities the blind saw.)

These lines are highlighted by a number of poetic devices, including the homeoteleuton of the "-on" ending that links the final words of every other line.[43] Furthermore, the final, unalliterating verbs of lines 577, 579, and 580 determine the alliteration of the lines following ("h," "w" and "b"), while the cross alliteration of "b" and "s" in line 581 similarly serves to draw in the final word of the previous line (*gebundene*). This term participates in the formula *witum gebunden*, which is identical to *Judith*

---

39 *Beowulf* 1743a.

40 There is, interestingly, one instance of this formula being used of construction when it describes a sword that is *wrættum gebunden* (bound by gems) in *Beowulf* 1531b. See chapter 3, p. 79.

41 Robinson, *"Beowulf" and the Appositive Style*, p. 71.

42 These include *Andreas* 1379b; *Christ III* 1538b; *Christ and Satan* 58b, 103a, and 323b; *Elene* 771b; *Judith* 114b; *Juliana* 433b; and, arguably, Hrothgar's Sermon in *Beowulf* 1743a.

43 The repetition of nouns with "-um" endings also links 577a and 578a, as well as 580b and 581a.

115b's reference to the casting of Holofernes into hell.[44] The presence of *wite* in poetic descriptions of hell and prison elsewhere is common.[45]

Of course, the *Andreas*-poet's persistent use of such imagery means it is not out of place here. Indeed, if this were the only instance of miracles described in such a way, we might assume that the poet had added the imagery of binding for the sake of poetic parallelism. However, similar imagery also occurs in *Guthlac B*'s account of the saint's miracles:

> Mære wurdon
> his wundra geweorc   wide ond side,
> breme æfter burgum   geond Bryten innan,
> hu he monge oft   þurh meaht godes
> gehælde hygegeomre   hefigra wita,
> þe hine unsofte,   adle gebundne,
> sarge gesohtun   of siðwegum,
> freorigmode.   (881b–8a)

(His work of miracles became renowned far and wide, famous in cities throughout Britain, how he often through the might of God healed many mournful in spirit of burdensome afflictions, those who, sorrowful, sought him from afar with difficulty, bound by disease, sad in mind.)

The sadness of the sick in both this and the *Andreas* passage seems to be a result not merely of weakness and weariness, but of the fact that they are held captive and bound by their illness. While in *Andreas* the suffering ones are bound by the more general *witum* (torments/punishments), here in *Guthlac B*, they are bound by *adl* (disease). This is one of two instances of the formula as *adle gebundne*, the other of which occurs in *Christ III*, in a description of Christ separating the good souls from the damned:

---

44 See chapter 5, pp. 150–2.

45 A search of the *DOE Corpus* yields 129 poetic instances of *wite* and related compounds. The greatest concentration is in religious poems: *Christ and Satan* (16), *Genesis A* (14), *Genesis B* (12), *Christ III* (10), *Andreas* (10), *Elene* (6) and *Daniel* (6). *Hell* and *wite* directly collocate 24 times: *Christ and Satan* 156b–8a, 160b–1a, 340b–2a, and 425–6a; *Genesis A* 38–9a; *Genesis B* 303–4, 318–19, 323b–4, 329b–31a, and 367b–8a; *Christ III* 1269 and 1622b–3; *Andreas* 1052b and 1298b–9a; *Soul and Body I* 32b, 47b and *II* 29b, 44b; *Christ I* 264b–5a; *Juliana* 615–17; *Judith* 115b–16; *Judgement Day II* 188b–90; and *The Lord's Prayer III* 36b.

Ge þæs earnedon   þa ge earme men,
woruldþearfende,   willum onfengun
on mildum sefan.   Ðonne hy him þurh minne noman
eaðmode to eow   arna bædun,
þonne ge hyra hulpon   ond him hleoð gefon,
hingrendum hlaf   ond hrægl nacedum;
ond þa þe on sare   seoce lagun,
æfdon unsofte,   adle gebundne,
to þam ge holdlice   hyge staþeladon
mid modes myne.   (1349–58a)

(You earned this when you willingly received with a merciful heart, miserable men, poor in worldly goods. When the humble-minded asked you for
favours in my name, when you helped them and provided them with shelter,
bread to the hungry, and clothing to the naked; and those who lay sick in
soreness, suffering violently, bound by disease, you faithfully strengthened
their spirit with the love of your heart.)

The similarities between this passage and that of *Guthlac B* are striking,
particularly the formulaic use of *adle gebundne*, which is preceded by *unsofte* in the a-verse of both.

What is of further interest is the fact that disease is the only common de-
nominator in all three of these lists of miracles/deeds. In the *Andreas* passage, Christ is credited with giving speech to the mute, hearing to the deaf,
sight to the blind, and healing the lame and leprous. In the *Guthlac B* passage, the saint is attributed with general healing only. And in the *Christ III*
passage, the good souls are attributed with providing shelter, food, and
clothing to the poor, and healing the sick.

If we compare all three of these texts to their exemplars and analogues,
we see first that this passage has been expanded in *Andreas*. Although an
exact source for *Andreas* is not extant,[46] we can compare it to its closest
Latin and Greek analogues. The Latin *Recensio Casanatensis* lists Christ's
miracles: *Cecos fecit videre, claudos ambulare, leprosos mundavit, paral-
iticos curavit, de aqua vinum fecit. Accepit quinque panes et duos pisces, et
populum fecit discumbere super fenum, benedixit ac fregit, et saturavit plus*

---

46 See chapter 5, p. 128n36.

quam quinque milia hominum (15–18) (He made the blind see, the lame walk, cleansed the lepers, healed the paralysed, made water into wine. He took five loaves and two fishes and had the people sit down on the hay, he blessed and broke it and sated more than five thousand people).[47] The Greek *Praxeis Andreou kai Matheian eis ten Polin ton Anthropophagon* includes a similar list of miracles: making the blind see, the lame walk, the deaf hear, cleansing lepers, changing water into wine, and the miracle of the loaves and the fishes.[48] Although the miracles listed in the *Andreas* passage are generally accounted for in the Latin and Greek analogues, neither of these traditions employs the metaphor of disease as a binder.[49] The Old English prose versions omit the list of miracles altogether.

The identification of the source of *Guthlac B* has provoked much less scholarly controversy than *Andreas*; it is generally agreed to be based on Felix's Latin *Vita sancti Guthlaci*.[50] Chapter 45 of the Latin text describes Guthlac's miracles, which relate to *quos aut corporum egritudo aut inmundorum spirituum infestatio aut commissorum errorum professio, aut aliorum quorumcumque criminum quibus humanum genus adluitur causa vexabat* [...] *Nam nullus ab illo egrotus sine remedio, nullus vexatus sine salute, nullus tristis sine gaudio, nullum taedium sine exortatione, nulla maestitia sine consolatio, nulla anximonia sine consilio ab illo reversa est*[51] (those who were troubled by disease of the body or by the possession of foul spirits or by the profession of committed sins or by reason of any of the other faults by which the human race is beset [...] For no sick person went away from him without remedy, no afflicted person without health, no sad person without gladness, no weary person without exhortation, no grieving person without consolation, no troubled person without counsel). These sad and sick people are paralleled in the Old English poem. However, in the Latin there is once again no mention of the binding nature

---

47 Blatt, *Die lateinischen Bearbeitungen der Acta Andreae et Matthiae apud anthropophagos*, p. 53.

48 For the Greek, see Blatt, *Die lateinischen Bearbeitungen der Acta Andreae et Matthiae apud anthropophagos*, p. 53. For an English translation, see Boenig, *Acts of Andrew*, p. 7.

49 Nor does *The Hêliand*'s description of Christ's miracles in lines 2268b–83, which focuses on the severity of physical, mental, and supernatural illnesses that Christ was capable of healing.

50 Roberts, *Guthlac Poems*, p. 36.

51 *Felix's Life of Saint Guthlac*, p. 138.

of disease. Nor is there any such mention in the Old English prose version, in which Guthlac heals the sick, returns the possessed to their rightful minds, and cures the diseased.[52]

Perhaps the most interesting case is that of *Christ III*. This particular poem has a great many proposed sources,[53] but only two that relate to this specific passage. One of these is a Latin hymn, the first stanza of which Bede quotes in his *De arte metrica*. Albert S. Cook argues that this is the primary source of the poem, an assertion that later scholars have questioned.[54] In this hymn, Christ's discussion with the good souls relates only to how they helped the poor, which indicates that, if this were the primary source, the Old English poem would have expanded the text significantly.[55] The Latin *Vulgate*, on the other hand, includes a full list of the good deeds that these souls have performed, a list which points to an interesting difference on the part of the Old English poem: *tunc dicet rex his qui a dextris eius erunt venite benedicti Patris mei possidete paratum vobis regnum a constitutione mundi. esurivi enim et dedistis mihi manducare sitivi et dedistis mihi bibere hospes eram et collexistis me. nudus et operuistis me infirmus et visitastis me in carcere eram et venistis ad me* (Matthew 25:34–6) (Then the king will say to those who will be on his right hand: Come, blessed of my Father, possess the kingdom prepared for you from the foundation of the world. For I was hungry, and you gave to me to eat, I was thirsty, and you gave to me to drink, I was a stranger, and you took me in. Naked, and you clothed me; sick, and you visited me, I was in prison, and you came to me). The list of deeds here matches that of the poem – providing shelter, food, and clothing to the poor, and healing the sick – but it contains no reference to binding (as

---

52 Gonser, *Das angelsächsische Prosa-Leben des heiligen Guthlac*, p. 152.
53 For more on these, see Cook, *Christ of Cynewulf*; as well as his "Cynewulf's Principal Source for the Third Part of 'Christ'"; Biggs, *Sources of Christ III*; and Allen and Calder, *Sources and Analogues*, pp. 84–107.
54 Biggs, *Sources of Christ III*, p. 1; and Grau, *Quellen und Verwandtschaften*, pp. 48–52.
55 Cook, *Christ of Cynewulf*, p. 171, lines 19–24. Christ's discussion with the bad souls does, however, mention sickness in addition to poverty: *"nudo vestem non dedistis, neglexistis languidum"* [...] *Peccatores dicent: "Christe, quando te vel pauperem, / te, Rex magne, vel infirmum contemnentes sprevimus"* (27–32) ("[when I was] naked, you did not [give me] clothes, sick, you neglected me [...] The sinners will say: "Christ, when did we scorn you as a pauper, great king, disdaining you as infirm?"). Cook, *Christ of Cynewulf*, pp. 171–2.

found in the passages in *Andreas* and *Guthlac B*). The one additional element is the visiting of prisoners.

Based on a comparison with these verses, it would seem that the Old English poetic passage both expands and contracts the Biblical tradition of Christ's miracles. *Christ III* clearly elaborates upon the description of the sick, portraying them as both suffering violently and being bound by disease, and in doing so employs the formulaic structure outlined above. It is possible that the removal of the reference to prison that should follow also stems from this formulaic structure. In all else, the passage follows the Biblical pattern, and so the poet's choice not to include a reference to prison after the mention of disease may relate to the conflation of these two traditions of binding. Because of the strong associations between binding and imprisonment, the poet may not have deemed it necessary to refer directly to prison, which was, itself, a foreign concept in Anglo-Saxon England.[56]

It is interesting to note that, of the many miracles and good deeds of Christ and his followers, the ones that were chosen for emphasis in three different Old English poems were the healing of the sick and the curing of disease. It is further interesting that, in doing so, all three poems utilize the same formulaic language of disease as a binder. Within this formulaic context, disease is described using typical binding imagery, with the binding participating exactly as we expect given other instances of such imagery in descriptions of prisons and hell.

The portrayal of disease using the formula *x-hord onleac/onlocen* is, however, somewhat unconventional.[57] The most common and best known variation of this formula is *wordhord onleac* (unlocked the speech-hoard), which occurs five times in Old English poetry.[58] Related to this is *modhord onleac* (unlocked the mind-hoard).[59] Other compounds without the *hord*-element, but related in sense, include *larcræftas onlocen* (unlocked

---

56 Indeed, Christ's address to the good and bad souls in *The Hêliand* refers not to visiting people in prison, but to helping those who are chained up. See lines 4395b–402a and 4423–9a.

57 See Tyler, *Old English Poetics*, p. 68.

58 *Andreas* 316b and 601b; *Beowulf* 259b; *Metres of Boethius (Metre 6)* 1b; *Widsith* 1b. See also *Vainglory's wordhord onwreah* (3a) (uncovered the speech-hoard) and *Riddle 84's hordword onhlid* (53a) (unclosed the speech-hoard).

59 *Andreas* 172b.

knowledge)[60] and *leoðucræft onleac* (unlocked poetic skill).[61] In all of these formulaic instances, the unlocking of a noun related to knowledge or words is quite clearly depicted in a positive light.

Guthlac B, on the other hand, employs the formula in relation to disease three times, all to a very different, negative, end: disease repeatedly unlocks the saint's body (*lichord onlocen/lichord onleac/feorhhord onleac*).[62] Each of these three passages also simultaneously employs imagery of binding. The first describes the onset of the saint's illness:

> Wæs se bancofa
> adle onæled,   inbendum fæst,
> lichord onlocen.   Leomu hefegedon,
> sarum gesohte.   He þæt soð gecneow
> þæt hine ælmihtig   ufan neosade,
> meotud fore miltsum.   He his modsefan
> wið þam færhagan   fæste trymede
> feonda gewinna.   Næs he forht seþeah,
> ne seo adlþracu   egle on mode,
> ne deaðgedal.

(954b–63a)

(His bone-enclosure was inflamed by disease, his body-hoard, fast with internal bonds, [was] unlocked. His limbs grew heavy, set upon by pains. He knew the truth that the almighty, the lord, in his mercy visited him from above. He strengthened his spirit firmly against the enclosing terrors, the attacks of the devils. Yet he was not afraid, nor [was] the disease's attack troublesome to his mind, nor the severing of death.)

Here, the saint's bone-enclosure is described as *inbendum fæst* (fast with internal bonds). Yet the very next half-line seems to negate the assertion that his body is fast within; indeed, the body of the saint, rather than being bound by disease, is unlocked by it. In this passage, the bonds are positive

---

60 *Solomon and Saturn I* 3a.

61 *Elene* 1250a. A similar formula is *x-locan onspeon*, where the opening of enclosures indicates the disclosing or acceptance of secret (whether evil or divine) knowledge. See *Andreas* 470b: *wordlocan onspeonn* (opened the word-enclosure) and 671b: *hordlocan onspeon* (opened the hoard-enclosure); *Elene* 86b: *hreðerlocan onspeon* (opened the heart-enclosure); and *Juliana* 79b: *ferðlocan onspeon* (opened the heart-enclosure).

62 For a discussion of the body motifs in *Guthlac B*, see Rosier, "Death and Transfiguration," pp. 84–8; and Jagger, "Body, Text and Self," pp. 213–40.

and constructive – they are what hold the body together. Yet, with the attack of disease, Guthlac faces a disintegration of his bodily bonds, which once held so firmly together. Thus, death is described as a *-gedal*, a severing of body from soul.

The next passage to describe Guthlac's disease, this time in the voice of the saint himself, also describes it in terms of unlocking, with nearly verbatim repetition of three half-lines:[63]

> Ic wille secgan   þæt me sar gehran,
> wærc in gewod   in ðisse wonnan niht,
> lichord onleac.   Leomu hefegiað,
> sarum gesohte.   Sceal þis sawelhus,
> fæge flæschoma,   foldærne biþeaht,
> leomu lames geþacan,   legerbedde fæst
> wunian wælræste.   (1027–33a)

(I will say that in this dark night pain struck me, suffering crept in, unlocked my life-hoard. My limbs grow heavy, set upon by pains. This soul-house, the doomed flesh-home, must be covered by an earth-house, my limbs by a roof of loam, fast in a sick-bed, [it must] dwell in the grave.)

Here the body is no longer held fast by its internal bonds, but is instead unlocked by a disease that keeps it *legerbedde fæst* (fast in a sick-bed). Immediately following this passage, compounds with *-gedal* occur twice in quick succession: *sawelgedal* (1035a) (severing of soul) and *lifgedal* (1046a) (severing of life). Indeed, there are twelve compounds with *-gedal* in total running throughout the *Guthlac* poems, but concentrated for the most part towards the end of *Guthlac B*.[64] This is the highest proportion

---

63 The only differences are the use of the past participle *onlocen* and preterite *hefegedon* in the previous passage where this passage uses the preterite and present tenses, respectively.

64 In addition to the *sawelgedal* and *lifegedal* of this passage, the severing of death is signaled at line 235a (*deaþa gedal*) of *Guthlac A*, as well as 963a (*deaðgedal*) of *Guthlac B*. Similarly, the term *nydgedal* (the inevitable severing [of death]) occurs at *Guthlac A* 445b and *Guthlac B* 934a and 1168a. *Guthlac B* also contains references to *gastgedal* (862b, 1138b) (the severing of the spirit), *feorhgedal* (1178a, 1200a) (the severing of life), as well as the *þeodengedal* (1350a) (separation from one's lord) that Guthlac's servant suffers at his death. This focus builds on other more casual descriptions in the poem's Latin source depicting death as separating soul from body. See Rosier, "Death and Transfiguration," p. 84; Jagger, "Body, Text and Self," pp. 213–21; and Bjork, *Old English Verse Saints' Lives*, p. 91. See also the description of the Mermedonians' cannibalism as a loosing of body and soul in *Andreas* 147–51.

of -*gedal* terms in any Old English poem, and it indicates an emphasis on imagery of bodily disintegration, unlocking, and severing.[65]

The final time the saint's disease is described occurs right before his death. Guthlac has predicted that he will die on the seventh day after he fell ill, and he is true to his word:

> Com se seofeða dæg
> ældum ondweard,   þæs þe him in gesonc,
> hat, heortan neah,   hildescurum
> flacor flanþracu,   feorhhord onleac,
> searocægum gesoht.
>
> (1141b–5a)

(The seventh day came into being for men, since the flying attack of arrows in battle-showers sank into him, hot, near his heart, unlocked his life-hoard, set upon him with cunning keys.)

Here again we have the unlocking of Guthlac's body, this time with the additional imagery of cunning keys. As Seth Lerer has emphasized, speaking of other religious poetry and prose, keys are symbols of wisdom and enlightenment,[66] an interpretation which draws us back to the usual usage of *x-hord onleac*. The following passage from *Exodus* demonstrates his point:

> Dæg weorc/Dægword[67] nemnað
> swa gyt werðeode,   on gewritum findað
> doma gehwilcne,   þara ðe him drihten bebead
> on þam siðfate   soðum wordum,
> gif onlucan wile   lifes wealhstod,
> beorht in breostum,   banhuses weard,
> ginfæsten god   gastes cægon.

---

65   See also Saint Paul's desire *dissolvi et cum Christo esse* (to be dissolved/loosed and be with Christ) in the *Vulgate*, Philippians 1:23.

66   *Literacy and Power*, pp. 112–25; and "Riddle and the Book." See also Salvador, "Key to the Body," pp. 63–72.

67   The manuscript reads *dæg weorc*, but following Gollancz, *Cædmon Manuscript*, p. lxxvii, Krapp emends to *Dægword*, according to the argument that this is a translation of the Latin name of the Chronicles, *dierum verba*, and is thus a reference to Deuteronomy; *Junius Manuscript*, pp. 105, 216.

Run bið gerecenod,   ræd forð gæð.   (519b–26)[68]

(They call it the work of the day/Deuteronomy, which the people still find in
the Scriptures – each of the laws which the Lord announced to them, by means
of true words, during the journey, if the interpreter of life, the guardian of the
bone-house, bright in the breast, wishes to unlock the great fastness with the
keys of the spirit. The mystery will be explained, wisdom will go forth.)

Most instances of both the formula *x-hord onleac/onlocen* and the imagery
of keys unlocking hoards occur in a positive religious context. *Guthlac B*,
on the other hand, takes that diction and converts it to refer to disease attacking the body. The keys in the *Guthlac B* passage are thus described as
a *flacor flanþracu* (flying attack of arrows), which sinks into him *hildescu-
rum* (in battle-showers) and is *hat, heortan neah* (hot, near his heart). Not
only is this imagery similar to that found in the *Metrical Charm, Wið
Færstice*, which refers to supernatural agents whose projectiles cause illness, but the symptoms outlined in *Guthlac B* are also comparable to those
caused by poison.[69]

   A comparison may be made between Guthlac's illness and Beowulf's
suffering prior to his death by the dragon venom that spreads rapidly from
his wound throughout his entire body. Poison, rather than severing the
sinews and flesh that keep the body whole, attacks internally, coursing
through his blood and burning from within:

> Ða sio wund ongon,
> þe him se eorðdraca   ær geworhte,
> swelan ond swellan;   he þæt sona onfand,
> þæt him on breostum   bealonið(e) weoll
> attor on innan.   (2711b–15a)

(Then the wound, which the earth-dragon had earlier wrought on him, began
to burn and swell; he immediately discovered that in his breast there welled a
malicious evil, poison from within.)

---

68 See also the passage from *Solomon and Saturn I* mentioned in the introduction to this
    survey, pp. 7–8.
69 See also Hrothgar's Sermon, where the unguarded soul who is *bisgum gebunden* (1743a)
    (bound by cares) falls victim to the arrows of evil spirits.

The verb *weallan*, to "well," "flow," "boil," "burn,"[70] is notable because it is linked to the hydraulic model of the mind, in which cardiocentric boiling is connected to extreme emotions (both positive and negative).[71] Here, of course, we are seeing the symptoms of illness, but, given Leslie Lockett's argument for holistic views of the mind/body within Anglo-Saxon culture,[72] it should come as no surprise that negative bodily and mental states would be associated.

Beowulf's injury, furthermore, echoes Guthlac's disease in its reference to heat and the penetration of the breast near the heart. In line 2422a, Beowulf's body is described as a soul-hoard that is severed from life, not unlike the *lichord/feorhhord onleac* formulas in *Guthlac B*. In their descriptions of disease and death, therefore, *Guthlac B* and *Beowulf* are highly reminiscent of one another. Yet what sets the two heroes – one spiritual and one secular – apart is Guthlac's welcoming of death. Shortly before the onset of Guthlac's illness, we are told that the Holy Spirit visits him:

> þa wæs frofre gæst
> eadgum æbodan   ufan onsended,
> halig of heahþu.   Hreþer innan born,
> afysed on forðsið.   Him færinga
> adl in gewod.   He on elne swa þeah
> ungeblyged bad   beorhtra gehata
> bliþe in burgum.   Wæs þam bancofan
> æfter nihtglome   neah geþrungen,
> breosthord onboren.   Wæs se bliþa gæst
> fus on forðweg.   (932b–45a)

(then the holy spirit was sent from above as a comfort to the blessed one, the messenger from the heights. His breast burned from within, hastened on the forward journey. Suddenly disease advanced within him. Even so, he waited with courage undismayed for brighter promises, happy in the dwellings. During the darkness of night his bone-enclosure was severely oppressed, his breast-hoard weakened. His happy spirit was eager for the way forward.)

---

70 Bosworth and Toller, *Anglo-Saxon Dictionary*, s.v. See also Potter, "'Wylm' and 'weallan' in *Beowulf*"; and Jagger, "Body, Text and Self," p. 32.
71 Lockett, *Anglo-Saxon Psychologies*, pp. 59–62.
72 Ibid., pp. 150–78.

And so Guthlac's disease is quite clearly an act of divine intervention, the illness having been brought to the exhausted saint through the visitation of the Holy Spirit. Thus, while the violent imagery of the disease, which both unlocks the body's bonds and binds it fast in its sick-bed, aligns the text with Beowulf's own rather unwilling death, here it serves to paint the saint as a martyr (despite the fact that he dies of illness rather than by execution). Furthermore, since Guthlac's eagerness for death is clear in the poem, the use of the formula *x-hord onleac*, which in all other cases indicates the positive distribution of knowledge, is not so very out of place. By unlocking the body, the disease looses the soul so it may travel to heaven. Just as when hoards of knowledge and words are unlocked, so when life-hoards are released, access to a greater power is achieved. Of course, this positive spin only applies to an eager martyr like Guthlac. This difference is significant, underlying as it does the choice to employ body-unlocking formulas only in *Guthlac B*, despite similar references to life-hoards in other poems, including *Beowulf*.[73]

Given that binding and loosing are generally considered to be opposites in Old English, the coexistence of these forces in the poetry, at times even in the same poem, is significant for our approach to Anglo-Saxon culture. The complex and contrasting ways in which formulas of disease are put to use in Old English poetry demonstrate a much more nuanced world view than the supposed binary of binding and loosing presumes.

Bodily Bonds and Mental Constriction

The formulaic association between disease and binding is also mirrored in Old English depictions of other afflictions. Many of them are again linked to hell, as in the case of hunger,[74] which appears in collocations with *bindan*

---

73 Admittedly, Beowulf is also accepting of his fate; however, there is a distinct difference between his heroic and stoic acceptance of death and Guthlac's eager desire for it.

74 Hunger appears to be a standard hellish affliction, as demonstrated by its association with hell in *Solomon and Saturn II* 289b–95, and by heaven's association with a lack of hunger in *Phoenix* 611–14a and *Judgement Day II* 256–67. Hunger and the other standard afflictions appear in the latter poem's sources at line 130 of the Latin poem, *De die iudicii*, and line 260 of the Old English prose homily, *Be domes dæge*; see Caie, *Old English Poem 'Judgement Day II,'* pp. 132, 107, respectively.

that echo the *x gebunden* formula.[75] *Hungor* and *hungrig* are popular terms in Old English, with a search of the *DOE Corpus* yielding forty-one poetic references, most of which occur in religious contexts. *Hungor* also collocates twice with the past participle of *hæftan* (to capture/constrain), where it describes both actual and allegorical starvation,[76] and twice with *clam* (chain), where it refers to the afflictions of imprisonment and winter.[77] In the case of *The Seafarer*, the chains of hunger associated with the isolation of winter may refer to literal hunger, but also perhaps to the seafarer's hunger for company and spiritual solace.

The loneliness linked to the physical state of hunger speaks to the use of binding in relation to all manner of mental afflictions. Although the division of bodily and mental afflictions is perhaps anachronistic, given Lockett's recent work on Anglo-Saxon mind-body holism, I will discuss the mind as a separate entity here in order to underline the range of types of affliction that are associated with binding. In addition to using images of boiling and heat linked with the hydraulic model of the mind, Old English poetry frequently depicts mental affliction in terms of constriction.[78] This constriction may arise from the pressure caused by boiling, or it may be present in a separate capacity:

> even when heat and seething are absent, the functioning of the mind-in-the-breast can be impaired by constriction from other sources. Conversely, since mental heat and seething are not unequivocally harmful phenomena, they need not lead to constriction. In this light, it is likely that even the most abstract references to psychological narrowness are implicitly connected to the idea that mental constriction injures the mind-in-the-breast, even when that connection is obscured by imagery that the present-day reader recognizes more readily, including the topos of enslavement to sin.[79]

---

75 *Soul and Body I* 31b and *Soul and Body II* 28b make reference to *hungre gebunde*, where the verb appears in its second-person preterite form. The context here is one of spiritual, rather than physical, starvation. An instance in *Maxims I* 38 refers to a man who has no food, collocating the past participle of *bindan* and *nyd* (need).

76 *Andreas* 1156b–8a; *Elene* 611–18.

77 *Elene* 691–6b; *Seafarer* 8b–12a.

78 Lockett, *Anglo-Saxon Psychologies*, pp. 73–83. See also Low, "Anglo-Saxon Mind," pp. 96–9; Harbus, *Life of the Mind*, p. 135; and Mize, "Representation of the Mind as an Enclosure."

79 Lockett, *Anglo-Saxon Psychologies*, p. 79.

The constriction of the mind by sorrow and distress is articulated both in elaborated passages, such as lines 39–40 of *The Wanderer*: *ðonne sorg ond slæp somod ætgædre / earmne anhogan oft gebindað* (then sorrow and sleep both together often bind the miserable solitary thinker), and in formulas: *sorgum gebunden* appears in both *Deor* 24b and *The Metres of Boethius* (*Metre 26*) 96b,[80] with variations of *x gebunden* being common. The description in *Metre 5* of the distress caused by evil and worldly troubles reads:

> Forðæm simle bið
> se modsefa   miclum gebunden
> mid gedrefnesse,   gif hine dreccean mot
> þissa yfla hwæðer,   innan swencan.[81]   (38b–41)

(Therefore the mind is always greatly bound by distress, if either of these evils should torment it, afflict it from within.)

The reference to *innan* (within) situates this distress as an internal affliction that takes place within the mind, as opposed to an external affliction endured by the body. This does not, however, indicate a clear-cut separation between mental and bodily afflictions, since the physical effects of poison and disease are also emphatically depicted as internal attacks. Thus, a binary of binding that places the internal alongside the constructive and pits them against the external and constrictive is inadequate. In this

---

80 The equivalent passage in chapter 38 of the prose B-text has only *sorgiende*; Godden and Irvine, *Old English Boethius*, 1:351, line 40 (as Bredehoft briefly notes, *Authors, Audiences, and Old English Verse*, pp. 93, 95). It does, however, refer to chains and fetters (*racentan/cospas*) shortly before (as does the verse text (*cyspan/racente*)); see 1:350, line 30 for the prose, and lines 77b–8a of the verse.

81 This passage is almost identical – minus the formulaic phrasing and apposition of torments – to its prose equivalent in chapter 6 of the B-text: *forðam þæt mod siemle bið gebunden mid gedrefedness þær þissa twega yfela auður ricsað* (16–18) (therefore the mind is always bound by distress where either of these two evils rules); Godden and Irvine, *Old English Boethius*, 1:251. Both are very similar to the Latin of Book 1, Metre 7:
> Nubila mens est
> uincta que frenis
> haec ubi regnant. (29–31)
> (Where these reign, the mind is clouded, bound with chains.) *De consolatione philosophiae*, p. 26.

particular case, internal bonds are not positive, structure-enhancing elements, but negative, constraining afflictions.

The worldly troubles that afflict the mind can also be seen in Old English depictions of sin. An example is provided in Hrothgar's famous "sermon," which demonstrates the importance of mental and spiritual alertness:

> oð þæt him on innan   oferhygda dæl
> weaxeð ond wridað;   þonne se weard swefeð,
> sawele hyrde;   bið se slæp to fæst,
> bisgum gebunden,   bona swiðe neah,
> se þe of flanbogan   fyrenum sceoteð.   (1740–4)

(until a portion of proud thoughts grow and flourish within him. When the guardian sleeps, the protector of souls; that sleep is too fast, bound by cares, the slayer very near, he who wickedly shoots from an arrow-bow.)

This is not the literal sleep of the body, but rather the metaphorical sleep of the proud soul who is focused too much on his or her own presence in the world.[82] The formula *x gebunden* is once again employed in a negative context to depict the hold that worldly cares may have over a leader of people. The imagery of an evil shooter also links this passage back to *Christ II*'s reference to sin and *Guthlac B*'s depiction of disease, discussed above. This passage's association with religious poems such as these helps to explain its significance to the scholarly debate over *Beowulf*'s relationship with Christianity/paganism. The editors of Klaeber Four argue that it "offers another striking example of the amalgamation of different cultural influences, representing what appears to be a native heroic theme imbued with Christian precepts and sentiments."[83] Others read it as an example of traditional wisdom; Elaine Tuttle Hansen interprets it as part of a tradition of parental advice poems,[84] while Hansen argues that, similar to a bestowal of knowledge by a wise king, this passage represents an attempt to honour Beowulf "with another precious gift."[85]

---

82 See also *Christ III*'s depiction of Judgement Day as a thief in the dark, seizing those who are *slæpe gebundne* (873b) (bound by sleep).
83 P. 213.
84 "Hrothgar's 'Sermon'." See also Bodek, "Beowulf."
85 "Hrothgar's 'Sermon'," p. 66.

Hrothgar's qualifications to speak in this way are made evident through references to his wisdom and old age.[86] The language with which his age is described is of particular interest here because it includes a variation on the same *x gebunden* formula. Having returned home, Beowulf recounts the events of his journey and describes Hrothgar's reaction to his victory against Grendel:

hwilum eft ongan   eldo gebunden,
gomel guðwiga   gioguðe cwiðan,
hildestrengo;   hreðer (in)ne weoll,
þonne he wintrum frod   worn gemunde.   (2111–14)

(again sometimes the old battle-warrior, bound by age, began to lament his youth, his battle-strength; his heart welled within, when he, wise in winters, remembered many things.)

It is significant that the only use of this formula to describe age – which is often positively associated with wisdom[87] – comes in the voice of Beowulf himself. This indicates something of the hero's own approach to aging, which he views as an affliction, an interpretation in line with the other contexts in which the *x gebunden* formula occurs. Interpreting the passage in this manner, furthermore, speaks to Beowulf's resistance towards taking on the role of aged parental figure, something that is especially demonstrated through his continued heroism and decision to fight the dragon even at an advanced age, not to mention his rather late, death-bed "adoption" of Wiglaf.

Given the poem's clear interest in Scandinavia, Beowulf's sentiments about age can be read, to some extent, in relation to Carol J. Clover's work on Old Norse gender. Clover adapts Thomas Laqueur's one-sex model, so that gender is imagined as either *blauðr* (soft/weak) or *hvatr* (bold/active/vigorous), rather than dependent on biological difference.[88] According to her discussion,

---

86 He is referred to as *frod*: 279a, 1306b, 1724a, 2114a; *snottor*: 190b, 1313b, 1384a, 1475a, 1786b, 2156a; and *wis*: 1318a, 1400b, 1413a, 1698b.
87 See the note above.
88 "Regardless of Sex," pp. 1–2; and Laqueur, *Making Sex*.

to the extent that we can speak of a social binary, a set of two categories, into which all persons were divided, the fault line runs not between males and females per se, but between able-bodied men (and the exceptional woman) on one hand and, on the other, a kind of rainbow coalition of everyone else (most women, children, slaves, and old, disabled, or otherwise disenfranchised men).[89]

This division between powerful and powerless is perhaps even more stark for members from one group who move to the second, as is the case for aging men: "In a literature not given to pathos and little interested in the old, these moments – in which former heroes are shown doddering about, or bedridden, or blind and impotent – stand out in strong relief."[90]

This concept of age weakening the boldness and activity of once strong men is evident in *Beowulf*'s celebration of the youthful hero and in the depiction of the loss of physical power that the wise Hrothgar laments.[91] The formula employed here, *x gebunden*, in linking all of the other physical and mental afflictions with old age, points to Beowulf's world view. Of course, it is not only Beowulf who associates these afflictions and age; indeed, old age appears in a word pair with disease four times in Old English poetry. The formula *adl ne yldo* (disease nor old age) is used to speak of God's nature (i.e., he is not subject to them) in *Maxims I* 10a and *Beowulf* 1736a, with variations of it occurring in relation to the soul in *Riddle 43* (soul and body) (4a: *yldo ne adle*) and the human condition in *The Seafarer* (70a: *adl oþþe yldo*). The link between disease and old age is rooted in infirmity and loss of control. Whereas religious heroes revel in the earthly loss of control that brings them closer to God, this is not something generally desirable to lay people.

In addition to these formulaic contexts, which demonstrate the conventional nature of Old English poetry's obsession with control, an expanded reference to old age as a binder occurs in *Solomon and Saturn II*:

Yldo beoð on eorðan   æghwæs cræftig;
mid hiðendre   hildewræsne,

---

89 "Regardless of Sex," p. 13.
90 Ibid., pp. 14–15.
91 See also the discussion of Anglo-Saxon perceptions of age in Rothauser, "Winter in Heorot"; and Sánchez-Martí, "Age Matters," pp. 220–5.

rumre racenteage   receð wide,
langre linan,   lisseð eall ðæt heo wile.   (114–17)

(Old age is, of all things on earth, mighty; with plundering battle-bonds, great fetter-ties, [she] reaches widely, with a long rope, subdues all that she will.)

These lines represent a response to Saturn's riddle about the disastrous effects of time. As Thomas D. Hill has demonstrated, a Latin analogue to this riddle exists in the *Collectanea Pseudo-Bedae*,[92] although that particular text only includes a riddle with no response. According to Daniel Anlezark, the expected answer from the riddling tradition seems to be "wind," rather than "old age."[93] We have already seen in chapters 4 and 6 that wind and storms are described in terms of binding, which serves to underline the similarity of imagery between alternate solutions. The personification of old age here as a creature of violence who binds and restrains her victims contains echoes of prison imagery (fetters, ropes and *racenteage*),[94] as well as martial imagery, with the mighty creature employing *hildewræsne* (battle-bonds) to subdue her living targets. While the passage from *Beowulf* discussed above implies that old age binds the body so as to cut it off from the glories of youth, here the poet's use of martial terminology allows the elderly to depart like warriors (which, of course, Beowulf does). The expansion of the metaphor demonstrates the living nature of the metaphorical binding of old age in this text.

If old age binds, it is only one step further to suggest that pain and death are also binders. This is something we see in *Beowulf*'s description of Grendel's arm-loss:

Hwæþere he his folme forlet
to lifwraþe   last weardian,
earm ond eaxle.   No þær ænige swa þeah

---

92 "Saturn's Time Riddle." See also Anlezark, *Dialogues of Solomon and Saturn*, pp. 125–6. The Latin text reads: *Dic mihi quae est illa res quae coelum totamque terram repleuit, siluas et surculos confringit, omniaque fundamenta concutit: sed nec oculis uideri, aut manibus tangi potest?* (Tell me what it is that fills the entire sky and earth, breaks forests and sprouts, and shakes all the foundations: but cannot be seen by eyes, or touched by hands). *Collectanea Pseudo-Bedae*, p. 130, no. 79.
93 *Dialogues of Solomon and Saturn*, p. 35.
94 See chapter 5, p. 142, and chapter 9, p. 263.

> feasceaft guma   frofre gebohte:
> no þy leng leofað   laðgeteona
> synnum geswenced,   ac hyne sar hafað
> in niðgripe[95]   nearwe befongen,
> balwon bendum.   (970b–7a)

(However he left his hand for the protection of his life, to guard his track, his arm and shoulder. Nevertheless, he did not obtain any comfort, the miserable man: nor therefore will the hostile assailant live long, troubled by crimes, but pain has narrowly enveloped him with its malicious grip, with baleful bonds.)

It is interesting that Grendel's impending death is described through this particular personification of pain as an assailant who grips and binds its victim, because, of course, both Beowulf and Grendel are frequently associated with hands and gripping.[96] The formula *x bendum* in the last line cited above appears elsewhere, with one example amplifying this passage's collocation of *nearwe* and *bendum*: *Riddle 52*'s (flail) *nearwum bendum* (3b) refers to the bonds that hold the captives, criminals or slaves prisoner.[97] In diction relating to prison and hell, *nearwe* is a common term, and the fact that these bonds are modified by the adjective *bealu* (evil) further reinforces placement of this scene in the context of hell, where Grendel awaits judgment for his crimes. The removal of his arm and the fact that he is *synnum geswenced*[98] (troubled by crimes) imply in addition the context of legal mutilation, which marked a person's crime on the body.[99]

Formulaic references to imprisonment can also be linked to death's fettering in *Exodus*. The fate of the Egyptians who are trapped in the sea while pursuing the Israelites is described thus: *Mægen wæs on cwealme / fæste gefeterod* (469–70a) (Their might was fettered fast in death). A

---

95 The MS reads *in mid gripe*, but its lack of alliteration has prompted most editors to emend it.

96 See Carens, "Handscóh and Grendel"; and Rosier, "Uses of Association."

97 See chapter 6, pp. 164–7.

98 Variations of the *x geswenced* formula include *hundum geswenced* (*Beowulf* 1368b); *sarum geswenced* (*Guthlac B* 1137a); and *sorgum geswenced* (*Andreas* 116a; and *Metres of Boethius (Metre 3)* 8a). *Judgement Day II* 256 also includes a collocation of *sorg*, *sar* and *-swencan*, along with *yldo*.

99 See Bremmer, "Grendel's Arm and the Law"; and Lockett, "Role of Grendel's Arm." For more on legal mutilation, see O'Brien O'Keeffe, "Body and Law," and chapter 5, pp. 124–5.

collocation of *fæst* and *-feterian* also occurs in *Riddle 52* at line 4, although here the word order is reversed. In addition to these two collocations, a reference in *Solomon and Saturn I* to a confining device in prison also pairs the nominal form, *feter*, with the verb, *-fæstnian*.[100] More immediately relevant, however, is the translation of *Psalm 106* in the *Paris Psalter*:

> þa þe her on ðystrum   þrage sæton
> and on deaðes scuan   deorcum lifdan,
> gebundene   bealuwe feterum
> on wædle wrace   and on iserne.   (26–9)

(those who sat in the darkness for a time and lived in the dark shadow of death, bound by baleful fetters in miserable poverty and in iron.)

Here, *feter*, *isern*, *bealu*, and *-bindan* are all connected to death in an elaboration of the reference in *Vulgate* Psalm 106:10 to *habitantes in tenebris et umbra mortis alligatos inopia et ferro* (those dwelling in darkness and the shadow of death, bound in want and iron). Given that *Christ III* also refers to Christ releasing the good from *deaþes bend* (1041b) (death's bond) on Judgment Day, the evidence implies a Biblical origin for the association between bonds, fetters, and death. However, both the elaboration of the psalm and the use of formulaic diction in passages not overtly religious in nature point to an extension of the Christian idea in Old English, a conscious incorporating of it into the existing imagery and language of binding.

One final application of this association between binding and affliction builds on the formulaic context outlined above and culminates in the imaginative expression of drunkenness in *Riddle 27* (mead). This poem turns on its head the convention of using binding formulas to depict lack, instead offering a portrayal of excess:

> Nu ic eom bindere
> ond swingere,   sona weorpe
> esne to eorþan,   hwilum ealdne ceorl.

---

100 See chapter 3, p. 88. See also the collocation of *feter* and the adverb *fæste* in *Paris Psalter* (*Psalm 78*) 39. The Old English psalm is based on *Vulgate* Psalm 78:10–11, which uses the past participle of *vincire* (to bind/fetter) to refer to prisoners in Jerusalem.

> Sona þæt onfindeð,   se þe mec fehð ongean,
> ond wið mægenþisan   minre genæsteð,
> þæt he hrycge sceal   hrusan secan,
> gif he unrædes   ær ne geswiceð,
> strengo bistolen,   strong on spræce,
> mægene binumen;   nah his modes geweald,
> fota ne folma.   Frige hwæt ic hatte,
> ðe on eorþan swa   esnas binde,
> dole æfter dyntum   be dæges leohte.   (6b–17)

(Now I am a binder and a scourger, at once I throw a man to the ground, sometimes an old churl. He who fights against me and contends with my mighty force immediately discovers that he must seek the ground with his back, if he does not abandon such foolishness, robbed of his strength, strong in speech, deprived of power; he does not have control over his mind nor his feet and hands. Ask what I am called, who on earth thus binds men, foolish after blows, by the light of day.)

After a brief description of the riddle solution's value to men, the poem shifts to depict the danger it poses as a *bindere ond swingere* (binder and scourger). Its binding is clearly figurative, with an emphasis on alcohol's ability to remove a man's control over himself and render him powerless. This poem also does not participate in the formulaic contexts of the other afflictions examined in this section, instead presenting an object that its possessors might think a blessing, but which actually turns out to pose a threat. The lack of formulaic expression could arguably result from mead's status as an active binder, rather than a passive recipient of binding (i.e., *x gebunden*). However, there are other formulaic contexts that do not utilize the past participle, which could have been employed here (i.e., *x-bendum fæst* or *x-bendum*), indicating that the poet is less concerned with an active/passive binary, and more with the poetic revivification of formulaic diction.

This reimagining takes the form of a thief who robs men of their strength (*strengo bistolen*), power (*mægene binumen*), and self-control (*nah his modes geweald, / fota ne folma*). The personification is enhanced by the phrase, *be dæges leohte* (by the light of day), implying the major difference between a real thief and this metaphorical one is that the latter acts openly, with its victims' awareness and complicity. Jennifer Neville notes that the poem's initial depiction of labour and value lead the audience to expect an artefact of some kind, "a safely 'denatured' and passive object."[101] The frustration of this expectation, thus, "destabilises the supposedly safe area inside the human circle of light by maintaining that the object still retains the dangerous power of the natural world."[102] Elinor Teele points out that the riddle, in addition to depicting nature's power, portrays "the power of mastered objects, altered by humans into a new unnatural form, to usurp their master's position."[103] Despite the constructive and controlling efforts of humans, it is they who are bound and controlled here. She further concludes that the use of binding in the poem may relate to sin, emphasizing the fall of humanity and its origin in Adam and Eve's gluttony.[104] This is upheld by the use of the doublet *bindere / ond swingere* in religious contexts,[105] where demons bind and beat, indicating that "[m]ead has assumed the role of the punishing devil, humorously striking its errant charges for their licentiousness. As the idea of drinking as a sin naturally suggested a devilish role for drink itself, so sin masters the sinner."[106]

Of course we may have seen binding in an alcohol riddle before, if we accept the "John Barleycorn" or "ale" solutions of *Riddle 28*.[107] In that poem (which directly follows the present riddle in the manuscript), the relationship between humans and alcohol is inverted: alcohol is portrayed as the victim of human violence. Although I am not convinced of this solution for *Riddle 28*, we should not dismiss outright the possibility that these may be two different approaches to a complicated topic – where alcohol is portrayed as being capable of producing both social cohesion and antisocial behaviour. If they do treat two different views of the same object – or even if the manuscript's compiler simply placed them together under the belief that they did – then it is significant that binding characterizes both. In the world of Old English poetry, everything can bind and be bound.

---

101 *Representations of the Natural World*, p. 201.
102 Ibid.
103 "Heroic Tradition," p. 173.
104 Ibid.
105 Rhyming forms of *bindan* and *swingan* collocate in *Christ III* 1621–2a; and *Juliana* 336–7a.
106 Teele, "Heroic Tradition," p. 173.
107 See chapter 6, pp. 167–72.

Binding the Heart and Mind Against Affliction

While we have seen that Anglo-Saxon poets constantly employ formulaic binding to describe negative, constraining effects, there is also a current in Old English poetry that depicts a positive side to mental constriction. Just as the unprepared mind is to be eschewed, the prepared spirit, which holds itself fast and firm, is to be emulated. The language of binding, with its connotations of construction and architectural stability, can be suitably employed here too. A striking example occurs in *Resignation*:

> hwæþre ic me ealles þæs   ellen wylle
> habban ond hlyhhan   ond me hyhtan to,
> frætwian mec on ferðweg   ond fundian
> sylf to þam siþe   þe ic asettan sceal,
> gæst gearwian,   ond me þæt eal for gode þolian
> bliþe mode,   nu ic gebunden eom
> fæste in minum ferþe.   (70–6a)

(regardless of all this I will have courage and laugh and trust in myself, equip myself for the way forward and hasten to that journey which I must set out on, prepare my spirit, and suffer all that for God with a happy mind, now I am bound fast in my heart.)

In her edition, Klinck takes *gebunden* to mean "committed, obliged," citing W.S. Mackie's literal translation in contrast to her own metaphorical interpretation.[108] However, given the other uses of *bindan*, especially in collocations with *fæst*, the sense of this passage seems to be one of a firmness that comes from proper construction and careful maintenance of the soul. This is fully in line with more literal instances of things that are bound, and so there is no reason to differentiate them – rather, the fact that common language is used to describe them should be highlighted because it emphasizes the permeation of *bindan* in all aspects of construction and constriction.

The firm bonds of the heart and mind are also invoked in *Beowulf*, at the hero's departure from Denmark. In this passage, Hrothgar, who, as we

---

108 *Old English Elegies*, p. 193.

have already seen is generally characterized with reference to his wisdom
and age, is described as overwhelmed by emotion:

> Wæs him se man to þon leof
> þæt he þone breostwylm   forberan ne mehte,
> ac him on hreþre   hygebendum fæst
> æfter deorum men   dyrne langað
> born wið blode.   (1876b–80a)

(The man was beloved to him so that he might not hold back the breast-
surging, but in his heart, fast with mind-bonds, a secret longing for the dear
man burned in his blood.)

Lockett examines this instance in relation to the hydraulic model of the
mind, arguing that the *breostwylm*, which has in the past been read as
the flow of tears, actually refers to the boiling of the breast with emotion.[109] This reading is supported by the fact that Hrothgar manages to
keep his longing *dyrne* (secret), which would not be possible if he were
visibly weeping. The binding, then, relates to Hrothgar's control over his
emotions:

> Beowulf is so beloved that when he departs, Hrothgar cannot prevent his
> breast from boiling, *but* his hidden longing remains firmly tethered in the
> breast. The heat of Hrothgar's emotion, while wilfully constrained inside
> the pectoral container, burns all the more fiercely and transmits its heat to
> the blood. The word *hygebendum* evokes a mechanism by which an indi-
> vidual might counteract the outward pressure of the seething mind-in-the-
> breast, as if the mind-tethers were muscles that could be flexed at will to
> keep words and tears from escaping from the breast, but at the risk of in-
> creasing the heat and pressure inside the chest cavity.[110]

Thus, internal bonds are often as concerned with constriction as they are
with structural connection.

Apart from this instance of *breostwylm*, the only other occurrence of
the term appears in several Old English translations of Psalm 21:10, where

---

109 *Anglo-Saxon Psychologies*, p. 83.
110 Ibid.

the breast-surging relates to a "full breast; (mother's) milk."[111] This seems significant given Clover's reading of Hrothgar and aging members of society as occupying the same gendered space as women. However, given that *bosm* (breast/embrace) is also frequently linked to the father – indeed to God the father[112] – the implication may be more related to his paternal feelings towards Beowulf rather than an indication of a one-sex model of gender. Nevertheless, the strength of Hrothgar's emotions are depicted as something which must be kept secret and bound fast, with unchecked passion clearly marked as dangerous through references that connect burning and *wylm* to fire and poison.

A description of the binding of one's heart and mind is also found in *Homiletic Fragment II*:

> Gefeoh nu on ferðe   ond to frofre geþeoh
> dryhtne þinum,   ond þinne dom arær,
> heald hordlocan,   hyge fæste bind
> mid modsefan.   (1–4a)

(Rejoice now in spirit and grow as a comfort to your lord, and raise your glory, hold the hoard-enclosure, bind fast your mind with your heart.)

The formulaic nature of these depictions is clear when the two poems are read together. Just as this passage collocates *hyge* (mind), *fæst*, and *bindan*, so too does line 1978b of *Beowulf*: *hygebendum fæst* (1978b) (fast with mind-bonds). However, here the mind and spirit are less dangerous commodities that must be imprisoned than they are valuable enclosures

---

111 *DOE*, s.v. *breostwylm*, sense a.

112 Ibid., sense 2. Of the nine collocations of *bosm* and *fæder*, eight have a religious context: Ælfric's homilies, *Feria IIII de fide Catholica*, in *Catholic Homilies: First Series*, ed. Clemoes, p. 338, line 96; *Sexagesima*, in *Catholic Homilies: Second Series*, ed. Godden, p. 54, line 61; *Feria II in Letania maiore*, in *Second Series*, p. 186, line 210; *Feria tertia in Letania maiore*, in Bazire and Cross, *Eleven Old English Rogationtide Homilies*, p. 99, line 181; homily 1, *Annunciatio S. Mariae*, in Morris, *Blickling Homilies*, p. 5; Numbers 11:12, in *Old English Version of the Heptateuch*, p. 310; Gregory the Great's *Pastoral Care*, in *King Alfred's West-Saxon Version*, pp. 46/7, section 5, lines 3–4; and Prayer 18 from Holthausen, "Altenglische Interlinearversionen lateinischer Gebete und Beichten," p. 242, line 2. Appearing in a non-religious context, the terms collocate in *Riddle 37* (bellows) 7–8.

(*hordlocan*), which must be protected.[113] It is perhaps the playing with this common trope that led to its expansion in the poetic depictions in *Soul and Body I* and *II* of the soul enclosed and held captive by the body.

The overtly religious nature of these passages sets them off from *The Wanderer*, alongside which they can be read.[114] *The Wanderer* depicts a particularly heroic approach to binding one's emotions – similar to that evinced by Hrothgar – and herein lies the key to the wanderer's distress. The lonely warrior initially speaks of his attempts to curb his emotions:

> Ic to soþe wat
> þæt biþ in eorle   indryhten þeaw,
> þæt he his ferðlocan   fæste binde,
> healde his hordcofan,   hycge swa he wille.
> Ne mæg werig mod   wyrde wiðstondan,
> ne se hreo hyge   helpe gefremman.
> Forðon domgeorne   dreorigne oft
> in hyra breostcofan   bindað fæste;
> swa ic modsefan   minne sceolde,
> oft earmcearig,   eðle bidæled,
> freomægum feor   feterum sælan   (10b–21)

(I know as a truth that it is a lordly custom in a nobleman that he should bind fast his mind-enclosure, hold his hoard-chamber, think as he will. Nor may a weary mind withstand fate, nor can the troubled mind perform help. Therefore the glory-eager ones often bind fast that which causes grief in their breast-coffer; so I, often miserable in sorrow, deprived of my homeland, far from friendly kinsmen, have had to bind my heart with fetters).

This passage contains a much higher concentration of hoard (*-loca/-cofa/ hord*), mind/heart (*ferð-/mod-/hyge/breost-/-sefa*), and constriction terms (*fæst/bindan/feterum/sælan*). In addition to reading it in terms of the hydraulic mind and the ideal of cardiocentric restraint,[115] scholars have

---

113 See also *The Hêliand* 1651–5a for an association between heaven and a mental treasure hoard.

114 Andy Orchard outlines the verbal overlap between these lines and the opening of *The Wanderer*; "Re-Reading *The Wanderer*," pp. 16–17.

115 Lockett, *Anglo-Saxon Psychologies*, pp. 79–83.

noted the poem's movement from restraint to freedom,[116] which is ironically paralleled by a progression from frenzied motion and wandering to stasis.[117] However, a link between the wanderer's attempt to bind his mind and the unbinding of the world around him has also been emphasized:

> The binding imagery ties the poem together, joining the concept of the decaying external world with that of the wanderer's mental state. At the same time, the imagery demonstrates the oppositions in the poem: the tightly bound mind maintained in opposition to the storm, the ultimate image of chaotic nature.[118]

Ruth Wehlau further refers to this personal binding as "the only available response to the slow unbinding of Creation, over which one has no power."[119] However, the poem makes it clear that this attempt by the wanderer to hold his emotions at bay actually causes a great deal of distress.

William C. Johnson maintains that the wanderer's assumption that binding his thoughts will act as a consolation in the bound world "is, of course, wrong; and the poet's dramatizing of futile acts of binding becomes a criticism of them and the view of life they imply. Stoicism of this sort has no answer for death, for its binding is not the *fæstnung* (115), 'firm peace, security,' of the Father in Heaven."[120] There is much to be said for this approach, especially if we read the poem according to its imagery of hoards and enclosures. As Wehlau notes, here the mind's fastness relates not to protection (like that in *Juliana*), but to restraint,[121] thus implying that the wanderer's mistake lies in his misinterpretation of religious wisdom. The image present in the statement in *Homiletic Fragment II* that people should bind the mind and hold the *hordlocan* (hoard-enclosure) is one of protecting the mind, heart, and spirit within the fortress of the body. Thus, we have a rare portrayal of positive constriction that ultimately relates to the body's natural construction. This is not the sort of constriction we see in imagery of slavery, prison, hell, etc., and yet the wanderer treats his mind as a sort of prison for his thoughts, using fetters to hold them in place.

---

116 Ibid., p. 10.
117 Ibid., p. 11; and Hait, "Wanderer's Lingering Regret," p. 281.
118 Wehlau, *Riddle of Creation*, p. 50.
119 Ibid., p. 48.
120 "*Werig* and *Dreorig* in *The Wanderer*," pp. 59–60.
121 *Riddle of Creation*, p. 47.

Andy Orchard argues that the wanderer's journey towards wisdom involves a journey from constraint to mental freedom and stability, which aligns the poem with a movement away from a secular past towards Christian values.[122] However, if we accept that the wanderer converts to Christianity and, through it, develops into the wise man at the end of the poem, then we might be surprised to see that his new wisdom does not entirely negate a philosophy of mental restraint:

> Til biþ se þe his treowe gehealdeþ,   ne sceal næfre his torn to rycene
> beorn of his breostum acyþan,   nemþe he ær þa bote cunne,
> eorl mid elne gefremman.   (112–14a)

(Good is he who holds his faith, a warrior should never too quickly make known his grief from his heart, until he, a nobleman, knows the remedy beforehand, [how] to act with courage.)

The advice still holds that rash bouts of emotion are unwise for warriors; however, there is an acknowledgment that some expression may be permitted should a remedy be at hand. Thus, the constraint of emotions is not entirely rejected, but qualified, perhaps to be read in the religious context of protective binding emphasized in *Homiletic Fragment II*.

This mental control is also ultimately linked to speech, as the verb *acyþan* (to make known) demonstrates. The maintaining of strict boundaries between what is thought and what is said is thus key to this second passage. However, the previous reference to binding the mind describes not the careful withholding of speech, but rather its wholesale suppression:

> Nis nu cwicra nan
> þe ic him modsefan   minne durre
> sweotule asecgan.   (9b–11a)

(There is now no one living to whom I dare express my heart openly.)

It is, therefore, the inability to speak and the separation from the *larcwidum* (38a) (teaching-words) of his lord that cause the wanderer to suffer

---

122 "Re-Reading *The Wanderer*," p. 26.

in silence and in constraint.[123] The link highlighted here between the mind and language is particularly interesting because language is also characterized as bound and woven in Old English poetry, as the following chapter demonstrates.

A final instance of emotional binding is noteworthy because it presents an entirely different context. *Paris Psalter (Psalm 146)* refers to God's ability to heal in the following terms: *Se hæleð eac heortan geðræste / and heora unrotnesse ealle gewriðeð* (7–8) (he also heals afflicted hearts and entirely binds up their sorrow). This is a fairly direct translation of *Vulgate* Psalm 146:3, which praises God *qui sanat contritos corde et alligat plagas eorum* (who heals the broken in heart and binds up their wounds). The psalm evokes a medical metaphor in which wounds to the inner being are healed through a binding that parallels the wrapping of injuries. Indeed, the Old English verb *wriðan* is frequently invoked in this context,[124] and so it comes as no surprise to find the term used here. However, *geþræstan*, which is generally confined to prose, is striking here because "binding" and "constraining" are listed among its possible meanings, many of which are decidedly negative ("to crush," "destroy," "afflict," "twist," "torment," etc.).[125] The use of the verb in this psalm, alongside a verb of bandaging, implies that the translator is contrasting differing states of internal binding. It is tempting to read previous examples, in which the emotions are depicted as constrained, protected, and fettered, in light of the medical context evoked here, and conclude that for Anglo-Saxon writers, the heart, despite many injuries and afflictions, can be bound up and bandaged like any other body part.

The above discussions of the bonds that both tie the body together and afflict it, and protect the mind and attack it, indicate a complex approach to internal binding. The differing applications of the terminology demonstrate binding's dual life as constructive and constrictive. Ultimately, the presence of all of these types of bodily and mental bonds in the literature conveys the desire to exercise some form of control over the internal world – whether by giving it a structure or assigning responsibility for affliction.

---

123 Wehlau, *Riddle of Creation*, p. 47.
124 See above, p. 196n7.
125 Boswoth and Toller, *Anglo-Saxon Dictionary*, s.v.

8 Language and Knowledge

While today we may imagine language as emanating from the mouth, the Anglo-Saxon understanding of the mind strongly associated speech with the chest.[1] As Eric Jager has observed: "[v]erbal prowess is collocated in the chest along with the vital powers and moral virtue, making the chest a "center of action," and a symbolic repository of heroic values."[2] This association of chest and language underlies the common poetic depiction of the mind as a *wordhord*, an image that Jager argues aligns speech with the treasure-hoards that are central to the functioning of heroic society.[3] Britt Mize has further revised previous discussions of the compound *wordhord*, noting that, rather than "a collection of words," it should be understood as signifying "the discursive treasury – a mind full of valuable potential utterances – that is 'unlocked' in the act of speech."[4] Wise language and the knowledge it conveys are thus marked as valuable assets.

In addition to emphasizing the significance of wise words and their meaning, this treasure metaphor indicates one of the most interesting aspects of Old English poetry's approach: this is a concrete vision of

---

1 Indeed, it is interesting that all the Old English references to the binding of the tongue occur in prose texts which demonstrate a clear Latin influence. See *DOE*, s.v. *bend*, sense 1.b.i.a.: "*tungan bend* 'bond of the tongue', i.e. speechlessness"); and s.v. *gebend*: "bond, cord; figurative: *gebend tunges* 'bond of the tongue'." See also Lockett, *Anglo-Saxon Psychologies*, pp. 1–178.

2 "Speech and the Chest in Old English Poetry," p. 849.

3 Ibid.

4 "Manipulations of the Mind-as-Container Motif," p. 31. See also his "Representation of the Mind as an Enclosure," pp. 69–71.

language.[5] Statements are seen as object-like entities that can be bound together, (inter)woven and locked up. This concretization of language is evident in compounds such as *reordberend*[6] (speech-bearer) – a "person" term – reminiscent of the array of "warrior" terms that compound *-berend* with an element of weaponry or armour.[7] Similarly, verbs accompanying "speech" terms in the poetry include *mengan* (to mix)[8] and *wrixlan* (to exchange).[9] Given the frequent use of *mengan* in medical contexts, this verb can be said to carry a sense of combining ingredients, frequently liquid ones,[10] while *wrixlan* has a similar physical sense to it when used of exchanging objects.[11] Metaphors of weaving and binding also play into this concretization, with the speaker or poet occasionally referred to as one who binds or weaves speeches or poetic compositions together.

This particular association between words and weaving has in the past been explained by the centrality of textile production in Anglo-Saxon life and the household.[12] Maren Clegg Hyer, in particular, surmises that

---

5 Mize also discusses this reification in "Representation of the Mind as an Enclosure," pp. 75–6; and "Manipulations of the Mind-as-Container Motif," p. 31.

6 With the most frequent poetic occurrences of all *-berend* compounds, this term is found nine times: *Andreas* 419b; *Christ I* 278b and 381b; *Christ III* 1024b and 1368a; *Daniel* 123a; *Dream of the Rood* 3a, 89b; and *Elene* 1282a.

7 These include *sweordberend* (sword-bearer): *Genesis B* 1056; *æscberend* (spear-bearer): *Andreas* 45, 1074, 1536; and *Genesis B* 2040; *garberend* (spear-bearer): *Battle of Maldon* 260; and *Exodus* 227; and *helmberend* (helmet-bearer): *Beowulf* 2516, 2638; and *Descent into Hell* 37. Compounds with the first element referring to life or the spirit are also popular; see *feorhberend*: *Genesis B* 1953; and *Riddle 39* 5; *sawlberend*: *Beowulf* 1002; and *gæstberend*: *Christ III* 1598; *Gifts of Men* 1; and *Riddle 20* 8.

8 It collocates once with *-cwide* (words): *Solomon and Saturn II* 255b; once with *frinan* (to ask): *Solomon and Saturn I* 58–9; and once with *gerscipe* (conversation? – see the *DOE* for more on the ambiguity of this term's meaning): *Riming Poem* 11b.

9 It collocates with *word* six times: *Beowulf* 366a and 874a; *Riddle 60* 10a; *Soul and Body I* 115a and *II* 110a; and *Vainglory* 16a; with *giedd* twice: *Maxims I* 4a; and *Vainglory* 15b–16a; with *spræc* twice: *Riddle 60* 9b–10a; and *Rune Poem* 57b; with *cwide* once: *Beowulf* 366–7a; and with *reord* twice: *Phoenix* 127–8a; and *Riddle 8* 1–2.

10 Indeed, elsewhere in the poetry, *mengan* collocates with *mere-* (sea): *Beowulf* 1449; *Husband's Message* 43a; and *Metres of Boethius* (*Metre 5*) 9–10; and with *blod* (blood): *Beowulf* 847–8, 1593–4; and *Paris Psalter* (*Psalm 105*) 109–10.

11 See also Mize, "Representation of the Mind as an Enclosure," pp. 75–6.

12 "Textiles and Textile Imagery in Old English," pp. 214–5. Hyer also explores a range of analogous associations in Latin, Greek, and Germanic texts, and points out that a similar metaphor is attested in Irish and Vedic texts. She further notes that the weaving of words occurs universally, rather than simply in Indo-European sources, something that suggests this tradition may be independently common to textile cultures. See

entertainment taking place around the loom may have helped to link the concepts of weaving, music, and poetry together, while similarities between the physical structure and sound produced by the lyre and the loom may have further fostered such a connection.[13] The link to everyday domestic experience is perhaps less relevant for Old English poetry because, as outlined in chapter 1, the poetic references to woven cloth are emphatically concerned with high status rather than quotidian usage. The focus of weaving and binding terminology in these texts reveals an interest in a concept of craftsmanship that both poet and poetry revere and elevate.

John Leyerle's much anthologized article on the structure of *Beowulf* invokes word-weaving as evidence for a connection between textiles, interlaced metalwork, and narrative form – that is, he argues that the episodic and digressive nature of *Beowulf*'s narrative stems from an Anglo-Saxon cultural aesthetic that prizes artistic interlace.[14] However, as I demonstrate below, close reading of Old English poetry's use of weaving and binding metaphors indicates a concern with smaller-scale joining of concepts, rather than narrative-wide scope. Despite its influence, this theory of interlace appears to reflect a modern metaphor rather than an Anglo-Saxon one. That being said, metaphors of weaving and binding do play into a common Anglo-Saxon approach to crafted objects, so Leyerle's link between artful language and skilful metalwork is a useful one. Previous chapters have established the Old English poetic fascination with material objects whose creation requires a high calibre of skill, and it is not a great stretch for the poet – one who held a prized position – to imagine his or her own skilled work through a similar metaphor.[15] Thus, when Old English poets depict language in terms of weaving and binding, it is imperative that we keep in mind this status-related context of craft and construction.

---

pp. 223–6. Given the irrefutable ties between Old English and Anglo-Latin, the Latin examples provide the most relevant basis for comparison. It is with the Latin tradition that many discussions of text/textile wordplay begin because, of course, the Latin verb *textere* (and the noun deriving from it, *textus*) initially referred to weaving, later coming to indicate writing as well. Such wordplay is common to the Anglo-Latin corpus; see Clover, *Medieval Saga*, p. 93.

13 Hyer, "Textiles and Textile Imagery in Old English," pp. 214–17.

14 "Interlace Structure of *Beowulf.*"

15 That the poet is revered as a craftsman of great skill is made clear in references such as those in *Beowulf* 89b–91, 496b–8 and 1063–70; *Deor* 35–42; and *Fortunes of Men* 77–84, as well as in the examples discussed below.

Word-weaving and -binding

It is in the light of such construction that the most elaborate Old English poetic depiction of woven words occurs. In the epilogue to *Elene*,[16] the poet Cynewulf refers to himself as a metaphorical weaver:

> Þus ic frod ond fus   þurh þæt fæcne hus
> wordcræftum wæf   ond wundrum læs,
> þragum þreodude   ond geþanc reodode[17]
> nihtes nearwe.   Nysse ic gearwe
> be ðære [rode][18] riht   ær me rumran geþeaht
> þurh ða mæran miht   on modes þeaht
> wisdom onwreah.   Ic wæs weorcum fah,
> synnum asæled,   sorgum gewæled,
> bitrum gebunden,   bisgum beþrungen,
> ær me lare onlag   þurh leohtne had
> gamelum to geoce,   gife unscynde
> mægencyning amæt   ond on gemynd begeat,
> torht ontynde,   tidum gerymde,
> bancofan onband,   breostlocan onwand,
> leoðucræft onleac.   Þæs ic lustum breac,
> willum in worlde.   (1236–51a)

(Thus I, experienced and ready, through that deceitful house [i.e., body] wove with the craft of words and miraculously gathered, at times deliberated and carefully sifted my thoughts by night. I did not sufficiently know the truth

---

16 For a discussion of the conventionality of this and other medieval epilogues, see Gradon, *Cynewulf's "Elene,"* pp. 20–2; and Anderson, *Cynewulf*, pp. 18–19. For a contrasting approach to the epilogue's originality, see Fish, "Theme and Pattern," pp. 22–4; and Calder, *Cynewulf*, pp. 134–6.

17 The meaning of this verb is contested. Bosworth and Toller list only "?" under its definition, while Hall defines it as "to sift? search out?," suggesting it may be related to *redian* (to reach, discover, effect). See *Anglo-Saxon Dictionary* and *Concise Anglo-Saxon Dictionary*, s.v. *reodian*.

18 This term does not appear in the manuscript, but is generally added by editors based on context and the line's alliteration. See Gradon, *"Elene,"* p. 71; Krapp, *Vercelli Book*, pp. 100, 149; and Nelson, *Judith, Juliana, and Elene*, p. 182.

about that [cross], before wisdom, through its illustrious might, uncovered in my mind's thought a greater knowledge. I was stained by my deeds, tied up by sins, afflicted by sorrows, bound and oppressed by bitter cares, before he granted knowledge to me in luminous form, as a comfort to an old man, the mighty king bestowed a glorious gift and poured it into my mind, revealed its brightness, at times increased it, unbound my bone-chamber, unwound my breast-enclosure, unlocked poetic craft. I enjoyed that happily, with delight in the world.)

This passage invokes word-weaving exactly as we might expect it to: as a metaphor for the joining together of statements in poetic composition. The significance of the link between poetic skill and divine inspiration is made clear, and the well-organized nature of Cynewulf's mind is set in opposition to the affliction of the unenlightened and those trapped in bodily states. Not only is Cynewulf a weaver, but his poetic ability is also depicted as treasure locked up (*leoðucræft onleac*) in the now open hoard of his mind (*bancofan onband/breostlocan onwand*).

The metaphorical nature of this weaving image can be confirmed through careful attention to the poetics of this passage, a set of verses whose stylistic highlighting is particularly notable.[19] Not only does every line doubly alliterate,[20] but there is also a great variety of alliterating sounds: f, þ, n, r, s, g and t each govern the alliteration of one line, while b, l and m govern two lines and w governs three. The lines whose alliterating sounds repeat include references to weaving (*wæf*) and uncovering (*onwreoh*) skilful words (*wordcræftum*), will (*willum*) and wisdom (*wisdom*); (un-) binding (*gebunden/onband*), the body/chest (*bancofan, breostlocan*), and afflictions (*bitrum/bisgum*); bestowing (*onlag*) and unlocking (*onleac*) knowledge (*lare*); the mind (*modes, gemynd*) and God's might (*mæran miht/mægencyning*). The repetition of these letters in a passage that is in part marked by its range is easily explicable when we take into account

---

19 For discussions of the poetics of these lines, see Rogers, "Rhymes in the Epilogue to *Elene*"; Zacher, "Cynewulf at the Interface," pp. 351–3; and Olsen, *Speech, Song, and Poetic Craft*, pp. 76–9. For more on Cynewulf's style in general, see Calder, *Cynewulf*, pp. 139–70; and Steen, *Verse and Virtuosity*, pp. 116, 118, 122, 124–6.

20 B.R. Hutcheson calculates the frequency of double alliteration in *Elene* at a fairly low 43 per cent, making the concentration of such alliteration in this passage particularly noteworthy; see *Old English Poetic Metre*, p. 271.

the importance of all of these words and concepts, particularly in a religious context.

The passage is further emphasized through its use of rhyme, consonance, and assonance,[21] which connect the final words of the a- and b-verse of most lines (*fus/hus, þreodude/reodode, nearwe/gearwe, riht/geþeaht, miht/þeaht, onwreah/fah, asæled/gewæled, gebunden/beþrungen, onlag/had, amæt/begeat, ontynde/gerymde, onband/onwand, onleac/breac*). Ornamental alliteration also links lines 1246 and 1247 ("g": *gamelum/geoce/gife/begeat*), as well as 1249 and 1250 ("b" and "l": *ban-/onband/breost-/breac; -locan/leoðu-/onleac/lustum*), while interlinear rhyme and assonance occur in several places (*nihtes/riht/miht; -cræftum/wæf/læs; geþeaht/þeaht/onwreah; ær/mæran; lare/onlag/had; unscynde/-cyning/gemynd/ontynde/gerymde; -cofan/-locan; ban-/onband/onwand*).[22]

In addition to these effects, the passage also includes a great deal of formulaic language. Notably, several of the formulas are related to construction and craft:

wordcræft x: *Elene* 592a
x gebunden: *Andreas* 580b, 947a, 1379b and 1396b; *Beowulf* 1531b, 1743a
   and 2111b; *Christ III* 873b and 1538b; *Christ and Satan* 58b, 103a
   and 323b; *Deor* 24b; *Elene* 771b; *Judith* 114b; *Juliana* 433b; *Metres
   of Boethius (Metre 20)* 67b and 153b; *(Metre 26)* 96b; *Riddle 56* 6a;
   Seafarer 8b; *Soul and Body I* 31b; and *Soul and Body II* 28b
x onleac: *Andreas* 172b, 316b and 601b; *Beowulf* 259b; *Elene* 1250a; *Metres
   of Boethius (Metre 6)* 1b; *Solomon and Saturn I* 3a; and *Widsith* 1b.
x onwreah: *Vainglory* 3a

---

21 For more on rhyme in this passage and in Cynewulf's other works, see Rogers,
   "Rhymes in the Epilogue"; Zacher, "Cynewulf at the Interface," p. 351; Anderson,
   Cynewulf, p. 16; Steen, *Verse and Virtuosity*, p. 126; and Conner, "On Dating
   Cynewulf," p. 24. For discussions of rhyme in a wider context, see Bredehoft, *Early
   English Metre*, pp. 57–62 and 79–80; as well as his "Old English and Old Saxon
   Formulaic Rhyme"; and Stanley, "Rhymes in English Medieval Verse."
22 Zacher argues against the reading that line 1237 contains assonance, instead maintaining that this line visually puns the final words of each half-line; "Cynewulf at the
   Interface," p. 352. However, the presence of -*cræft* in addition to *wæf* and *læs*, as well as
   myriad other assonant phrases, indicates the importance of taking into account a wider
   variety of contexts than simply the words in half-line final positions.

Further formulas include:

nihtes nearwe: *Fates of the Apostles* 104a; and *Guthlac B* 1210a (*niht* and
   nearwe also collocate in *Beowulf* 422; *Exhortation to Christian Living*
   53; and *Seafarer* 7a)
gife unscynde: *Elene* 1200b
will- in (x) worulde: *Andreas* 304a and 356a; and *Vainglory* 72a
x -sæled: *Beowulf* 2764a; *Christ II* 736a; *Exodus* 471a; *Genesis A* 2197a;
   Genesis B 765a; and *Judith* 114a
x -wæled: *Andreas* 1361a
x -þrungen: *Andreas* 990b; *Elene* 949a; *Genesis A* 2511a; *Guthlac B* 934b,
   943b; *Phoenix* 341a; *Seafarer* 8b (here rhyming with *gebunden* (9b) as
   well); and *Vainglory* 56b
x to geoce: *Beowulf* 1834a; *Christ I* 124a; *Elene* 1138a; *Guthlac A* 367a;
   Homiletic Fragment I 46a; *Seafarer* 101a; and *Waldere A* 25a
x gerymde: *Dream of the Rood* 89a

A scholarly tendency to view the formula as purely functional can be identified in the remarks of Éamonn Ó Carragáin on this passage's invocation
of *wordcræft wæf* and *wordhord onleac*: "These two references are brief
and conventional. Cynewulf is not primarily interested in techniques of
poetic composition. The epilogue is clearly intended to emphasize his efforts as a meditative reader, rather than his skill as a poet."[23] This abrupt
dismissal is unfounded, as the above discussion of poetics demonstrates.
Rather, Cynewulf's emphasis on formulaic language helps to highlight this
passage, as does his employment of concentrated poetic artistry and rhetorical flourish.[24]

Thomas A. Bredehoft has recently argued that rhyme and secondary
alliteration are commonly employed as ornamental effects, especially in
cases where the poet wishes to emphasize construction motifs.[25] The

---

23 "Cynewulf's Epilogue to *Elene* and the Tastes of the Vercelli Compiler," p. 191. See the
    introduction to this survey, pp. 8–10. For a discussion of formulaic diction as vibrant
    rather than static.
24 For more on poetic highlighting, see Orchard, "Artful Alliteration."
25 *Early English Metre*, pp. 65, 68, 93, 149. Seth Lerer also discusses binding imagery in
    relation to poetic construction, although he is less concerned with poetic devices; see
    Literacy and Power, pp. 112–25.

existence of Bredehoft's "linguistic or poetic interlacing"[26] (distinct from Leyerle's understanding of the term) is corroborated by the passage cited above from *Elene*. In fact, these lines sweep aside Bredehoft's caveat that interlace provides a useful reference-point for modern readers, "even if the Anglo-Saxon poet or audience might not have conceptualized the use of these secondary effects as interlace."[27] Cynewulf's characterization of poetic craft as a type of weaving indicates that at least some Anglo-Saxons did conceptualize poetry in terms of interlaced objects – in this case, textiles.

Further examples exist in the form of word-binding, with several such instances occurring in *Beowulf*. Indeed, the description of the storyteller in Hrothgar's court who eulogizes Beowulf's monster-fights neatly echoes Cynewulf's image of composition:

> Hwilum cyninges þegn,
> guma gilphlæden,   gidda gemyndig,
> se ðe eal fela   ealdgesegena
> worn gemunde,   word oþer fand
> soðe gebunden;   secg eft ongan
> sið Beowulfes   snyttrum styrian
> ond on sped wrecan   spel gerade,
> wordum wrixlan.   (867b–74a)

(Sometimes a retainer of the king, a man filled with tales of glory, mindful of songs, he who greatly remembered a large number of ancient legends, arranged different words, truthfully bound – the warrior again began to wisely put into motion Beowulf's undertaking and to successfully utter a skilful tale, to exchange words.)

Here we have a clear reference to a concrete vision of poetic composition. Not only does the poet bind words together, much like an architect or craftsman binds materials into a useful creation, but he also exchanges (*wrixlan*) them, which further implies their physicality. The skill and wisdom of this *gemyndig* (mindful) poet are made clear through the terms *snyttrum* (wisely), *on sped* (successfully), and *gerad* (skilful). The poet's

---

26 *Early English Metre*, p. 65.
27 Ibid., p. 149.

process of creation is thus depicted using imagery very like that of object-construction as discussed in chapter 3.

In addition to the poet's specific reference to the storyteller's ability to bind words together, he employs ornamental poetic effects that we can read as further instances of linguistic interlace. While this passage contains fewer rhyming words – except perhaps for *munde* and *gebunden* – there is a great deal of assonance, particularly in alliterating words (*cystum/cyninges; gilp-/gidda; eal/eald-; worn/word; snyttrum/styrian; wrecan/spel*[28]). Furthermore, half of these eight lines employ double alliteration; this time, rather than a variety of alliterating letters, we have a concentration of specific sounds that appears to be deliberate. Thus, at the very point of focus on the binding together of words, the poet employs an alliterative envelope pattern: line 870 alliterates on "w," the next three lines alliterate on "s," and they are followed by another line alliterating on "w." Formulaic language is, once again, prominent, with formulas related both to construction and the materiality of language (*x gebunden,*[29] *wordum wrixlan*[30]), mindfulness (*x gemyndig,*[31] *x gemunde*[32]), and the hero (*x Beowulfes*[33]). Together, these effects demonstrate that, as with the *Elene* passage, the *Beowulf*-poet is here highlighting a description of interlaced language through rhetorical devices that reflect the verses' content.

---

28 Technically, the long "e" in *sped* does not assonate, however its visual similarity appears to be no mistake.

29 *Andreas* 580b, 947a, 1379b, and 1396b; *Beowulf* 1743a and 2111b; *Christ III* 873b and 1538b; *Christ and Satan* 58b, 103a, and 323b; *Deor* 24b; *Elene* 771b; *Judith* 114b; *Juliana* 433b; *Metres of Boethius (Metre 20)* 67b and 153b; *(Metre 26)* 96b; *Riddle 56* 6a; *Seafarer* 8b; *Soul and Body I* 31b; and *Soul and Body II* 28b.

30 See *Beowulf* 366a; *Riddle 60* 10a; *Soul and Body I* 115a; *Soul and Body II* 110a; and *Vainglory* 16a.

31 *Andreas* 1001b, 1263b, and 1312b; *Beowulf* 613b, 1173b, 1530a, 2082b, 2171b, and 2689b; *Elene* 213b, 266b, 818a, 901b, and 939b; *Exodus* 549b; *Genesis A* 1780a, 1899a, 1943b, 2164b, 2374b, and 2465b; *Guthlac B* 1294a (a related collocation, rather than a formula); *Judith* 74b; *Juliana* 601b; *Kentish Hymn* 31b; *Metres of Boethius (Metre 22)* 55b; *Paris Psalter (Psalm 76)* 24b and 31b; *(Psalm 104)* 21b and 114b; *(Psalm 110)* 13b; *Kentish Psalm 50* 147b; *Seasons for Fasting* 163b; and *Wanderer* 6b.

32 *Battle of Maldon* 225b; *Beowulf* 1129b, 1141b, 1259b, 2114b (*worn gemunde*), 2391b, 2431b, 2488b, and 2678a; *Genesis A* 1795b and 2433b; *Guthlac A* 97b and 750b; *Husband's Message* 14b; *Judgement Day II* 12b; *Metres of Boethius (Metre 1)* 79b; and *Paris Psalter (Psalm 105)* 124b.

33 *Beowulf* 795a and 1971a (identical formula).

Related to this instance is a second example from *Beowulf*, this time in Unferth's rather unflattering speech to the hero.[34] The lead-up to the famous flyting reads:

Unferð maþelode,   Ecglafes bearn,
þe æt fotum sæt   frean Scyldinga,
onband beadurune.   (499–501a)

(Unferth spoke, the son of Ecglaf, who sat at the feet of the lord of the Scyldings, he unbound battle-secrets.)

Here, it seems likely that Unferth's unbinding of words relates more to constriction than to construction: to the letting loose of language from its enclosure rather than to the careful skill of a textile or related craft. However, the exact nature of what Unferth is unbinding is not clear, since *run* can refer to an engraved symbol or letter, as well as a secret. For this unique instance of the compound *beadurun*, the *DOE* reads: "secret quarrel, literally 'battle-secret'; *onbindan beadurune* 'to begin a bellicose speech' or 'to begin the conflict'." Given the context, as well as that of *Elene* 27b's similar compound *wælrun* (which refers to the wolf's howling song as it anticipates battle), the definition "secret" would seem to be appropriate here. This conclusion is further supported by the many formulas that describe the opening or unlocking of speech- and mind-hoards.[35] Rather than elegantly binding words into poetry, Unferth (whose actions may or may not be sanctioned by Hrothgar) is aggressively sending forth information that verges on the taboo.[36]

------

34 For more on Unferth and the flyting, see Church, "Beowulf's "ane ben""; Clover, "Germanic Context"; Eliason, "Þyle and Scop"; Enright, "Warband Context"; Ogilvy, "Unferth: Foil to Beowulf?"; Parks, "Flyting and Fighting"; as well as his "Flyting Speech in Traditional Heroic Narrative"; Rosier, "Design for Treachery"; and Silber, "Rhetoric as Prowess in the Unferð Episode." For more on this passage in the context of twentieth-century verse translations, see Magennis, *Translating Beowulf*, pp. 37–8, 103–4, 130–1, 156–7, 185–7.

35 See chapter 7, pp. 213–30.

36 Carol J. Clover notes that battle metaphors are also evident in the Old Norse flytings. "Germanic Context," p. 460. See also Mize, "Manipulations of the Mind-as-Container Motif," pp. 28–30 for more on this passage.

Once again, these lines are notable for their poetics, although this time not because of ornamental rhyme or alliteration. Rather, here we have a concentration of formulas in three of the four half-lines that precede the binding reference: *Unferð maþelode*,[37] *Ecglafes bearn*,[38] and *frean Scyldinga*.[39] Interestingly, after this concentration of formulas in singly alliterating lines, the reference to (un-)binding occurs in a line with double alliteration. The second half-line, *wæs him Beowulfes sið* (501b), includes a collocation of *sið* and *Beowulfes*, which also appear concurrently in a formula in the passage depicting the storyteller's binding together of Beowulf's exploits. Along with the repeated binding language, such formulaic overlap indicates that these two passages are more closely related than has previously been recognized.

While the presence of similar diction ties these two passages together, their use of binding is nevertheless differentiated. Because of this, it is worth noting that the Unferth-passage occurs before Beowulf's exploits, while the description of the storyteller praised for his ability to bind words together comes after. The focus on constructive binding sets this later poet apart from Unferth who, in constructing his case against Beowulf, actually unbinds knowledge, releasing it (not unlike the mind-hoard so constrained in chapter 7's discussion of *The Wanderer*), in a way that ultimately connects his flyting to the removal of constrictions. We may, thus, read Unferth as de-constructing Beowulf's story through the secrets he looses. When Beowulf is able to successfully live up to his boasts and prove that his reputation is merited, his story may be re-bound and re-constructed through the words of the retainer-poet.

A final instance of word-binding – this one clearly constrictive – occurs in *Riddle 42*'s call for a solution:

---

37 The formula *x maþelode* is particularly common throughout *Beowulf*: 286a, 348a, 360a, 371a, 405a, 456a, 499a, 529a, 631a, 925a, 957a, 1215a, 1321a, 1383a, 1473a, 1651a, 1687a, 1817a, 1840a, 1999a, 2425a, 2510a, 2631a, 2724a, 2862a, and 3076a; also occurring in *Battle of Maldon* 42a and 309a; *Elene* 332a, 404a, 573a, 604a, 627a, 642a, 655a, 685a, and 806a; *Genesis A* 1820a and 2893a; *Genesis B* 347a and 522a; and *Riddle 38* 5a.

38 Variations of this formula also occur in *Battle of Maldon* 267a; and *Beowulf* 590b, 1465b, and 1808a.

39 The formula *x Scyldinga* occurs throughout *Beowulf*: 30b, 53b, 58b, 148a, 170a, 291a, 371b, 428a, 456b, 464b, 500b, 597b, 663a, 778b, 913a, 1019a, 1069b, 1108b, 1154a, 1321b, 1418a, 1563b, 1601a, 1653a, 1675a, 1871a, and 2026b.

>   Hwylc þæs hordgates
> cægan cræfte   þa clamme onleac
> þe þa rædellan   wið rynemenn
> hygefæste heold   heortan bewrigene
> orþoncbendum?   (11b–15a)

(Who has unlocked, with the skill of the treasure-door's key, the chains that held the riddle mind-fast from the interpreters of secret things, concealed in the heart by skilful bonds?)

This passage relies on the idea lying behind the formulaic *wordhord* – that wisdom is enclosed and must be unlocked before it can be understood.[40] Expanding on this concept, the final lines of the poem depart from the solution (a cock and hen mating) to address the impenetrability of riddling meaning, held as it is by *orþoncbendas* (skilful bonds). As with the above passages, these verses associate knowledge and bonds; without Unferth to unbind the poem's secrets, the audience itself is challenged to unlock the poem's treasure. As Seth Lerer has argued, keys are commonly referred to in the context of wisdom in religious poetry and prose,[41] an association resonant in the formula *x-hord onleac*. Thus, while the chains (*clamme*) and bonds (*-bendum*) that the riddle-audience must unlock at first suggest physical or mental constriction, the use of the treasure metaphor and the fact that the bonds are skilful further implies a sense of craftsmanship on the part of the poet. The riddle holds the solution fast in a work whose construction is similar to that of objects crafted by a smith.[42]

Lerer also reads these lines concretely, as a reference to bookbinding. Thus, he argues that the physicality inherent in the term *orþonc* and the

---

40 For more on this context, see especially Mize, "Manipulations of the Mind-as-Container Motif," pp. 26–7; as well as his "Representation of the Mind," pp. 60–1.

41 See chapter 7, p. 210. He further argues that the use of similar imagery in *Riddle 42*'s tongue-in-cheek depiction of a cock and hen mating is a play on the usual context of religious wisdom for such language; see *Literacy and Power*, pp. 112–25; and "Riddle and Book."

42 There are seven other poetic occurrences of *orþonc*, all of which refer to skilfully or mysteriously crafted things: Grendel's *glof* (*Beowulf* 2087a); Creation (*Christ and Satan* 18a); the ornamented feathers of the phoenix (*Phoenix* 304a); the elements of the plough (*Riddle 21* 12a); a musical instrument (*Riddle 70* 3a); (possibly) an oyster (*Riddle 78* 8a); and the remains of a building (*Ruin* 16a).

fact that it is associated with craft (especially through contexts of binding and sewing) could well indicate "the appearance of the covers enclosing an Anglo-Saxon manuscript," as opposed to simply abstract bonds of secret knowledge.[43] This reading accounts well for *Riddle 42*, but it does not apply to any of the above contexts of weaving and binding words and speech. The binding that punctuates Unferth's speech and the Danish retainer's story (and the skill that characterizes each of the speakers) seems to be generally associated with language and knowledge, whether or not it is written. Hence I would argue that, while Lerer's reading of *Riddle 42* is intriguing, a broader context of word-weaving and -binding exists in Old English poetry. This is a context in which words and the secrets they hold may be woven or bound together like constructed objects, or bound up like constricted bodies, to be loosed only by one who fully understands them.[44]

The overt focus of the passages above on the weaving and binding of words speaks to the importance of construction and constriction terminology in Old English poetry and poetics. Furthermore, the highlighting of these passages through stylistic devices demonstrates the practical importance of understanding Old English poetics. The fact that these poets lavish so much artistry upon self-reflexive descriptions of speech and poetic composition implies that, rather than simply viewing formulaic language and rhetorical effects as utilitarian and structural, they recognized the importance of and took pleasure in playing with the formulaic conventionality that was so essential to poetic style.[45] Cynewulf's epilogue in particular takes several traditional approaches to weaving and binding and combines them, expanding each convention and creating links between imagery that is frequently used to different and multiple ends. Thus, the weaving of words is grouped together with discussions in previous chapters of the ties of the body and bonds of sin in a way that implies that true knowledge comes as a result not of earthly attempts to construct, but of divine loosing and the revelation of knowledge that accompanies this removal of bonds. Only then may spiritual knowledge be woven into a form that can be conveyed to the faithful. Without

---

43 *Literacy and Power*, p. 120.

44 See also *The Hêliand*'s reference to unlocking the meaning of words in lines 2574b–80a, as well as the *Order of the World* lines 17–20.

45 See Tyler, *Old English Poetics*, pp. 111–12.

recognition of the conventionality of this language, the living, dynamic use of these metaphors might have escaped us.

Weaving Evil Counsel

Given what we know of Old English poetry's approach to language as an object of skilful construction, the following set of weaving metaphors may come as a surprise. Perhaps the very opposite of the high status poetry that the poets mentioned above carefully crafted and enthusiastically depicted, the set of metaphors with which this section is concerned relates to the portrayal of evil words and plotting as a woven entity.

The majority of these examples make use of the verbs *wefan* and *webbian*, both of which possess a range of meanings in addition to their primary sense, "to weave." They can be defined generally or figuratively as "to construct," "put together," "arrange," "plan," and "contrive."[46] These seemingly separate though related semantic fields indicate that these passages may contain instances in which the verbs have been bleached of their original meaning; certainly the translations that gloss over the sense of weaving altogether imply such a consensus on the part of some scholars.[47] Establishing whether or not these examples remained actively figurative will, thus, be the primary aim of the following discussion.

The first instance occurs in *Genesis A*, in which Satan is described as an evil counsellor who pollutes the other angels through his plotting:

> Him þær sar gelamp,
> æfst and oferhygd,   and þæs engles mod
> þe þone unræd ongan   ærest fremman,
> wefan and weccean.   Þa he worde cwæð,
> niþes ofþyrsted,   þæt he on norðdæle
> ham and heahsetl   heofena rices
> agan wolde.   (28b–34a)

(There the wound came into being in them, envy and arrogance, and the pride of that angel who first began to advance evil counsel, to weave/contrive and stir up [trouble]. Then he said vocally, exceedingly thirsty for hostility, that

---

46 Bosworth and Toller, *Anglo-Saxon Dictionary*, s.v. *wefan* and *webbian*.
47 See, for example, *Genesis A* 31a and *Elene* 309a in Bradley, *Anglo-Saxon Poetry*, pp. 13, 172; and Kennedy, *Genesis*, p. 2.

he wanted to have a home and a high seat in the northern portion of the kingdom of heaven.)

There is little indication in this passage or in any other description of Satan and the fallen angels that the weaving metaphor is a living one. It is not particularly elaborated, being invoked, rather, in a series of metaphors that are linked by their physicality: sin is likened to a painful wound (*sar*), evil counsel to the act of weaving (*wefan*), and desire for hostility to a powerful thirst (*ofþyrsted*).

Furthermore, unlike the examples discussed in the previous section, language and weaving are not caught up in the passage's poetic effects. Although *wefan* and *worde* do appear in a line with double alliteration, the concentration of ornamental language is arguably focused at the end of the passage, on the description of heaven. Here we have the common formula *heofena rices*,[48] the elements of which also appear frequently as a compound or in collocation with one another.[49] In addition, *heofon* collocates elsewhere with *ham* and *heah*,[50] as it does here. *Ham* and *heahsetl*, the latter being a common compound in religious poetry,[51] also belong to the formula *x and heahsetl*,[52] and collocate with one another elsewhere.[53] If we accept that formulaic language is often used in order to highlight passages, it becomes unlikely that the weaving metaphor is being emphasized here. Indeed, *wefan* may have been included solely for the sake of supplying "w" alliteration in a line containing the term *worde*, making it ornamental, though leaving open the question of whether it is a living metaphor.

There are, however, additional instances of weaving verbs invoked in relation to evil speech, two of which appear in the same formula. Once

---

48 *Andreas* 1683b; *Christ and Satan* 277b and 617a; *Daniel* 441b; *Genesis B* 254b; *Judgement Day II* 22b; *Exhortation to Christian Living* 21a; and *Solomon and Saturn I* 37b, 52a. This phrase also appears frequently in prose.

49 A search of the *DOE Corpus* yields a further 75 instances of the compound *heofonrice*.

50 *Phoenix* 483; *Paris Psalter (Psalm 102)* 53–4; *Natale sancti Georgii martyris*, in Ælfric's *Lives of Saints*, 1:318, lines 180–1; and homily 2, *Dominica Prima in quinqvagesima*, in Morris, *Blickling Homilies*, p. 25. See also the *DOE Corpus* for the hundreds of *heofon/ham* and *heofon/heah* collocations.

51 *Christ II* 555a; *Christ III* 1217a and 1335a; *Judgement Day II* 118a; *Lord's Prayer II* 39a; *Metres of Boethius (Metre 4)* 2b and 38a; *(Metre 25)* 5a; *(Metre 29)* 73b; *Paris Psalter (Psalm 88)* 86a; *(Psalm 102)* 54a; *(Psalm 131)* 36a; and *Phoenix* 515a. See also its use in non-religious contexts: *Beowulf* 1087a and *Maxims I* 69b.

52 *Beowulf* 1087a.

53 *Christ and Satan* 218–19; and *Paris Psalter (Psalm 102)* 53–4.

again we have an example in *Elene* that is not attested in the poem's source,[54] here in the titular character's speech to the wise men of Judea:

> Swa ge modblinde   mengan ongunnon
> lige wið soðe,   leoht wið þystrum,
> æfst wið are,   inwitþancum
> wroht webbedan.   (306–9a)

(Thus in your blind hearts you began to mix lies with truth, light with darkness, malice with honour, with evil thoughts you wove/plotted slander/injustice.)

Again, there is not a great deal here to indicate that this weaving reference is a living metaphor.[55] The passage employs a few poetic effects, such as double alliteration and the parallel structure of opposition (*x wið x*) in three half-lines. The use of formulaic language for this weaving reference is also interesting, but in isolation from other formulas or poetic effects such as rhyme, assonance or ornamental alliteration, the suggestion remains that this particular formula may have been conventionalized or even directly copied. The use of *mengan* (to mix) in relation to abstract concepts that should not be united does, however, emphasize the materiality of both good and evil thoughts, and, by extrapolation, the slanderous language used to convey such thoughts. With a focus in the text on the bringing together of these various concepts, it would certainly be appropriate that a metaphor of connection such as weaving should be employed. The mixing of lies, truth, light, darkness, malice, and honour could well, therefore, merit such an association of weaving and conspiracy, with each element representing one thread in the overall plot.[56]

The second example of this formula has an even more intriguing formulaic context. This instance from *Andreas*, also non-existent in the poem's

---

54 The source for *Elene* is considered to be a non-extant Latin version of the *Vita Cyriaci*. Numerous recensions of this narrative exist in Greek, Syriac, and Latin, and are found throughout medieval Europe. See Gradon, "*Elene*," pp. 15–22; and Allen and Calder, *Sources and Analogues*, pp. 59–69. Although the beginning of this passage appears in the source, the last two half-lines do not.

55 Although it has certainly been read as such. See van der Wurff, "Cynewulf's *Elene*"; and Olsen, *Speech, Song, and Poetic Craft*, p. 142.

56 For a similar context of constructing evil words, see also the use of the term *wrohtsmiþ* (slander-smith) in *Andreas* 86a and *Guthlac B* 905a.

analogues, occurs when the saint describes to his disguised lord the high priest's treatment of Christ and the apostles:

> Huscworde ongan
> þurh inwitðanc   ealdorsacerd
> herme hyspan,   hordlocan onspeon,
> wroht webbade   (669b–72a)

(With insulting speech the high priest began through evil thoughts to revile us, unfastened his hoard-enclosure, wove/plotted slander/injustice.)

The poetic structure is tight here, with double alliteration in every line but one,[57] and with four of the six half-lines following a distinctly rhythmical noun-verb pattern (*Huscworde ongan*; *herme hyspan*; *hordlocan onspeon*; *wroht webbade*). Once again, "w"-alliteration begins the passage and ends it, and there is also a noticeable use of "o"-assonance, with repeated clusters of "or" and "on" (*-worde/hord-*; *ongan/ onspeon*; *-locan/wroht*). These lines, like the examples above of word-weaving and -binding, are intricately constructed.

Furthermore, the passage retains a strong formulaic context, through the presence of *þurh x þanc*[58] and, perhaps more relevantly, *x-locan onspeon*.[59] This formula clearly speaks to the concrete vision of language, as do several other common language-formulas that are semantically related: *wordhord onleac*[60] (unlocked the speech-hoard), *modhord onleac*[61] (unlocked the mind-hoard), *larcræftas onlocen*[62] (unlocked knowledge), *leoðucræft onleac*[63] (unlocked poetic skill), and *wordhord onwreah* (uncovered the speech-hoard).[64] Perhaps most pertinent to the current discussion is another example from *Elene*, where *x-locan onspeon* occurs just lines

---

57 The first half-line alliterates with the end of the unquoted previous sentence: *wuldre gewlitegod*.

58 *Azarias* 191a; *Christ I* 315b; *Creed* 50a; *Genesis B* 532a, 631a and 1078b; and *Metrical Charm 1* 33b.

59 *Andreas* 470b; *Elene* 79b; and *Juliana* 86b.

60 *Andreas* 316b and 601b; *Beowulf* 259b; *Metres of Boethius (Metre 6)* 1b; and *Widsith* 1b.

61 *Andreas* 172b.

62 *Solomon and Saturn I* 3a.

63 *Elene* 1250a.

64 *Vainglory* 3a.

above a weaving term in the famous formula *fæle friðowebba* (faithful peace-weaver), which will be discussed in chapter 10. As we have already seen from *Elene*'s epilogue, Cynewulf is clearly fond of formulas that emphasize the uncovering and unlocking of knowledge, as well as the unbinding and opening up of the speech-containing mind. It seems likely, therefore, that this example from *Andreas*, whose author is known to borrow directly from Cynewulf,[65] is not simply a dead textile metaphor, but a vibrant one, and one that clearly interacts with the poetically high-lighted language around it. Given Cynewulf's formulaic approach to material language, the same may be said for the previous example of the formula in *Elene*.

This reading is further supported by a similar instance in *Beowulf*, where *bregdan* is employed with the figurative meaning "to weave (devil-ish knots / malicious net)."[66] The passage reads:

> Swa sceal mæg don,
> nealles inwitnet   oðrum bregdon
> dyrnum cræfte,   deað ren(ian)
> hondgesteallan.   (2166b–9a)[67]

(So must a kinsman act, not at all braid an evil net for another with secret craft, contrive the death of a hand-companion.)

Even scholars who do not agree that poetic effects amount to a sort of linguistic interlace – and therefore read no further into the previous examples of *wefan/webbian* than simply the meaning "to contrive" – are likely to concede that this statement presents a clear textile metaphor. This is because, rather than compounding *inwit* (evil) with *þanc* (thought/intention) as both of the previous examples did, here we have the unique compound *inwitnet* (evil net). The presence of this term indicates that *bregdon* is not acting as a general "making" or "contriving" verb; rather

---

65 See chapter 5, p. 133n58.

66 *DOE*, s.v. *bregdan*, sense 2.b.

67 The *DOE* links this usage of *bregdan* to that of weaving "devilish knots" in Ælfric's *Sermo ad populum, in octavis pentecosten dicendus*, in *Homilies of Ælfric*, 1:423: *se syrwienda deofol swicað æfre embe us, and on þæs mannes forðsiðe fela cnottan him bryt* (163–4) (the plotting devil is always moving about us, and on man's forward journey he braids many knots for him).

the poet is invoking a metaphorical image in which evil words and plotting thoughts are imagined as a textile object whose purpose is ensnarement.[68] Since this example of the creation of an evil plot through the braiding or weaving of a net appears to be a living metaphor, the previous examples discussed may well be a part of the same tradition. Of course, the metaphorical nature of each example may vary – perhaps it would be more useful to look at them as points on a scale, with some instances being highlighted by the poet, while others merely employ conventional language. It is therefore difficult to say whether the vibrant examples of the metaphor came first and were then conventionalized or whether conventional language spawned imaginative revivification (or indeed both processes functioned concurrently).

As this net image indicates, we are once again dealing with an idea of language and knowledge as concrete, material objects, whose components may be woven and braided not only into beautiful poetry, but also into conspiratorial lies. Emerging from this discussion is the question of why two such opposing ideas are yoked together through similar imagery and diction. The answer to this duality appears to lie in the nature of the Old English approach to craftsmanship in general. The key passages discussed in both of the sections above link language to human skill: *cræft* or *searo*.[69] Notably, however, both of these terms, at the lexicographical level, possess

---

68 For other nets associated with death, see *Exodus* 202a's ambiguous *wælnet* (slaughter-net), *Andreas* 64a's reference to Matthew's imprisonment in a *searonet* (skilful net), and *Beowulf* 406a's use of the same term to refer to a mail-coat. *Bregdan*, interestingly, is particularly associated with nets elsewhere in Old English literature. Thus when the huntsman in Ælfric's *Colloquy* elaborates on his methods of trapping animals, he says: *ic brede me max* (57) (I braid a mesh/net). *Ælfric's Colloquy*, p. 23. This sentence, which translates the Latin *plecto mihi retia* (I plait a net/snare), occurs under sense 2. of the *DOE*'s entry on *bregdan*: "to weave, intertwine (something)." The *DOE* also aligns it with another instance of a form of *bregdan* glossing *plecto* in Ælfric's grammar and glossary: *ic brede net oððe ic gewitnige* (I braid a net or I punish). *Ælfrics Grammatik und Glossar*, p. 176, line 3. Elsewhere, *bregdan* is invoked in relation to the construction of mail-coats (see chapter 2), as well as the intertwining of ornamented rings (*Phoenix* 306 and 602–3a), celestial spheres (at year 1104 of *Anglo-Saxon Chronicle: MS E*, ed. Irvine, 7:113, line 6) and the fibres of a basket (*Dominica VIII post Pentecosten*, in *Ælfric's Catholic Homilies, Second Series*, ed. Godden, p. 234, line 123). Together these instances imply that the verb held connotations that were distinct from *wefan* and *webbian*, our main "weaving" verbs, although overlap did occur. Note especially that the nominal *gebregd* glosses *textum* (cloth) in the context of a fabric made of rope, in Meritt, *Old English Prudentius Glosses*, p. 92, no. 852.

69 See chapter 6, pp. 181–3, for references to *searo*.

a range of contradictory meanings. Thus, *cræft* may indicate anything from the positive "skill," "art," "talent," and "artifact" to the negative "trick," "fraud," and "deceit."[70] Similarly, *searo* can be applied in contexts of "art," "skill," "armour," "equipment," "machine," "engine [of war]," as well as "contrivance," "device," "snare," and "treachery."[71] What we are seeing here is anything but a black and white approach to the human-object relationship. Rather, this range of applications indicates a nuanced understanding of human construction and constructed objects, where the crafty nature of the construction process is always noted, but the uses to which those objects – or in this case concretized words – are put varies with the individual. Just as treasures like armour and weapons are positive in the hands of the hero and negative in the hands of the enemy, so too can textiles and enclosures act positively as shields from the elements or indicators of wealth, and negatively as methods of entrapment.[72] In Old English poetry, this dual nature of crafted objects is mapped onto the abstract concepts of language and knowledge, resulting in a set of imagery that reflects its meaning through its interlaced application.

---

70 Bosworth and Toller, *Anglo-Saxon Dictionary*, s.v. *cræft*. See also the many senses catalogued under its *DOE* entry.
71 Bosworth and Toller, *Anglo-Saxon Dictionary*, s.v. *searu*.
72 See also the discussion of Grendel's *glof* in chapter 3, pp. 83–90.

9 Creation, Magic, and Fate

As the previous chapter's discussion of language has demonstrated, there is a precedent in Old English poetry for the depiction of highly valued abstract concepts in terms of concrete crafted objects. It thus comes as no surprise that the creation of the world is similarly imagined in terms of skilled construction. A great deal of groundwork on such creation metaphors has already been undertaken by Ruth Wehlau, who discusses in particular the representation of God as an architect.[1] She perceives the emphasis in Old English literature to be on the order and control that a creator exerts, substantiating this with references to binding and joining. These actions are, she argues, "an essential part of creation, a synthesis that creates a new order out of an old chaos, and God's creation of the universe is seen in these terms primarily, rather than as a creation ex nihilo."[2] Weaving, too, as this survey has shown us, is equally bound up in the idea that skilfully made objects afford their maker or owner power and control over the world. Creation itself is depicted as a woven entity in one instance discussed below, an example that emphasizes the connection between the constructive impulses of both weaving and binding. Given that God is frequently depicted as a craftsman, it makes sense for his work to be represented in terms of skilled workmanship, including weaving.

---

1 See chapter 4, p. 97 and chapter 6, p. 184.

2 *Riddle of Creation*, p. 33. I shall not examine every instance Wehlau surveys, in part because this ground has already been covered, and in part because she often deals with a different set of vocabulary (*fæstnian, scieppan*, etc.) than is the focus here.

Magic and fate, sharing similar supernatural and creative tendencies, have long been linked to weaving and binding in medieval Europe.[3] These associations are both old and cross-cultural, with the symbology of weaving frequently representing both growth and creation.[4] It is partly because of this that ropes, nets, webs, and fabric are often linked to the life of the individual, as well as to the entirety of the universe.[5] The Old English poetic choice to depict powerful abstract forces in terms of human knowledge and abilities is seen in this context also, though here woven creation, magic, and fate are part of a far more widespread symbolism. One of the most persuasive explanations for such a symbolism is Karen Bek-Pedersen's:

> Once it has been laid down, one cannot escape one's fate; once the heddles have been threaded and the warp set up, the backbone of the pattern has been decided. As the warp contains the basic truth about the finished cloth, so a person's fate constitutes the basic truth about their personality, about who they really are, about the choices they will make during their life.[6]

The depictions of creation, magic, and fate to which this survey now turns demonstrate the constructive impulses of weaving and binding, while still maintaining the element of control with which these sets of imagery are profoundly engaged.

---

3 See especially Hall, *Elves in Anglo-Saxon England*, pp. 97, 119; and Eliade, *Images and Symbols*, p. 115. Both scholars discuss certain etymologies that demonstrate a connection between binding, medicine, and magic. For examples of binding and loosing magic in Old Norse, Old High German, Anglo-Latin, and Old English prose, see below; as well, Stephanus Eddius's *Life of Bishop Wilfrid*, p. 28. For medieval examples and scholarly discussions where women's weaving is associated with magic, see Krusch and Levison, *Passiones vitaeque sanctorum aevi Merovingici et antiquiorum aliquot*, pp. 706–7; Burchard of Worms, *Decretum*, col. 836B and 961; Flint, *Rise of Magic*, pp. 226–7; and Meaney, *Anglo-Saxon Amulets and Curing Stones*, pp. 181–8. For Old Norse associations between weaving, magic, and supernatural figures, see especially *Darraðarljóð*, in Poole, *Viking Poems*, pp. 116–19; *Jómsvíkingasaga*, in Blake, *Saga of the Jomsvikings*, ch. 8, p. 10; *Helgakviða Hundingsbana* I, in Neckel, *Edda*, 1:126, sts. 2–4; Bek-Pedersen, "Are the Spinning *Nornir* Just a Yarn?"; as well as her *Norns in Old Norse Mythology*, pp. 105–64; Davidson, *Myths and Symbols in Pagan Europe*, pp. 70, 94, 164; as well as her *Roles of the Northern Goddess*, pp. 91–124; and Lionarons, "Dísir, Valkyries, Völur, and Norns"; as well as her "Women's Work and Women's Magic." For a discussion of European literary examples that relate fate to spinning, binding, and weaving, see Onians, *Origins of European Thought*, pp. 352–8.

4 Long, "Webs and Nets," 15:367–8.

5 Ibid.

6 "Fate and Weaving," p. 36.

Woven Creation

In dealing with woven creation, we have, perhaps surprisingly, only one Old English poetic example to consider. This instance occurs in *Riddle 40* (creation), a long adaptation[7] of Aldhelm's Anglo-Latin *Enigma 100, De creatura*. The Anglo-Latin tradition and its influence on Old English discussed in chapter 2 are once again highly relevant here. The Latin text reads:

> Et uersa uice protendor ceu Serica pensa
> In gracilem porrecta panum seu stamina pepli.
> Senis, ecce, plagis, latus qua panditur orbis,
> Vlterior multo tendor, mirabile fatu.   (59–62)

(On the contrary, I am spread out like fine Chinese silk, extended like thin cloth or the threads of a robe. Behold, I stretch much farther than the six regions that are spread out across the extent of the world, wonderful to say.)

The Old English reads:

> Ic eorþan eom   æghwær brædre
> ond widgelra   þonne þes wong grena;
> ic uttor eaþe   eal ymbwinde,
> wrætlice gewefen   wundorcræfte.   (82–5)

(I am broader than the whole earth and wider than this green plain; I easily encircle everything, miraculously woven with wondrous skill.)

Here, the textile image is a metaphor rather than a simile; creation is quite clearly *gewefen* (woven). While this reference to weaving likely stems from the Latin text's depiction of cloth, the differences between the two references are interesting. The Latin lines are concerned with the out-spread nature of cloth, with attention given to the type and fineness of that cloth. The Old English, on the other hand, refers directly to weaving, and applies this woven nature to creation itself. It is not spread out *like* cloth; rather, it *is* skilfully woven, with every thread incorporated into the grand

---

7 "Adaptation" is more apt than "translation" here because the Old English poem is longer than the Latin and alters the text in many places. Indeed, toward the middle of the poem, it departs from direct translation and begins to paraphrase only. For more on the style of the Old English translator, see O'Brien O'Keeffe, "Exeter Riddle 40."

pattern. The difference may be partly due to Old English poetry's preference for metaphor rather than simile, but there is a significant distinction
in the choice to emphasize the method of construction as opposed to the
product. Although Old English poetry does make use of terms for silk and
fine cloth elsewhere, here the translator chooses to signal value not through
the object itself, but through the human skill required to create it.

Furthermore, although the presence of a somewhat more elaborated
textile simile in the Latin text means that the figurative nature of the Old
English weaving reference need not be questioned, the poetics of the passage remain noteworthy. Weaving may well have been emphasized here
because it allows for a linguistic play on words via ornamental "w"-allit-
eration (*widgelra/wong/-winde/wrætlice/gewefen/wundor-*). There are
also several instances of assonance, both internal to half-lines and as links
between them (*eorþan/eom*; *eaþe/eal*). A further instance of assonance
connects lines 82 and 85, creating an envelope pattern of sorts (*æghwær/
brædre/wrætlice*[8]). One half-line includes a formula attested elsewhere in
religious poetry: *wundorcræfte*,[9] and there is an interesting case of overlap
with an earlier passage in the poem:

> Ic eorþan eom   æghwær brædre,
> ond widgielra   þonne þes wong grena;
> folm mec mæg bifon   ond fingras þry
> utan eaþe   ealle ymbclyppan.   (50–4)

(I am broader than the whole earth and wider than this green plain; a hand
can seize me and three fingers can easily enclose me entirely.)

These are clearly a reference to lines 27–8 of the Latin text:

> Latior, en, patulis terrarum finibus exto
> Et tamen in media concludor parte pugilli.

(Lo, I stand broader than the wide-spread ends of the earth, yet I am confined
within the fist.)

---

8 Although the "æ" in -*cræft* is short, it may also contribute to this pattern on a visual level.
9 *Andreas* 13b and 645b; *Fates of the Apostles* 55b; and *Juliana* 575b.

While the repetition of one or two of these half-lines within the Old English poem may be taken as formulaic,[10] the re-use of two entire lines (50–1 and 82–3) indicates potential scribal error. Alternatively, it may point to experimentation on the part of the poet, since it is at line 85 (following the textile image) that the translator begins to depart from direct translation of the Latin, turning instead to looser adaptation and paraphrase.[11]

While the above lines are the only directly overlapping ones, the beginning of the poem also contains many words in common with the weaving-metaphor passage. Here we have an invocation of God's status as both creator and controller of the world:

Ece is se scyppend,　se þas eorþan nu
wreðstuþum wealdeð　ond þas world healdeð.
Rice is se reccend　ond on ryht cyning
ealra anwalda,　eorþan ond heofones,
healdeð ond wealdeð,　swa he ymb þas utan hweorfeð.
He mec wrætlice　worhte æt frymþe,
þa he þisne ymbhwyrft　ærest sette.　　　　　　　　　(1–7)

...

Þisne middangeard　meahtig dryhten
mid his onwalde　æghwær styreð;
swa ic mid waldendes　worde ealne
þisne ymbhwyrft　utan ymbclyppe.　　　　　　　　　(12–15)

(The shaper is eternal, he who now controls and holds this earth to its foundations. The ruler is powerful and king by right, the lone wielder of all, he holds and controls earth and heaven, just as he encompasses about it. He wondrously created me in the beginning, when he first built this world. [...] The mighty lord controls in every respect this middle-earth with his power; thus I by the word of my leader entirely enclose this globe.)

Aside from *eorþan*, which is bound to occur throughout the poem given the riddle's subject, the passage has the following elements in common with

---

10　Certainly the content of 83b is formulaic, since *wong* and *grene* frequently collocate elsewhere: *Andreas* 774–6a; *Genesis A* 1657b; *Guthlac A* 231a–2, 477a, and 746a; *Menologium* 206b; *Metres of Boethius (Metre 20)* 77b–8a; *Phoenix* 13 and 78; *Riddle 12* 2b; and *Riddle 66* 5a.

11　This change in the translation style is discussed in Anderson, "Aldhelm and the Leiden Riddle," p. 171.

lines 82–5: *wrætlice, ymb-, eal-, ut-*, as well as a verb of making (here *worhte*). The outer encircling implied by *ymb-* and *ut-* in particular recurs throughout the poem,[12] and there is one further passage that invokes *wrætlice* twice, as well as the verb *windan* (to wind) and the noun *scyppend* (shaper).[13] It is notable that such general references to craft and construction are also applied to weaving in the passage above, because it signals this form of creation as an object of high status, a notion emphasized in particular in chapter 1. Of course, the ultimate focus in the opening lines is on God's power and might,[14] which marks him out as creator (*scyppend*), controller (*anwalda/waldend*),[15] ruler (*reccend*), lord (*dryhten*), and king (*cyning*).[16]

Thus, God is imagined in human terms, with the poem's overall emphasis being on his craftsmanship – hence the unique reference to the woven state of creation – and his ability to control the world he has created. Notably, then, the construction-constriction duality that runs through weaving and binding terminology more generally is seen here with regard to God. Of course, God's command of the world is a benevolent one; he is imagined in terms of his leadership, much like a good human lord. The association between construction and the Anglo-Saxon poetic emphasis on order shines through.

Binding Magic

Magic is perhaps the ultimate attempt to control the external world; its association with weaving and binding, therefore, is to be expected. There is a surprising amount of information about Anglo-Saxon magic that survives, given the Christian church's stance on such matters.[17] And yet, while there is an elaborate tradition of binding and weaving magic in wider European contexts, there are actually very few instances in the Old English poetic record that clearly demonstrate this connection.

Ambiguous instances that have been construed by scholars in the past to indicate magic are more common, as in the case of *Riddle 33* (iceberg): *Heterune bond* (7b) (bound a hateful rune/secret). This phrase has been translated differently by all of its interpreters because *run* can mean,

---

12 See lines 42b, 47b, and 53 (this instance follows the directly overlapping lines).
13 See lines 98–104.
14 See lines 20–22, 38–41, 86–91, 98–101.
15 See line 89b.
16 See line 39b.
17 Of special interest here is the Anglo-Saxon charm tradition. See Storms, *Anglo-Saxon Magic*; and Pettit, *Anglo-Saxon Remedies, Charms, and Prayers*.

among other things, "mystery," "secret" or "runic character,"[18] and its *-e* ending could be any of five feminine endings (accusative/genitive/dative singular or nominative/accusative plural). Hence, Elinor Teele translates: "it bound a hateful mystery,"[19] Craig Williamson: "[she] carried a curse,"[20] Anita Riedinger: "bound up a hateful secret,"[21] Kevin Crossley-Holland: "she bound them [ships] with a baleful charm,"[22] Patrick Murphy: "It bound up a terrible secret!"[23] and F.H. Whitman: "it spread evil charms."[24] The *DOE* entry reads: "figurative: *heterune bindan,* a crux; perhaps 'to contain, keep hidden a baleful secret'," suggesting: "(perh. translate 'it [an iceberg] bound up a baleful secret', ? ref. to the menace of the bulk of an iceberg, kept hidden beneath the surface of the sea)."[25] Tiffany Beechy claims that ""heterune bond" ["bound with a hate-rune"] takes up the engraving image of *grof* from the line before, suggesting the writing of a curse – writing specifically, because of *grof* ["engraved"]; it is the only previous clue the new verse can attach itself to."[26] If we take the image to be the carving of a rune, described as binding magic, then this instance is a uniquely overt reference to this sort of magic being used for negative ends. R.I. Page also points out that *-rune* often occurs as the second element in a compound describing a person with magical powers.[27] However, in these cases, the magical nature of the person seems to be indicated by the first element, rather than by *-rune*, which may simply mean "one skilled in mysteries," as in *hellerune* (one skilled in the mysteries of the dead/hell – thus a demon or a necromancer).[28] Hence, *heterune* could refer to the subject of the riddle as one skilled in hatred. Given that the following line reads *sægde searocræftig ymb hyre sylfre gesceaft* (8) (the cunning one told of her own creation), this half-line seems to refer more to binding words (here written letters) together into a composition than to rune-magic.[29]

The identification of magic proves less problematic elsewhere because surviving occurrences mostly take the form of charms in medical literature.

---

18 Hall, *Concise Anglo-Saxon Dictionary,* s.v. *run.*
19 "Heroic Tradition," p. 127.
20 *Feast of Creatures,* p. 91.
21 "Formulaic Style," p. 39.
22 *Exeter Book Riddles,* p. 36.
23 *Unriddling the Exeter Riddles,* p. 9.
24 *Old English Riddles,* p. 187.
25 s.v. *bindan,* sense D. 4.
26 *Poetics of Old English,* p. 96. The square brackets are Beechy's own.
27 "Anglo-Saxon Runes and Magic," p. 21.
28 Ibid.
29 See chapter 8.

The majority of these are prose, with only twelve deemed poetic enough to be dubbed *Metrical Charms*, and while there is a great deal of binding in the prose tradition,[30] there is only one instance of binding and no instances of weaving in the poetic charms. Given that evidence for this particular aspect of binding is so sparse, this survey cannot rely on formulaic language in order to identify specific patterns; I have, therefore, singled out for discussion several passages that clearly refer to magic, while also employing diction that frequently collocates with binding and weaving references. Such examples may be loosely categorized as constructive and constrictive, although they are all unique in both imagery and context.

A passage in *Beowulf* contains what has in the past been considered a straightforward reference to curse-magic. It describes a magical spell using vocabulary of winding or intertwining, rather than weaving or binding, although Bosworth and Toller include binding among *bewindan*'s many definitions: "To wind or bind around or about, entwine, wrap, enwrap, encircle, surround, wind, turn." Similar to the instances of the braiding of mail-coats discussed in chapter 2, this passage describes a treasure hoard that is intertwined with and wound about by magic:

> þonne wæs þæt yrfe   eacencræftig,
> iumonna gold   galdre bewunden,
> þæt ðam hringsele   hrinan ne moste
> gumena ænig,   nefne God sylfa,
> sigora soðcyning   sealde þam ðe he wolde
> – he is manna gehyld –   hord openian,
> efne swa hwylcum manna   swa him gemet ðuhte.   (3051–7)

---

30 A search of the *DOE Corpus* leads to seventy-one instances of binding in the charms, remedies and medical texts, generally in the context of binding up – or binding something to – a body part. In deriving this statistic, I have included forms of *-bindan*, *bewindan* and *-bend* in *Leechbook I*, *Leechbook II*, *The Lacnunga*, *Peri Didaxeon* and *Medicina de quadrupedibus*, as well as various collections of charms and remedies edited by Storms in *Anglo-Saxon Magic* and by Cockayne in *Leechdoms, Wortcunning, and Starcraft*. These take the form of instructions to bind or unbind body parts, as well as to bind various remedies to body parts. They are also employed as terms referring to the nature of the disease, particularly in the case of intestinal disorders. There are also a number of variants of the same statement regarding a *feter* that refer to a horse's restraint (in conjunction with its bridle) in charms against theft (Charms 11 A, 11 B and 12, in Storms, *Anglo-Saxon Magic*, pp. 202–6). For more information on the specific usages, see the relevant *DOE* definitions for *bindan*, sense A., A.1., B.2., B.2.a, C.2., and D.7.; *gebindan*, sense B.2. and B.2.a.; *gebind*, sense 2.; *gebunden*, sense B.1.b.; *bebindan*, sense 1. and 2.; *bewindan*, sense 1., 1.a., 1.a.i, 1.b., and 1.b.i; and *feter*, sense 1.c.

(then that heritage, exceedingly large, the gold of ancient men, was wound
about by a spell, so that no man might touch the ring-hall, unless God himself,
the true king of victories, should grant to whomever he wished – he is the protector of men – to open the hoard, to whichever man seemed fitting to him.)

The editors of Klaeber Four note that the "curse laid on the gold is first
mentioned in a substantially heathen fashion, though with a saving clause
of Christian tenor."[31] It is interesting that in modern English curses are
"laid" upon something, while in this instance, the spell is actually encircling, intertwined with and wound about its object in the same way that
serpents wind about Holofernes' body in hell.[32]

Furthermore, although the relevant phrase here, *galdre bewunden*, is not
strictly speaking a construction metaphor, it does relate to Part I's examples
of weaving or binding objects together, in that the magic is depicted as
physically encircling the hoard. Elsewhere in *Beowulf*, *bewindan* is fairly
concrete, with the past participle frequently being used of objects like the
helmet that is *wirum bewunden* (1031a) (wound about with wires), life
flæsce bewunden (2424b) (wound about by flesh) or the grasping of an object, which is described as *mundum bewunden* (3022b), and *mid mundum
bewand* (1461b) (wound about by hands). It is also used abstractly of lam-
entation at Beowulf's burial, when the flames are *wope bewunden* (3146a)
(wound about by weeping). However, in the broader context of both poetry and prose, *bewindan* is used of winding, wrapping, and surrounding
both concrete and immaterial things. Although the *DOE* places this particular instance under the definition "to wind, entwine (something) round
with (something *dat.*, *mid* and *dat.*, *instr.*); *bewindan utan* 'to wind round';
also figurative,"[33] it may be better aligned with the enclosing of life within
flesh, which the *DOE* defines as "to enclose, shut up (something *acc.*)."[34]
Equally apt is the sense of wrapping and covering used to describe bandaging wounds, swaddling clothes, and death shrouds.[35]

Just as the exact sense of *bewindan* is difficult to place here, as it is in general, so too is the depiction of the magic that is described. Paul Beekman
Taylor argues that this spell on the treasure hoard is an example of black
magic or an anti-charm, a type of magic that "impede[s] nature's course and

---

31 Klaeber Four, p. 264.
32 See chapter 5, pp. 150–2.
33 s.v. *bewindan*, sense 1.a.i.
34 Ibid., sense 1.b.iv.
35 Ibid., sense 1.b.

man's interests."[36] However, it must be noted that in the Anglo-Saxon world, nature's course does not generally mesh with man's interests, as chapter 4 has demonstrated. The riddles perhaps make this point most clearly when they depict construction as a human attempt to control and manipulate nature, which is considered to be hostile to mankind. Thus, the fact that this spell utilizes a construction metaphor seems to align it with the man-made world, rather than the natural world. Furthermore, since elsewhere in the poem the formula *x bewunden* refers to things that are relevant to human civilization (constructed objects, the body, hand grips, and even weeping), the spell seems to be invoked in terms of its relation to humanity.

Initially it seems foolish to claim that this spell is portrayed in a positive light in the poem because it does appear to impede the interests of humans. It cuts off a vast quantity of treasure from the gift-giving economy, and may or may not cause the death of the hero, as many have argued in the past.[37] However, J.F. Doig argues against the general scholarly trend to view the spell placed on the treasure as an ancient curse inflicted upon anyone who breaches the boundary.[38] He maintains that the damnation of those trifling with the hoard is a consequence, rather than a curse caused by the men who left the treasure:

> the spell is clearly intended [...] to have the binding effect of preventing entry to the hoard. As the poet points out, this would be the result of the spell unless God Himself intervened on behalf of the favored man. There is no curse, in the romantic sense understood by translators; instead there is a hoard guarded by a spell, which cannot hold out Beowulf or his emissaries because he enjoys the favor of God.[39]

Raymond P. Tripp, Jr expands upon this statement, arguing that the prohibitive spell is only placed upon the hoard when the Geats bury their king, rather than at some time in the past.[40] He maintains that if God is the

---

36 *Sharing Story*, p. 85.

37 See Klaeber Four, pp. 264, 266–7; Bliss, "*Beowulf*, Lines 3074–3075"; Goldsmith, *Mode and Meaning*, pp. 228–30; Helder, "Beowulf and the Plundered Hoard," pp. 322–5; and Stanley, "Hæþenra hyht."

38 Anderson similarly argues that the passage does not refer to a curse, maintaining instead that the context is one of the legal rights of a king to possess a discovered treasure trove; see "Treasure Trove in *Beowulf*," pp. 151–7.

39 "*Beowulf* 3069b," p. 5.

40 "Lifting the Curse on *Beowulf*," p. 2. Cooke echoes this in his "Who Cursed Whom and When," p. 209.

only one who can allow people to breach the spell and the spell is ancient, then it would follow that God must also have allowed the dragon and thief to access the hoard before Beowulf.[41] According to Tripp, the ancient date which most scholars ascribe to the spell is derived solely from the word *þonne* (then), and from the assumption that it occurs in apposition with line 3050b's reference to *þusend wintra* (for a thousand winters).[42] Since the spell is mentioned only after the Geats see the treasure, their dead lord, and the dragon, Tripp concludes that they view the treasure as the cause of their problems: "It is the abuse of treasure which has brought them to their present plight; and they do the logical – if not necessarily effective – thing: they attempt to "ban" treasure by laying a spell, a prohibition, upon it, so that it will never be abused again."[43] If we accept this reading, then the spell may indeed be portrayed in a positive light, as yet another construction that serves the purposes of the humans who created it. However, it is also noteworthy that the treasure hoard is again invoked in lines 3069–73, this time without a hint of magic. There, those who meddle with the treasure are simply declared guilty of crimes, in a passage invoking the powers of hell. This indicates a strong link between the use of binding and winding imagery and constrictive fettering.

Constriction traditionally plays a greater role when it comes to magic, although, as noted above, examples in Old English are few and far between. One example we do have occurs in the charm *Wið Dweorh* (Against a Dwarf/Fever), a well known and controversial poetic charm. Indeed, debate surrounds its purpose as well as the meanings of a number of its lexical choices. There have been a range of suggestions as to what ailment the charm targets: warty eruption, tumour, convulsive disease, nightmare, fever, and witch-riding.[44] These interpretations are all interesting, but the evidence from other Old English medical texts suggests that the meaning of *dweorh* is "fever," and the supernatural dwarf seems to have been reduced to "a residual linguistic fossil."[45] The text itself consists of prose instructions for the making of an amulet from ecclesiastical wafers, followed by a poem that the practitioner is instructed to chant to the patient. The relevant lines read:

---

41 "Lifting the Curse on *Beowulf*," p. 4.

42 Ibid., pp. 4–5.

43 Ibid., 6.

44 Nelson, "Charm Against Nightmare," p. 17; and Gay, "Anglo-Saxon Metrical Charm 3," p. 174.

45 Pettit, *Anglo-Saxon Remedies*, 1:xxxiii. See also Cameron, *Anglo-Saxon Medicine*, p. 152.

Her com ingangan inspidenwiht.⁴⁶
Hæfde hi(m) his haman⁴⁷ on handa, cwæð þ(æt) þu his hæcgest wære.
Leg[d]e þe his teage an sweoran. Ongunnan hi(m) of þæm lande liþan.⁴⁸

(Here came walking in an *inspiden* creature. He had his bridle in his hands, he said that you were his horse. He laid his bonds on your neck. They began to travel from that land.)

---

46 This term is a crux and there have been many attempts to define or emend it. The most popular is *inspiderwiht* (spider creature), first proposed by Cockayne, *Leechdoms, Wortcunning, and Starcraft*, 3:43, and followed by Grendon, "Anglo-Saxon Charms," p. 167; Storms, *Anglo-Saxon Magic*, pp. 51, 166–7; Skemp, "Old English Charms," p. 294; Glosecki, *Shamanism and Old English Poetry*, p. 187; Nelson, "Charm Against Nightmare," p. 17; Gay, "Anglo-Saxon Metrical Charm 3," p. 175; and Neville, *Representations of the Natural World*, p. 104. This is followed by an emendation to *in[w]ri[ð]enwiht*, which was proposed by Grattan and Singer, who claimed that the "incubus seems to take the form of a corpse swathed in grave-clothes." *Anglo-Saxon Magic and Medicine*, p. 162. Bonser accepts this suggestion, translating the term as a creature "all swathed." *Medical Background of Anglo-Saxon England*, pp. 165–6. This reading would be particularly fitting, given the use of *-wriðan* in the charms and medical remedies that instruct the binding and wrapping up of body-parts and wounds. However, as Heather Stuart has pointed out, there is no evidence in the Old English medical texts to support the concept of such a supernatural creature. "Spider," pp. 39–40. She instead emends to *unspedigwiht* (wretched creature) on the basis that it satisfies the metrical requirements, is similar to the use of *ermig* (miserable) in the metrical charm against a wen, and can be explained palaeographically. Pettit, however, rejects all of these suggestions, arguing that Stuart's is "too complicated and speculative to be convincing," and that, as Stuart noted, there is no evidence for the existence of the term *spider* in Old English. *Anglo-Saxon Remedies*, 2:186–8. The prefix is also difficult to explain, and in the end Pettit concludes that the "MS reading is probably corrupt, with only *wiht* ('creature') being clear." *Anglo-Saxon Remedies*, 2:186–7. While I accept Pettit's cautionary reading, I do find intriguing the most recent interpretation, which emends to *inswiden wiht* (burning within/fever spirit) and posits an Old English cognate to Old Norse *sviða* (to burn/roast). See Hutcheson, "*Wiþ Dweorh*."

47 This term has also posed problems for critics, with its usual definition being "a covering." Bosworth and Toller, *Anglo-Saxon Dictionary*, s.v. There have been several explanations for its use here, one of which relies on Old Norse *hama*, a shape-shifting coat. Skemp, "Old English Charms," p. 295. Pettit quickly rejects this solution, arguing: "the *inspidenwiht* cannot have been wearing its putative *hama* – and so (presumably) have been transformed by it – if it were carrying it *on handa*." *Anglo-Saxon Remedies*, 2:190. Instead, Pettit maintains that the most likely interpretation in this context is "bridle" or "harness," despite the fact that the *Oxford English Dictionary* does not record this use of "hame" before 1300. *Anglo-Saxon Remedies*, 2:189.

48 This text is taken from Pettit's edition, 1:72, 74. Although he does not provide numbers, these are lines 9–11 (with the prose instructions included in the line referencing), according to the version in the ASPR.

Teag is the most relevant term for this survey's purposes, with the following attested meanings: "tie," "band," "case," "coffer," "basket," "box," and "enclosure."[49] Given the context, Edward Pettit suggests "reins" might be appropriate;[50] however, I have translated this term as "bonds," because of the common collocation of nouns of binding and *lecgan*.[51] Indeed, since illness is elsewhere depicted as binding the body in Old English poetry, and since injuries are also frequently bound, the presence of bonds is highly appropriate here.[52]

Interestingly, however, this is the only instance of *-teag* in the charms and medical remedies, although animal restraints are referred to as *feteran* in charms against theft.[53] Outside of charms, *-teag* is twice invoked in relation to poetic hell-bonds[54] and once in relation to the bonds of old age – this time as an element in the compound *racenteag* (fetter-bond).[55] This compound is also particularly common in later Ælfrician works, especially in his *Lives of Saints*, where it appears twelve times.[56] In prose and glosses, *racenteag* (with thirty-eight instances) is much more common than either *racente* (with sixteen instances) or *teag* (with eight instances).[57] These

---

49 Bosworth and Toller, *Anglo-Saxon Dictionary*, s.v. *teah*.

50 *Anglo-Saxon Remedies*, 2:192.

51 See chapter 6, pp. 177 and 188 and chapter 7, p. 198.

52 Unfortunately, given that there is not enough evidence for the existence of a spider in the poem, and given that the "fever" reading has more scholarly backing than "nightmare," I cannot accept Jennifer Neville's suggestion that "the 'garment' and 'fetters' seem to derive from dwarves' associations with spiders and spinning. In general, the charm seems to describe a dwarf that 'rides' its victims, like the traditional nightmare." *Representations of the Natural World*, p. 104. However, given this survey's interest in weaving and textiles, the suggestion is intriguing.

53 Charms 11 A, 11 B, and 12, in Storms, *Anglo-Saxon Magic*, pp. 202–6, line 2.

54 *Christ II* 733b; and *The Panther* 60b. See chapter 5, pp. 142 and 147.

55 *Solomon and Saturn II* 116a. See chapter 7, pp. 218–19.

56 See the following in Skeat's edition: *Natale sancte Eugenie uirginis*, 1:36, line 198; *Passio sancti Iuliani et sponse eius Basilisse*, 1:100, line 183, 108, line 306; *De sancta Lucia, virgine*, 1:218, line 140; *Passio sancti Albani, martyris*, 1:426, line 180; *Natale sancti Apollonaris, martyris*, 1:480, line 142; *Natalis sanctorum Abdon et Sennes*, 2:54, line 13; *Passio S. Dionysii et sociorum eius*, 2:184, line 239; *Vita S. Martini episcopi et confessoris Anglicae*, 2:222, line 35 (verbal form), 290, line 1145; *Passio Chrisanti et Dariae*, 2:386, line 164; *Passio sancti Thomae apostoli*, 2:406, line 117; and *Passio sancti Vincentii martyris*, in *Old English Homilies from MS. Bodley 343*, ed. Irvine, p. 101, line 48. The compound appears six additional times in Ælfric's *Catholic Homilies, Second Series*, ed. Godden: *Dominica III post Pentecosten: alia narratio de euangelii textu*, p. 218, lines 150, 152; *In festiuitate sancti Petri apostoli*, p. 221, lines 12, 16; *Natale sancti Iacobi apostoli*, p. 242, line 50; and *Depositio sancti Martini*, p. 288, line 16.

57 According to a search of the *DOE Corpus*.

prose instances describe everything from the fettering of the devil to the crucifixion of Christ and suffering of saints and martyrs. Thus, the context of this passage stands out among both poetic and prose instances of binding and bonds. It is not even similar to the other charm and remedy texts describing bridles, fetters, and bonds. As noted above, the other dwarf remedies refer to fever and do not contain imagery of living creatures or personified diseases. The only analogues containing remotely similar imagery are those that concern the *mare* (mare/nightmare), which attacks its victims by riding them. The Old English charm from Bald's *Leechbook* reads: *Gif mon mare ride: genim elehtran 7 garleac 7 betonican 7 recels bind on næsce; hæbbe him mon on 7 he gange in on þas wyrte* (If a mare rides someone: take lupine and garlic and betony and (frank-)incense. Bind them in fawn-skin; let that one have [them] on him and let him walk in on these plants).[58] Notably, these texts are only aligned by the act of riding and the presence of a supernatural creature, the latter feature being debatable in the *Metrical Charm*, which may simply be a narrative depiction of the combat between patient/physician and personified fever.

As for what is being fettered, the most common view is that the dwarf (or the fever it represents) has placed fetters upon the patient[59] – that is, he has bound the sick person with disease. However, Pettit suggests instead that the incantation is being sung into the patient's body, and thus the beginning of the charm addresses the dwarf/fever[60] – that is, the disease itself is being fettered. This fettering may be compared with the protective drawing of lines around or remedial bandaging of a diseased (though not

---

58 Pettit, *Anglo-Saxon Remedies*, 2:180. Pettit also notes the "more dramatic" Old Norse instances of creatures riding victims, quoting the only actual description of an attack wherein a man is killed by a *mara* in *Ynglinga saga*: *Þá gerðisk honum svefnhǫfugt ok lagðisk hann til svefns. En er hann hafði lítt sofnat, kallaði hann ok sagði, at mara trað hann. Menn hans fóru til ok vildu hiálpa honum. En er þeir tóku uppi til hǫfuðsins, þá trað hon fótleggina, svá at nær brotnuðu. Þá tóku þeir til fótanna; þá kafði hon hǫfuðit, svá at þar dó hann* (Then he became drowsy and lay down to sleep. And when he had slept a little he called out and said that a 'mare' was treading on him. His men went to him and wanted to help him. But when they came to his head, then it bore down on his legs, so that they were almost broken. Then they came to his feet; then it smothered his head so that he died there). Text and translation as quoted in *Anglo-Saxon Remedies*, 2:180.

59 Ibid., 2:173–4.

60 Ibid., 2:175.

visibly wounded) part of the body practised by certain ancient cultures.[61] The idea behind this practice, as Nigel F. Barley notes, lies in the integrity of bodily boundaries: "For protection against hostile powers, to prevent their reinforcement during treatment or re-entry afterwards, boundaries are reaffirmed."[62] Boundaries are important – the bonds of the body must hold firm so as to prevent the unlocking of the body by disease. Thus, it is not particularly relevant for this discussion of magic and binding whether the charm describes a sick person fettered by illness or a physician fettering the illness itself. Both interpretations are linked to the other instances of binding and disease in Old English poetry. However, it is also important to note the uniqueness of *Wið Dweorh*, which does not generally resemble these other poetic instances. It possesses a very different set of vocabulary and imagery, and it lacks the formulaic context that marks other poetic instances of disease-binding.

A second poetic instance of binding has been read in relation to magic, although because it is not a charm its context is open to debate. This is a passage from the end of *Solomon and Saturn I*, which seems to recall a Germanic tradition of fettering and loosing charms:[63]

Hwilum he gefeterað   fæges mannes,
handa gehefegað,   ðonne he æt hilde sceall
wið lað werud   lifes tiligan.
Awriteð he on his wæpne   wællnota heap,
bealwe bocstafas,   bill forscrifeð,
meces mærðo.   Forðon nænig man scile
oft orðances   ut abredan
wæpnes ecgge,   ðeah ðe him se wlite cweme –
ac symle he sceal singan,   ðonne he his sweord geteo,
Pater Noster,   and ðæt palmtreow

---

61 See Grendon, "Anglo-Saxon Charms," p. 121; Eliade, *Images and Symbols*, p. 111; and Storms, *Anglo-Saxon Magic*, p. 86.
62 "Anglo-Saxon Magico-Medicine," p. 70.
63 For examples and discussions of supernatural fettering in Old Norse, see *Hávamál*, in Neckel, *Edda*, 1:41, st. 149; *Brot*, in Neckel, p. 195, st. 16; *Ynglinga saga*, in Snorri Sturluson, *Heimskringla*, p. 8, ch. 7; Vilmundarsson and Vilhjálmsson, *Harðar Saga*, p. 87, ch. 36; and Davidson, *Myths and Symbols*, pp. 70, 96. For Old High German associations between binding and magic, see the First and Second Merseburg Charms in Giangrosso, "Merseburg Charms"; Edwards, *Beginnings of German Literature*; and Fuller, "Pagan Charms in Tenth-Century Saxony?"

biddan mid blisse,   ð‹æt› him bu gife
feorh and folme,   ðonne his feond cyme.   (158–69)

(Sometimes he fetters the doomed man, weighs down the hands, when he must strive for his life in battle against a hostile troop. He writes upon his weapon a group of fatal inscriptions, baleful letters, condemns the edge, the glory of the sword. Therefore no man should thoughtlessly draw out the weapon's edge, although its beauty pleases him – but he should always sing, when he withdraws his sword, the *Pater Noster*, and joyfully pray to the palm-tree, that it should give him life and limb, when his foe comes.)

Although it is difficult to determine to whom all of the third-person pronouns refer, the *he* in the first half-line seems to be a reference to the demons. These are described as a group and individually in the verses preceding this passage, with each evil act they perform signalled by the same opening phrase as above (*Hwilum hie/he*).[64] Context, therefore, indicates that the *he* who carries out the actions of fettering and inscribing the blade refers to a demon. According to this reading, the inscription on the sword may be aligned with death-runes and the *Pater Noster* with a counter-spell.[65] Such an interpretation is upheld by the juxtaposition of the inscribed letters in this passage with the runes of lines 89–145. The personified runes in the earlier passage apply to the letters of the *Pater Noster*, the utterance of which is said to *ealra feonda gehwane fleondne gebrengan / ðurh mannes muð* (147–8a) (put to flight every single fiend through the mouth of man).[66] The poem, therefore, provides a positive Christian alternative to runic magic which is firmly aligned with both the devil and human suffering.

Another reading of this passage does not take the opening lines as apposed examples of demonic meddling. Given the lines' ambiguity, it is possible that the *he* who writes on the sword refers to the owner of the blade himself. If this is the case, then the written letters appear to represent the warrior's attempt to ensure his success in battle by means of

---

64 See lines 146–57, with opening *hwilum hie/he* clauses at 151b, 152a, and 155a.

65 Nelson, "King Solomon's Magic," p. 32. See also Anlezark, *Dialogues of Solomon and Saturn*, p. 25. For more on the relationship between Christianity and magic, see Jolly, *Popular Religion*.

66 For more on the personification of the *Pater Noster*, see Jonassen, "Pater Noster Letters."

victory-runes. Marie Nelson's discussion of this passage briefly alludes to such an interpretation, arguing that the positive connotations of the phrase *meces mærðo* (glory of the sword) may point to a less nasty set of runes than those associated with death.[67] However, the description of the letters as *wællnota heap* (a group of fatal inscriptions) and *bealwe* (baleful), along with their ability to condemn (*forscrifeð*) the blade, strongly implies that, even if they are intended to be a warrior's victory-runes, they are aligned with the devil. Supernatural evil is seen, therefore, to be firmly connected with magical inscription, which together act to incapacitate weapons and warriors alike.

The association between magic and fettering has a broad Germanic context, as noted above. However, there are also several specific Old Norse examples that depict the magical blunting of sword edges. Particularly noteworthy here are the stanzas in *Hávamál* that refer first to blunting swords and second to escaping fetters:

Þat kann ek it þriðia: ef mér verðr þǫrf mikil
    hapts við mína heiptmǫgo,
eggiar ek deyfi   minna andskota,
    bítat þeim vápn né vélir.

Þat kann ek it fiórða: ef mér fyrðar bera
    bǫnd at boglimom,
svá ek gel,   at ek ganga má;
    sprettr mér af fótom fiǫturr,
    en af hǫnom hapt.[68]

(I know a third one which is very useful to me, / which fetters my enemy; / the edges of my foes I can blunt, / neither weapon nor club will bite for them. // I know a fourth one if men put / chains upon my limbs; / I can chant so that I can walk away, / fetters spring from my feet, / and bonds from my hands.)[69]

Despite their similar content, it should be noted that these Old Norse stanzas do not overtly refer to written magic. Indeed, Óðinn's list of

---

67 Nelson, "King Solomon's Magic," p. 32.
68 Neckel, *Edda*, 1:41, sts. 148–9.
69 Translation from Larrington, *Edda*, p. 35. See also *Sigrdrífomál*'s description of women who sit by the road deadening swords, in Neckel, *Edda*, 1:191, st. 27.

magical spells describes this knowledge in terms of *ljóð*, or songs.[70] Of course, given that a discussion of runes directly precedes the list of songs, a connection to written magic – although not spelled out – does appear to be present. In the passage cited above from *Solomon and Saturn I*, it is noteworthy that the inscribed letters featured there are also never explicitly referred to as runes, but rather as *bocstafas*. However, the term *bocstæf*, which is generally interpreted as a written letter or character,[71] is strongly associated with runes and trees in its other poetic occurrences.[72] Given that *boc* means "beech-tree," in addition to simply "book,"[73] this association is not surprising. These factors, along with the existence of the analogous compound, *runstæf*, indicate, if not a direct equivalence, then at least a strong connection between runes and the type of inscribed letter invoked in *Solomon and Saturn I*.

There is, of course, a traditional context for sword-runes, which exist in the European archaeological record – the Thames *scramasax* being, perhaps, the most famous example.[74] Lines 1687–98a of *Beowulf*, in which Hrothgar examines the giant-wrought blade Beowulf has used to defeat Grendel's mother, are also relevant to this discussion. There, the runes appear to refer to the original owner of the sword, although Page notes that they "may have served the additional purpose of extending the remarkable powers of this weapon."[75] Despite the fact that the context of this *Beowulf* passage is distinct from that of *Solomon and Saturn I*, it is interesting that these lines directly precede Hrothgar's account of Heremod, an account which culminates in his famous sermonic warning to stay alert in the face of diabolic temptation and attack.

---

70 Neckel, *Edda*, 1:41, st. 146.

71 See *DOE*, s.v. *bocstæf*.

72 The compound *bocstæf* is also invoked at line 99a, in the middle of the runic *Pater Noster* passage (runes occur at lines 89b, 93a, 94a, 96a, 98a, 108a, 111a, 118a, 123a, 123b, 127a, 134a, and 135b). Elsewhere, the term appears in *Daniel* 723a and 739b, alongside references to *worda gerynu* (722b), *runcræftige men* (733b) and *seo run* (740b); *Elene* 88, where it refers to the letters inscribed upon the tree that Constantine sees in his divine vision; and *Seasons for Fasting* 25, where it collocates with *beam* (22a) in a passage describing Christ's crucifixion. This final poem also contains references to the interpretation of runes and mysteries at lines 6b, 52a, 82b (which collocates *geryne* with *boc*) and 117b.

73 *DOE*, s.v. *boc²*, senses 1–1.a. and *boc¹*, senses A–A.4.g.

74 Moltke, *Runes and their Origin*, pp. 27, 95–107.

75 "Anglo-Saxon Runes," p. 30.

A final Old English instance of magical binding also concerns demonic powers, although here it is quite clear that a human is the binder. Ælfric's homily *Natale sancti Stephani protomartyris* refers to a distressed widow who intends to curse her troublesome child: *Þa wearð seo modor biterlice gegremod [...] fram hire anum cilde to ðan swiðe . þæt heo on eastertide eode to cyrcan . and wolde ðone sunu þe hi getirigde mid wyriungum ge-bindan*[76] (102–5) (Then the mother became so bitterly annoyed by one of her children that she went to church at Easter time and wished to bind with curses the son who vexed her). The devil meets her on her way to church and convinces her to curse not only her son, but her other children as well, which she does: *eode þa to ðam fantfæte . and tolysde hire feax . and bedypte on ðam fante . and mid micelre hatheortnysse ealle hire bearn manfullice wirigde*[77] (115–17) (she went to the font-vessel, and loosed her hair, and dipped it into the font, and with great fervour wickedly cursed all her children). Although *gebindan* is invoked in relation to curses here,[78] the actual method of cursing is vague. We are not told if the woman employs a written spell, although, given the passage's attention to detail (especially with regard to the loosing and dipping of her hair),[79] we might expect to have heard if the woman had brought writing implements with her. It is impossible to determine absolutely, yet the apparent lack of writing implements or other objects seems to rule out not only a connection to runic magic, but also to the pre-Christian tradition of binding through curse-tablets, a practice that recent scholars have argued was not prevalent in Germanic magic.[80] However, what is clear is that we are once again dealing with the nexus between Christianity and magical ritual: in order for the curse to work, the woman must make use of objects present in a church.

In considering together the foregoing examples where binding is associated with magic, it is apparent that we are not dealing with nearly as

---

76 *Catholic Homilies: Second Series*, ed. Godden, p. 15.

77 Ibid.

78 This is the only instance of *gebindan* listed by the *DOE* under sense C.6.a: "*mid wyrgungum gebindan* 'to bind with curses; curse (someone *acc.*)'," although it may be related to C.6: "in spiritual or ecclesiastical use, referring to doctrinal association of 'binding' with 'condemnation', and 'loosing' with 'absolution' (cf. Mt 16:19)."

79 The treatment of the woman's hair is itself a point of interest given that loosing is frequently invoked in opposition to binding.

80 MacLeod and Mees, *Runic Amulets*, pp. 231–2, 254. For more on binding magic and curses, see Flint, *Rise of Magic*, pp. 228–31; and Gager, *Curse Tablets*, pp. 3–30.

cohesive a tradition as those associated with the hell-bonds or natural binding treated in previous chapters. This is in part due to the sharply dissimilar natures and goals of each text. Indeed, how can we compare the narrative depiction of protective magic in *Beowulf* with the verbal charm against a *dweorh* (dwarf/fever) whose intent is to drive illness away from a real patient? More comparable, perhaps, are the lines in *Solomon and Saturn I* and Ælfric's homiletic references to evil binding magic because their goal is to deter bad behaviour and celebrate victory over the devil. Yet the significant differences between the wisdom text's dialogic form and frequently esoteric frame of reference and the homily's instructive accessibility set the two texts apart from one another. The implication from these differing literary references is that, despite such magic being both multifaceted and possibly widespread, the recording of texts similar to those that do survive may not have been deemed either prudent or, perhaps, necessary. Given the practical application of magical binding, it stands to reason that such content may simply have been out of place in the sorts of poetic texts that Old English poets and scribes prized. Of course, the possibility remains that other texts referring to magic may simply not have survived the test of time for a variety of reasons.

Weaving Fate

Evidence for the Old English concept of *wyrd* is likewise thin on the ground. This term is etymologically related to Old Norse *Urðr*, the name of one of the Norns,[81] making it a target for many Anglo-Saxon scholars of the nineteenth and early-mid twentieth centuries attempting to identify traces of paganism in Old English literature. Eric G. Stanley, who has documented the progression of ideas about *wyrd*, notes that the term glosses the Latin Parcae and occurs in Old English translations of Boethius's *De consolatione philosophiae* (where it refers to the divine Fortuna).[82] Not only is it "difficult to establish at each occurrence the extent to which *wyrd* is

---

81   For more on these Old Norse fate deities, see Davidson, *Myths and Symbols*, pp. 96, 164–5; as well as her *Roles of the Northern Goddess*, pp. 119–22 and 145–6; Jochens, *Old Norse Images of Women*, pp. 39–41; and Lionarons, "Dísir, Valkyries, Völur, and Norns." For a problematization of past scholarly approaches to the norns, see especially Bek-Pedersen, "Are the Spinning *Nornir* Just a Yarn?"; and *Norns in Old Norse Mythology*.

82   *Search for Anglo-Saxon Paganism*, p. 92.

personified," but it is "difficult also to establish to what extent the personification of *wyrd* is indebted to classical mythology."[83] Stanley further notes that some scholars use the Parcae's association with spinning and cutting thread as evidence for a separate tradition of *wyrd* that is not derived from these classical deities – *wyrd* being associated only with weaving in the Old English examples.[84] Yet these two concepts were clearly connected in the Anglo-Saxon mind, at least enough for one to gloss the other. Consequently, it should be noted that, while assuming one knows anything about Anglo-Saxon pagan deities is risky at best, rejecting the metaphors with which we are presented seems to be needlessly short-sighted. While it is likely that we are dealing primarily with an abstract concept by this time in Old English literature, rather than a deity, *wyrd* may still be personified for poetic purposes through references to its ability to weave.[85]

Perhaps just as single-minded as the scholars who interpret *wyrd* in terms of paganism are those who take it to be solely a manifestation of Christian Providence. B.J. Timmer, one of the main supporters of this theory, argues that the loss of the original mythological sense of *wyrd* allowed the term "to pass from heathen into Christian times and to form a bridge between the old and the new creed: the idea of unalterability of the events of our life, at one time expressed by the heathen word *wyrd*, is also common to the Christian faith, so that *wyrd* then expresses the course of events as ordained by God's Providence."[86] F. Anne Payne, following Timmer, refers to *wyrd* as "merely God's other face," asserting that as "God's work, Wyrd has no imaginable form, [and] cannot have been personified as a deity."[87] While this approach is perhaps more grounded in the reality of Anglo Saxon religion and culture, it is also an overreaction; the association between *wyrd* and classical deities that is evident in the glosses, as well as the use of poetic personification, which will be discussed below, both indicate that the term could be employed in other contexts.

Indeed, following the strictly pagan and strictly Christian readings of *wyrd*, a more syncretistic approach is now the norm. With the recognition that "[e]ven today the concept of fate is not totally at odds with

---

83 Ibid., p. 94.

84 Ibid.

85 Not unlike the descriptions of the natural world's ability to bind, discussed in chapter 4.

86 "*Wyrd* in Anglo-Saxon Prose and Poetry," p. 227.

87 "Three Aspects of *Wyrd* in *Beowulf*," p. 18.

Christianity,"[88] recent criticism maintains that the debate over *wyrd*'s Christian versus pagan nature rather misses the point, since the term likely came to possess a range of connotations.[89] Furthermore, given *wyrd*'s etymological connection to *weorðan* (to become/happen), the term may also be defined as simply "that which happens."[90] Scholars advocating strictly pagan or Christian readings of *wyrd* are thus at risk of over-analysing some examples of the term. The lengthy debate over how *wyrd* functions in Old English literature has reinforced two important ideas. First, we do not know very much about pre-Christian beliefs in Anglo-Saxon England, even if traces of them have survived the conversion period to enter the written record. Second, this lack of information makes it all the more imperative that we stick to the surviving written evidence instead of making assumptions. It is with this in mind that the discussion below will approach instances where *wyrd* is associated with weaving and binding.

The first example of binding occurs in *Solomon and Saturn II*:

Saturnus cwæð:
Saga ðu me, Salomon cyning,   sunu Dauides,
hwæt beoð ða feowere   fægæs rapas?
SALOMON CVÆÐ:
Gewurdene wyrda
ðæt beoð ða feowere   fæges rapas.   (154–7)

(Saturn said: "Say to me, King Solomon, son of David, what are the four ropes of the doomed one?" Solomon said: "Fates/events that have come to pass, those are the four ropes of the doomed one.")

Although the reference here is not to a form of *bindan* or *bend*, the mention of doom/death[91] in relation to *rapas* (ropes)[92] quite strongly implies

---

88 Major, "Christian *wyrd*," p. 6.

89 See especially Major, "Christian *wyrd*"; and Kasik, "Use of the Term *Wyrd* in *Beowulf*."

90 Stanley, *Anglo-Saxon Paganism*, p. 93.

91 The *DOE* defines *fæge* as: "at the point of death, doomed to die; traditionally translated 'doomed (to death), fated (to die)'." s.v., sense 1. *Fæge* appears frequently in poetry and occasionally in prose, with the *DOE* listing fifty occurrences in total. This instance is one of four collocations with *wyrd*, the other three occurring in *Guthlac B* 1057b–9 and 1345b–6a; and *Beowulf* 572b–3.

92 We may compare this to the sinners in *Christ I* who are *hearde genyrwad/gebunden bealorapum* (364b–5a) (harshly constrained, bound with baleful ropes).

bondage, making the passage relevant to the current discussion.[93] As for where this instance of *wyrd* stands in the debate over its definition, it is notable that the term is certainly not personified here, being equivocated as it is with the ropes themselves.[94] This indicates a definition with the sense of "events" or "things that have happened." However, *wyrd*'s association with the ropes does lend it a figurative sense, a playful metaphoricity that is further highlighted by the use of polyptoton that links *wyrd* and the past participle of *weorðan* (the verb from which it derives) in the same half-line. This figurative language points towards the poet's riddling tendencies, an approach that is common in this and other wisdom texts. To solve the riddle, we may look to the passages that surround these lines: directly preceding it, there is a description of proud and evil people who strive against God[95] and, following it, a reference to Christ, judgment, and Doomsday.[96] According to this context, we may read the passage with the sense: "people are constrained by the things that have happened" or even "actions have binding consequences." Such a reading aligns the text more with constriction than construction, setting this particular instance of the term firmly apart from a tradition of *wyrd*-weaving.

Associations of *wyrd* and weaving occur three times in Old English poetry, in *The Riming Poem*, *Guthlac B* and, as mentioned in chapter 2, the mail-coat riddles. The first poem has generally been taken as a Christian lament for earthly transience and the passing of youth into age.[97] It has also been read as a conversion poem, much like *The Wanderer*, wherein a gloomy approach to transience marks the movement from secular life to Christianity.[98] For Alexandra Hennessey Olsen, the overall opposition of the poem is "the contrast between the heroic world, in which items of value betray their possessor, and the immutable Christian world, in which

---

93 See T.A. Shippey's remarks on the fatalism of these lines: "[Solomon's] curtness and precision give an air of final certainty to human bondage, not decreased by the surrounding references to Doomsday, and perhaps in any case playing on the peculiar terror of binding and paralysis occasionally present elsewhere in Germanic literature." *Old English Verse*, p. 64.

94 In lines 265–71, fate is invoked through the elaborate and extended metaphor of a powerful woman who causes suffering for humankind. However, the passage contains no reference to either weaving or binding.

95 See lines 149–53.

96 See lines 158–9.

97 See Mackie, "Old English "Rhymed Poem," p. 507; and Macrae-Gibson, *Old English Riming Poem*, p. 65.

98 Olsen, "Heroic World," p. 56.

no betrayal is possible either for the individual or for the nation which trusts in God."[99] The differing interpretations of the poem need not, however, directly affect our reading of the description of weaving fate, which occurs following a passage on the joys of kingship:

Me þæt wyrd gewæf,   ond gewyrht forgeaf,
þæt ic grofe græf,   ond þæt grimme scræf[100]
flean flæsce ne mæg,   þonne flanhred dæg
nydgrapum nimeþ,   þonne seo neaht becymeð
seo me eðles ofonn   ond mec her eardes onconn.[101]   (70–4)

(Fate wove that for me, and gave me the task, that I should carve out a grave, and flesh may not escape that grim cavern, when the arrow-swift day seizes with forceful grips, then the night approaches, which begrudged me my homeland and accused me here in my land.)

---

99 Ibid., p. 57.

100 Following Sievers, "Zum Angelsächsischen Reimlied," p. 354, Mackie emends the second manuscript instance of *græf* to *scræf* on the grounds that nowhere else in the poem does a word rhyme with itself. "Rhymed Poem," pp. 516–17. Following suit are the most recent editors, Macrae-Gibson, *Riming Poem*, pp. 34, 53; and Muir, *Exeter Anthology*, 1:264 and 2:579. I have accepted this reading here, even though Krapp and Dobbie retain the manuscript reading. *Exeter Book*, p. 168.

101 Where the manuscript reads *onfonn*, most scholars emend to *ofonn* for the purposes of alliteration and sense (although this of course does not take into account the appropriateness of *onfonn* as a rhyme for *onconn*). See especially Lehman, "Old English Riming Poem," p. 448; and Macrae-Gibson, *Riming Poem*, p. 54. Perhaps more problematic than the sense of this half-line is the translation of *ond mec her eardes onconn*. Here, Macrae-Gibson proposes "[the night] mocks my home here," although he lists "accuses" as the definition for *onconn* in his glossary. *Riming Poem*, pp. 35, 59. Lehman translates "and accused me of [having] a dwelling here." "Riming Poem," p. 445. Wentersdorf entirely reconstructs this passage, suggesting it should read: *þonne seo neaht becymeð / seo me eðles of onn, [ealle adle conn, / minre hæftniede onn,] ond mec herheardes on conn*, and be translated: "then death will draw near and deny me my earthly home; [it will discover all my infirmities, desire to take me captive,] and accuse me of idolatry." "Old English *Rhyming Poem*," pp. 293–4. The manuscript reading does include an "h" before *eardes*, which has been emended out for sense and sound (see Lehman, "Riming Poem," pp. 443, 448), lending some credibility to Wentersdorf's otherwise rather radical reading. In all, if we work according to the accepted emendations, the words and grammar make this passage difficult to translate; hence I have supplied a preposition rather than taking the genitive in its usual sense.

The imagery here relates to the darkness and constriction of the grave and death, hence the appropriateness of employing binding and weaving terminology. As for *wyrd*, it is mentioned in passing, without elaboration, making it difficult to establish whether or not fate is personified and described as weaving an outcome for the speaker or whether *gewæf* is semantically bleached, becoming simply a general "making" term.[102] As with the previous chapter's discussion of language, we may turn to poetics in an attempt to discover whether or not these lines are invoking weaving terminology conventionally. Most of these lines employ different letters or clusters that doubly alliterate, including the "w" of both *wyrd* and *wefan*. Unfortunately, however, we cannot interpret the presence of rhyme as evidence for poetic highlighting, since rhyming is a consistent feature throughout this poem. On the whole, these lines lack formulaic diction,[103] except in the case of *grimme* and *græf*, which collocate elsewhere.[104] The

---

102 There is another arguably bleached example of weaving in *Riddle 84*. Here, water is characterized as a powerful woman who *þæt wuldor wifeð, worldbearna mægen* (33) (weaves glory, the might of world-children). It is difficult to make sense of this line, but since what follows is a prepositional phrase discussing a wise man (34–5), line 33 probably relates to the preceding lines (which describe water's actions), as opposed to those following. The main concern is whether *þæt wuldor* and *mægen* are nominative or accusative because both nouns are neuter and could therefore be either. I have taken them as accusative here, with water, which has been characterized as feminine throughout, as the subject. Williamson also takes water as the subject in his translation, although he transforms the verb form *wifeð* into a noun: "She is the weaver / Of world-children's might." *Feast of Creatures*, p. 142. Whitman seems also to have had trouble with this passage, since he simply stops translating at line 32, although his transcription of the Old English poem continues for some twelve lines before the damage to the manuscript becomes so pervasive that only parts of words and phrases are clear. *Old English Riddles*, pp. 218–19. At any rate, water appears to be the subject here, and, if this is the case, then she is depicted as a creator who is responsible for creating the glory and might of men.

103 An argument could be made for a collocation of *wyrht-* and *forgeaf*, since these words appear in close proximity in several of Ælfric's homilies: *In die sancto Pentecosten*, in *Ælfric's Catholic Homilies, First Series*, ed. Clemoes, p. 358, line 116; *Natale sancti Mathei apostoli et euangelistae*, in *Ælfric's Catholic Homilies, Second Series*, ed. Godden, p. 275, lines 96–7; *De falsis diis*, in *Homilies of Ælfric*, 2:680, line 76; and *De sex etatibus huius seculi*, in *Sex aetates mundi*, p. 196, line 47. That being said, all of these examples, which relate to the works of humans before Noah's flood, employ *forgeaf* with the sense of "forgave" rather than simply "gave" (as in this passage from the *Riming Poem*), indicating a significant dissimilarity between these texts.

104 See *Christ and Satan* 707a: *grim græfhus* (grim grave-house), and also, perhaps the collocation of *grafan* (to dig) and *grim-*, which occurs once again in relation to hell in *Christ III* 1003a: *græfeð grimlice*.

other instances of such a collocation invoke the context of hell, which is particularly appropriate to this elegiac description of the grave, hell being elsewhere strongly associated with pits and narrow, earthly enclosures.[105] However, even if we take the formulaic nature of line 71 – which also involves polyptoton in the form of the noun *græf* and the verb *grafan* – as evidence for poetic highlighting, the fact remains that the emphasis is on the earthly digging of a grave, rather than on a textile-making fate. Indeed, *wefan* may well have been employed here solely because it rhymes with *forgeaf*, the governing nature of rhyme being responsible for many of the poem's seemingly odd decisions. Thus it is perhaps impossible to conclude much from this reference, except that an abstract concept of fate is linked to a potentially weakened form of weaving.

The second example of such an association occurs in *Guthlac B* when the saint's servant sings him a death-song:

> Ellen biþ selast   þam þe oftost sceal
> dreogan dryhtenbealu,   deope behycgan
> þroht þeodengedal,   þonne seo þrag cymeð,
> wefen wyrdstafum.   (1348–51a)

(Courage is best for the one who most often must endure the loss of a lord, deeply contemplate the suffering of separation from his ruler, when the time comes, woven by the decrees of fate.)

As in *The Riming Poem*, fate and weaving are yoked together by the context of loss and death. Here the focus is on those left behind, with the heavy use of heroic diction – through terms such as *ellen* (courage), *dryhten* (lord), and *þeoden* (ruler) – marking the servant's description of the death of his master. Indeed, one might argue that the emphasis on courage is similar to that espoused by Beowulf when he consoles Hrothgar over Æschere's death and urges him towards action rather than mourning: *Ne sorga, snotor guma. Selre bið æghwæm / þæt he his freond wrece þonne he fela murne* (1384–5) (Do not sorrow, wise man; it is better for each that he avenge his friend, than that he mourn too much). The description of the loss of the lord also echoes the wanderer's situation, although without

---

105 See chapter 5, pp. 139–56.

the explicit references to the constraining of emotions.[106] However, the use of *-gedal* (severing) clearly ties this passage to the poem's previous descriptions of disease as a separator of soul and body,[107] demonstrating continuity in *Guthlac B*'s use of diction and register.

The weaving is not only associated with *wyrd* here, but also with *stafas*, a term that as a simplex refers to a "letter," "written character" or "literature," and here in compound form to a "decree."[108] The link to writing is an interesting one, because it may imply fate's personification. Furthermore, the written connotations which *stæf* carries especially stand out here because of the association between weaving and language, discussed in chapter 8. A similar poetic highlighting to those examples is also employed here, with several instances of assonance ("eo": *dreogan/deope/ þeoden-*; "ea": *sceal/-bealu*; "y": *dryhten-/behycgan/cymeð/wyrd*) and double alliteration throughout all lines but the first. In addition, despite their differing vowel lengths, there is a certain aural similarity between the first syllables of *ellen* and *selast* in the opening half-line. Yet despite all of this, the reference to fate and weaving appears here only in passing. Furthermore, rather than construction, the passage's overriding focus concerns separation, leaving us with the possibility that (as with *The Riming Poem*) the metaphor of weaving fate has become less dynamic and more entrenched in the language.

Much more dynamic, however, is the example of fate in *Riddle 35* (mailcoat) and *The Leiden Riddle*, the West Saxon and Northumbrian translations of Aldhelm's Latin enigma, *De lorica*, discussed in chapter 2. Where the Latin reads: *Nec crocea Seres texunt lanugine uermes* (4) (nor do Chinese worms weave me from their yellow floss), the Old English has: *Wyrmas mec ne awæfan wyrda cræftum,/þa þe geolo godwebb geatwum frætwað* (9–10) (The worms which adorn fine yellow cloth with trappings did not weave me together with the skills of the fates). *The Leiden Riddle* employs the singular form for fate, *uyrdi*. This passage provides us with a definite and provable Latin influence, because the Old English versions are translations of an Anglo-Latin text. And yet the idea of fate is entirely supplied by the Old English translator who employs the same collocation of *wyrd* and *-wefan* as in the examples above.

---

106 See chapter 7, pp. 213–30.

107 Ibid., pp. 209–10.

108 Bosworth and Toller, *Anglo-Saxon Dictionary*, s.v. *stæf, wyrdstæf*. See also the discussion of *bocstæf* above, p. 268.

Since the concept of fate may be evident in Aldhelm's silkworm enigma, *De bombicibus*,[109] one could argue that the translator drew inspiration for this particular rendering from another Aldhelmian poem. However, the silkworm enigma refers to fate in the singular: *Vt globulos fabricans tum fati sorte quiescam* (4) (So that, fashioning little balls, I may then rest as ordained by fate). Perhaps another likely influence was his spindle enigma, *De fuso*, which reads *Per me fata uirum dicunt decerpere Parcas* (5) (Through me, they say, the Fates determine the destinies of men). This poem offers irrefutable proof that Anglo-Latin writers engaged with the classical tradition of fate deities being associated with textiles. Furthermore, it is not a great leap to argue that the Old English translator of *De lorica* may also have read other Aldhelmian works on similar subject matter, taking them as inspiration for a divergent translation. Therefore, to accept Thomas Klein's translation "with the skills accorded to them by providence (or nature)"[110] or Erika von Erhardt-Siebold's "with inborn skill,"[111] given the plural form of *wyrda* in *Riddle 35* and the clear evidence for the understanding of fate deities in related works, may be to stubbornly avoid what was not actually an issue to the Anglo-Saxons. Furthermore, if the skills of the silkworms are attributed to the classical Fates in *Riddle 35*, even if only for poetic purposes, then this complicates arguments that weaving and spinning associations should be kept firmly separate when discussing concepts of fate.[112] Here, the relation between textiles and fate seems strong enough, regardless of whether it refers to either spinning or weaving or both. And so, while the other occurrences of weaving fate may or may not be passing references which have lost their status as vibrant, living metaphors, the portrayal of fate in a poem devoted to the concept of weaving is strong evidence that such an association was very much present in the awareness of some Anglo-Saxons, whatever the roots of that association.

The above poetic comparisons have together allowed us to closely examine the use and meaning of the weaving and binding imagery that is expressed in relation to creation, magic, and fate. Although the Old English references to each of these abstract concepts are somewhat sparse and

---

109 Klein, "Old English Translation," p. 349.

110 Ibid.

111 "Old English Loom," p. 13.

112 As Stanley points out in *Anglo-Saxon Paganism*, p. 94, this is the argument of Richard Jente in his *Die mythologischen Ausdrücke im altenglischen Wortschatz*, p. 199.

frequently employ this imagery in a non-formulaic or unique way, they are ultimately united by associations between supernatural or divine forms of control. Such associations could be reduced to the conventional or picked up by poets versed in the Old English and Anglo-Latin traditions in order to imbue the topic at hand with a sense of status and power. Whether constructive or constrictive, these examples can be tied to the literal weaving or binding that the previous chapters have outlined, the physicality of which helped to explain phenomena that were above and beyond the control of everyday people.

10 Peace[1]

The power and control associated with the abstract concepts discussed in the preceding chapters are also integral to one final use of weaving and binding imagery in Old English poetry: that of peace. Given the centrality of warfare in Anglo-Saxon society, it makes sense that representations of peace should also employ this conventional yet intrinsically flexible set of diction and imagery. Indeed, physical binding has a natural place in the context of warfare,[2] and the bond of peace is an established metaphor in prose religious contexts.[3] Furthermore, even the typically positive act of weaving may be bound up with violence in medieval literature, as chapter 1's discussion of the loom riddle demonstrated.

Our understanding of peace is frequently defined by our understanding of war, something that Stacy S. Klein touches upon in a discussion specific to the context of Old English. She argues that the contradictions inherent in a society that praises heroism in war alongside efforts to "weave" peace "are produced not only by the Anglo-Saxons' respective valuations of war and peace but also by their fundamental understandings of these concepts."[4] As J.M. Wallace-Hadrill has argued, war and peace were "two

---

1 A version of this article has been published as "Formulaic *Friþuwebban*" in *JEGP* 114.3. Copyright 2015 by the Board of Trustees of the University of Illinois.
2 See chapter 5, pp. 121–5.
3 See chapter 6, p. 177n83.
4 *Ruling Women*, p. 100.

poles of a single concept" for earlier civilizations.[5] The fact that warfare is typically more associated with constrictive binding in Old English does, however, set the weaving of peace apart, wrapped up as it is in the construction of a positive textile image that draws together the people it concerns.

Before the application of peace-weaving imagery may be analysed, however, the concept itself must be rigorously discussed. This is because the idea of the "peace-weaver" has developed beyond the literary depictions in which this compound is invoked, in many ways defining modern conceptions of the role of women throughout the Anglo-Saxon world. Capturing scholarly interest early in the nineteenth century,[6] peace-weaving has been marshalled as evidence for everything from the misogynistic bartering of women between tribes to an idealized position from which Anglo-Saxon women doled out advice, favour, and, of course, a steady flow of mead. While scholarly opinions about the representation of women have continued to develop and change, the label "peace-weaver" has stuck, crystallizing into a critical model that is distinct from the Old English references to *friþuwebban* (peace-weavers) – a compound with only three poetic references.[7] While it is perhaps inevitable that intense critical attention focused on a concept with so few occurrences should leave behind the term's literary context, both the feminine and masculine

---

5 "War and Peace in the Earlier Middle Ages," p. 157.

6 For more on the early historiography of peace-weaving, see Baker, *Honour, Exchange and Violence*, pp. 103–26.

7 It should be noted that we are actually dealing with two related compounds: the masculine *friþuwebba*, which occurs once in *Elene* 88a, and the feminine *friþuwebbe*, which occurs twice in *Beowulf* 1942a and *Widsith* 6a. Bosworth and Toller's definitions of these terms lay the groundwork for peace-weaving scholarship's focus on gender, by translating the masculine form as "a peace-weaver, an angel" and the feminine form as "a peace-weaver, woman." *Anglo-Saxon Dictionary*, s.v. *friðo-webba* and *freoðu-webbe*. This sets out a subtle distinction, which implies that, although the masculine form is used once of *an* angel, the feminine form is applicable to "woman" in general, and so perhaps to "all women." The *DOE* is more neutral, defining the masculine form as: "weaver of peace (referring to an angel); [in the formula] *fæle friþuwebba* 'faithful peace-weaver'," and the feminine as: "(female) weaver of peace; honorific or epithet for a (high-ranking) woman; *fæle friþuwebbe* 'faithful peace-weaver'." s.v. *friþu-webba* and *friþu-webbe*. Perhaps sensibly, Hall avoids engaging with the debate entirely, translating both compounds together as "peace-maker." *Concise Anglo-Saxon Dictionary*, s.v. *friðo-webba*.

forms of the Old English compound still have much to tell us on their own terms. It is with this in mind that the following discussion will, after briefly surveying the history of peace-weaving scholarship, revisit Old English *friþuwebba/e* in order to examine each occurrence of the term within its formulaic context. Careful attention to this context will demonstrate that the Old English weaving metaphor, while clearly restricted to figures of high status, is not necessarily gender-specific.

The Critical Model of Peace-weaving

Scholarly ideas about peace-weaving have developed in relation to changes in the field of feminist criticism and gender studies.[8] Richard Burton's early mention of *friþuwebbe*, which problematically refers to the compound as "an oft recurring expression," indicates that there was already a rough scholarly consensus regarding the term's meaning in the nineteenth century.[9] This consensus focused on "the frequent part played by woman when given in marriage between hostile tribes, peace being patched up thereby, to last for a longer or shorter time."[10] The potentially powerful nature of peace-making is something with which scholarship on Anglo-Saxon women has particularly engaged.[11] Especially noteworthy here is Larry M. Sklute's 1970 analysis of the poetic instances of the Old English term, in which he recognizes the diplomatic function attributed to each of the figures is named as *friþuwebban*: "it is a poetic metaphor referring to the person whose function it seems to be to perform openly the action of making peace by weaving to the best of her art a tapestry of friendship

---

8 For a useful survey of peace-weaving and Old English gender studies up to the early 1990s, see Olsen, "Gender Roles"; and Bennett, "From Peace Weaver to Text Weaver." For more recent discussions, see Frantzen, *Anglo-Saxon Keywords*, pp. 209–12; and Baker, *Honour, Exchange and Violence*, pp. 103–26.

9 Burton, "Woman in Old English Poetry," p. 6.

10 Ibid. This interpretation was clearly influential, as its presence in much later scholarship indicates. See, for example, Buck, "Pre-Feudal Women"; Welsh, "*Branwen, Beowulf, and the Tragic Peaceweaver Tale*"; Fee, "*Beag and Beaghroden*," p. 285; and Ingham, "From Kinship to Kingship."

11 See Sklute, "*Freoðuwebbe* in Old English Poetry"; Kliman, "Women in Early English Literature"; Dietrich, "Introduction to Women"; Enright, *Lady with a Mead Cup*, pp. 21–37; and Klein, *Ruling Women*, pp. 87–123.

and amnesty."[12] This reading, though defined here in terms of the femi-nine form of the compound is, of course, equally applicable to the mascu-line form's occurrence, as Sklute notes.[13]

Later scholarship is concerned less with the metaphor itself than with the social function of peace-making, as we see in Klein's work. Her analy-sis argues that the *Beowulf*-poet critiques the masculine, militaristic soci-ety that the poem depicts and its hero so highly values. Within this context, peace-weaving

> demands that one redefine the place traditionally allotted to the domestic world within a heroic ethos – in which home and hall typically provide the rationale for battle (one fights to protect women), the impetus to battle (one is impelled to battle by whetting women), or the audience for battle (women celebrate victory or mourn failure) – and recognize women as central forces, rather than marginal supports, in the production of social order.[14]

Klein's argument develops out of an earlier vein of criticism that discusses peace-weaving as a passive social role, setting women apart from the mas-culine-centred warrior culture depicted in *Beowulf* and other poems.[15] Thus both Jane Chance and Gillian R. Overing discuss the failure of peace-weavers in a society that is defined by conflict. It should be noted

---

12 Sklute, "*Freoðuwebbe* in Old English Poetry," p. 208. The influential nature of this article is evident from its reprinting in a 1990 volume of new readings of women in Old English – that is, twenty years after it first appeared in print (and following an explo-sion of feminist criticism), it was still considered relevant enough to be placed among new interpretations.

13 Later interpretations of peace-weaving as a gendered role also argue for analogy in the way the angel acts as "intermediary between man and God, just as woman acts as intermediary, at least politically and socially, between tribe and tribe, retainer and lord, or individual to individual." Chance, *Woman as Hero*, p. 5. See also Baker, *Honour, Exchange and Violence*, p. 136.

14 Klein, *Ruling Women*, p. 104.

15 See Chance, "Structural Unity in *Beowulf*"; Chance, *Woman as Hero*, pp. xiv, 10, 100, 106; Haruta, "Women in *Beowulf*"; and Overing, *Language, Sign and Gender*, pp. xxiii–xxvi, 68–107. Maren Clegg Hyer, however, rejects the active-passive binary, choosing instead to focus on the constructive-destructive nature of the metaphorical textile-making that the texts she discusses depict. See "Textiles and Textile Imagery in Old English," pp. 98–154. Finally, Shari Horner discusses the way *Beowulf*'s depictions of various female figures build upon and gloss the peace-weaver motif in order to nor-malize the poem's construction of femininity. See *Discourse of Enclosure*, pp. 65–100.

that Chance, whose influential monograph makes her one of the fore-mothers of the critical model, uses the Old English term *friþuwebbe* rather freely in her discussion of peace-weaving. Thus, the following quotation implies that the context of line 1942 involves the passing of a mead cup:

> The mead-sharing ritual and the cup-passer herself come to symbolize peace-weaving and peace because they strengthen the societal and familial bonds between lord and retainers. First, the literal action of the *freoðuwebbe* (peace weaver, 1942) as she passes the cup from warrior to warrior weaves an invisible web of peace: the order in which each man is served, according to his social position, reveals each man's dependence upon and responsibility toward another.[16]

The fact that we never see a *friþuwebbe* passing a cup in Old English (neither at the line quoted by Chance nor elsewhere) demonstrates the importance of keeping the Old English term and the critical model separate from one another. Of course, the critical model has been revised since it informed the interpretation of the female figures that Chance's monograph analysed, but it is still worth reiterating that scholarship's "peace-weaver" and the Old English *friþuwebba/e* are not one and the same.

Indeed, it is surprising that a more general term like "peace-maker" has not displaced "peace-weaver" in discussions of Anglo-Saxon women's political and social roles because it encompasses a wider range of Old English depictions of women in which weaving is not mentioned.[17] The

---

16 *Woman as Hero*, p. 98.

17 This label would cover, for instance, characters like Wealhtheow (who is referred to as a *friþusibb* (peace-pledge) in *Beowulf* 2017a) and possibly the foster-mother of the cuckoo (who is called a *friþe mæg* (protective woman) in *Riddle 9* 9a). On the translation of the latter, see *DOE*, s.v. ? *friþ*. With regard to the former, Wealhtheow is already generally discussed in relation to peace-weaving, despite the differing connotations of *friþusibb*. The differences between these two compounds are treated briefly in Hill, *Anglo-Saxon Warrior Ethic*, pp. 64, 153n8; and Porter, "Social Centrality of Women in *Beowulf*," section II. Hill's differentiation is in reaction to Sklute's earlier analysis, which conflates the two terms. Indeed, his translation of *friþusibb* as "peace-bond" implies an additional overlap between the second elements of the two compounds, as is clear from his use of "bond" in his definition of *friþuwebbe*: "the idea of weaving bonds of peace by means of personal behavior or action." "*Freoðuwebbe* in Old English Poetry," p. 208. In actuality, *friþusibb* is only connected to the concept of "peace," and not with either bonds or weaving, and should rather be translated as "peace-peace," "protection-peace" or "peace/protection-relationship," with the repetition of similar

use of the label, then, seems to speak to scholarship's ongoing desire to anchor the abstract work of diplomacy within a more traditional type of women's work.[18] Indeed, in addressing the question of why the metaphor of weaving was associated with diplomacy, Hyer states: "the daily life of high-status females such as Wealhtheow or her historical Anglo-Saxon counterparts would have involved considerable devotion to spinning and weaving. Since a noble woman's role [...] also requires diplomatic, community-building efforts, it is most probably her gender that provides the initial association between the textile outbuildings' literal looms and the main hall's metaphorical one."[19] It should be noted that Hyer's discussion of peace-weaving approaches the compounds from the direction of weaving metaphors rather than gender studies – that is, she is more interested in the use of textile imagery in Old English literature than the critical model of the "peace-weaver" – and so we might expect a broader picture of the Old English terms than the critical model allows. Yet the resulting focus is once again on women, this time as producers of textiles, both actual and metaphorical.

However, the weaving element of the metaphor does not necessarily imply a similar group of agents performing both the actions of creating textiles and creating peace. Although I am not disputing the link between weaving and women in Anglo-Saxon England,[20] this is not the only association that weaving carries in Old English poetry. As discussed in chapter 1, we have seen that when it comes to descriptions of actual woven textiles, in every instance the Old English poetic tradition emphasizes their status as objects of worth. Hence we see weaving-terminology in the context of treasures, weapons and armour, tapestries and temple veils.[21] These examples, as well as the metaphorical uses to which weaving terminology is

---

elements acting as an intensifier. See *DOE*, s.v. *friþ(u)*; and Bosworth and Toller, *Anglo-Saxon Dictionary*, s.v. *sib*. Alaric Hall similarly problematizes Sklute's translation of *friþusibb*, noting the semantic differences between this compound and *friþuwebbe*. See "Hygelac's Only Daughter," p. 85.

18 Frantzen also notes and problematizes this association, in *Anglo-Saxon Keywords*, p. 210.

19 "Textiles and Textile Imagery in Old English," p. 120. Although this quotation is not directly repeated in Hyer's published articles, the same undercurrent is present in "Textiles and Textile Imagery in the Exeter Book," pp. 35, 38; and "Woven Works," p. 184.

20 See chapter 1, p. 34n59.

21 See chapters 1–2 for discussions of references from *Metres of Boethius (Metre 8)* 24b–5a; *Exodus* 588a; *Riddle 56*; *Riddle 35*; *The Leiden Riddle*; Aldhelm's *De lorica*; *Beowulf* 994b–5; and *Christ III* 1134b.

applied (glory, creation, fate, and language),[22] tell us that woven objects were highly valued in Old English poetry, serving as evidence for human skill. What this wider context of poetic weaving implies, then, is that peace-weaving is equally valuable and socially important. And so we can safely say that Old English *friþuwebba/e* points to peace as highly significant and to the construction of peace as a task of some status. However, the term does *not* imply that the attempted construction of peace is inherently linked to women. Indeed, Cynewulf's epilogue to *Elene* demonstrates a clear association between weaving and poetic composition,[23] but no one has tried to argue that the act of composing poetry in Anglo-Saxon England was predominantly a female role.[24] While the critical model of the peace-weaver has led to many interesting readings of women in Anglo-Saxon literature and culture, it is clear that when it comes to examining the *friþuwebban*, gender should not be our sole focus.

---

22 See chapters 8–9 for discussions of *Riddle 84* 32a; *Riddle 40* 85a; Aldhelm's *De creatura* 59–62; *Riming Poem* 70a; *Guthlac B* 1351a; *Riddle 35* 9–10; *Leiden Riddle* 9–10 (but not Aldhelm's *De lorica*); and *Elene* 1237a.

23 See chapter 8, pp. 234–8.

24 However, in *Writing Power in Anglo-Saxon England*, pp. 117–21, Catherine A.M. Clarke has suggested that the invocation of weaving in *Elene*'s epilogue feminizes Cynewulf. In doing so, she draws on Lionarons' argument that "Cynewulf's "masculine" task of writing poetry [...] is metaphorically described in terms of a task culturally coded as feminine in Germanic culture, that of weaving." Lionarons, "Cultural Syncretism," p. 67. However, this discussion is problematic in places, particularly where Lionarons refers to the angel as "characterized by the traditionally and grammatically feminine epithet *friðowebba*" (at p. 53). This instance of the compound is masculine and the rare use of the feminine form cannot prove "traditional" associations in Old English. Taking Lionarons' work as a starting point, Clarke's own reading approaches Cynewulf's word-weaving as a feminization that ties in with what she argues is typical Marian imagery, especially the *clavis David* (key of David) in the Advent Antiphons and *Christ I*. Her argument is certainly interesting and would be more compelling if the texts she compared contained specific overlapping imagery and if locking and unlocking imagery were not used in so many other contexts in which gender is not at issue. Indeed, the physicality that Clarke argues marks the unlocking of Cynewulf's inspiration could equally be linked to the many other Old English accounts of bodily binding and release, such as those in *Andreas* and *Guthlac B*, as well as to the formulaic depiction of the mind as a locked *wordhord* (speech-hoard). Furthermore, should the idea that weaving automatically invokes femininity be accepted, we would also have to extend this feminization to God. As discussed in the preceding chapter, in *Riddle 40* – a poem replete with references to God as creator – creation is referred to as *wrætlice gewefen wundorcræfte* (85) (miraculously woven with wondrous skill). The skill associated with the production of metaphorical cloth by weaving could be seen as an analogue for Cynewulf's own composition process.

Old English *Friþuwebban*

Turning now to the Old English examples of the compounds, the first in-stance of the feminine form in *Widsith* reads:

> He mid Ealhhilde,
> fælre freoþuwebban,   forman siþe
> Hreðcyninges   ham gesohte
> eastan of Ongle,   Eormanrices,
> wraþes wærlogan.   (5b–9a)

(He with Ealhhild, the faithful peace-weaver, for the first time sought, east from the Angles, the home of the glorious king, Eormanric, the cruel oath-breaker.)

At first glance, *friþuwebbe* appears to be a casual epithet for Ealhhild, with the immediate narrative context being more focused on Widsith's travels to foreign lands. Although the description of Ealhhild does not occur as part of an extended metaphor and does not shed a great deal of light on her charac-ter (which is elaborated upon in lines 97–102), it does, of course, refer to a woman of high rank who is married to (or about to marry) the king of the Goths – hence its usefulness to the critical model of peace-weaving. In gen-eral, however, this short introduction appears to give us little to go on.

And yet, keeping in mind the importance of context in determining whether or not formulas possess traditional meaning, it is worth pushing these lines further. If a number of such formulas laden with traditional meaning are placed together, this clustering arguably serves to highlight the passage, drawing links to greater thematic patterns or associations. The need to pay close attention to the formulaic poetics of this passage be-comes clear when we note the presence of a second formula, *wraþ wærlo-ga*. This formula is applied to Eormanric, as well as to the devil in *Andreas* 613a and 1297a,[25] and provides an interesting counterpoint to Ealhhild's peace-weaving. The juxtaposition of creating peace (a valuable commodity

---

25 *Wærloga* appears twice in prose and sixteen times in poetry: Homily 50 ("Larspell"), in *Wulfstan*, p. 266, line 29; Homily 60 ("Be hæðendome"), in *Wulfstan*, p. 310, line 6; *Andreas* 71a, 108a, 613a, and 1297a; *Genesis A* 1266a, 2411b, 2505b, and 2532a; *Christ III* 1561b; *Guthlac A* 298a, 623a, and 911a; *Judith* 71b; *Juliana* 455a; *Whale* 37a; and, of course, *Widsith* 9a. Except for this *Widsith* instance, the occurrences refer exclusively to enemies of Christianity and God.

to the Anglo-Saxons) and cruelly breaking oaths (which is arguably one of the worst crimes available in the heroic and religious worlds of Old English poetry), indicates a more thoughtful use of the formula *fæle friþuwebbe* than might otherwise be gathered from a quick scan of these lines. The reference to Eormanric's legal failings highlights the nature of marriage as a secular and religious compact, and further points to Ealhhild's expected diplomatic function as queen.[26] Another interesting compound, *friþuwær*, ties together Ealhhild and Eormanric's epithets. This compound, which is exclusive to poetry, denotes a peace agreement or pact, especially "a covenant with God."[27]

The context of law and compact also draws a closer connection to the second instance of the formula, here employing the masculine form, *friþuwebba*. This reference occurs in *Elene's* depiction of the angel who comes to the war-weary Constantine in a dream:

> He wæs sona gearu
> þurh þæs halgan hæs,   hreðerlocan onspeon,
> up locade,   swa him se ar abead,
> fæle friðowebba.   (85b–8a)

(He was immediately ready, through the holy one's bidding, he unfastened his heart-enclosure, looked up, as the messenger commanded him, the faithful peace-weaver.)

This passage is notable for its use of enclosure terms, which links it to the poem's epilogue.[28] Significantly, the epilogue also pairs a weaving metaphor

---

26 The term *wær* is also attested both in relation to covenants with God and oaths between husband and wife in Old English. For poetic references to religious covenants, see *Andreas* 211–14a and 415–16; *Christ II* 583b–5; *Daniel* 10–13a; *Elene* 818b–24a; and *Genesis A* 2816b–23. For poetic references to marital oaths, see *Maxims I* 100a; and *Husband's Message* 49–53. For more on pledge-terms used in relation to both marriage and religious covenants, see Ammon "Pledges and Agreements," pp. 7, 23, 29, 75–129. E. Gordon Whatley also notes that *friþowebba* "is normally found in contexts [...] where covenants, treaties – protective relationships between nations or people – are at issue." "Figure of Constantine," p. 183.

27 *DOE*, s.v. *friþu-wær*, sense c. The term appears with this sense in *Andreas* 1630b; and *Exodus* 306b. It appears in the context of other feuds and covenants in *Paris Psalter* (*Psalm 118*) 472a; and *Beowulf* 1096a and 2282b.

28 This passage is discussed in chapter 8, pp. 234–8. For more on this context of mental enclosure, see chapter 7. Links between these two passages have also been recognized

(1237a: *wordcræftum wæf* (wove with the craft of words)) with formulaic half-lines following the pattern "noun (of the chest/knowledge) + verb (of uncovering/unlocking)": *wisdom onwreah* (1242a) (uncovered wisdom), *bancofan onband* (1249a) (unbound the bone-chamber), *breostlocan onwand* (1249b) (unwound the breast-enclosure), and *leoðucræft onleac* (1250a) (unlocked poetic craft). These references envelop a section of verses that describe the bodily and mental constriction and affliction that Cynewulf suffered before his spiritual unlocking. Both passages, then, include a dual focus on construction and constriction.

It is important to note the wider formulaic context of the enclosure terminology from this particular passage. Variations of *x-locan onspeon* occur in *Juliana*: *ferðlocan onspeon* (79b) (unfastened the heart-enclosure) and in *Andreas'* references to wise speech: *wordlocan onspeonn* (470b) (unfastened the speech-enclosure) and *hordlocan onspeon* (671b) (unfastened the hoard-enclosure). A similar context may be read in the semantically related formulas that deal with revealing wisdom, which are discussed in chapters 7 and 8.[29] The most famous example is, of course, *wordhord onleac* (unlocked the speech-hoard). It is especially notable, then, that *Widsith*, which employs *friþuwebba/e* in the same formula as *Elene*, also includes the formula *wordhord onleac* at 1b: only a few lines above *friþuwebbe*. The interrelated nature of this diction implies that the angel in the above *Elene* passage may be designated a *friþuwebba* in order to emphasize a poetic association: that is, the link between high status textile imagery and enclosures of wisdom.

Looking closer at the formula in which *friþuwebba/e* appears can also provide us with useful insights into the Old English understanding of peace-weaving. The above discussion has so far concentrated on the second element, but the first is equally important. According to the *DOE*, the adjective *fæle* means, "of people / angels / God: faithful, trusty; also, more generally: kind, beloved, pleasant."[30] The dictionary also notes that it appears "in specific alliterative collocations: *fæle friþuscealc / friþuweard /*

---

before; thus, Antonina Harbus argues that Cynewulf purposefully draws parallels between his own and Constantine's revelations. "Text as Revelation," p. 651. This builds on suggestions that the diction of the poem's epilogue links Cynewulf to both Constantine and Judas (note that Judas is depicted as crafty with words at lines 419a and 592a). See Fish, "Theme and Pattern," pp. 22–3; Frese, "Art of Cynewulf's Runic Signatures," pp. 324–7; and Calder, *Cynewulf*, p. 135.

29 Pp. 210–11, 247.

30 s.v. *fæle*, sense 1.

friþuwebba/friþuwebbe 'faithful minister of peace/guardian of peace/ peace-weaver'."[31] Here, and in all other instances in which *fæle* occurs – notably almost exclusively in poetry and specifically in psalms[32] – the context relates to a figure who protects or creates peace. Its other three formulaic occurrences appear in *Genesis A* (2303a and 2499a:[33] *fæle freoðoscealc* (faithful servant of peace)), and *Guthlac A* (173a: *fæle freoðuweard*) (faithful guardian of peace). All of these instances refer to angels.

These examples demonstrate that it is the *fæle* (faithful) and *friþu-* (peace) elements that are essential to this formula, while the invocation of variable elements – servant (*-scealc*), guardian (*-weard*), and weaver (*-webba/e*) – is linked to individual poetic context.[34] Furthermore, just as the term *wærloga* generally describes enemies of Christianity,[35] *fæle* almost always refers to religious figures – frequently angels, Christ, God, and saints – making its use highly appropriate in *Elene*. A similar context may, perhaps, be gleaned from the *Widsith* passage, if we read the ritual nature of marriage as linking Ealhhild with a religious figure. Such an association may lie in the language of law and compact which governs both the understanding of religion and marriage in Anglo-Saxon England,[36] with the implication that peace is the key function for all people of status and morality who enter into such compacts.[37] Certainly, the formulaic diction that contrasts Ealhhild with her oath-breaking husband also elevates her morally. Thus, an understanding of the formulaic context of both the *Widsith* and *Elene* passages indicates that peace-weaving is especially concerned with individuals of elevated status and social or

---

31 s.v. *fæle*, sense 1.a.

32 For the thirty-five other poetic occurrences and one prose instance, see *DOE*, s.v. *fæle*.

33 Note also that this angel's speech refers to the enemies of Lot as *wærlogan* (oathbreakers) at 2505b, tying it closely to the *Widsith* passage.

34 This variability makes it possible to argue that it is in fact Ealhhild's gender that demands the use of *-webbe* (as traditionally gendered labour) instead of one of the other terms used in other instances of this formulaic system. However, such an argument is problematized by *Elene*'s reference to a male angel as a *-webba* and to Cynewulf as a weaver of words.

35 See above, p. 287.

36 See above, p. 288.

37 This works nicely with Klein's reading of marriage alliances and the Christian conversion: "[Bede] refigures such entrenched Anglo-Saxon queenly roles as secular peaceweaver and catalyst for dynastic alliances, suggesting that royal women might be used, instead, to weave peace with God and to forge alliances between kings and clergy." *Ruling Women*, p. 19.

moral importance. This conclusion matches Sklute's assessment of peace-weaving as a diplomatic task, although he does not note a religious context and still refers to it as a "womanly" occupation.[38] Since the diplomatic role is one that is available to women in Old English poetry, it makes sense for us to find some of them described as *friþuwebban*.

While both *Widsith* and *Elene* imply that peace, rather than gender, is key to the formulaic system, *Beowulf*'s use of *friþuwebbe* is linked more to war and death.[39] Here we have an ironic peace-weaver, in the form of Fremu:[40]

> Modþryðo wæg
> Fremu, folces cwen,   firen' ondrysne;
> nænig þæt dorste   deor geneþan
> swæsra gesiða,   nefne sinfrea,
> þæt hire an dæges   eagum starede,
> ac him wælbende   weotode tealde
> handgewriþene;   hraþe seoþðan wæs
> æfter mundgripe   mece geþinged,
> þæt hit sceadenmæl   scyran moste,
> cwealmbealu cyðan.   Ne bið swylc cwenlic þeaw
> idese to efnanne,   þeah ðe hio ænlicu sy,
> þætte freoðuwebbe   feores onsæce
> æfter ligetorne   leofne mannan.
> Huru þæt onhohsnod[e]   Hemminges mæg.   (1931b–44)

---

38 Sklute, "*Freoðuwebbe* in Old English Poetry," p. 209.

39 The context of the following passage has also caused a great deal of speculation about Grendel's mother; however, it should be noted that she does not collocate with either peace or weaving in the poem. Her association with Fremu (see n41 on name below) derives from the fact that she is an active and aggressive female character, which makes her useful to the critical model of peace-weaving. Thus, for Chance, Fremu and Grendel's mother are "anti-types of the peace-weaving queen [who] behave like kings, using the sword to rid their halls of intruders or unwanted 'hall-guests'." *Woman as Hero*, p. 106. For further discussions of Fremu and Grendel's mother, see Damico, *Beowulf's Wealhtheow*, pp. 46–51; Hyer, "Textiles and Textile Imagery in Old English," pp. 132–4; Klein, *Ruling Women*, pp. 105–11; and Overing, *Language, Sign and Gender*, pp. 101–7.

40 Formerly known as "(Mod)thryth," she is renamed in Klaeber Four, pp. 224–6. The suggestion was originally offered by Kock, in "Interpretations and Emendations," p. 103, and was taken up by Fulk, in "Name of Offa's Queen." Fulk argues convincingly that *modþryðo wæg* simply means "acted arrogantly" with the irregular noun *fremu* at 1932a being the character's name.

(Fremu, the queen of the people, arrogantly carried out a terrible crime; there was no one of her own company brave enough except a great lord who dared to look upon her with his eyes by day, but he would soon learn that hand-twisted slaughter-bonds were in store for him; quickly then after the seizure by hand it was decided by the blade, the patterned-sword would settle that, perform deadly punishment. Nor is such a queenly custom for a noblewoman to perform, though she be peerless, that a peace-weaver should deprive a beloved man of life due to an imagined insult. Indeed the kinsman of Hemming put an end to that.)

As above, this passage is highlighted by formulaic diction with traditional meaning,[41] including several terms related to construction and constriction. Although this passage contains the only instance of *wælbend* (slaughter-bond) in Old English, other compounds with *bend* are prolific, especially in formulaic contexts.[42] Indeed, *wælbend* could easily have been substituted for the otherwise attested *witebend* (punishment-bond)[43] without affecting the alliteration of the line. Thus, its presence emphasizes the murderous, as opposed to punitive, context of these particular bonds.

Another significant term is *handgewriþene*, which is also attested only here. There are, however, other examples of similar verbs denoting object-production in collocations or compounds with hands, as we have seen in chapter 2's discussion of the mail-coat formulas, *heard hondlocen* and *hondum gebroden*. The latter of these is also used of a banner in *Beowulf* 1443b, as is *-locen leoðo-x*: *hondwundra mæst, / gelocen leoðocræftum*

---

41   Note especially collocations of *folc* and *cwen*: *Beowulf* 641a, 1932a and 2016b–17a; *swæs* and *gesiða*: *Beowulf* 29a, 2040a, and 2518a; *eage* and *starian*: *Beowulf* 1781a and *Christ and Satan* 139b; *mund* and *grip*: *Beowulf* 380b, 753a, and 1534a; *cwealm* and *bealu*: *Beowulf* 2265b and *Christ III* 1425b–6a; and *leof* and *manna*: *Beowulf* 297b, 1915b, 1994a, 2080a, 2127a, and 3108a, *Genesis B* 1656b and 2589a, *Guthlac B* 1173a, and *Soul and Body I* 152b. These lines are further highlighted by an interesting repetition of consonant sounds at a key point: the consonance on "d" at the end of most of the stressed syllables in 1936 (*wælbende/weotode/tealde*) morphs into a repetition of "þ" in the following line (*handgewriþene/hraþe/seopðan*).

42   See, for example, *orþancbend* (*Riddle 42* 15a) and *searubend* (*Beowulf* 2086b), all the elements of which appear in collocation with one another in the *Beowulf* passage; *leoðubend* (*Andreas* 100b, 164a, 1033b, 1373b, and 1564b; *Genesis B* 382b; and Old Saxon *Hêliand* 3797a, 4927a, and 5268b); and *isenbend* (*Genesis B* 371b; and *Beowulf* 774b and 998b).

43   See *Andreas* 108b and 1561a; and *Christ and Satan* 48b–9a.

(2768b–9a) (the greatest of hand-wonders, skilfully interlocked).[44] All of these instances describe objects of great worth through the context of the skilful intertwining of their craftsmanship. They can be set in contrast to Fremu's binding, as well as to the only other instance of a collocation of a hand-term and *-wriðan*, which notably invokes the binding-verb in reaction to the presence of *wæl*:

Ic hine hrædlice   heardan clammum
on wælbedde   wriþan þohte,
þæt he for mundgripe   minum scolde
licgean lifbysig,   butan his lic swice.   (963–6)

(I intended to bind him quickly with firm grips on the slaughter-floor, so that because of my hand-grasp he would have to lie struggling for life, unless his body should escape.)

Given that the only slaughter to have taken place in Heorot is that of Grendel killing the Danish warriors (and, of course, one Geat), it stands to reason that Beowulf's binding of the monster is intended as a punishment for such actions – that is, this is not simply a description of a battle-field, in whose violence both opponents are equally implicated.[45] Thus, when Fremu attempts to make use of similarly skilful, hand-crafted bonds without legitimate cause, the act is depicted as an unconditionally negative one – one that emphasizes the ironic context of this particular peace-weaver. Since a peace-weaver is someone who acts towards the construction of peace through diplomacy, we can assume that the poet is commenting that while Fremu should be *constructive*, she is constrictive instead. As a woman whose status places her in the ideal position to become a diplomat, Fremu's resistance to the taking on of this role and her actions, which directly contradict the role, are criticized.[46]

---

44 See chapter 1, p. 25.

45 This binding may be literal or metaphorical; death is associated with fetters and bonds in *Exodus* 469–70a, *Christ III* 1041b and *Paris Psalter (Psalm 106)* 26–9.

46 Although Baker's questioning of the binary that associates violence with evil figures and peace with good ones is a useful corrective (p. 155), I do not agree with his argument that Fremu's violent act is "perfectly comprehensible in the context of a social system in which the defence of one's honour is all but mandatory." *Honour, Exchange and Violence*, p. 153. Regardless of whether Fremu later becomes a good queen, her inciting of violence is clearly depicted as a *firen* (wicked deed/crime).

Once again, scholarly approaches to this passage have generally focused on gender roles. A prominent example is Overing, who argues that it is Fremu's hostility towards her own objectification that causes her to act so violently.[47] For her, Fremu's rebellion hinges upon: "her refusal to be looked at, to become an object, which necessarily results in her rejection of the female peace-weaver role."[48] While this may certainly be the case, I would like, by way of conclusion, to draw attention to one final example of a figure in Old English poetry who refuses to be looked at. This character is the male antagonist of *Judith*, Holofernes:[49]

> Þær wæs eallgylden
> fleohnet fæger   ond ymbe þæs folctogan
> bed ahongen,   þæt se bealofulla
> mihte wlitan þurh,   wigena baldor,
> on æghwylcne   þe ðær inne com
> hæleða bearna,   ond on hyne nænig
> monna cynnes,   nymðe se modiga hwæne
> niðe rofra   him þe near hete
> rinca to rune gegangan.   (46b–54a)

(There was an entirely golden, fair fly-net, hung around the leader of the people's bed, so that the baleful one, the ruler of warriors, could look through it upon everyone who came in there, the children of heroes, and no one of humankind could look upon him, unless the proud one should call one of the warriors, bold in battle, to go near to him for secret counsel.)

Holofernes' use of another potentially constrictive textile object – a net[50] – through which he may look out but which allows none to look on him, can be read as a parallel situation of a high status leader who takes

---

47 *Language, Sign and Gender in Beowulf*, pp. 103–4.

48 Ibid., p. 250.

49 Arguments have, been made, however, that his gender is also being questioned. See discussions of his symbolic castration in Hermann, *Allegories of War*, pp. 189–98; and Kim, "Bloody Signs."

50 For more on this passage, see Berkhout and Doubleday, "Net in *Judith*"; and Griffith, *Judith*, p. 65. Other nets in Old English poetry include the fetters that the Mermedonians place upon Matthew in *Andreas* 63–4a and 943a; the ensnaring net of contrivance warned against in *Beowulf* 2167a; hell in *Paris Psalter (Psalm 140)* 38b;

advantage of his position by instilling fear in his men.[51] Reading these two passages together, the emphasis seems to be on the lack of accessibility that both characters entrench in their communities. Thus, the discrepancy between Fremu's perceived role and her actions may stem not only from her gender, but also from her high rank. Indeed, the poet comments that her action is not a *cwenlic þeaw*, a *queenly* custom;[52] he does not say it is not a womanly custom.[53]

As the above discussion has demonstrated, our understanding of the only three instances of Old English *friþuwebban* in the written record may be greatly enhanced by an analysis that emphasizes the intertextual close reading of related sets of formulaic diction. While the critical model of the peace-weaver has proven productive in broader discussions of the role of women in Anglo-Saxon literature and culture, the Old English metaphor itself has much to tell us about the particular passages in which it appears. The formulaic framework of the *friþuwebban*, furthermore, makes it clear that the context, while not inherently gender specific, is very much concerned with status, moral superiority, and good leadership. In the end, special attention paid to the diction of these texts can help us to tease out understandings of Anglo-Saxon literature that may otherwise go unnoticed.

---

a fair few mail-coats in *Beowulf* 406a, 1547a, 1553a, 1889b, and 2754b, and *Exodus* 202a and 236b; as well as the protective veil by which the Israelites are sheltered from the burning heavens in *Exodus* 74a; a fishing net in *Metres of Boethius (Metre 19)* 11a; and the fragile spider's web in *Paris Psalter (Psalm 89)* 28b.

51 This passage proves that a similar sort of criticism was available to both male and female characters in Old English poetry; indeed, punishing your subordinates for looking at you, no matter your gender, is not a sign of heroic governance. Klein similarly takes issue with readings that attribute to *Beowulf* a fear over female-specific aggression: "That both Grendel's mother and Thryth are fiercely prohibited from particular forms of masculine behavior that involve retributive violence stands as a thinly veiled assertion on the part of the poet that this is a kind of masculinity that should, perhaps, not be replicated." *Ruling Women*, p. 109.

52 The reference here is to *cwēn*, as opposed to *cwene* (although the *DOE* notes that the forms are sometimes difficult to distinguish). While *cwēn*, like *cwene*, can refer to "a woman" or "a wife," it much more commonly refers to ruling women or women of secular/spiritual nobility, both in poetry and prose. For more examples of the term's usage, see *DOE*, s.v. *cwēn*.

53 Indeed, even the term *ides* (lady) refers not simply to womanhood but to nobility, perhaps having once invoked a supernatural sort of power. See Meaney, "*Ides* of the Cotton Gnomic Poem."

Weaving and Binding: Conclusions on Human Experience and World View

This survey's analysis of the formulaic diction and imagery of weaving and binding has focused on an Anglo-Saxon context, and on a poetic context in particular. Such a focus emphasizes that through the examining of related diction and imagery, scholars can begin to understand more about poetic constructions of reality, while avoiding the anachronistic application of modern metaphors to earlier texts. Of course, these constructive and constrictive representations also have lives outside of this particular corpus, as has been noted throughout this study. Although texts from any culture that weaves and binds are bound to contain loose analogues, given this study's concentration on formulaic diction the most relevant parallels are those from Old English prose, Latin, Old Norse, and Old Saxon texts. In this concluding discussion, I will briefly touch upon some final examples in order to demonstrate how the analyses undertaken in the preceding chapters tie into this wider tradition, and how this wider tradition itself holds great potential for further research into the areas that this study has mapped in relation to Old English verse.

What ultimately unites both the acts of weaving and binding cross-culturally is the power that such construction and constriction bestow upon humanity and personified entities. Yet, we must also keep in mind that when these acts are related through literature they are themselves constructions under the control of whoever spoke, composed, adapted or translated them. Thus, the composer of the Old Saxon *Hêliand* works on multiple levels when depicting the reaction to Christ's parable about separating the wheat from the chaff:

Bâdun thô sô gerno   gôdan drohtin
antlûcan thea lêra,   that sia môstin thea liudi forð,
hêlaga hôrean.   (2578–80a)[1]

(Then they eagerly asked the good leader to unlock his holy teaching, so that henceforth the people might be able to follow it.)

First, s/he attributes to Christ a form of higher knowledge that requires unlocking, a familiar trope in Old English wisdom literature. Spiritual – and here, specifically, metaphorical – discourse is thus imagined as a physical object that can be accessed by those who possess its key. However, the passage also demonstrates that it is possible to spread this access through teaching, which is precisely what the *Hêliand*-poet aims to do. This is not a case of a question put to the audience to solve, like the challenge of *Riddle 42*;[2] rather, it is a story that begs an explanation from Christ and from the poet him/herself. It is, after all, the poet who acts as a mediator when composing a poem about Christ's life. Thus, by depicting Christian learning through a wisdom trope that associates knowledge with a constructed object whose contents are strictly controlled, the poet points to his/her own poem as a created object whose contents are unlocked for the audience.

Given the close relationship of their corpora, the above example from Old Saxon is easy to discuss in relation to Old English poetry. The far larger Old Norse tradition, however, offers a more wide-ranging base from which to derive parallels. Perhaps the most notable literary depiction of an object – woven, this time – to be invoked in a constructive-constrictive context is from *Darraðarljóð*, stanza 2 of which reads:

Sjá er orpinn vefr
Ýta þǫrmum
ok harðkljáðr
hǫfðum manna;
eru dreyrrekin

---

1 Behaghel, *Heliand und Genesis*, pp. 90–1.
2 See chapter 8, pp. 241–3.

dǫrr at skǫptum,
járnvarðr yllir
en ǫrum ?*hǽ*laðr?.
Skulum slá sverðum
sigrvef þenna.[3]

(The fabric is warped/with men's intestines/and firmly weighted/with
men's heads;/bloodstained spears serve/as heddle rods,/the shed rod is
ironclad/and ?pegged? with arrows./With our swords we must strike/this
fabric of victory.)

Although this poem does not refer to wisdom explicitly – whether verbal-
ized or written – it does involve the speech act of a group of the supernatural figures. These figures attempt to control the dissemination of their
speech by concealing their work in a *dyngja* (weaving hut), as the prose
frame of *Njáls saga* reveals. Unlike the Old Saxon example in which wisdom is unlocked by a willing teacher, the silent observer is left to piece
together the meaning of the incident he witnesses. The incident involves
the simultaneous weaving of fabric from human body parts and reciting of
a skaldic poem that details the work of weaving and the outcome of a
battle. Whether or not we believe these figures to be active or passive
agents of fate, by speaking the victory before it has taken place, they are,
in effect, weaving the outcome. They are constructing a literal and verbal
object that aims to control an event.

Though not a strict parallel, this poem brings to mind another famous
literary association of a constructed object, constriction, and a verbal act.
This Anglo-Saxon example from Bede's *Historia Ecclesiastica Gentis
Anglorum* relates the story of the captive Imma who is freed from his
bonds when his brother, believing him to be dead, has Masses said for his
soul. The Latin version relates how the man's baffled captor asks: *quare
ligari non posset, an forte litteras solutorias, de qualibus fabulae ferunt,
apud se haberet, propter quas ligari non posset*[4] (why he could not be

---

3 The edited text and translation are both from Poole, *Viking Poems on War and Peace*,
   p. 116 (the question marks refer to Poole's emendations and suggestions for terms
   whose definitions are subject to debate). For an edition of the poem in its saga context,
   see Sveinsson, *Brennu-Njáls saga*, pp. 454–9.
4 *Bede's Ecclesiastical History of the English People*, p. 402, Book 4.22.

bound, whether he perhaps had about himself loosing letters, about which the stories speak, because of which he could not be bound). The Old English translation of this text expands the Latin question, asking instead: *hwæðer he þa alysendlecan rune cuðe, 7 þa stafas mid him awritene hæfde, be swylcum men leas spel secgað 7 spreocað, þæt hine mon forþon gebindan ne meahte*[5] (whether he knew the loosing runes, and had with him the staves written out, about which men speak and tell false tales, so that therefore he could not be bound).[6] The *litterae solutoriae* and *alysendlecan rune* are depicted as words believed to possess the power to protect their carrier from being bound. The power to defy constriction resides, then, in the combination of a constructed object and written words. Of course, the Imma-passage is designed to combat such a belief, by attributing the true power to the words of the Mass, an official line that Bede attempts to disseminate by recording it in his greater history. However, his translator also tries to control the reading of this particular passage by emphasizing the falseness of the belief in loosing letters or runes: rather than mere stories, these are specifically *leas* (false) tales. The importance of the power of binding and in this case unbinding is clear from this passage's attempt to wrest control away from non-canonical beliefs and put the credit where Bede believes it is due: still with words, though not the words that Imma's captor assumes.

A final example of the powerful nature of these processes occurs in an Anglo-Latin poetic context. Tatwine's preface to his collection of forty enigmata employs a textile metaphor in an intriguing way, opening with: *Sub deno quater haec diuerse enigmata torquens / Stamine metrorum exstructor conserta retextit* (Turning these enigmata in the opposite direction after forty, their constructor unravels how they are intertwined by a thread/warp of verses). The careful construction of his collection is likened to either the warp of a woven fabric or an individual thread, providing as it does the structure by which he links his separate works together. The particular technique to which Tatwine alludes is his use of acrostics and telestichs to open each enigma: in working one's way through the first

---

5 *English Version of Bede's Ecclesiastical History*, 2:328.

6 The tradition does not end with Bede, but continues when Ælfric incorporates the story into a homily on the efficacy of the mass: *Þa axode se ealdorman þone hæftling hwæðer he ðurh drycræft. oððe ðurh runstafum his bendas tobræce* (159–60) (Then the nobleman asked the captive whether he broke his bonds apart by means of sorcery or rune-staves). *Catholic Homilies, Second Series*, ed. Godden, p. 204.

letter of each poem and then back again through the final letters of their opening lines, these very verses about the intertwining of threads are spelled out a second time.

This passage initially struck me as an instance of word-weaving like those discussed in chapter 8, in line perhaps with the crafty skill depicted in Cynewulf's epilogue to *Elene* or with the storyteller's binding together of words to illuminate Beowulf's heroic deeds. But it is more than that, as the reference to *retexere* (to unravel/unweave) makes clear. Not only does Tatwine construct his collection, but he also takes it apart and makes its structure clear to his reader. Furthermore, rather than the weaving together of words into a tale, Tatwine outlines a rhetorical framework that connects separate texts into a broader narrative in a necessarily textual manner. The written words hold the key to solving the opening lines; indeed, it would likely be impossible to recognize the acrostic pattern of these enigmata if delivered orally. Like the books mentioned in the *Solomon and Saturn I* passage discussed in the introduction to this survey, then, we are once again dealing with a physical object that acts as an enclosure of wisdom, rather than the Old English poetic image of an abstract mental space. Both types of enclosure are of value, but the continued dissemination of the former is more easily controlled by its author – or *exstructor* (constructor) in this case – as Tatwine's rhetorical flourish emphasizes. For, by tying his poems securely together, Tatwine ensures that his collection remains intact.

What then do the unlocking of the Old Saxon parable, the weaving of the Old Norse speech act, the Latin and Old English prose loosing letters and the woven acrostics of the Latin poetic collection have in common with the Old English poems upon which this survey has focused? Although the self-reflexivity of these examples' narrative-weaving, -binding and -unlocking is much more overt, it is tempting to read the formulaic over-lapping and links between Old English poetic texts in similar terms. For even if the poems discussed in the preceding chapters are not explicitly concerned with writing or speech (although, of course, some are), they are certainly defined by the words they employ and the rhetorical effects they invoke to highlight certain passages.

In addition to serving as a means of establishing links, however, the particular sets of diction upon which this survey has focused may also be employed in order to differentiate. Indeed, readers will note that some of the texts discussed explore weaving and binding imagery to a greater extent than others. Given the riddles' focus on the object world and on the movement from nature to culture upon which the construction process relies, it will come as no surprise that riddling texts frequently make use of this diction. Indeed, the riddles may be relied upon to engage most critically with such imagery because they are frequently voiced in the first-person. Thus, reshapings through binding or weaving are imagined in vivid terms reflecting an experience of life that was anchored in pain and affliction. The presence of constrictive imagery in religious texts in general and in saints' lives in particular speaks to an outlook that accepted the biblical tradition of binding and loosing as literal. The fact that the Old English poems engage with such a tradition in an innovative way – amplifying images of imprisonment in translations from prose and Latin – indicates that this diction was essential to the poetics of these genres. One text notable for employing weaving and binding diction that spans the full range of contexts discussed in this survey is *Beowulf*. Considering the poem's interests in power struggles, it could be argued that heroic poetry is bound to employ this formulaic diction. Yet the majority of *Beowulf*'s references to weaving and binding occur in the context of objects, a characteristic which ties this poem more closely to the riddles than to other texts with interests in epic heroism. By breaking down the genres that we apply to Old English literature, surveys of specific sets of imagery, therefore, may point to new relationships between texts bound together by formulaic diction.

Another notable relationship that emerges is the one between construction and constriction themselves. This survey has demonstrated that these dual concerns in no way represent a hard and fast binary. Objects like the loom of *Riddle 56* and Grendel's *glof* are united by mutual interests in their bound or woven construction and in the painful binding they effect. Similarly, the oxen and oxhide of *Riddles 12, 38, and 72* tread the line between constricted creatures and constructed objects, where personification emphasizes an overlap with the human condition. Indeed, human bodies are equally depicted as interwoven systems of sinews and veins, constructions of a powerful creator, and victims of the mental and bodily bonds that seem to afflict everything with a voice in Old English poetry. But perhaps the most intriguing example of construction and constriction coming together is the portrait of Fremu as an ironic, violent peace-weaver. If Fremu is a weaver of anything, it is the hand-woven *wælbendas* (slaughter bonds) that she uses to punish one of her men in what the *Beowulf*-poet clearly depicts as an overreaction. Her short story is concluded by a return to the diplomatic behaviour expected of her high station and, with it, more peaceful forms of social control.

These examples and the others surveyed in this study demonstrate, in particular, the anthropocentric emphasis of Old English poetry. The human situation imagined in these texts is one that is fraught with afflic-tion and continually bound. It is because of this permanent state of bind-ing that humans in turn inflict their situation upon things around them, weaving and binding objects in nature in order to create useful things over which to exercise control. The language of object-crafting, then, provides a context for understanding the design of more complex things, like the body and mind, fate and magic, and even creation itself. And so it is that Anglo-Saxon poets construct reality in their texts. Humans become things and things become humans, and the boundaries between them are con-stantly called into question through the shared language of weaving and binding. Although we can point to instances that demonstrate either a con-strictive or a constructive impulse, given the multi-purpose nature of the language, the slippage between what is a human and what is a thing and the ability of everything to be both at once, it would seem that construc-tion and constriction in Old English poetry are significantly and essen-tially tied together. They both speak to an Anglo-Saxon fascination with exercising power and control, and through it somehow managing to bring stability to an unstable world – at once an aspiration and an impossibility for all but the omnipotent *eallwealda* (all-ruling one). That God's actions (and those of his demonic adversaries) are themselves imagined in human terms only serves to highlight that such power is ultimately conceived of in relation to human experience.

Bibliography

Editions, Translations, Dictionaries

Ælfric of Eynsham. *Ælfric's Colloquy*. Edited by G.N. Garmonsway. London: Methuen, 1939.

- *Ælfric's Catholic Homilies, The First Series*. Edited by Peter Clemoes. EETS s.s., 17. Oxford: Oxford University Press, 1997.
- *Ælfric's Catholic Homilies, The Second Series*. Edited by Malcolm Godden. EETS s.s., 5. London: Oxford University Press, 1979.
- *Ælfrics Grammatik und Glossar*. Edited by Julius Zupitza. Berlin: Weidmannsche Buchhandlung, 1880.
- *Angelsächsische Homilien und Heiligenleben*. Edited by Bruno Assmann. Kassel: Wigland, 1889.
- *Ælfric's Lives of Saints*. Edited by Walter W. Skeat. EETS o.s., 76, 82, 94, 114. London: Trübner, 1881–1900. Reprinted in 2 vols. London: Oxford University Press, 1966.
- *Homilies of Ælfric: A Supplementary Collection*. Edited by John C. Pope. EETS o.s., 259–60. London: Oxford University Press, 1967–8.
- *Sex aetates mundi: Die Weltzeitalter bei den Angelsachsen und den Iren, Untersuchungen und Texte*. Edited by Hildegard L.C. Tristram. Anglistische Forschungen 165. Heidelberg: C. Winter, 1985.

Aldhelm of Malmesbury. *Prosa de virginitate cum glosa latina atque anglosaxonica*. Edited by Scott Gwara. CCSL 124–124A. Turnhout: Brepols, 2001.

- *Through a Gloss Darkly: Aldhelm's Riddles in the British Library MS Royal 12.C. xxii*. Edited by Nancy Porter Stork. Toronto: Pontifical Institute of Mediaeval Studies, 1990.

Allen, Michael J.B., and Daniel G. Calder, eds. and trans. *Sources and Analogues of Old English Poetry I: The Major Latin Texts in Translation*. Cambridge: D.S. Brewer, 1976.

Ambrose. *Hexameron*. Edited by Karl Schenkl. CSEL 32.1. Vienna: Hoelder-Pichler-Tempsky, 1896.

The Anglo-Saxon Chronicle: A Collaborative Edition: MS A. Edited by Janet Bately. Vol. 3. Cambridge: D.S. Brewer, 1986.

– *MS B*. Edited by Simon Taylor. Vol. 4. 1983.

– *MS C*. Edited by Katherine O'Brien O'Keeffe. Vol. 5. 2001.

– *MS D*. Edited by G.P. Cubbin. Vol. 6. 1996.

– *MS E*. Edited by Susan Irvine. Vol. 7. 2004.

Anlezark, Daniel, ed. and trans. *The Old English Dialogues of Solomon and Saturn*. Anglo-Saxon Texts 7. Cambridge: D.S. Brewer, 2009.

Attenborough, F.L., ed. and trans. *The Laws of the Earliest English Kings*. Felinfach: Llanerch, 2000.

Bazire, Joyce, and James E. Cross, eds. *Eleven Old English Rogationtide Homilies*. Toronto Old English Series 7. Toronto: University of Toronto Press, 1982.

Bede. *Bede's Ecclesiastical History of the English People*. Edited and translated by Bertram Colgrave and R.A.B. Mynors. Oxford: Clarendon, 1969.

– *The Old English Version of Bede's Ecclesiastical History of the English People*. Edited and translated by Thomas Miller. EETS o.s., 95, 96, 110, 111. London: Trübner, 1890–8. Reprinted in 2 vols. London: Oxford University Press, 1959.

Behaghel, Otto, ed. *Heliand und Genesis*. 9th ed. Tübingen: Max Niemeyer, 1984.

Blake, N.F., ed. *The Phoenix*. Old and Middle English Texts. Manchester: Manchester University Press, 1964.

– Ed. and trans. *The Saga of the Jomsvikings*. London: T. Nelson, 1962.

Blatt, Franz, ed. *Die lateinischen Bearbeitungen der Acta Andreae et Matthiae apud anthropophagos*. Zeitschrift für die neutestamentliche Wissenschaft 12. Giessen: A. Topelman, 1930.

Boenig, Robert, ed. and trans. *The Acts of Andrew in the Country of the Cannibals: Translations from the Greek, Latin, and Old English*. Garland Library of Medieval Literature, series B, 70. London: Garland, 1991.

Boethius. *De Consolatione Philosophiae, Opuscula Theologica*. Edited by Claudio Moreschini. Bibliotheca scriptorum Graecorum et Romanorum Teubneriana. Munich: Saur, 2000.

Bonnet, Max, ed. *Acta Apostolorum Apocrypha II*. Vol. 1. Leipzig: Mendelssohn, 1898.

Bosworth, Joseph, and T. Northcote Toller. *An Anglo-Saxon Dictionary*. Oxford: Oxford University Press, 1898. *Supplement* by T. Northcote Toller. Oxford: Oxford University Press, 1921. Digital edition. 2010. Faculty of Arts, Charles University, Prague. Web.

Bradley, S.A.J., ed. and trans. *Anglo-Saxon Poetry*. London: Dent, 1982.

Bright, James, ed. *Anglo-Saxon Reader*. New York: Holt, 1891.

Burchard of Worms. *Decretum*. Patrologia Latina: The Full Text Database. Vol. 140. Ann Arbor, MI: ProQuest, 1996–2011. Web.

Büttner, Miriam Gudrun. "The Education of Queens in the Eleventh and Twelfth Centuries." PhD diss., University of Cambridge, 2003.

Byock, Jesse L., trans. *The Saga of the Volsungs*. London: Penguin Books, 1990.

Byrhtferth of Ramsey. *Byrhtferth's Enchiridion*. Edited by Peter S. Baker and Michael Lapidge. EETS s.s., 15. Oxford: Oxford University Press, 1995.

Caie, Graham D., ed. *The Old English Poem "Judgement Day II."* Anglo-Saxon Texts 2. Cambridge: D.S. Brewer, 2000.

Chickering, Howell D., Jr, ed. and trans. *Beowulf: A Dual-Language Edition*. Garden City, NY: Anchor Books, 1977.

Cockayne, Thomas, ed. *Leechdoms, Wortcunning, and Starcraft of Early England*. 3 vols. London: Holland Press, 1961.

Cook, Robert, trans. *Njal's Saga*. London: Penguin Books, 2001.

Craster, H.H.E. "Some Anglo-Saxon Records of the See of Durham." *Archaeologia Aeliana*, Series 4, 1 (1925): 189–98.

Crawford, S.J., ed. *The Old English Version of the Heptateuch*. EETS o.s., 160. London: Oxford University Press, 1922. Reprinted with additions by N.R. Ker, 1969.

Crossley-Holland, Kevin, trans. *The Exeter Book Riddles*. Rev. ed. London: Enitharmon Press, 2008.

Daly, Lloyd William, and Walther Suchier, eds. *Altercatio Hadriani Augusti et Epicteti philosophi*. Illinois Studies in Language and Literature 24. Urbana: University of Illinois Press, 1939.

Dietrich, F.E.C., ed. *Kynewulfi poetae aetas: aenigmatum fragmento e codice lugdunensi edito*. Marburg: Elwerti, 1860.

Doane, A.N. *The Saxon Genesis: An Edition of the West Saxon Genesis B and the Old Saxon Vatican Genesis*. Madison: University of Wisconsin, 1991.

Dobbie, Elliott van Kirk, ed. *Beowulf and Judith*. ASPR 4. New York: Columbia University Press, 1953.

– Ed. *The Minor Poems*. ASPR 6. New York: Columbia University Press, 1942.

Dobbie, Elliot van Kirk, and George Philip Krapp, eds. *The Exeter Book*. ASPR 3. New York: Columbia University Press, 1936.

Earle, J.A. *Hand-Book to the Land Charters and Other Saxonic Documents*. Oxford: Clarendon, 1888.

Farrell, R.T. *Daniel and Azarias*. London: Methuen, 1974.

Fehr, Bernhard von, ed. "Altenglische Ritualtexte für Krankenbesuch, heilige Ölung und Begräbnis." In *Texte und Forschungen zur englischen Kulturgeschichte: Festgabe für Felix Liebermann*, edited by Heinrich Boehmer et al., 20–67. Halle: Max Niemeyer, 1921.

Felix. *Vita Sancti Guthlaci*. In *Felix's Life of Saint Guthlac: Introduction, Text, Translation and Notes*. Edited and translated by Bertram Colgrave. Cambridge: Cambridge University Press, 1956.

Finch, R.G., ed. and trans. *The Saga of the Volsungs*. London: Nelson, 1965.

Fischer, Bonifatius, Roger Gryson, Jean Gribomont, H.F.D. Sparks, Walter Thiele and Robert Weber, eds. *Biblia sacra: iuxta Vulgatam versionem*. 5th ed. Stuttgart: Deutsche Bibelgesellschaft, 2007.

Fulk, R.D., Robert E. Bjork and John D. Niles, eds. *Klaeber's Beowulf*. 4th ed. Toronto: University of Toronto Press, 2008.

Getty, Sarah S., ed. "An Edition with Commentary of the Latin/Anglo-Saxon *Liber scintillarum*." PhD diss., University of Pennsylvania, 1969.

Glorie, F., ed. and trans. *Variae Collectiones Aenigmatum Merovingicae Aetatis*. CCSL 133–133A. Turnhout: Brepols, 1968.

Godden, Malcolm, and Susan Irvine, eds and trans. *The Old English Boethius: An Edition of the Old English Versions of Boethius's De Consolatione Philosophiae*. 2 vols. Oxford: Oxford University Press, 2009.

Gonser, Paul, ed. *Das angelsächsische Prosa-Leben des heiligen Guthlac*. Anglistische Forschungen 27. Heidelberg: C. Winter, 1909.

Goosens, Louis, ed. *The Old English Glosses of MS. Brussels, Royal Library 1650*. Brussels: Paleis der Academiën, 1974.

Gradon, P.O.E., ed. *Cynewulf's "Elene."* Rev. ed. Exeter: University of Exeter Press, 1996.

Gregory the Great. *Cura Pastoralis*. In *King Alfred's West-Saxon Version of Gregory's Pastoral Care*. Edited by Henry Sweet. EETS o.s., 45, 50. 2 vols. London: Oxford University Press, 1871.

Grendon, Felix. "The Anglo-Saxon Charms." *JAF* 22.84 (1909):105–237.

Griffith, Mark S., ed. *Judith*. Exeter Medieval English Texts and Studies. Exeter: University of Exeter Press, 1997.

Hall, J.R. Clark. *A Concise Anglo-Saxon Dictionary*. 4th ed. Toronto: Toronto University Press, 1960.

– Trans. *Beowulf: A Metrical Translation*. Cambridge: Cambridge University Press, 1926.

Healey, Antonette diPaolo, Dorothy Haines, Joan Holland, David McDougall, and Ian McDougall, with Pauline Thompson and Nancy Speirs. *The Dictionary of Old English: A-G Online*. Web interface by Peter Mielke and Xin Xiang. Toronto: Dictionary of Old English Project, 2007. Web.

Healey, Antonette diPaolo, John Price Wilkin, and Xin Xiang. *The Dictionary of Old English Corpus on the World Wide Web*. Toronto: Dictionary of Old English Project, 2009. Web.

Hecht, Hans, ed. *Bischof Waerferths von Worcester Uebersetzung der Dialoge Gregors des Grossen*. Darmstadt: Wissenschaftliche Buchgesellschaft, 1965.

Helgason, Jón, ed. *Heiðreks saga: Hervarar saga ok Heiðreks konungs.* Copenhagen: J. Jørgensen, 1924.

Hessels, J.H., ed. *An Eighth-Century Latin-Anglo-Saxon Glossary.* Cambridge: Cambridge University Press, 1890.

Holthausen, Ferdinand, ed. "Altenglische Interlinearversionen lateinischer Gebete und Beichten." *Anglia* 65 (1941): 230–54.

– *Altenglisches etymologisches Wörterbuch.* Heidelberg: C. Winter, 1934.

Irvine, Susan, ed. *Old English Homilies from MS Bodley 343.* EETS o.s., 302. Oxford: Oxford University Press, 1993.

Isidore of Seville. *Etymologiarum sive Originum libri XX.* Edited by W.M. Lindsay. 2 vols. Oxford: Clarendon Press, 1911.

Jack, George, ed. *Beowulf: A Student Edition.* Oxford: Clarendon Press, 1994.

Kennedy, Charles W., trans. *Elene.* Old English Series. Cambridge, ON: In Parentheses Publications, 2000.

– *Genesis.* Old English Series. Cambridge, ON: In Parentheses Publications, 2000.

Ker, N.R., ed. "Grammatical and Glossarial Fragments Transcribed in British Museum, Cotton Vitellius c. ix, ff. 213-15 in s. xvi ex." In *Catalogue of Manuscripts Containing Anglo-Saxon.* Oxford: Clarendon Press, 1957.

Klinck, Anne L., ed. *The Old English Elegies: A Critical Edition and Genre Study.* Montreal: McGill-Queen's University Press, 1992.

Kluge, F., ed. "Zur Geschichte der Zeichensprache: Angelsächsische Indicia Monasterialia." *Techmers internationale Zeitschrift für Sprachwissenschaft* 2 (1885):116–37.

Krapp, George Philip, ed. *The Junius Manuscript.* ASPR 1. New York: Columbia University Press, 1931.

– Ed. *The Paris Psalter and the Meters of Boethius.* ASPR 5. New York: Columbia University Press, 1932.

– Ed. *The Vercelli Book.* ASPR 2. New York: Columbia University Press, 1932.

Krusch, Bruno, and Wilhelm Levison, eds. *Passiones vitaeque sanctorum aevi Merovingici et antiquiorum aliquot.* Monumenta Germaniae Historica. Scriptores rerum Merovingicarum 4. Hannover: Hahn, 1896–1920.

Larrington, Carolyne, trans. *The Poetic Edda.* Oxford: Oxford University Press, 1996.

Lehmann, Ruth P.M., ed. and trans. "The Old English Riming Poem: Interpretation, Text and Translation." *JEGP* 69 (1970):437–49.

Lewis, Charlton T., and Charles Short. *A Latin Dictionary.* 1879. Oxford: Clarendon Press, 1945.

Liebermann, Felix, ed. *Die Gesetze der Angelsachsen.* 3 vols. Halle: Max Niemeyer, 1903–16.

Lindelöf, Uno Lorenz. *Der Lambeth-Psalter.* Acta societatis scientiarum Fennicae 35, i and 43, iii. Helsinki: Druckeri der Finnischen Litteraturgesellscaft, 1909–14.

Liuzza, R.M., trans. *Beowulf: A New Verse Translation*. Peterborough, ON: Broadview Distribution, 2000.

Mackie, W.S., ed. *The Exeter Book. Part II: Poems IX–XXXII*. EETS o.s., 194. London: Oxford University Press, 1934.

Macrae-Gibson, O.D., ed. and trans. *The Old English Riming Poem*. Cambridge: D.S. Brewer, 1983.

Menner, Robert J., ed. *The Poetical Dialogues of Solomon and Saturn*. New York: Modern Language Association of America, 1941.

Meritt, H.D. *The Old English Prudentius Glosses at Boulogne-sur-Mer*. Stanford Studies in Language and Literature 16. Stanford: Stanford University Press, 1959.

Mitchell, Bruce, and Fred C. Robinson, eds. *Beowulf: An Edition with Relevant Shorter Texts*. Malden, MA: Blackwell, 1998.

Morris, Richard, ed. *The Blickling Homilies of the Tenth Century*. EETS o.s., 58, 63, 73. London: Trübner, 1874–80. Reprinted in 1 vol. London: Oxford University Press, 1967.

Muir, Bernard J., ed. *The Exeter Anthology of Old English Poetry*. 2 vols. Exeter: University of Exeter Press, 1994.

Murphy, Ronald G., trans. *The Heliand: The Saxon Gospel*. Oxford: Oxford University Press, 1992.

Neckel, Gustav, ed. *Edda: Die Lieder des Codex Regius nebst Verwandten Denkmälern*. 2 vols. Heidelberg: C. Winter, 1927.

Nelson, Marie, ed. and trans. *Judith, Juliana, and Elene: Three Fighting Saints*. American University Studies 4, English Language and Literature 135. New York: Peter Lang, 1991.

Orchard, Andy, ed. *The Anglo-Saxon Riddle Tradition*. Dumbarton Oaks Medieval Library. Cambridge, MA: Harvard University Press. Forthcoming.

Oxford English Dictionary Online. Oxford: Oxford University Press, 2010. Web.

Pettit, Edward, ed. and trans. *Anglo-Saxon Remedies, Charms, and Prayers from British Library MS Harley 585: The Lacnunga*. 2 vols. Lewiston, NY: E. Mellen Press, 2001.

Pheifer, J.D., ed. *Old English Glosses in the Épinal-Erfurt Glossary*. Oxford: Clarendon Press, 1974.

Pinsker, Hans, and Waltraud Ziegler, eds. *Die altenglischen Rätsel des Exeterbuchs*. Anglistische Forschungen 183. Heidelberg: Winter, 1985.

Pseudo-Bede. *Collectanea Pseudo-Bedae*. Edited and translated by Martha Bayless and Michael Lapidge. Scriptores Latini Hiberniae 14. Dublin: School of Celtic Studies, Dublin Institute of Advanced Studies, 1998.

Roberts, Jane, ed. *The Guthlac Poems of the Exeter Book*. Oxford: Clarendon Press, 1979.

Robertson, Agnes J., ed. and trans. *The Laws of the Kings of England from Edmund to Henry I*. Cambridge: Cambridge University Press, 1925.

Rypins, Stanley, ed. *Three Old English Prose Texts in MS Cotton Vitellius A. xv.* EETS o.s., 161. London: Oxford University Press, 1924.

Schröer, A., ed. *Die angelsächsischen Prosabearbeitungen der Benediktinerregel*. Kassel, 1885. Reprinted with appendix by Helmut Gneuss. Darmstadt: Wissenschaftliche Buchgesellschaft, 1964.

Shippey, T.A., ed. and trans. *Poems of Wisdom and Learning in Old English*. Cambridge: D.S. Brewer, 1976.

Smith, A.H., ed. *Three Northumbrian Poems*. London: Methuen, 1933.

Snorri Sturluson. *Heimskringla: Noregs Konunga sǫgur*. Edited by Finnur Jónsson. Copenhagen: G.E.C. Gads Forlag, 1911.

Stephanus, Eddius. *The Life of Bishop Wilfrid*. Edited and translated by Bertram Colgrave. Cambridge: Cambridge University Press, 1927.

Storms, Godfrid, ed. *Anglo-Saxon Magic*. The Hague: Martinus Nijhoff, 1948.

Stryker, W.G., ed. "The Latin-Old English Glossary in MS. Cotton Cleopatra A.III." PhD diss., Stanford University, 1951.

Sveinsson, Einar Ól. ed., *Brennu-Njáls saga*. Íslenzk fornrit 12. Reykjavík: Hið Íslenszka Fornritafélag, 1954.

Swanton, Michael J., ed. and trans. *Anglo-Saxon Prose*. London: Dent, 1975.

– Ed. and trans. *Beowulf*. Manchester: Manchester University Press, 1978.

Thesaurus of Old English. Edited by Jane Roberts, Christian Kay and Lynne Grundy. Costerus n.s., 131. 2 vols. Amsterdam: Rodopi, 2000.

Timmer, B.J., ed. *The Later Genesis*. Oxford: Scrivener Press, 1948.

Tolkien, Christopher, trans. *The Saga of Heidrek the Wise*. London: Nelson, 1960.

Tupper, Frederick, ed. *The Riddles of the Exeter Book*. Boston: Ginn, 1910.

Vilmundarsson, Þórhallur and Bjarni Vilhjálmsson, eds. *Harðar saga*. Íslenzk fornrit 13. Reykjavík: Hið Íslenszka Fornritafélag, 1991.

Warner, Rubie D.-N., ed. *Early English Homilies from the Twelfth-Century MS. Vespasian D.XIV*. EETS o.s., 152. London: Oxford University Press, 1917.

Whitman, F.H., ed. and trans. *Old English Riddles*. Ottawa: Canadian Federation for the Humanities, 1982.

Williams, Mary Jane McDonald. "The Riddles of Tatwine and Eusebius." PhD diss., University of Michigan, 1974.

Williamson, Craig, trans. *A Feast of Creatures: Anglo-Saxon Riddle-Songs*. Philadelphia: University of Pennsylvania Press, 1982.

– Ed. *The Old English Riddles of The Exeter Book*. Chapel Hill: University of North Carolina Press, 1977.

Wrenn, C.L., ed. *Beowulf with the Finnesburg Fragment*. Rev. ed. London: Harrap, 1973.

Wulfstan of York. *The Homilies of Wulfstan.* Edited by Dorothy Bethurum. Oxford: Clarendon Press, 1957.
– *Wulfstan: Sammlung der ihm zugeschriebenen Homilien nebst untersuchungen über ihre Echtheit.* Edited by A.S. Napier. Sammlung englischer Denkmäler. Berlin: Weidmann, 1883. Reprinted with appendix by Klaus Ostheeren. Berlin: Weidmann: 1967.
Wyatt, A.J., ed. *The Old English Riddles.* Boston: D.C. Heath and Co. Publishers, 1912.

Secondary Works

Abels, Richard. *Lordship and Military Obligation in Anglo-Saxon England.* Berkeley: University of California Press, 1988.
Abraham, Lenore. "The Devil, the Yew Bow, and the Saxon Archer." *Proceedings of the PMR Conference* 16–17 (1992–3):1–12.
Abrahams, Roger D. "The Literary Study of the Riddle." *Texas Studies in Literature and Language* 14.1 (1972):177–97.
Ammon, Matthias. "Pledges and Agreements in Old English: A Semantic Field Study." PhD diss., University of Cambridge, 2010.
Amodio, Mark C., and Katherine O'Brien O'Keeffe, eds. *Unlocking the Wordhord: Anglo-Saxon Studies in Memory of Edward B. Irving, Jr.* Toronto: University of Toronto Press, 2003.
Anderson, Earl R. *Cynewulf: Structure, Style and Theme in his Poetry.* Rutherford, NJ: Associated University Presses, 1983.
– "Grendel's *Glof* (*Beowulf* 2085b-88) and Various Latin Analogues." *Mediaevalia* 8 (1982):1–8.
– "The Roman Idea of a Comitatus and Its Application to *The Battle of Maldon.*" *Mediaevalia* 17 (1994 for 1991):15–26.
– "Treasure Trove in *Beowulf*: A Legal View of the Dragon's Hoard." *Mediaevalia* 3 (1978 for 1977):141–64.
– "The Uncarpentered World of Old English Poetry." *Anglo-Saxon England* 20 (1991):65–80.
Anderson, George K. "Aldhelm and the Leiden Riddle." In *Old English Poetry: Fifteen Essays*, edited by Robert P. Creed, 167–76. Providence: Brown University Press, 1967.
Anderson, Theodore M. "The Thief in *Beowulf*." *Speculum* 59 (1984):493–508.
Arnold, C.J. *An Archeology of the Early Anglo-Saxon Kingdoms.* New ed. London: Routledge, 2005.
Baker, Peter S. *Honour, Exchange and Violence in Beowulf.* Cambridge: D.S. Brewer, 2013.

Barley, Nigel F. "Anglo-Saxon Magico-Medicine." *Journal of the Anthropological Society of Oxford* 3.2 (1972):67–76.

– "Structure in the Cotton Gnomes." *NM* 78 (1977):244–9.

Bazelmans, Jos. *By Weapons Made Worthy: Lords, Retainers, and Their Relationship in 'Beowulf'*. Amsterdam Archaeological Studies 5. Amsterdam: University of Amsterdam, 1999.

Beechy, Tiffany. *The Poetics of Old English*. Farnham: Ashgate, 2010.

Bek-Pedersen, Karen. "Are the Spinning *Nornir* Just a Yarn?" *Viking and Medieval Scandinavia* 3 (2007):1–10.

– "Fate and Weaving: Justification of a Metaphor." *Viking and Medieval Scandinavia* 5 (2009):23–39.

– *The Norns in Old Norse Mythology*. Edinburgh: Dunedin, 2011.

Belanoff, Patricia. "The Fall (?) of the Old English Female Poetic Image." *PMLA* 104.5 (1989):822–33.

Bennett, Helen. "From Peace Weaver to Text Weaver: Feminist Approaches to Old English Studies." In *Twenty Years of The Year's Work in Old English Studies: A Session from the Program of the Old English Division at the 1988 Modern Language Association Convention*, edited by Katherine O'Brien O'Keeffe, 23–42. Old English Newsletter Subsidia 15. Binghamton, NY: CEMERS, 1989.

Berger, Harry, Jr, and H. Marshall Leicester, Jr. "Social Structure as Doom: The Limits of Heroism in *Beowulf*." In *Old English Studies in Honor of John C. Pope*, edited by Robert B. Burlin and Edward B. Irving, Jr, 37–79. Toronto: University of Toronto Press, 1974.

Berkhout, Carl T., and James F. Doubleday. "The Net in *Judith* 46b–54a." *NM* 74 (1973):630–4.

Biggam, Carole P. "*Grund* to *Hrof*: Aspects of the Old English Semantics of Building and Architecture." In *Lexicology, Semantics and Lexicography: Selected Papers from the Fourth G.L. Brook Symposium, Manchester, August 1998*, edited by Julie Coleman and Christian J. Kay, 103–26. Amsterdam: John Benjamins, 2000.

Biggs, Frederick M. "The Passion of Andreas: "Andreas" 1398–1491." *SP* 85.4 (1988):413–27.

– *The Sources of Christ III: a Revision of Cook's Notes*. Old English Newsletter Subsidia 12. Binghamton, NY: CEMERS, 1986.

Bitterli, Dieter. *Say What I Am Called: The Old English Riddles of the Exeter Book and the Anglo-Latin Riddle Tradition*. Toronto: University of Toronto Press, 2009.

Bjork, Robert E. *The Old English Verse Saints' Lives*. Toronto: University of Toronto Press, 1985.

Bliss, A.J. "*Beowulf*, Lines 3074-3075." In *J.R.R. Tolkien, Scholar and Storyteller: Essays in Memoriam*, edited by Mary Salu and Robert T. Farrell, 41–63. Ithaca, NY: Cornell University Press, 1979.

Bloomfield, Morton W. "The Form of *Deor*." *PMLA* 79.5 (1964):534–41.

– "Understanding Old English Poetry." *Annuale Mediaevale* 9 (1968):5–25.

Bodek, Richard. "Beowulf." *Explicator* 62 (2004):130–2.

Bonjour, Adrien. "Beowulf and the Beasts of Battle." *PMLA* 72 (1957):563–73.

Bonser, Wilfrid. *The Medical Background of Anglo-Saxon England: A Study in History, Psychology, and Folklore*. London: Wellcome Historical Medical Library, 1963.

Bredehoft, Thomas A. "Ælfric and Late Old English Verse." *ASE* 33 (2004):77–107.

– *Authors, Audiences, and Old English Verse*. Toronto: University of Toronto Press, 2009.

– *Early English Metre*. Toronto: University of Toronto Press, 2005.

– "Old English and Old Saxon Formulaic Rhyme." *Anglia* 123.2 (2005):204–29.

Bremmer, Rolf H., Jr. "Grendel's Arm and the Law." In *Studies in English Language and Literature: 'Doubt Wisely'*, edited by M.J. Toswell and E.M. Tyler, 121–32. London: Routledge, 1996.

Bridges, M.E. *Generic Contrast in Old English Hagiographical Poetry*. Anglista 22. Copenhagen: Rosenkilde and Bagger, 1984.

Brown, Ray. "The Exeter Book's Riddle 2: A Better Solution." *ELN* 29.2 (1991):1–4.

Burris, H.W., Jr. "Geometric Figure Terms: their Universality and Growth." *Journal of Anthropology* 1.2 (1979):18–41.

Calder, Daniel G. *Cynewulf*. Boston: Twayne, 1981.

– "The Vision of Paradise: a Symbolic Reading of the Old English *Phoenix*." *ASE* 1 (1972):167–81.

Cameron, Esther and Quita Mould. "Devil's Crafts and Dragon's Skins? Sheaths, Shoes and Other Leatherwork." In *The Material Culture of Daily Living in the Anglo-Saxon World*, edited by Gale R. Owen-Crocker and Maren Clegg Hyer, 93–115. Exeter: University of Exeter Press, 2011.

Cameron, M.L. *Anglo-Saxon Medicine*. CSASE 7. Cambridge: Cambridge University Press, 1993.

Carens, Marilyn M. "Handscóh and Grendel: the Motif of the Hand in *Beowulf*." In *Aeolian Harps: Essays in Literature in Honor of Maurice Browning Cramer*, edited by Donna G. Fricke and Douglas C. Fricke, 39–55. Bowling Green, OH: Bowling Green University Press, 1976.

Cavell, Megan. "The Binding of Religious Heroes in *Andreas* and the *Hêliand*." *English Studies* 96 (2015):507–24.

– "Formulaic *Friþuwebban*: Re-examining Peace-weaving in the Light of Old English Poetics." *JEGP* 114.3 (2015):355–72.

– "Looming Danger and Dangerous Looms: Violence and Weaving in Exeter Book *Riddle 56*." *Leeds Studies in English* 42 (2011):29–42.

– "Sails, Veils, and Tents: The *Segl* and Tabernacle of Old English *Christ III* and *Exodus*." *Medieval Clothing and Textiles*. Forthcoming.

– "Old English 'Wundenlocc' Hair in Context." *MÆ* 82 (2013):119–25.

Cavill, Paul. *Maxims in Old English Poetry*. Cambridge: D.S. Brewer, 1999.

Chadwick, Nora K. "The Monsters and *Beowulf*." In *The Anglo-Saxons: Studies in Some Aspects of Their History and Culture Presented to Bruce Dickins*, edited by Peter Clemoes, 171–203. London: Bowes and Bowes, 1959.

Chance (Nitzsche), Jane. "The Structural Unity in *Beowulf*: The Problem of Grendel's Mother." *Texas Studies in Literature and Language* 22 (1980):287–303. Reprinted in *New Readings on Women in Old English Literature*, edited by Helen Damico and Alexandra Hennessey Olsen, 248–61. Bloomington: Indiana University Press, 1990.

– *Woman as Hero in Old English Literature*. Syracuse, NY: Syracuse University Press, 1986.

Cherniss, Michael. "The Progress of the Hoard in *Beowulf*." *PQ* 47 (1968):473–86.

Cherry, John. "Leather." In *English Medieval Industries*, edited by John Blair and Nigel Ramsay, 295–318. London: Hambledon Press, 1991.

Church, A.P. "Beowulf's 'ane ben' and the Rhetorical Context of the 'Hunferth Episode'." *Rhetorica* 18 (2000):49–78.

Clark, George. "Beowulf's Armour." *ELH* 32.4 (1965):409–41.

Clark, S.L., and Julian N. Wasserman. "The Imagery of *The Wanderer*." *Neophilologus* 63 (1978):291–6.

Clarke, Catherine A.M. *Writing Power in Anglo-Saxon England: Texts, Hierarchies, Economies*. Cambridge: D.S. Brewer, 2012.

Clemoes, Peter. "*Mens Absentia Cogitans* in *The Seafarer* and *The Wanderer*." In *Medieval Literature and Civilization: Studies in Memory of G.N. Garmonsway*, edited by D.A. Pearsall and R.A. Waldron, 62–77. London, 1969.

Clover, Carol J. "The Germanic Context of the Unferþ Episode." *Speculum* 55.3 (1980):444–68.

– *The Medieval Saga*. Ithaca: Cornell University Press, 1982.

– "Regardless of Sex: Men, Women, and Power in Early Northern Europe." *Representations* 44 (1993):1–28.

Coatsworth, Elizabeth. "Stitches in Time: Establishing a History of Anglo-Saxon Embroidery." *Medieval Clothing and Textiles* 1 (2005):1–27.

Coatsworth, Elizabeth, and Gale R. Owen-Crocker, *Medieval Textiles of the British Isles, AD 450–1100: An Annotated Bibliography*. Oxford: Archaeopress, 2007.

Cochran, Shannon Ferri. "The Plough's the Thing: A New Solution to Old English Riddle 4 of the Exeter Book." *JEGP* 108.3 (2009):301–9.

Condren, Edward I. "Deor's Artistic Triumph." *SP* 78.5 (1981):62–76.

Conner, Partrick W. "On Dating Cynewulf." In *Cynewulf: Basic Readings*, edited by Robert E. Bjork, 23–55. New York: Garland, 1996.

Cook, Albert S. *The Christ of Cynewulf.* Boston: Ginn & Company, 1900.

– "Cynewulf's Principal Source for the Third Part of 'Christ'." *MLN* 4.6 (1889):171–6.

Cook, Patrick. "*Woriað þa Winsalo*: The Bonds of Exile in 'The Wanderer'." *Neophilologus* 80 (1996):127–37.

Cooke, William. "Who Cursed Whom, and When? The Cursing of the Hoard and Beowulf's Fate." *MÆ* 76.2 (2007):207–24.

Cramp, Rosemary. "The Hall in *Beowulf* and in Archaeology." In *Heroic Poetry in the Anglo-Saxon Period: Studies in Honor of Jess B. Bessinger, Jr.*, edited by Helen Damico and John Leyerle, 331–46. Studies in Medieval Culture 32. Kalamazoo, MI: Medieval Institute Publications, 1993.

Creed, Robert P. "Widsith's Journey through Germanic Tradition." In *Anglo-Saxon Poetry: Essays in Appreciation, For John C. McGalliard*, edited by Lewis E. Nicholson and Dolores Warwick Frese, 376–87. Notre Dame: University of Notre Dame Press, 1975.

Cronan, Dennis. "Alliterative Rank in Old English Poetry." *SN* 58 (1986):145–58.

Cross, J.E. "The Conception of the Old English *Phoenix*." In *Old English Poetry: Fifteen Essays*, edited by Robert P. Creed, 129–52. Providence: Brown University Press, 1967.

Damico, Helen. *Beowulf's Wealhtheow and the Valkyrie Tradition.* Madison, WI: University of Wisconsin Press, 1984.

– "The Valkyrie Reflex in Old English Literature." In *New Readings on Women in Old English Literature*, edited by Helen Damico and Alexandra Hennessey Olsen, 176–90. Bloomington: Indiana University Press, 1990.

Damon, John Edward. *Soldier Saints and Holy Warriors: Warfare and Sanctity in the Literature of Early England.* Aldershot: Ashgate, 2003.

Dance, Richard. "The Old English Language and the Alliterative Tradition." In *Companion to Medieval Literature*, edited by Corinne Saunders, 34–50. Oxford: Blackwell, 2010.

Davidson, Hilda Roderick Ellis. *Myths and Symbols in Pagan Europe: Early Scandinavian and Celtic Religions.* Manchester: University of Manchester Press, 1988.

– *Roles of the Northern Goddess.* London: Routledge, 1998.

– *The Sword in Anglo-Saxon England: its Archaeology and Literature.* Oxford: Clarendon Press, 1962.

Davis, Adam. "Agon and Gnomon: Forms and Functions of the Anglo-Saxon Riddles." In *De Gustibus: Essays for Alain Renoir*, edited by John Miles Foley,

Chris J. Womack, and Whitney A. Womack, 110–50. The Albert Bates Lord Studies in Oral Tradition 11. New York: Garland, 1992.

Davis, Craig R. *Beowulf and the Demise of Germanic Legend in England*. New York: Garland, 1996.

Davis, Glenn. "The Exeter Book Riddles and the Place of Sexual Idiom in Old English Literature." In *Medieval Obscenities*, edited by Nicola McDonald, 39–54. York: York Medieval Press, 2006.

Dawson, Richard MacGregor. "The Structure of Old English Gnomic Poems." *JEGP* 61.1 (1962):14–22.

Dendle, Peter. *Satan Unbound: The Devil in Old English Narrative Literature*. Toronto: University of Toronto Press, 2001.

Denno, Jerome. "Oppression and Voice in the Anglo-Saxon Riddles." *Papers Presented at the 35th International Congress on Medieval Studies, 2000*. Kalamazoo Riddle Group. n.pag. Web.

Diamond, R.E. "Theme as Ornament in Anglo-Saxon Poetry." *PMLA* 76.5 (1961):461–8.

Diekstra, F.N.M. "*The Seafarer* 58-66a: The Flight of the Exiled Soul to its Fatherland." *Neophilologus* 55 (1971):433–46.

Dietrich, Franz. "Die Räthsel des Exeterbuchs: Würdigung, Lösung und Herstellung." *Zeitschrift für Deutsches Altertum* 11 (1859):448–90.

Dietrich, Sheila C. "An Introduction to Women in Anglo-Saxon Society (c. 600–1066)." In *The Women of England from Anglo-Saxon Times to the Present: Interpretive Bibliographical Essays*, edited by Barbara Kanner, 32–56. Hamden, CT: Archon Books, 1979.

Doane, A.N. "Three Old English Implement Riddles: Reconsiderations of Numbers 4, 49, and 73." *Modern Philology* 84.3 (1987):243–57.

Doig, J.F. "*Beowulf* 3069b: Curse or Consequence?" *ELN* 19.1 (1981):3–6.

Edwards, Cyril W. *The Beginnings of German Literature: Comparative and Interdisciplinary Approaches to Old High German*. Studies in German Literature, Linguistics, and Culture. Rochester, NY: Camden House, 2002.

Ekwall, Eilert. Review of *Three Northumbrian Poems*, by A.H. Smith. *MLR* 29 (1934):78–82.

Eliade, Mircea. *Images and Symbols: Studies in Religious Symbolism*. Translated by Philip Mairet. London: Harvill Press, 1961.

Eliason, Norman E. "The Þyle and Scop in *Beowulf*." *Speculum* 38.2 (1963): 267–84.

Enright, Michael. *Lady with a Mead Cup: Ritual, Prophecy and Lordship in the European Warband from La Tène to the Viking Age*. Dublin: Four Courts Press, 1996.

– "The Warband Context of the Unferth Episode." *Speculum* 73.2 (1998):297–337.

Erhardt-Siebold, Erika von. "Aldhelm in Possession of the Secrets of Sericulture." *Anglia* 60 (1936):384–9.

– "The Old English Loom Riddles." In *Philologica: The Malone Anniversary Studies*, edited by Thomas A. Kirkby and Henry Bosley Woolf, 9–17. Baltimore: Johns Hopkins Press, 1949.

Fanning, Steven. "Tacitus, *Beowulf*, and the *Comitatus*." *Haskins Society Journal* 9 (1997):17–38.

Fee, Christopher. "*Beag* and *Beaghroden*: Women, Treasure and the Language of Social Structure in *Beowulf*." *NM* 97.3 (1996):285–94.

Fell, Christine. *Women in Anglo-Saxon England*. London: British Museum Publications, 1984.

Fish, Varda. "Theme and Pattern in Cynewulf's *Elene*." *NM* 76 (1975):1–25.

Flint, Valerie I.J. *The Rise of Magic in Early Medieval Europe*. Oxford: Clarendon Press, 1991.

Foley, John Miles. *Immanent Art: From Structure to Meaning in Traditional Oral Epic*. Bloomington: Indiana University Press, 1991.

– *Traditional Oral Epic: The* Odyssey, Beowulf, *and the Serbo-Croatian Return Song*. Berkeley: University of California Press, 1990.

Forbes, Helen Foxhall. "The Power of Binding and Loosing: the Chains of Sin in Anglo-Saxon Literature and Liturgy." *Quaestio Insularis* 8 (2007):51–65.

Frank, Roberta. "*Beowulf* and Sutton Hoo: The Odd Couple." In *Voyage to the Other World: The Legacy of Sutton Hoo*, edited by Calvin B. Kendall and Peter S. Wells, 47–64. Minneapolis: University of Minnesota Press, 1992.

Frankis, P.J. "*Deor* and *Wulf and Eadwacer*: Some Conjectures." *MÆ* 31 (1962):161–75.

Frese, Dolores Warwick. "The Art of Cynewulf's Runic Signatures." In *Anglo-Saxon Poetry: Essays in Appreciation for John C.* McGalliard, edited by Lewis E. Nicholson and Dolores Warwick Frese, 312–34. Notre Dame, IN: University of Notre Dame Press, 1975.

Frey, Leonard. "Exile and Elegy in Anglo-Saxon Christian Epic Poetry." *JEGP* 62 (1963):293–302.

Friesen, Bill. "Visions and Revisions: The Sources and Analogues of the Old English *Andreas*." PhD diss., University of Toronto, 2008.

Fry, Donald K. "Exeter Book Riddle Solutions." *OEN* 15.1 (1981):22–33.

– "Old English Formulaic Themes and Type-Scenes." *Neophilologus* 52 (1968):48–54.

– "Old English Formulas and Systems." *ES* 48 (1967):193–204.

Fulk, Robert D. *A History of Old English Meter*. Philadelphia: University of Pennsylvania Press, 1992.

– "The Name of Offa's Queen: *Beowulf* 1931–2." *Anglia* 122.4 (2004):614–39.

Fuller, Susan D. "Pagan Charms in Tenth-Century Saxony?" *Monatshefte* 72 (1980):162–70.

Garner, Lori Ann. *Structuring Spaces: Oral Poetics and Architecture in Early Medieval England*. Notre Dame, IN: University of Notre Dame Press, 2011.

Gay, David E. "Anglo-Saxon Metrical Charm 3 against a Dwarf: A Charm against Witch-Riding?" *Folklore* 99.2 (1988):174–7.

Gerritsen, Johan. "Þurh þreata geþræcu." *ES* 35 (1954):259–62.

Giangrosso, Patricia. "The Merseburg Charms." In *Medieval Germany: An Encyclopedia*, edited by John Jeep, 112–13. New York: Garland, 2001.

Glosecki, Stephen O. *Shamanism and Old English Poetry*. New York: Garland, 1989.

Gneuss, Helmut. "The Study of Language in Anglo-Saxon England." In *Textual and Material Culture in Anglo-Saxon England: Thomas Northcote Toller and the Toller Memorial Lectures*, edited by Donald Scragg, 75–105. Publications of the Manchester Centre for Anglo-Saxon Studies 1. Cambridge: D.S. Brewer, 2003.

Göbel, Heidi, and Rüdiger Göbel. "The Solution of an Old English Riddle." *SN* 50.2 (1978):185–91.

Godden, Malcolm. "Literary Language." In *The Cambridge History of the English Language*, edited by Richard M. Hogg, vol. 1, 490–535. Cambridge: Cambridge University Press, 1992.

Goldsmith, Margaret E. *The Mode and Meaning of Beowulf*. London: Athlone Press, 1970.

Gollancz, Israel. *The Cædmon Manuscript of Anglo-Saxon Biblical Poetry, Junius XI in the Bodleian Library*. London: British Academy, Oxford University Press, 1927.

Grattan, John, and Charles Singer. *Anglo-Saxon Magic and Medicine: Illustrated Specially from the Semi-Pagan Text Lacnunga*. London: Oxford University Press, 1952.

Grau, Gustav. *Quellen und Verwandtschaften der älteren germanischen Darstellungen des jüngsten Gerichtes*. Studien zur englischen Philologie 31. Halle: Max Niemeyer, 1908.

Greenfield, Stanley B. "Esthetics and Meaning and the Translation of Old English Poetry." In *Old English Poetry: Essays on Style*, edited by Daniel G. Calder, 91–110. Contributions of the UCLA Center for Medieval and Renaissance Studies 10. Berkeley: University of California Press, 1979.

– "The Formulaic Expression of the Theme of 'Exile' in Anglo-Saxon Poetry." *Speculum* 30 (1955):200–6. Reprinted in *Essential Articles for the Study of Old English Poetry*, edited by Jess B. Bessinger, Jr and Stanley J. Kahrl, 352–62. Hamden, CT: Archon Books, 1968.

– "'Gifstol' and Goldhoard in *Beowulf*." In *Hero and Exile: The Art of Old English Poetry*, edited by George H. Brown, 33–42. London: Hambledon Press, 1989.

– "The Old English Elegies." In *Continuations and Beginnings: Studies in Old English Literature*, edited by Eric G. Stanley, 142–75. London: Nelson, 1966. Reprinted in *Hero and Exile: The Art of Old English Poetry*, edited by George H. Brown, 93–123. London: Hambledon, 1989.

Greentree, Rosemary. "The Wanderer's Horizon: A Note on *Ofer Waþema Gebind*." *Neophilologus* 86 (2002):307–9.

Griffith, Mark S. "Convention and Originality in the 'Beasts of Battle' Typescene." *ASE* 22 (1993):179–99.

– "Poetic Language and the *Paris Psalter*: The Decay of the Old English Tradition." *ASE* 20 (1991):167–86.

Hait, Elizabeth A. "The Wanderer's Lingering Regret: A Study of Patterns of Imagery." *Neophilologus* 68 (1984):278–91.

Hall, Alaric. *Elves in Anglo-Saxon England: Matters of Belief, Health, Gender and Identity*. Woodbridge: Boydell, 2007.

– "Hygelac's Only Daughter: A Present, a Potentate and a Peaceweaver in *Beowulf*." *SN* 78 (2006):81–7.

Hansen, Elaine Tuttle. "Hrothgar's 'Sermon' in *Beowulf* as Parental Wisdom." *ASE* 10 (1982 for 1981):53–67.

– *The Solomon Complex: Reading Wisdom in Old English Poetry*. McMaster Old English Studies and Texts 5. Toronto: University of Toronto Press, 1988.

– "Women in Old English Poetry Reconsidered." *Michigan Academician* 9 (1976):109–17.

Harbus, Antonina. *The Life of the Mind in Old English Poetry*. Costerus n.s. 143. Amsterdam: Rodopi, 2002.

– "Text as Revelation: Constantine's Dream in *Elene*." *Neophilologus* 78.4 (1994):645–53.

Haruta, Setsuko. "The Women in *Beowulf*." *Poetica (Tokyo)* 23 (1986):1–15.

Helder, Willem. "Beowulf and the Plundered Hoard." *NM* 78 (1977):317–25.

Hermann, John P. *Allegories of War: Language and Violence in Old English Poetry*. Ann Arbor: University of Michigan Press, 1989.

– "The Recurrent Motifs of Spiritual Warfare in Old English Poetry." *Annuale Mediaevale* 22 (1985 for 1982):7–35.

– "Some Varieties of Psychomachia in Old English." *American Benedictine Review* 34 (1983):74–86 and 188–222.

Heyworth, Melanie. "The Devil's in the Detail: A New Solution to Exeter Book Riddle 4." *Neophilologus* 91 (2007):175–96.

Hieatt, Constance B. "The Harrowing of Mermedonia: Typological Patterns in the Old English *Andreas*." *NM* 77.1 (1976):49–62.

Hill, John M. *The Anglo-Saxon Warrior Ethic*. Gainesville: University Press of Florida, 2000.

Hill, Joyce. "Þæt Wæs Geomuru Ides! A Female Stereotype Examined." In *New Readings on Women in Old English Literature*, edited by Helen Damico and Alexandra Hennessey Olsen, 235–47. Bloomington: Indiana University Press, 1990.

Hill, Thomas D. "Figural Narrative in *Andreas*." *NM* 70 (1969):261–73.

– "Saturn's Time Riddle: An Insular Latin Analogue for *Solomon and Saturn II* lines 282-291." *RES* 39.154 (1988):273–6.

– "The Tropological Context of Heat and Cold Imagery in Anglo-Saxon Poetry." *NM* 69 (1968):522–32.

– "The Unchanging Hero: A Stoic Maxim in *The Wanderer* and Its Contexts." *SP* 101 (2004):233–49.

– "Wise Words: Old English Sapiential Poetry." In *Readings in Medieval Texts: Interpreting Old and Middle English Literature*, edited by David Johnson and Elaine Treharne, 166–82. Oxford: Oxford University Press, 2005.

Hodges, Henry W.M. *Artifacts: An Introduction to Early Materials and Technology*. London: John Baker, 1964.

Hoffmann, Marta. *The Warp-Weighted Loom: Studies in the History and Technology of an Ancient Implement*. Studia Norvegica 14. Oslo: Universitetsforlaget, 1964.

Holtsmark, Anne. "Vefr Darraðar." *Maal og Minne* (1939):74–96.

Honegger, Thomas. "Form and Function: the Beasts of Battle Revisited." *ES* 79.4 (1998):289–98.

Hoops, Johannes. *Beowulfstudien*. Heidelberg: C. Winter, 1932.

Horner, Shari. *The Discourse of Enclosure: Representing Women in Old English Literature*. Albany, NY: State University of New York Press, 2001.

Howe, Nicholas. "Aldhelm's *Enigmata* and Isidorian Etymology." *ASE* 14 (1985):37–60.

– *The Old English Catalogue Poems*. Anglistica 23. Copenhagen: Rosenkilde, 1985.

Hume, Kathryn. "The Concept of the Hall in Old English Poetry." *ASE* 3 (1974):63–74.

– "The 'Ruin Motif' in Old English Poetry." *Anglia* 94 (1976):339–60.

Hutcheson, B.R. *Old English Poetic Metre*. Cambridge: D.S. Brewer, 1995.

– "*Wiþ Dweorh*: An Anglo-Saxon Remedy for Fever in its Cultural and Manuscript Context." *Amsterdamer Beiträge zur älteren Germanistik* 69 (2012):175–202.

Hyer, Maren Clegg. "Textiles and Textile Imagery in the *Exeter Book*." *Medieval Clothing and Textiles* 1 (2004):29–40.

– "Textiles and Textile Imagery in Old English Literature." PhD diss., University of Toronto, 1998.

Hyer, Maren Clegg, and Gale R. Owen-Crocker. "Woven Works: Making and Using Textiles." In *The Material Culture of Daily Living in the Anglo-Saxon World*, edited by Gale R. Owen-Crocker and Maren Clegg Hyer, 157–84. Exeter: University of Exeter Press, 2011.

Ingham, Patricia Clare. "From Kinship to Kingship: Mourning, Gender, and Anglo-Saxon Community." In *Grief and Gender: 700–1700*, edited by Jennifer C. Vaught and Lynne Dickson Bruckner, 17–31. New York: Palgrave Macmillan, 2003.

Irvine, Martin. "Cynewulf's Use of Psychomachia Allegory: the Latin Sources of Some 'Interpolated' Passages." In *Allegory, Myth, and Symbol*, edited by Morton W. Bloomfield, 39–62. Harvard English Studies 9. Cambridge, MA: Harvard University Press, 1981.

– *The Making of Textual Culture: 'Grammatica' and Literary Theory, 350–1100*. Cambridge: Cambridge University Press, 1994.

Irvine, Susan. "Hanging by a Thread: Ælfric's Saints' Lives and the *hengen*." In *Hagiography in Anglo-Saxon England: Adopting and Adapting Saints' Lives into Old English Prose (c. 950–1150)*, edited by Loredana Lazzari, Patrizia Lendinara and Claudia Di Sciacca, 67–94. Textes et Études du Moyen Âge 73. Barcelona-Madrid: Fédération Internationale des Instituts d'Études Médiévales, 2014.

Irving, Edward B., Jr. "Heroic Experience in the Old English Riddles." In *Old English Shorter Poems*, edited by Katherine O'Brien O'Keeffe, 199–212. New York: Garland, 1994.

– "Heroic Role-Models: Beowulf and Others." In *Heroic Poetry in the Anglo-Saxon Period: Studies in Honor of Jess B. Bessinger, Jr.*, edited by Helen Damico and John Leyerle, 347–72. Studies in Medieval Culture 32. Kalamazoo, MI: Medieval Institute Publications, Western Michigan University, 1993.

– "Image and Meaning in the Elegies." In *Old English Poetry: Fifteen Essays*, edited by Robert P. Creed, 153–66. Providence: Brown University Press, 1967.

Isaacs, Neil D. *Structural Principles in Old English Poetry*. Knoxville: University of Tennessee Press, 1968.

Jager, Eric. "Speech and the Chest in Old English Poetry: Orality or Pectorality?" *Speculum* 65.4 (1990):845–59.

Jagger, Holly. "Body, Text and Self in Old English Verse: A Study of "Beowulfian" and "Cynewulfian" Rhetoric." PhD diss., University of Toronto, 2002.

Jente, Richard. *Die mythologischen Ausdrücke im altenglischen Wortschatz*. Anglistische Forschungen 56. Heidelberg: C. Winter, 1921.

Jochens, Jenny. *Old Norse Images of Women*. Philadelphia: University of Pennsylvania Press, 1996.

Johnson, William C. "The Ruin as Body-City Riddle." *PQ* 59 (1980):397–441.
– "*Werig* and *Dreorig* in *The Wanderer*: The Semantics of Death." *In Geardagum* 7 (1986):45–69.
Jolly, Karen Louise. *Popular Religion in Late Saxon England: Elf Charms in Context.* Chapel Hill: University of North Carolina Press, 1996.
Jonassen, Frederick B. "The Pater Noster Letters in the Poetic *Solomon and Saturn.*" *MLR* 83 (1988):1–9.
Jones, Alison. "*Daniel* and *Azarias* as Evidence for the Oral Formulaic Character of Old English Poetry." *MÆ* 35 (1966):95–102.
Kasik, Jon C. "The Use of the Term *Wyrd* in *Beowulf* and the Conversion of the Anglo-Saxons." *Neophilologus* 63 (1979):128–35.
Kim, Susan. "Bloody Signs: Circumcision and Pregnancy in the *Old English Judith.*" *Exemplaria* 11.2 (1999):285–307.
Klaeber, Frederick. "Beowulfiana." *Anglia* 50 (1926):107–22 and 195–244.
Klein, Stacy S. *Ruling Women: Queenship and Gender in Anglo-Saxon Literature.* Notre Dame: University of Notre Dame Press, 2006.
Klein, Thomas. "The Old English Translation of Aldhelm's Riddle *Lorica.*" *RES* n.s., 48.191 (1997):345–9.
Kliman, Bernice W. "Women in Early English Literature, *Beowulf* to the *Ancrene Wisse.*" *Nottingham Medieval Studies* 21 (1977):32–49.
Kock, Ernst A. "Interpretations and Emendations of Early English Texts." *Anglia* 44 (1920):97–114.
Kuhn, S.M. "Was Ælfric a Poet?" *PQ* 52 (1973):643–62.
Laborde, E.D. "Grendel's Glove and his Immunity from Weapons." *MLR* 18 (1923):202–4.
Lakoff, George, and Mark Johnson. *Metaphors We Live By.* Chicago: University of Chicago Press, 1980.
Langeslag, Paul. "Seasonal Setting and the Human Domain in Early English and Early Scandinavian Literature." PhD diss., University of Toronto, 2012.
Lapidge, Michael. *Anglo-Latin Literature 600–899.* London: Hambledon Press, 1996.
– "*Beowulf* and Perception." *Proceedings of the British Academy* 111 (2001):61–97.
– "Cynewulf and the *Passio S. Iulianae.*" In *Unlocking the Wordhord: Anglo-Saxon Studies in Memory of Edward B. Irving, Jr*, edited by Mark C. Amodio and Katherine O'Brien O'Keeffe, 147–71. Toronto: University of Toronto Press, 2003.
– "Stoic Cosmology and the Source of the First Old English Riddle." *Anglia* 112.1–2 (1994):1–25.
Laqueur, Thomas. *Making Sex: Body and Gender from the Greeks to Freud.* Cambridge, MA: Harvard University Press, 1990.

Larrington, Carolyne. *A Store of Common Sense: Gnomic Theme and Style in Old Icelandic and Old English Wisdom Poetry*. Oxford English Monographs. Oxford: Clarendon Press, 1993.

Lee, Christina. "Body and Soul: Disease and Impairment." In *The Material Culture of Daily Living in the Anglo-Saxon World*, edited by Gale R. Owen-Crocker and Maren Clegg Hyer, 293–308. Exeter: University of Exeter Press, 2011.

Lees, Clare, and Gillian R. Overing. *Double Agents: Women and Clerical Culture in Anglo-Saxon England*. Philadelphia: University of Pennsylvania Press, 2001.

Lerer, Seth. "Grendel's Glove." *ELH* 61 (1994):721–51.

– *Literacy and Power in Anglo-Saxon Literature*. Lincoln, NE: University of Nebraska Press, 1991.

– "The Riddle and the Book: Exeter Book Riddle 42 in its Contexts." *Papers on Language and Literature* 25 (1989):3–18.

Lévi-Strauss, Claude. *The Raw and the Cooked*. Translated by John and Doreen Weightman. London: Cape, 1970. Reprint, Chicago: University of Chicago Press, 1990. Originally published as *Le Cru et le Cuit*. Paris: Plon, 1964.

Leyerle, John. "The Interlace Structure of *Beowulf*." *University of Toronto Quarterly* 37 (1967):1–17.

Lieber, Michael D. "Riddles, Cultural Categories, and World View." *JAF* 89 (1976):255–65.

Lionarons, Joyce Tally. "Cultural Syncretism and the Construction of Gender in Cynewulf's *Elene*." *Exemplaria* 10 (1998):51–68.

– "Dísir, Valkyries, Völur, and Norns: The Weise Frauen of the Deutsche Mythologie." In *The Shadow-Walkers: Jacob Grimm's Mythology of the Monstrous*, edited by T.A. Shippey, 271–97. Tempe, AZ: Arizona Center for Medieval and Renaissance Studies, 2005.

– "Women's Work and Women's Magic as Literary Motifs in Icelandic Sagas." In *Constructing Nations, Reconstructing Myth: Essays in Honour of T.A. Shippey*, edited by Andrew Wawn, Graham Johnson, and John Walter, 301–17. Making the Middle Ages 9. Turnhout: Brepols, 2007.

Lockett, Leslie. *Anglo-Saxon Psychologies in the Vernacular and Latin Traditions*. Toronto: University of Toronto Press, 2011.

– "The Role of Grendel's Arm in Feud, Law, and the Narrative Strategy of *Beowulf*." In *Latin Learning and English Lore: Studies in Anglo-Saxon Literature for Michael Lapidge*, edited by Katherine O'Brien O'Keeffe and Andy Orchard, vol. 1, 368–88. Toronto: University of Toronto Press, 2005.

Long, J. B. "Webs and Nets." *Encyclopedia of Religion*, edited by Mircea Eliade, vol. 15, 367–68. London: Macmillan, 1985.

Low, Soon Ai. "The Anglo-Saxon Mind: Metaphor and Common Sense Psychology in Old English Literature." PhD diss., University of Toronto, 1998.

Mackie, W.S. "The Old English Rhymed Poem." *JEGP* 21.3 (1922):507–19.

MacLeod, Mindy and Bernard Mees. *Runic Amulets and Magic Objects.* Woodbridge: Boydell, 2006.

Magennis, Hugh. "Gender and Heroism in the *Old English Judith*." In *Writing Gender and Genre in Medieval Literature: Approaches to Old and Middle English Texts*, edited by Elaine Treharne, 5–18. Cambridge: D.S. Brewer, 2002.

– *Images of Community in Old English Poetry*. CSASE 18. Cambridge: Cambridge University Press, 1996.

– *Translating Beowulf: Modern Versions in English Verse*. Cambridge: D.S. Brewer, 2011.

Magoun, Francis P., Jr. "Oral-Formulaic Character of Anglo-Saxon Narrative Poetry." *Speculum* 28 (1953):446–67.

– "The Theme of the Beasts of Battle in Anglo-Saxon Poetry." *NM* 56 (1955): 81–90.

Major, C. Tidmarsh. "A Christian *wyrd*: Syncretism in *Beowulf*." *ELN* 32.3 (1995):1–10.

Malmberg, Lars. "*The Wanderer: waþema gebind*." *NM* 71 (1970):96–9.

Maranda, Elli Köngäs. "Riddles and Riddling: An Introduction." *JAF* 89 (1976): 127–37.

Martin, B.K. "Aspects of Winter in Latin and Old English Poetry." *JEGP* 68 (1969):375–90.

Matto, Michael. "True Confessions: *The Seafarer* and Technologies of the *Sylf*." *JEGP* 103.2 (2004):156–79.

McCarthy, Mike. *Ships' Fastenings: From Sewn Boat to Steamship*. Ed Rachal Foundation Nautical Archaeology Series. College Station, TX: Texas A&M University Press, 2005.

McGowan, Joseph. "An Introduction to the Corpus of Anglo-Latin Literature." In *A Companion to Anglo-Saxon Literature*, edited by Philip Pusiano and Elaine Treharne, 11–49. Blackwell Companions to Literature and Culture. Oxford: Blackwell, 2001.

Meaney, Audrey L. *Anglo-Saxon Amulets and Curing Stones*. BAR, British Series 96. Oxford: Oxford University Press, 1981.

– "The Anglo-Saxon View of the Causes of Illness." In *Health, Disease and Healing in Medieval Culture*, edited by S. Campbell, B. Hall, and D. Klausner, 12–33. Toronto: University of Toronto Press, 1992.

– "The *Ides* of the Cotton Gnomic Poem." *MÆ* 48 (1979):23–39.

Mize, Britt. "Manipulations of the Mind-as-Container Motif in *Beowulf*, *Homiletic Fragment II* and *Alfred's Metrical Epilogue to the Pastoral Care*." *JEGP* 107.1 (2008):25–56.

– "The Representation of the Mind as an Enclosure in Old English Poetry." *ASE* 35 (2006):57–90.

– *Traditional Subjectivities: The Old English Poetics of Mentality.* Toronto: University of Toronto Press, 2013.

Moltke, Erik. *Runes and Their Origin: Denmark and Elsewhere.* Translated by Peter Foote. Rev. ed. Copenhagen: National Museum of Denmark, 1985.

Montelius, Oscar. *Civilisation of Sweden in Heathen Times.* Translated by Rev. F.H. Woods. 2nd ed. London: Macmillan, 1888.

Morey, Robert. "Beowulf's Androgynous Heroism." *JEGP* 95 (1996):486–96.

Murphy, Patrick J. *Unriddling the Exeter Riddles.* University Park, PA: Pennsylvania State University Press, 2011.

Nelson, Marie. "Four Social Functions of the Exeter Book Riddles." *Neophilologus* 75.3 (1991):445–50.

– "King Solomon's Magic: the Power of a Written Text." *Oral Tradition* 5 (1990):20–36.

– "An Old English Charm Against Nightmare." *Germanic Notes* 13.2 (1982): 17–18.

– "Old English Riddle 18 (20): a Description of Ambivalence." *Neophilologus* 66 (1982):291–300.

– "The Paradox of Silent Speech in the Exeter Book Riddles." *Neophilologus* 62.4 (1978):609–15.

Neville, Jennifer. *Representations of the Natural World in Old English Poetry.* CSASE 27. Cambridge: Cambridge University Press, 1999.

Niles, John D. *Beowulf: The Poem and its Tradition.* Cambridge, MA: Harvard University Press, 1983.

– "Formula and Formulaic System in *Beowulf.*" In *Oral Traditional Literature: A Festschrift for Albert Bates Lord,* edited by John Miles Foley, 394–415. Columbus, OH: Slavica Publishers, Inc., 1981.

– *Old English Enigmatic Poems and the Play of the Texts.* Studies in the Early Middle Ages 13. Turnhout: Brepols, 2006.

Ó Carragáin, Éamonn. "Cynewulf's Epilogue to *Elene* and the Tastes of the Vercelli Compiler: A Paradigm of Meditative Reading." In *Lexis and Texts in Early English,* edited by Christian J. Kay and Louise M. Sylvester, 187–201. Costerus 133. Amsterdam: Rodopi, 2001.

O'Brien O'Keeffe, Katherine. "Body and Law in Late Anglo-Saxon England." *ASE* 27 (1998):209–32.

– "Diction, Variation, the Formula." In *A Beowulf Handbook,* edited by Robert E. Bjork and John D. Niles, 85–104. Exeter: University of Exeter Press, 1997.

– "Exeter Riddle 40: the Art of an Old English Translator." *Proceedings of the PMR Conference* 5 (1983 for 1980):107–17.

– "Heroic Values and Christian Ethics." In *The Cambridge Companion to Old English Literature,* edited by Malcolm Godden and Michael Lapidge, 107–25. Cambridge: Cambridge University Press, 1991.

Oggins, Robin S. *The Kings and Their Hawks: Falconry in Medieval England*. New Haven: Yale University Press, 2004.

Ogilvy, J.D.A. "Unferth: Foil to Beowulf?" *PMLA* 79.4 (1964):370–5.

Olsen, Alexandra Hennessey. "Gender Roles." In *A Beowulf Handbook*, edited by Robert E. Bjork and John D. Niles, 311–24. Exeter: University of Exeter Press, 1997.

– "The Heroic World: Icelandic Sagas and the Old English *Riming Poem*." *Pacific Coast Philology* 14 (1979):51–8.

– *Speech, Song, and Poetic Craft: the Artistry of the Cynewulf Canon*. American University Studies, Series 4: English Language and Literature 15. Bern: Peter Lang, 1984.

Onians, R.B. *The Origins of European Thought*. Cambridge: Cambridge University Press, 1951.

Orchard, Andy. "Artful Alliteration in Anglo-Saxon Song and Story." *Anglia* 113 (1995):429–63.

– "Both Style and Substance: The Case for Cynewulf." In *Anglo-Saxon Styles*, edited by Catherine E. Karkov and George Hardin Brown, 271–305. SUNY Series in Medieval Studies. Albany: State University of New York Press, 2003.

– "Computing Cynewulf: The Judith-Connection." In *The Text in the Community: Essays on Medieval Works, Manuscripts, Authors, and Readers*, edited by Jill Mann and Maura Nolan, 75–106. Notre Dame, IN: University of Notre Dame Press, 2006.

– *A Critical Companion to Beowulf*. Cambridge: D.S. Brewer, 2003.

– "Enigma Variations: The Anglo-Saxon Riddle-Tradition." In *Latin Learning and English Lore: Studies in Anglo-Saxon Literature for Michael Lapidge*, edited by Katherine O'Brien O'Keeffe and Andy Orchard, vol. 1, 284–304. Toronto: University of Toronto Press, 2005.

– "Old English and Latin Poetic Traditions." In *Companion to Medieval Literature*, edited by Corinne Saunders, 65–82. Oxford: Blackwell, 2010.

– "Oral Tradition." In *Reading Old English Texts*, edited by Katherine O'Brien O'Keeffe, 101–23. Cambridge: Cambridge University Press, 1997.

– *The Poetic Art of Aldhelm*. CSASE 8. Cambridge: Cambridge University Press, 1994.

– "Re-Reading *The Wanderer*: The Value of Cross-References." In *Via Crucis: Essays on Early Medieval Sources and Ideas in Memory of J.E. Cross*, edited by Thomas N. Hall with assistance from Thomas D. Hill and Charles D. Wright, 1–26. Morgantown, WV: West Virginia University Press, 2002.

Overing, Gillian R. *Language, Sign and Gender in Beowulf*. Carbondale: Southern Illinois University Press, 1990.

Owen (-Crocker), Gale R. "Anglo-Saxon Costume." 3 vols. PhD diss., University of Newcastle upon Tyne, 1976.

– *Dress in Anglo-Saxon England.* Rev. ed. Woodbridge: Boydell, 2004.
– *The Four Funerals in Beowulf.* Manchester: Manchester University Press, 2000.
– "'Seldom ... does the deadly spear rest for long': Weapons and Armour." In *The Material Culture of Daily Living in the Anglo-Saxon World*, edited by Gale R. Owen-Crocker and Maren Clegg Hyer, 201–30. Exeter: University of Exeter Press, 2011.
– "Women's Costume in the Tenth and Eleventh Centuries and Textile Production in Anglo-Saxon England." In *The Archaeology of Anglo-Saxon England: Basic Readings*, edited by Catherine E. Karkov, 423–85. New York: Garland, 1999.
Owen-Crocker, Gale R., Elizabeth Coatsworth, and Maria Hayward, eds. *Encyclopedia of Medieval Dress and Textiles of the British Isles, c. 450–1450.* Leiden: Brill, 2012.
Page, R.I. "Anglo-Saxon Runes and Magic." *Journal of the British Archaeological Association* 27 (1964):14–31.
Parkes, M.B. "The Manuscript of the *Leiden Riddle*." *ASE* 1 (1972):207–17.
Parks, Ward. "Flyting and Fighting: Pathways in the Realization of the Epic Contest." *Neophilologus* 70 (1986):292–306.
– "The Flyting Speech in Traditional Heroic Narrative." *Neophilologus* 71 (1987):285–95.
Payne, F. Anne. "Three Aspects of *Wyrd* in *Beowulf*." In *Old English Studies in Honour of John C. Pope*, edited by R.B. Burlin and E.B. Irving, Jr, 15–36. Toronto: University of Toronto Press, 1974.
Pelteret, David A.E. *Slavery in Early Mediaeval England: From the Reign of Alfred until the Twelfth Century.* Studies in Anglo-Saxon History 7. Woodbridge: Boydell, 1995.
Pfrenger, Andrew M. "Grendel's *Glof*: *Beowulf* line 2085 Reconsidered." *PQ* 87.3 (2008):209–35.
Poole, Russell G. *Old English Wisdom Poetry.* Annotated Bibliographies of Old and Middle English Literature 5. Cambridge: D.S. Brewer, 1998.
– "The Textile Inventory in the Old English *Gerefa*." *RES* n.s., 40.160 (1989): 469–78.
– *Viking Poems on War and Peace: A Study in Skaldic Narrative.* Toronto: University of Toronto Press, 1991.
Porter, Dorothy Carr. "The Social Centrality of Women in *Beowulf*." *Heroic Age* 5 (2001): n.pag. Web.
Portnoy, Phyllis. "The Riddle of the Remnant: Solving OE *laf*." *Papers Presented at the 35th International Congress on Medieval Studies, 2000.* Kalamazoo Riddle Group. n.pag. Web.
Potter, Joyce. "'Wylm' and 'weallan' in *Beowulf*: a Tidal Metaphor." *Medieval Perspectives* 3 (1988):191–9.

Powell, Alison M. "Verbal Parallels in *Andreas* and its Relationship to *Beowulf* and Cynewulf." PhD diss., University of Cambridge, 2002.

Powell, Kathryn. "Orientalist Fantasy in the Poetic Dialogues of *Solomon and Saturn*." *ASE* 34 (2005):117–43.

Pugh, R.B. *Imprisonment in Medieval England*. Cambridge: Cambridge University Press, 1968.

Remley, Paul G. *Old English Biblical Verse: Studies in Genesis, Exodus and Daniel*. CSASE 16. Cambridge: Cambridge University Press, 1996.

Rendall, Thomas. "Bondage and Freeing from Bondage in Old English Religious Poetry." *JEGP* 73 (1974):497–512.

Reynolds, Andrew. "Executions and Hard Anglo-Saxon Justice." *British Archaeology* 31 (1998):8–9.

Riedinger, Anita. "*Andreas* and the Formula in Transition." In *Hermeneutics and Medieval Culture*, edited by Patrick J. Gallacher and Helen Damico, 183–91. Albany: State University of New York Press, 1989.

– "The Formulaic Relationship Between *Beowulf* and *Andreas*." In *Heroic Poetry in the Anglo-Saxon Period: Studies in Honor of Jess B. Bessinger, Jr.*, edited by Helen Damico and John Leyerle, 283–312. Studies in Medieval Culture 32. Kalamazoo, MI: Medieval Institute Publications, 1993.

– "The Formulaic Style in the Old English Riddles." *Studia Neophilologica* 76 (2004):30–43.

– "The Old English Formula in Context." *Speculum* 60 (1985):294–317.

Robinson, Fred C. *"Beowulf" and the Appositive Style*. Knoxville: University of Tennessee Press, 1985.

Rogers, H.L. "Rhymes in the Epilogue to *Elene*: A Reconsideration." *Leeds Studies in English* 5 (1971):47–52.

Rogers, Penelope Walton. *Cloth and Clothing in Early Anglo-Saxon England: AD 450–700*. York: Council for British Archaeology, 2006.

Rosier, James L. "Death and Transfiguration: *Guthlac B*." In *Philological Essays: Studies in Old and Middle English Language and Literature in Honour of Herbert Dean Meritt*, edited by James L. Rosier, 82–92. The Hague: Mouton, 1970.

– "Design for Treachery: The Unferth Intrigue." *PMLA* 77.1 (1962):1–8.

– "The Literal-Figurative Identity of the *Wanderer*." *PMLA* 79 (1964):366–9.

– "The Uses of Association: Hands and Feasts in *Beowulf*." *PMLA* 78 (1963):8–14.

Roth, H. Ling. *Ancient Egyptian and Greek Looms*. Halifax: Bankfield Museum, 1913. Web: Project Gutenberg http://www.gutenberg.org/files/25731/25731-h/25731-h.htm.

Rothauser, Britt C.L. "Winter in Heorot: Looking at Anglo-Saxon Perceptions of Age and Kingship through the Character of Hrothgar." In *Old Age in the*

Middle Ages and the Renaissance: Interdisciplinary Approaches to a Neglected Topic, edited by Albrecht Classen, 103–20. Fundamentals of Medieval and Early Modern Culture 2. Berlin: Walter de Gruyter, 2007.

Russell, Jeffrey Burton. *Lucifer: The Devil in the Middles Ages*. Ithaca: Cornell University Press, 1984.

Salvador (-Bello), Mercedes. "The Key to the Body: Unlocking Riddles 42-46." In *Naked Before God: Uncovering the Body in Anglo-Saxon England*, edited by Benjamin C. Withers and Jonathan Wilcox, 60–96. Morgantown: West Virginia University Press, 2003.

– "The Sexual Riddle Type in Aldhelm's Enigmata, the Exeter Book, and Early Medieval Latin." *PQ* 90.4 (2011):357–85.

Sánchez-Martí, Jordi. "Age Matters in Old English Literature." In *Youth and Age in the Medieval North*, edited by Shannon Lewis-Simpson, 205–26. Leiden: Brill, 2008.

Scheid, John, and Jesper Svenbro. *The Craft of Zeus: Myths of Weaving and Fabric*. Translated by Carol Volk. Cambridge, MA: Harvard University Press, 1996.

Schneider, Jane, and A. Weiner, eds. *Cloth and Human Experience*. Washington: Smithsonian Institution Press, 1989.

Shook, Laurence K. "Old-English Riddle 28—*Testudo* (Tortoise-Lyre)." *Mediaeval Studies* 20 (1958):93–7.

– "Old English Riddle No. 20: *Heoruswealwe*." In *Franciplegius: Medieval and Linguistic Studies in Honor of Francis Peabody Magoun, Jr.*, edited by Jess B. Bessinger and Robert P. Creed, 194–204. New York: New York University Press, 1965.

Sievers, Eduard. *Der Heliand und die angelsächsische Genesis*. Halle: Max Niemeyer, 1875.

Silber, Patricia. "Rhetoric as Prowess in the Unferð Episode." *Texas Studies in Literature and Language* 23.4 (1981):471–83.

Sisam, Kenneth. *The Structure of Beowulf*. Oxford: Clarendon Press, 1965.

Skeat, W.W. "On the Signification of the Monster Grendel in the Poem of Beowulf; with a Discussion of Lines 2076-2100." *Journal of Philology* 15.29 (1886):120–31.

Skemp, A.R. "The Old English Charms." *MLR* 6.3 (July 1911):289–301.

Sklute, Larry M. "Freoðuwebbe in Old English Poetry." *NM* 71 (1970):534–41. Reprinted in *New Readings on Women in Old English Literature*, edited by Helen Damico and Alexandra Hennessey Olsen, 204–10. Bloomington: Indiana University Press, 1990.

Stanley, Eric G. "Hæþenra hyht in *Beowulf*." In *Studies in Old English Literature in Honor of Arthur G. Brodeur*, edited by Stanley B. Greenfield, 136–51. Eugene: University of Oregon Books, 1963.

– "Heroic Aspects of the Exeter Book Riddles." In *Prosody and Poetics in the Early Middle Ages: Essays in Honour of C.B. Hieatt*, edited by M.J. Toswell, 197–218. Toronto: University of Toronto Press, 1995.

– "Old English Poetic Diction and the Interpretation of *The Wanderer, The Seafarer*, and *The Penitent's Prayer*." *Anglia* 73 (1955):413–66. Reprinted in *Essential Articles for the Study of Old English Poetry*, edited by Jess B. Bessinger, Jr and Stanley J. Kahrl, 458–514. Hamden, CT: Archon Books, 1968.

– "Rhymes in English Medieval Verse: From Old English to Middle English." In *Medieval English Studies Presented to George Kane*, edited by George Kane, Edward Donald Kennedy, Ronald Waldron, and Joseph S. Wittig, 19–54. Wolfeboro, NH: D.S. Brewer, 1988.

– *The Search for Anglo-Saxon Paganism*. Cambridge: Brewer, 1975.

Steen, Janie. *Verse and Virtuosity: The Adaptation of Latin Rhetoric in Old English Poetry*. Toronto: University of Toronto Press, 2008.

Stephens, John. "Weland and a Little Restraint: A Note on *Deor* 5-6." *SN* 41.2 (1969):371–4.

Stewart, Ann Harleman. "The Solution to Old English Riddle 4." *SP* 78.5 (1981):52–61.

Stoodley, Nick. *The Spindle and the Spear: A Critical Enquiry into the Construction and Meaning of Gender in the Early Anglo-Saxon Burial Rite*. BAR, British Series 288. Oxford: Hedges/Archaeopress, 1999.

Stuart, Heather. "'Spider' in Old English." *Parergon* 18 (August 1977):37–42.

Szarmach, Paul. "Abbot Ælfric's Rhythmical Prose and the Computer Age." In *New Approaches to Editing Old English Verse*, edited by Sarah Larratt Keefer and Katherine O'Brien O'Keeffe, 95–109. Cambridge: D.S. Brewer, 1998.

Tanke, John W. "The Bachelor-Warrior of Exeter Book Riddle 20." *PQ* 79 (2000):409–27.

Taylor, Keith P. "Mazers, Mead, and the Wolf's-head-tree: A Reconsideration of Old English Riddle 55." *JEGP* 94.4 (1995):497–512.

Taylor, Paul Beekman. *Sharing Story: Medieval Norse-English Literary Relationships*. New York: AMS Press, 1998.

Teele, Elinor. "The Heroic Tradition in the Old English *Riddles*." PhD diss., University of Cambridge, 2004.

ten Brink, Bernhard. *Beowulf: Untersuchungen*. Strassburg: Karl J. Trübner, 1888.

Thomas, P.G. "'Beowulf,' ll. 1604–5, 2085–91." *MLR* 17 (1922):63–4.

Tigges, Wim. "Signs and Solutions: A Semiotic Approach to the Exeter Book Riddles." In *This Noble Craft: Proceedings of the Xth Research Symposium of the Dutch and Belgian University Teachers of Old and Middle English and Historical Linguistics, Utrecht, 19–20 January, 1989*, edited by Erik Kooper, 59–82. Amsterdam: Rodopi, 1991.

Timmer, B.J. "*Wyrd* in Anglo-Saxon Prose and Poetry." *Neophilologus* 26 (1941):24–33, 213–28.

Toswell, M.J. "'Awended on Engliscum Gereorde': Translation and the Old English Metrical Psalter." *Translation and Literature* 5.2 (1996):167–82.

– "The Translation Techniques of the Old English Metrical Psalter, with Special Reference to Psalm 136." *English Studies* 75 (1994):393–407.

Tripp, Raymond P., Jr. "Language, Archaic Symbolism, and the Poetic Structure of *Beowulf*." *Hiroshima Studies in English Language and Literature* 19 (1972):1–21.

– "Lifting the Curse on *Beowulf*." *ELN* 23.2 (1985):1–8.

Tristram, Hildegard. "Stock Descriptions of Heaven and Hell in Old English Prose and Poetry." *NM* 79 (1978):102–13.

Tuggle, Thomas T. "The Structure of 'Deor'." *SP* 74.3 (1977):229–42.

Tyler, Elizabeth M. *Old English Poetics: The Aesthetics of the Familiar in Anglo-Saxon England*. York: York Medieval Press, 2006.

van der Wurff, W.A.M. "Cynewulf's *Elene*: the First Speech to the Jews." *Neophilologus* 66 (1982):301–12.

Viswanathan, S. "On the Melting of the Sword: *wæl-rápas* and the Engraving on the Sword-Hilt in *Beowulf*." *PQ* 58 (1979):360–3.

Wallace-Hadrill, J.M. "War and Peace in the Earlier Middle Ages." *Transactions of the Royal Historical Society*, 5th series, 25 (1975):157–74.

Walsh, Mary M. "The Baptismal Flood in the Old English *Andreas*: Liturgical and Typological Depths." *Traditio* 33 (1977):137–58.

Weber, Benjamin. "The Isidorian Context of Aldhelm's 'Lorica' and Exeter Riddle 35." *Neophilologus* 96.3 (2012):457–66.

Wehlau, Ruth. *"The Riddle of Creation:" Metaphor Structures in Old English Poetry*. Studies in the Humanities 24. New York: Peter Lang, 1997.

Welsh, Andrew. "*Branwen, Beowulf*, and the Tragic Peaceweaver Tale." *Viator* 22 (1991):1–13.

Wentersdorf, Karl. "The Old English *Rhyming Poem*: A Ruler's Lament." *SP* 82 (1985):265–94.

Whatley, E. Gordon. "The Figure of Constantine the Great in Cynewulf's *Elene*." *Traditio* 37 (1981):161–202.

Whitbread, L. "*Beowulf* and Archaeology: Two Footnotes." *NM* 68 (1967): 28–35.

– "The Binding of Weland." *MÆ* 25 (1956):13–19.

Whitman, F.H. "Significant Motifs in Riddle 53." *MÆ* 46 (1977):1–11.

Wilcox, Jonathan. "New Solutions to Old English Riddles: Riddles 17 and 53." *PQ* 69 (1990):393–408.

– "'Tell Me What I Am': The Old English Riddles." In *Readings in Medieval Texts: Interpreting Old and Middle English Literature*, edited by David Johnson and Elaine Treharne, 46–59. Oxford: Oxford University Press, 2005.

Williams, David. "The Exile as Uncreator." *Mosaic* 8.3 (1975):1–14.

Williams, Edith Whitehurst. "Annals of the Poor: Folk Life in Old English Riddles." *Medieval Perspectives* 3 (1988):67–82.

– "What's So New about the Sexual Revolution?: Some Comments on Anglo-Saxon Attitudes toward Sexuality in Women Based on Four Exeter Book Riddles." *Texas Quarterly* 18.2 (1975):46–55.

Wilson, David M. "Craft and Industry." In *The Archaeology of Anglo-Saxon England*, edited by David M. Wilson, 253–81. London: Methuen, 1976.

Wittig, Joseph. "Figural Narrative in Cynewulf's *Juliana*." *ASE* 4 (1974):37–55.

Wodzak, Victoria. "Of Weavers and Warriors: Peace and Destruction in the Epic Tradition." *Midwest Quarterly* 39 (1998):253–64.

Woolf, Rosemary. "The Devil in Old English Poetry." *RES* 4 (1953):1–12.

Wright, Thomas. *Biographia Britannica Literaria*. Vol. 1. London: J.W. Parker, 1842.

Wyld, Henry Cecil. "Diction and Imagery in Anglo-Saxon Poetry." *Essays and Studies* o.s. 11 (1925):49–91.

Zacher, Samantha. "Cynewulf at the Interface of Literacy and Orality: The Evidence of the Puns in *Elene*." *Oral Tradition* 17 (2002):346–87.

Zandvoort, R.W. "The Leiden Riddle." *English and Germanic Studies* 3 (1949–50):42–56.

Ziegler, Waltraud. "Ein neuer Losungsversuch fur das altenglische Ratsel Nr. 28." *Arbeiten aus Anglistik und Amerikanistik* 7.2 (1982):185–90.

Zymer, Tomasz. "Wyrd as the Determiner of Human Fate in Selected Passages from Old English Poetry." *Kwartalnik Neofilologiczny* 39.2 (1992):103–14.

Index

Toronto Anglo-Saxon Series

General Editor:
ANDY ORCHARD

Editorial Board
ROBERTA FRANK
THOMAS N. HALL
ANTONETTE DIPAOLO HEALEY
MICHAEL LAPIDGE
ROY LIUZZA
KATHERINE O'BRIEN O'KEEFFE